ENTWINED HOMELANDS, EMPOWERED DIASPORAS

SEPHARDI AND MIZRAHI STUDIES
Harvey E. Goldberg and Matthias Lehmann, editors

ENTWINED HOMELANDS, EMPOWERED DIASPORAS

Hispanic Moroccan Jews and Their Globalizing Community

AVIAD MORENO

INDIANA UNIVERSITY PRESS

This book is a publication of

Indiana University Press
Office of Scholarly Publishing
Herman B Wells Library 350
1320 East 10th Street
Bloomington, Indiana 47405 USA

iupress.org

© 2024 by Aviad Moreno

Cover photo courtesy of Daniel Moreno

All rights reserved

No part of this book may be reproduced or utilized in any form or by any means, electronic or mechanical, including photocopying and recording, or by any information storage and retrieval system, without permission in writing from the publisher. The paper used in this publication meets the minimum requirements of the American National Standard for Information Sciences—Permanence of Paper for Printed Library Materials, ANSI Z39.48-1992.

Manufactured in the United States of America

First Printing 2024

Cataloging information is available from the Library of Congress.

ISBN 978-0-253-06966-5 (hdbk.)
ISBN 978-0-253-06967-2 (pbk.)
ISBN 978-0-253-06968-9 (web PDF)

I dedicate this book to my beloved wife, Galit; my sons, Yehonatan and Or; my parents, Daniel and Naomi; and to my grandparents, Flora and Alberto, and Ida and Avraham

CONTENTS

Note on Transliteration   ix

Introduction   1
1. Hispanic Jews in Morocco   18
2. In (Re)Search of Origins   34
3. Morocco in Latin America, Latin America in Morocco   51
4. Zionism and the Hispanic Moroccan Diaspora   69
5. Moroccans in Venezuela: A New Global Hierarchy   93
6. Spain and the Postcolonial Diaspora   107
7. Hispanic Moroccans in Israel   126
8. A Global Hispanophone Diaspora   141

Epilogue   154

Conclusions   163

Acknowledgments   171

Notes   175

Bibliography   201

Name Index   233

Subject Index   239

NOTE ON TRANSLITERATION

PROPER NOUNS, SUCH AS THE NAMES of people, places, and institutions, that are mentioned only a few times appear in their common Spanish, French, and Portuguese spellings, reflecting the way they are commonly written in the primary sources. Thus, similar names may appear with different spellings depending on the specific sources they are drawn from and the language they are written in. More frequently mentioned proper nouns and terms (e.g., Tangier, Tetouan, Haketia) appear in their commonly used English spellings. Arabic and Hebrew proper nouns and terms are transliterated using common English scripts, omitting foreign diacritics and orthographies. Hebrew and Arabic bibliographic titles have been translated into English.

ENTWINED HOMELANDS, EMPOWERED DIASPORAS

INTRODUCTION

"UNLIKE OTHER SEPHARDIM AROUND THE WORLD, we [the Jews from northern Morocco] . . . have been Spanish once again for over 130 years [as the result of modern Spanish influence in North Africa]. We are therefore in a better position than anyone else to promote this reunion [between modern Spain and the Jews at the quincentennial anniversary of the 1492 Alhambra Decree], and to actively collaborate [internationally] in the demonstrations of rapprochement that will take place in 1992."[1] With these words, Abraham Hassan Cohen gave a new twist to the overall tendency of Sephardi communities to romanticize the Jewish past in pre-1492 Iberia. His words came at a time when many Sephardi groups worldwide were preparing for the quincentennial commemoration of the 1492 Alhambra Decree, which led to the conversion and expulsion of non-Catholic minorities from Spain, and the simultaneous "discovery" of the Americas by Christopher Columbus.[2] Hassan Cohen spoke these words in a speech at the Spanish embassy in Paris on July 5, 1990, during a planning session for the upcoming Sepharad '92 conference, a part of the international quincentennial celebrations.

Hassan Cohen was then serving as president of France-MABATT, an association in France of Spanish-speaking Jewish immigrants from northern Morocco. France-MABATT derived its name and organizational motivation from its Israeli counterpart, MABAT, the Hebrew acronym for Mifgash Benei Tanjir (Reunion of Tangier's Natives), founded in Tel Aviv in 1979.[3] France-MABATT not only drew inspiration from its Israeli equivalent but was forged through concrete transnational ties with the Israeli organization, after the latter had called upon Jews from northern Morocco to establish communities around the world commemorating *lo nuestro* (our thing), an expression in Spanish that indicates the cultural traits of Spanish-speaking Jews from "Spanish" or "northern" Morocco, mostly vis-à-vis the Arabic-speaking Jews from "the south" of Morocco.[4]

In his speech at the embassy, Hassan Cohen further emphasized the common denominator of lo nuestro and how it marked the differences between Jews from the north and the south of Morocco according to his observation: "We [from the north] continue to live like Spaniards [around the world]. In Israel they [fellow northern Moroccan Jews] are today still called Spaniards rather than just Sephardim.[5] In Spain we are totally Spanish and in the rest of the world we are Spanish emigrants."[6]

For Hassan Cohen, however, being "totally Spanish" did not mean shying away from his Moroccan or Jewish background—quite the contrary. "MABAT means in Hebrew: a gaze . . . onto everything that is Jewish, Hispanic, and Oriental," he explained as he continued to mark the differences, as he saw it, between Hispanic Moroccan Jews from northern Morocco and other Moroccan groups. Celebrating his modern Spanish identity entailed a celebration of the historic symbiosis between the three cultures, or, to use his own words, a "wonderful amalgam of East and West" in which both Jewish and Moroccan identities play an essential role in the shaping of world Spanish culture. According to Hassan Cohen, this unique combination was encapsulated by *Haketia*, a communal dialect, distinct from European languages like French or English, adopted by Jews elsewhere across the Middle East and North Africa (MENA) in light of modern colonialism in the nineteenth century. Developed in northern Morocco immediately after the 1492 expulsion, Haketia was an amalgam of pre-1492 Iberian Spanish, Arabic, and Hebrew mixed with words in Moroccan Arabic and Tamazight dialects that were added to it after the settlement of Jews in northern Morocco in the fifteenth century. Haketia marked the centuries-long attachment of Jews in northern Morocco to Spain, even when that country that expelled them continued to officially reject their right to form a new community in its mainland territory well into the twentieth century. Other groups of expelled Jews from Iberia who moved further south into Morocco stopped speaking a dialect whose main morphology and vast vocabulary was based on Spanish and adopted Arabic dialects instead.[7]

The diaspora of Jews from northern Morocco had another characteristic whose exploration adds complexity to the analysis of their community building over the last century and a half. They were among the pioneers of international migration from Morocco already in the early nineteenth century. Their main hubs were in the Iberian Peninsula and Latin America, most typically in Venezuela, Argentina, and the Peruvian and Brazilian Amazon. With roots in the early nineteenth century, the diaspora of Hispanic Moroccan Jews became very mobile in the twentieth century, establishing formal communities in Spain and Venezuela as well as in Israel, France, the United States and Canada. In the 1950s and 1960s, when the vast majority of Jews from the MENA region, including about 80 percent of all Moroccan Jews, made Israel their home, about two-thirds of Hispanic Moroccan Jews then still living in northern Morocco chose instead to immigrate to South and North America and Europe.[8] Together they constituted a Spanish-speaking diaspora that included intra-African migrants to Melilla, a Spanish territory on African soil that still constitutes one of the largest Jewish holds on North African soil, though it is geopolitically part of Spain.[9] Their immigration to Spain, a country with which they identified their ancestry, also marked a unique story of postcolonial migration.

In examining these and other underexplored synchronic and diachronic developments in the global diaspora of Jews from northern Morocco, *Entwined Homelands, Empowered Diasporas* offers a new framework for analyzing diaspora-making among Sephardi and MENA Jews in modern times. Hassan Cohen's expression of both a pre-1492 and modern Spanish identity, as a Moroccan Jewish immigrant leader in France heading an émigré organization formed through direct transnational connections with counterparts in Israel, represents this book's case well. However, it is only one among multiple examples showcasing how hybridity and interconnectivity continued to evolve and characterize the diaspora across postcolonial and national contexts in the latter half of the twentieth century. In the following sections, I will further elaborate on the innovation that lies in this study.

SPAIN, AN OLD/NEW JEWISH "HOMELAND"

Focusing on Hispanic Moroccan Jews, this book is among the first to explore Jewish dispersion in the context of Spanish colonialism, rather than in the more familiar context of postcolonial migrations from French and British dominated MENA countries to Israel, West Europe, and North America. This history is essential for understanding their sense of diaspora in the twentieth century, even among the members of the community who stayed in northern Morocco until the mid- or late-twentieth century.

A major trigger for the process of diaspora formation, at least in cultural and discursive terms, among Hispanic Moroccan Jews came with the 1859–60 Spanish-Moroccan War, in which Spain occupied Tetouan for a year and a half. The occupation dramatically influenced the relationship between modern Spain and the Jews of Morocco, including the ways in which each side publicly described the other. Following the Spanish occupation of 1859–60, Spanish politicians and colonial agents began to characterize the colonial mission as a *"reencuentro"*—a nostalgic "reencounter" between Jews, Muslims, and Christian Spaniards on Moroccan soil, marked by an expressed desire to "return" to the golden age of the Convivencia, when the three communities were said to have lived in harmony in medieval Spain.[10] Inspired by these earlier descriptions, Spanish senator Ángel Pulido (1852–1932) cultivated new forms of historical imagination at the beginning of the twentieth century. Captivated by the linguistic proximity of Judeo-Spanish (Ladino) across the Sephardi diaspora and the Castilian Spanish spoken in modern Spain, in 1905, Pulido published a book that carried in its very title the notion that members of the "Sephardi race" were in fact *Españoles sin patria* (stateless Spaniards).[11] Pulido was among the most enthusiastic advocates of a group of Spanish intellectuals and liberal politicians who came to be known as the Philo-Sephardi Movement. This group imagined the reencounter of Jews with Spain as a means of righting the injustice of the 1492 Alhambra Decree.

It is worth noting that, despite the historical circumstances in which the Spanish state officially continued to exclude expelled Jews and Muslims from mainland Spain, the same Spanish state actively promoted the concept of a Hispano-Moroccan brotherhood—based on kinship for Muslims and linguistic ties for Jews—when colonial interests were at stake. Drawing on Philo-Sephardi ideas, in Morocco more than elsewhere, this concept of brotherhood served clear political and practical purposes, which became even more evident after 1912, when Spain and France signed the Treaty of Fez and most of northern Morocco was officially declared a Spanish territory.[12] This state of affairs would continue under Spanish dominion until Morocco's independence in 1956.

Spain's colonial expansion into Morocco in the first half of the twentieth century followed the decline of its global empire, including the momentous loss of its last remaining American and Pacific colonies during the Spanish-American War of 1898, which led in turn to a long period of internal instability in Spain. A dispute over the merits of a new colonial campaign in Africa arose between the Spanish liberals and the so called "Africanists"—generals who advocated for colonial expansion to restore Spain's lost pride and economic prestige. Despite clear ideological differences between the parties, the Africanistas also embraced a discourse that justified the occupation of Morocco as a historic interfaith reunion. They emphasized the historical racial fusion between Iberians and North Africans in pre-1492 Iberia, along with the geographical and cultural proximities, including their linguistic ties with Sephardi Jews.[13]

Figure 0.1. Spanish Protectorate of Morocco ("Atlas general de España" by Casa editorial Bailly-Bailliere, Madrid 1914). © Alamy, image ID:2G8CX07.

The 21,243 square kilometers occupied by Spain in northern Morocco were rich in natural resources. But for Spain, fulfilling its colonial dream came with a particularly heavy price tag. The Spanish army encountered logistic hardships as well as severe resistance and significant loss of life. The Rif War, led by Abd al-Karim between 1920 and 1926, set back Spanish control in northern Morocco and exposed its military vulnerability vis-à-vis the French protectorate in the south.[14] At the time, several Spanish colonialists believed that Spanish-speaking Jews in the north could somewhat help Spain spread its influence and regain its erstwhile glory.[15]

This local aspiration was linked to ongoing efforts to engage with the broader Sephardi diaspora across the Mediterranean. In 1924, during the dictatorship of General Miguel Primo de Rivera (1923–30), a naturalization law set a period of six years during which Sephardi Jews in the Ottoman Empire were eligible to apply for Spanish citizenship. When the Second Spanish Republic (1931–39) was founded more than half a century after the Spanish Restoration (1874–1931), the new republic, which advocated for religious tolerance in Spain, continued to promote the idea of Jews as beneficial agents of Spain through nostalgic narratives about the renewal of the Convivencia. In 1935, on the occasion of the eighth centenary of the birth of Maimonides, and in the atmosphere of severe political instability, the Spanish government organized a series of events throughout the communities of the Mediterranean aimed at bringing Jews closer to the Spanish state.[16]

Many scholars have emphasized the cynical motivations, ambiguity, and hypocrisy associated with the Spanish continuous Philo-Sephardi discourse and related narrative about the "stateless Spaniards," pointing to the political and economic self-interest of the Spanish imperialists who fueled this campaign beginning in the nineteenth century.[17] This became even more apparent with Francisco Franco's rise to power following the military coup that marked the beginning of the Spanish Civil War in July 1936. After the end of the civil war in 1939, the Francoist regime conceived of Spanish colonialism as a process of isolating Spain from the rest of Europe. This led to the reinforcement of what anthropologist Gustau Nerín has called *Hispanotropicalism*. According to this notion, Spanish colonialism since the eighteenth century, unlike other European colonial projects, was based on affinities between the colonizer and colonized rather than the cultural superiority of Spain and its wish to exploit the colonies. High rates of miscegenation were understood as proof that Spanish colonizers were guided by the religious idea that all of humankind was created in God's image. While this discourse led to actual miscegenation in the Latin American context, in Morocco, it perpetuated narratives of a historic reencounter and portrayed Spain's intervention as an altruistic duty to protect its younger North African brethren.[18]

For Jews in northern Morocco, one of the most lasting aspects of that perceived reencounter was, as mentioned, its linguistics. Haketia, widely used by Jews in the area until the twentieth century, consisted mostly of Spanish words. Unlike their Jewish counterparts in southern Morocco, who spoke in local (Jewish) dialects of Arabic and Tamazight, the ethnic language of most Jews in the north distinguished them, at least linguistically, from the larger non-Jewish environment. In some ways, the process resembled the function of Ladino in non-Spanish-speaking environments across the Mediterranean and beyond, or the linguistic self-segregation of Yiddish speakers in non-German-speaking regions of Europe and the Americas. Until the beginning of the twentieth century, the use of Arabic by northern Moroccan Jews in everyday interactions with their non-Jewish environment was fairly widespread, as is evident from the penetration of numerous Arabic words into Haketia.[19] Following the reencounter with Spain, however, many local Jews who were still familiar with Arabic began to treat it as a more marginal language, modifying their manner of speech to better resemble modern Spanish. In an academic article published in 1945, the philologist Paul Bénichou, speaking of Haketia, remarked that "the dialect, or great parts of it, is no more than a mere memory, which continues to exist only among people from the earlier generation."[20]

Given the context of Spanish colonialism, this, perhaps somewhat dramatized, observation reflected a much more complex process of self-conscious linguistic transformation. On the one hand, the Jewish middle and upper classes of northern Morocco, and particularly those among them who developed an exceptional sense of kinship with modern Spain and the Hispanophone world, deemed Haketia too "archaic" and even a sign of underdevelopment, and as such a source of shame among the generation born around the early 1900s.[21] On the other hand, it was exactly this notion that motivated a strong impulse to document their dying Hispano-Arab heritage among the modernized intellectual elite. Fueled by academic studies, an intellectual elite imbued Haketia with a certain degree of expressed nostalgia for pre-1492 Jewish Spain. Groundbreaking efforts in this direction were undertaken by, among others, Pinhas Asayag, a Jewish journalist from Tangier and member of the local Jewish community council; José Benoliel, a philologist, poet, and teacher from Tangier; and Zarita Nahón, a disciple of the forefather of modern anthropology, Franz Boas.[22] Nahón's 1929 ethnographic account of *romancero*, a collection of Sephardic romances or Spanish ballad songs performed in Haketia in her community as a living link to its medieval Iberian roots, heralded a conceptual "sealing off" of Judeo-Spanish communities concentrated in northern Morocco from the rest of Morocco.

While local conditions under colonialism in Morocco were significant in influencing the encounter of Hispanic Moroccan Jews with the Hispanophone world and their Sephardi roots, they were also closely linked to global developments in the main Hispanic Moroccan Jewish hubs in Venezuela, Argentina, Brazil, and the US. Crucially, these destinations also shaped their new diasporic map. Moreover, political changes during the last fifteen years of Franco's regime (1960–75) and the post-Franco era that followed, as well as an unprecedented wave of Jewish migration from Morocco to Spain, elevated Spain's role as an epicenter for the production and dissemination of shared narratives of the community's ancestry in Spain.[23] Associated developments—ranging from the establishment of bilateral relations between Israel and Spain in 1986 to a series of transnational collaborative projects in 1992 marking five hundred years since the expulsion of Jews from Spain—affected Israel as well. From the 1980s onward, Israel became a small but vibrant hub for the dissemination of nostalgic narratives about Spain and Morocco as entwined homelands. Notably, Israel also became a major hub for Hispanic Moroccan Jews in the twentieth century. Considering Israel's historic and modern appeal to Jews across the world, this history thus has implications for the way we study diasporas.

REFRAMING MENA JEWISH DIASPORAS

Despite the vast and growing body of research on nineteenth- and twentieth-century MENA Jews, the existing scholarship is not oriented toward an understanding of these Jews as members of multipolar global diasporas, with transregional power relations and networks of communal solidarity. Until the 1960s, the conventional (nationalist) wisdom was that *homeland* and *diaspora* (often capitalized at the time) are fixed spatial categories, with homeland representing the ultimate place of origin from which an ethnic diaspora has dispersed and to which the latter's core identity is attached. The general spatial separation between homeland and diaspora was not thoroughly challenged until the 1990s,[24] when grand narratives that were once conceived as encompassing definitive histories of people and nations and their relations to geography—as in the Zionist nationalist understanding of the Jewish diaspora's return to the Land of Israel—were increasingly reconceived as cultural constructions that served political projects.[25] At the time, the *spatial turn* in the humanities and social sciences accompanied a series of other turns, for example, the *transnational* and *hybrid* turns in postcolonial criticism. These turns further challenged nationalist and colonialist concepts of space and dispersion by highlighting multiculturalism and syncretic identities that bore affinities to multiple nations and sites.[26] Against this backdrop, scholarship in Jewish and Israel studies has come a long way from the traditional understanding of the Jewish diaspora and homeland as dichotomous categories.[27]

However, the field of MENA studies, often labeled "area" studies, has until very recently generally neglected questions related to global migration and *multi-sited* diaspora-making.[28] In addition, a significant and groundbreaking scholarship over the past decade has focused on contextualizing Jews within their respective MENA societies, as opposed to perceiving them as self-contained and isolated Jewish communities.[29] When it comes to the study of Jewish diasporic groups from the MENA region in the twentieth century, however, the recent tendency in this field has been to study them within competing bipolar national (e.g., Moroccan or Zionist Israeli) contexts. This orientation echoes in part what Jessica Sperling defined as the swap of *methodological nationalism* for *methodological bi-nationalism*.[30] Many of the important historical studies that offer a critical view of Jewish national identities, in fact have highlighted the trends of integration of Jews into the national elites of newly independent

MENA countries in the latter half of the twentieth century. These studies have only infrequently addressed the transregional links created through migration outside of the "region" as a way of decentering Zionism.[31] In doing so, they align with the pioneering generation of Mizrahi Studies scholars, who, by overdetermining MENA Jewish experiences in Israel according to their marginalization by the Ashkenazi elite, have similarly perpetuated the tendency of differentiating the Israeli case from contemporary Jewish migrations from the MENA region to Europe and the Americas.[32]

In addition, despite the preoccupation of Jewish studies with the concepts of diaspora and exile, when it comes to MENA Jewish diasporas, much of the scholarship ends in the mid-twentieth century, just prior to the "great rupture" that is said to have separated Jews from their pre-migration environments during and in the aftermath of colonialism.[33] Consequently, little attention is given to the study of transnational MENA/Sephardi diaspora networks, in which Israel is one important hub by no means isolated from the rest.[34] The existing scholarship that goes over the mid-twentieth century dividing line concentrates on MENA Jewish migrations to France, Spain, and North, Central, and South American countries—where North African Jews are often referred to themselves as Sephardim. While this existing scholarship has made groundbreaking contributions in analyzing the transnational aspects of MENA and Sephardi Jewry, it has primarily focused on assessing their impact within regional and national contexts, with limited attention given to the broader synchronic consequences of transnationalism.[35]

Continuing a long legacy of methodological separation from the late nineteenth century onward—between the study of the golden age in Sepharad and the study of the post-expulsion Sephardi diaspora that resettled in the Orient, the Levant, and the Maghreb—much of the sub-field of Sephardi studies has sought to distinguish itself from modern MENA histories.[36] While recent works in Jewish studies have begun to bridge Sephardi and MENA diasporas, a tendency to study the migrations and transnational networks of Sephardi and MENA Jews only before the mid-twentieth century remains typical of this field.[37]

A budding corpus of studies do explore the post-1948 immigration of Jews to Israel in the wider context of modern Jewish migrations—especially during the period when the demographic centers of Jewish life shifted from Asia, Africa, and Eastern Europe to the Americas, Western Europe, and Israel. Yet, these studies leave aside the MENA region and tend to focus instead on Jewish migration from Europe, the former Soviet Union, and the US.[38]

Recent studies, mostly by Italian scholars, have begun to explore ties between specific hubs of MENA Jews, conceived as a diaspora that spans multiple postcolonial Mediterranean contexts in the second half of the twentieth century.[39] But few monographs today are dedicated to a single diasporic group with one or several defined homelands.[40] The diaspora of Hispanic Moroccan Jews, with their attachment to two historical homelands and to multiple global hubs throughout the twentieth century, offers a more transregional approach to MENA and Sephardi hometown diasporas. Nonetheless, the most up-to-date account of Spanish colonialism's attitude toward Jews in North Africa has been explored in a localized context, looking specifically at encounters between Spain and Morocco and leaving aside the European, Israeli, and South and North American contexts.[41]

Drawing on the case of Hispanic Moroccan Jews, this book offers insight into the way processes of diaspora formation interact with international migration patterns and the associated intra-diasporic hierarchies and global networks over the twentieth century and beyond. It delineates how a small group of generally first-generation migrants who shared the same urban space in northern Morocco's small cities and towns forged narratives of shared ancestral roots by referring to a multiplicity of historic and modern homelands alongside Spain, as a source for community empowerment.

THE BOOK'S CHAPTERS

Spanish colonialism in Africa, as historian Mimoun Azziza observes, was "a poor man's version of colonialism."[42] The loss of Spain's global empire in the Americas and the Pacific in the late nineteenth century, and the resulting economic downturn and political instability of the twentieth century, stood in contrast with the colonial expansion of neighboring Western European powers like France and Great Britain. This gap between Spain and other Western European nations widened even further during the period of economic rehabilitation that followed World War II. While France, the Netherlands, Germany, and Belgium together attracted around 350,000 Moroccan immigrants in the decade from 1965 to 1975, less than 10,000 Moroccans resided in the more geographically proximate Spain in 1975.[43] The encounter with modern Spain was thus largely realized through the process of Spanish settler immigration and the way it came to shape a new concept of community belonging among the Sephardim in northern Morocco. As a result of the exposure of Jews to Spanish settlers, the popularity of modern Spanish language fed, in a dialectical way, their self-definition via linguistic, social, and cultural "boundary work" designed to define their nuanced position in the Spanish colonial project vis-à-vis Spanish settlers.[44]

This book's two opening chapters sketch the way affinity to Spain was integrated into modern Jewish narratives of belonging in northern Morocco as both a colonial power and an imagined place of ancestry that supported community building. In chapter 1, I show how Tangier and Tetouan, the major urban centers where most Hispanic Moroccan Jews lived in the first half of the twentieth century, became hubs where Jews intermingled with Spanish colonial settlers in the domestic and leisure spheres on the basis of shared language. Social codes were significantly altered by colonial expansion and related intra-urban migration, which in turn also affected the everyday lives of northern Moroccan Jews as well as their desire to differentiate themselves by associating with the circles of the Jewish community.

In chapter 2, I explore how actors within the Jewish community facilitated the notion of Jewish ancestry in Spain by forging new institutions and ties with French, American, and Spanish ethnographers, and philologists of Haketia. This chapter delineates how ethnic formation accompanied the expansion of global networks of heritage preservation from the outset of colonization and through Franco's reign and Moroccan independence in 1956. Colonialism that could have been seen as a challenge to community identity in fact reinforced it. Taken together, chapters 1 and 2 serve as a foundation for understanding how Jewish communities in northern Morocco developed a strong affinity with the Hispanic world and entwined it with their modern Sephardi identities, even as other colonial influences—primarily French—were increasingly becoming part of their identities.

Chapter 3 addresses the influence of Jewish migration on the hometown awareness of Hispanic Moroccan Jews abroad as well as on the increasing prominence of South America in the formation of local Hispanic Jewish identities in northern Morocco in the 1920s through the 1950s. Shaped by circular migration ties and transnational hubs in Venezuela, Argentina, Brazil, and Peru, the notion of a unique connection to Latin America impacted community building, becoming a mythical reference point for Jewish Hispanic identity in Morocco. Significantly, I demonstrate how these dynamics unfolded in the context of a growing awareness that shared global Hispanic origins and could serve as a source of local empowerment.

Chapter 4 recounts how the rise of Zionism in northern Morocco, beginning in 1900, was consistent with the growing identification with Spanish culture and the global dispersion of Hispanic community networks until the mid-twentieth century. By exploring the development of Zionism as a tool for community interconnectivity from the early 1900s through Morocco's independence in 1956, the chapter challenges prominent studies of Jewish migration from the

MENA region. Such studies view the development of Zionism, on the one hand, and the construction of diasporic consciousness or local (non-Israeli) national identities, on the other hand, as opposed or contradictory processes.

Further developing the idea that the influence of Zionism did not run counter to international migration to destinations other than Israel, and to Jewish community building worldwide, chapter 5 looks more closely at the construction of Hispanic Moroccan identities in the 1960s and 1970s. I begin this chapter by showing how community building among Moroccan Jews in Venezuela, one of the most prominent hubs of Hispanic Moroccan Jews after 1948, was entwined with the growing influence of Israel as a source of solidarity across the Jewish diaspora and, more particularly, among Sephardi Jews. As I show, such a notion of solidarity was entwined with new hierarchies that conceived of Moroccan Jews as "Jewries in distress." To position themselves in a conceivably upper-hand position vis-à-vis other groups of Moroccans on the move, leaders in Venezuela appealed to their histories of international migration. Through that process, new interpretations of Zionism as well as Moroccan and Latin American identities, as recounted in the previous chapters, were formed to empower the local hub of the diaspora.

Focusing on postcolonial developments after Morocco's independence from Spain in 1956, chapter 6 looks at how the notion of the community's ancestry in Spain traveled to the renewing hubs, primarily to Spain and Venezuela. Drawing on communal sources, I show how narratives of ancestry in Spain, originally created to serve Spanish colonialism, were employed by Jewish leaders to empower their local diaspora communities in both countries. In Spain they helped them integrate into a new national discourse that was designed to rebrand the country as democratic and thus historically tolerant to Jews (and Muslims). Traveling to Venezuela, the notion of ancestry in Spain, and the merging of Moroccan identities into that notion helped the community integrate into Venezuelan narratives that bridged Latin America with Spain, including with its pre-1492 legacies.

Chapter 7 is dedicated to the several thousand Spanish Moroccan Jews who emigrated to Israel. In the late 1970s, they began to distinguish themselves from the larger Moroccan community in the country. While this differentiation had deep roots in pre-immigration Morocco as well as in the newer global hubs outside of Israel, the fact that the Israeli establishment stereotyped Moroccans as culturally backward intensified the construction of a separate narrative emphasizing the cultural difference of Moroccans with an ancestral connection to Spain. The community in Israel began to elevate the Hispanic part of its identity, including a connection to modern Spain, in order to emphasize how it was distinguished from (Arabic-speaking) Moroccan immigrants, who were negatively stereotyped in Israel. Yet in this process, Haketia, with its Arabic component and origins in Morocco, was employed to portray the community as authentically Moroccan with deeply rooted Spanish traits, demonstrating that, unlike their southern counterparts, Hispanic Moroccan Jews' European roots were not artificially imposed by modern (French) colonialism.

Local developments in Israel influenced the global network of advocates dedicated to spreading the nostalgic narrative about the community's origins. Chapter 8 recounts how the Israeli group of community leaders directly influenced the creation of sister organizations in the smaller hubs in France, the US, and Canada. This chapter exemplifies the connections between the local communities in the non-Spanish-speaking world and how they sought to use those links to strengthen their connection to the Hispanophone world.

To achieve this, it borrows the concept of the Global Hispanophone, addressing the ties between regions of the world that were bound by the Spanish Empire beyond Latin America, the Caribbean, and the Iberian Peninsula itself—namely, North Africa, Equatorial Guinea, and the Philippines and other regions that scholars rarely study alongside one another. Placing the Global Hispanophone paradigm in the context of postcolonial migration from Morocco in this chapter advances the study of local contexts hitherto marginal to major historical centers of Spanish influence, transcending existing boundaries and bringing the past and present of these far-flung regions into dialogue with others.[45] In all, this book focuses on the Spanish linguistic heritage and capabilities that enabled Jews in Spain and Latin America, but also in Israel, Morocco, and the non-Spanish-speaking countries of North America and Europe, to build connections and empower themselves as a diaspora.

THE MECHANISM OF DIASPORA MOBILIZATION

The history of Hispanic Moroccan Jews and their globalizing diaspora in the twentieth century bears implications for the study of diasporas beyond the Sephardi and Jewish contexts. To avoid the over-essentialization of *diaspora* as an analytical term, Rogers Brubaker insisted that three core elements define diasporas, even in times of globalization and multicultural and hyphenated experiences: *dispersion, homeland orientation,* and *boundary maintenance.* These three characteristics, in his mind, distinguished diasporas from other dispersed groups.[46] Rubin Cohen later described Brubaker's intervention as "the consolidation phase" of diaspora studies, stressing that this observation is not intended to maintain that diasporas are not socially constructed or to reembrace nationalist ideas about simplistic links between land, people, and culture—prominent until the 1960s—but rather to "find some dialogical possibilities between diaspora scholars and their social constructionist critics."[47] From this perspective, with the opening up of global space and hyphenated experiences, the relationship between diaspora and homeland may at times be "reversed," as when members of ethnic diasporas enact "homecomings" to historical centers of diaspora life.[48] More significantly, while previous approaches exclusively connected immigrants' place of origin with the new homeland or host country, this new literature conceives of transnational experiences as *multi-sited* and *multi-directional*.[49]

Combining the analysis of such multilayered experiences with the Spanish, and mostly the myth of a reencounter with Spain—embraced by a group of Jews that maintained their Iberian identities in Morocco and eventually came to represent one of the prominent Jewish communities in Spain and Israel in the last third of the twentieth century—raises more nuanced questions for the consolidation phase as defined by Cohen. Under such circumstances, what goal did a declared attachment to multiple ancestral centers serve in the identity construction of a small diaspora whose members predominantly migrated from a small territory in northern Morocco?

As many diaspora scholars have argued in recent years regarding the social structure of diasporas, diaspora formation and maintenance require a significant number of scattered individuals who adhere to the diaspora idea, even situationally, as the construct develops over time.[50] In other words, it is not enough to merely *be* from a specific place of origin to become a member of a diaspora—you also need to *act* on that awareness to become a member, to accept the collective narrative and often further disseminate it through networks and institutions. Or, as diaspora scholar Brian Keith Axel inquires, "Who in the most quotidian of ways, claims to be the subject of diaspora? ... What are the everyday conditions for the identification of a subject of diaspora?"[51] As I maintain relatedly throughout the book, modern diasporas are "mobilized" by interpersonal, semiformal and formal associations, organized events, and means of communication that mediate shared conceptions about roots and home.[52] Individuals actively develop their sense of being a diaspora through unifying narratives that flow within those networks and make sense of their collective "duty" to use those narratives to maintain connections and set boundaries with other groups.[53]

As the research for this book evolved, the centrality of this notion became increasingly clear. I began my research on the Hispanic Moroccan Jewish diaspora in 2009 by conducting twenty-seven interviews with men and women who immigrated to Israel from northern Morocco. For this preliminary research, I simply engaged two of my own interpersonal networks at the time. The first stemmed from my own family: my father, a native of Tangier, connected me with a distant relative with whom I had not previously been familiar. The second network was based on the professional connections of my former MA adviser, Prof. Tamar Alexander, then head of the Gaon Center for the Study of Ladino and Its Culture. During my studies for my master's degree in 2008, Prof. Alexander put me in touch with immigrants from northern Moroccan who had been active "preservers" of the community's heritage in Israel. After several interviews, my two initial networks—familial and professional—eventually merged, as exemplified by an interview I conducted with my adviser's colleague, who turned out to be a distant relative of mine.

The way in which I witnessed the networks blend into a single web of connections came to influence my approach to studying Hispanic Moroccan Jews and their diasporas in the twentieth century. I began to realize that common and repeated expressions recurred throughout the narratives about the community's past in Spain and Morocco and slowly revealed the structure of a popularized collective narrative that was deeply rooted in the diasporic experiences of these individuals and their relationships with the place I had come from—academia. The following anecdote may capture my point. Following my interview with Sara, an immigrant from Tetouan who resided in Beer-Sheva at the time of the interview, she offered to lend me an academic book authored by Shoshana (Susana) Weich Shahak. The book, *En Buen Siman! Panorama Del Repertorio Musical Sefaradí*, explored the *romancero* (Spanish ballad song collections) traditionally sung by Jews in northern Morocco.[54] When I opened it, I found between its pages an invitation to Sephardi Jews in North Morocco: Music, Language, and Culture, an academic event hosted by the Gaon Center in Beer-Sheva. The event had taken place in March 2006 with the participation of Profs. Alexander, Weich Shahak, Jimmy Weinblatt (then rector of Ben-Gurion University), and Yaakov Bentolila. Esti Keinan Ofri of the Kol Oud Tof Trio had performed northern Moroccan wedding melodies.

I attended the next Gaon Center event dedicated to northern Moroccan culture and history in March 2009, called Haketia Evening. Haketia was a key and repetitive topic in these collective stories told by community members, even when few of the people I met spoke it fluently. Some of those immigrants actually stressed overtly that they "did not speak Haketia [in Morocco]," hinting at the complexity of everyday life experiences in northern Morocco in their childhood, where their parents replaced Haketia with contemporary Spanish and other European languages, thus deeming Haketia archaic and even a source of shame. But paradoxically, these individuals were some of the most enthusiastic preserves of Haketia, as I learned. Estrella Jalfón de Bentolila, an enthusiastic documenter of Haketia in Israel, expressed this notion in the prologue to her 2011 memoir: "Prof. Jacob Bentolila . . . said in a conference in Ben-Gurion University 'when a language is only used in humorous writings it is because the language is in the agony of death pains.' It must be true, but it pained me.... The essay I wrote in 1992 [to commemorate the five hundred years of the Expulsion of Jews from Spain] had only few words in Haketia... but over the years I began to expand the vocabulary list.... At night when I had trouble sleeping, words came to me."[55] A number of proactive individuals stressed the importance of their (our) duty to salvage the community heritage that was considered dead in the modernizing urban spaces of northern Morocco, and in the contexts of their migration from Morocco. The salvage of Haketia was imbued with a sense of a nostalgic passage to forgotten shores.

Ultimately, the interviews I conducted in 2009 and 2010 do not provide much of the content of this book. Yet collecting those stories was an essential step in understanding the community's social dynamics and developing the project's theoretical framework and for tracing an array of more traditional and less conventional archival sources. Focusing on such community perspectives helped me shape the main questions of this book and sharpen my understanding of the global proliferation of community networks through the twentieth century.

The role of community networks in the construction of attachment to multiple homelands, and the way this multiplicity of attachments serves to hold the hubs of a small diaspora together and differentiate it from other groups as a source for empowerment, also lies at the heart of the book's methodological approach. Throughout this book, I analyze an abundance of ethnographic publications and the institutions that produced and stored them—institutions that, beyond merely providing information for my research, serve as sites of community formation. The sources include numerous records; more than 150 interviews, events, and radio shows recorded in multiple locations, including but not limited to Morocco, France, Canada, Venezuela, Spain, Israel, Portugal, and Switzerland; personal and community correspondence; and understudied community periodicals. The periodicals include, for example, some of the first Jewish Spanish periodicals in Morocco: *Adelante* (1929–31/32), and *Or-Luz* (1956). In the chapters on events in Venezuela, I analyze for the first time the long-running publication *Maguén-Escudo*, founded in Caracas by Moroccan Jews in 1970 and still in production today. I examine *MABAT Revista* (*Mabat Review*) and the circulars of the main organization of Hispanic Moroccans Jews in Israel during the 1980s and 1990s. I also utilize a wide array of ethnographic works and memoirs written about and for the community in Morocco, Venezuela, Israel, Spain, the US, and France.

Notably, many of these sources were accessible to me thanks to the desire of devoted individuals and community leaders who comprise the networks detailed in this book. They saw me and my research as a bridgehead for disseminating the community's own account of its history.[56] Albeit composed in specific geographical and temporal contexts, those networks reflect the dynamics that incubated the formation of a global community. Hassan Cohen's words at the opening of this chapter are, too, a single manifestation of a worldwide project undertaken by Hispanic Moroccan Jews and the monumental efforts they expended to bridge vast distances, real and imagined—efforts that this book hopefully does some justice.

ONE

HISPANIC JEWS IN MOROCCO

"ALL THE JEWS IN THE *JUDERÍA* speak Spanish and find great joy in speaking to Spaniards."[1] Antonio J. Onieva used these words to describe, in his Spanish tourist guidebook published in 1947, his experience while visiting the Judería, the Jewish quarter in Tetouan. Scholarship on Spanish colonialism in Morocco has examined how Spain's policy toward Sephardi Jews as its colonial agents incorporated the idea of "linguistic brotherhood." Dwelling on cultural and linguistic commonalities between Sephardim and Spaniards, as mentioned in the introduction, Spain justified its colonial expansion by deeming it a reencounter with Jews in North Africa. Few scholars, however, have analyzed the community's perspective on that reencounter. Furthermore, there has been a paucity of scholarly inquiry into the factors motivating a substantial number of northern Moroccan Jews to embrace the colonial Spanish culture and language, as well as an examination of the boundaries of this attraction and its impact on their perceptions of their ethnic Jewish identities.[2]

Looking at the colonial urban setting of northern Morocco, where Jews were not just subjects of a literary imagination but actively engaged in day-to-day interactions with Spaniards, this chapter explores how Hispanic identities became entwined with modern Jewish identities, even when they defined the boundaries between the groups in a fundamentally new way.

A JEWISH-COLONIAL LANGUAGE

Modern Spanish colonialism in Morocco commenced in the aftermath of the Spanish-Moroccan War of 1859–60. The agreement that ended the war enabled Spanish citizens to purchase land in Morocco tax-free. As a result, by 1880

Spanish settlers comprised the largest foreign group on Moroccan soil, numbering some sixty-three hundred, or 70 percent of the country's European population at the time.[3]

In 1913, a year after the establishment of the French and Spanish protectorates, about fifteen thousand of the thirty-six thousand European citizens living in Morocco were concentrated in Tangier. Among them eight thousand Spaniard who preferred Tangier even when Tetouan was declared the capital of the Spanish protectorate.[4] In late 1924, Tangier was declared an international administrative zone governed by several European powers and administratively detached from the Spanish protectorate zone. An even more dramatic increase of its Spanish population came during the Spanish Civil War (1936–39), as many Spanish republican refugees fled there from the Franco-controlled Spanish protectorate.[5] Alongside these Spanish republicans, Jews fleeing Nazi-dominated Europe also began to arrive. In 1936, the Tangier Jewish community created a special committee to keep track of the increasing number of refugees, reaching about seven hundred by 1939.[6]

The end of the Spanish Civil War in 1939 was followed by Franco's annexation of Tangier during World War II (1940–45), and then by a decade during which it reverted to its international status (1945–56). By the early 1940s, a well-established European community had emerged in Tangier. Many of them were pro-Franco Spaniards, who came to replace republican teachers and administrators who had sought refuge in the French territories of Morocco during the annexation years.

Economically and geopolitically speaking, Tangier's return to international status in 1945 attracted many laborers and settlers, further reshaping its demographic landscape through migration.[7] An official census carried out by the international administration indicated that by 1951, out of a total population of 162,000 inhabitants, fourteen thousand were Jews; thirty thousand were Spanish; eleven thousand were other Europeans; six thousand were of non-Jewish, non-European heritage; and the rest were Muslims.[8] On the eve of Moroccan independence in 1955, some 40 percent of Tangier's population was considered European. Concentrations were even higher in the city center, where two-thirds of the city's total European population of sixty thousand resided (see table 1.1).[9]

In the neighboring Spanish protectorate zone, demographic changes were even more dramatic. In the 1930s, the second Spanish republic invested money intended to transform the protectorate from a military outpost into a civilian society.[10] By 1952, some 80,588 Spanish immigrants resided there. They comprised a significant majority of the European minority in that region.[11] The Spanish administration also invested large sums in the planning and

Table 1.1. The population of Tangier, 1915–60

Year	Europeans	Muslims	Jews	Total
1915	14,000	37,000	19,000	70,000
1927	10,000	35,000	15,000	60,000
1933	17,520	46,000	6,480	70,000
1941	22,534	72,670	7,102	102,306
1955	60,000	75,000	15,000 (since 1952)	150,000
1960	***34,508	[~123,500]	**6,232	***164,232

Source: Albzzaz, 21.
** Service Central de Statistiques, *La Voix des Communautés*, June 1, 1961, 2.
*** Kutz, 22.

development of a new, modern part of Tetouan known as El Ensanche ("the extension").[12]

The influence of Spanish language and culture on the public sphere in the cities of Tangier, Tetouan, Larache, Alcazarquivir), and Arcila, as well as other smaller towns in northern Morocco, should be examined with this demographic balance in mind. From the 1930s through the 1950s, Jews in these urban centers increasingly integrated into the modern Hispanophone world through the language and culture that comprised a significant part of their everyday lives, even as other European influences, most prominently French, simultaneously shaped their cultural and social realms.

Spain's nostalgic colonial discourse regarding the linguistic brotherhood served as one of the practical strategies for the colonization of northern Morocco. It reflected a persistent effort to propagate Spanish culture, or Hispanidad, throughout North Africa. As Maite Ojeda Mata has argued, the Spanish protectorate authorities explicitly mandated the use of Spanish for the community's communal records and minutes' books. This was part of a broader policy aimed at "re-Hispanizing" Sephardi Jews.[13]

This aspiration, however, collided with a multicultural colonial situation in Morocco, particularly in Tangier. During the first decade of Spanish colonialism, intervention in the local education system, for example, was kept to a bare minimum, despite the declared goal of "re-Hispanizing" the Jews and challenging the dominance of the Alliance Israélite Universelle's (AIU) French-language schools. Like the Arab-French schools, the AIU schools were better financed than the Spanish colonial education system and more accessible to the largest urban populations.

Table 1.2. The population of Tetouan, 1913–60

Year	Europeans	Muslims	Jews	Total
1913	3,096	11,887	4250	19,247
1931	17,312	35,992	6172	59,476
1940	[~22,400]	39,580*	8056	70,078
1950	29,232	47,183*	4122	80,732
1960	–	–	4,103**	101,352**

Source: Israel Garzón, Los Judios, 171, 185.
* Source: López García, 33.
** par le Service Central de Statistiques, *La Voix des Communautés*, June 1, 1961, 2.

From the opening of its first branches in Tetouan in 1862 and Tangier in 1864, the AIU school system functioned as the de facto mainstream educational framework for local Jews. Before the establishment of the Spanish protectorate in 1912, Spanish was in fact taught in the AIU schools of Tangier and Tetouan. Members of the AIU Alumni Association promoted Spanish rather than Arabic as a Jewish language, seeing the former as the native language of Jews in northern Morocco. Following the onset of Spanish colonialism, however, AIU leaders shifted the schools' focus to French in light of the increasing colonial competition between the two European powers. Around that time, the AIU Alumni Association made efforts to promote French among alumni in Tangier who were native Spanish speakers.[14]

After 1936, Franco implemented a policy that involved greater intervention into the local education system. The policy reflected the regime's desire to channel Moroccan nationalism against France as a common enemy. The language of instruction in Spain's colonial schools in Morocco was changed to Arabic and greater emphasis was placed on Islamic studies. Separate colonial schools from those that served Spanish settlers in Morocco, designated as "Hispano-Arab" and "Hispano-Hebrew," (also knowns as "Hispano-Israelite") respectively. These schools were created for Muslims and Jews in order to reorient them culturally and politically toward their own communities while maintaining education under the supervision of the Spanish colonial regime. Both types of schools offered a curriculum similar to Spain's, with additional Jewish and Muslim educational contents. Local religious figures taught these cultural-specific subjects, and the approach was part of a strategy to avoid conflict and encourage voluntary collaboration in the colonial context.[15]

Despite Spanish policies and the opening of new Hispano-Arab and Hispano-Hebrew schools in northern Morocco, the French education system continued to play a more significant role in the cultural lives of a large number of schoolchildren in the first half of the twentieth century. The number of Jews in the Spanish education system in the protectorate zone was surprisingly small: just 88 students out of a total of 1,114 during the 1947–48 school year.[16] In 1952, out of 1,533 Jewish students in Tangier, 1,088 attended AIU French schools. In the Spanish protectorate zone that same year, 756 students, a sizable portion of the area's Jewish youth at that time of considerable Jewish emigration, attended AIU schools.[17]

In Tangier, the (non-Jewish) Lycée Français, the network of French state schools operating outside of France, was an option for Jewish parents who believed that their children would receive a better education in French state schools than they would in the AIU network. In 1947 alone, 156 Jewish pupils (along with only 74 Muslims) enrolled at the Lycée Renault, a local French high school affiliated with the Lycée Français.[18] Data from the website *Tangerinos*, a virtual community maintained by natives of Tangier around the world, demonstrate the popularity of non-Jewish French schools among the Jewish population of Tangier: 274 of the website's 435 Jewish subscribers (as deduced from their surnames) who listed their educational background stated that they attended non-Jewish European schools, mostly Regnault, Perrier, Saint Aulaire (later Ibn Batouta), and Berchet, all Lycée Français affiliates.[19] The centrality of these schools to the lives of many local Jews can also be inferred from the fact that even the Zionist Federation of Tangier clearly stated in its reports that the Lycée Français should be considered a central local institution from which potential immigrants to Israel could be recruited.[20]

A memoir published by the Haketia researcher Alegría Bendelac in 1986, some two decades after she left Morocco for the US, offers insight into the way French was regarded as a language of high culture among the Jewish elite of Tangier. Before enrolling her children in the Lycée Français, Bendelac's mother revived the French that she herself had studied at an AIU school as a young girl and required her daughters to use it at home. As Alegría grew up, she conversed in French with her sisters, reserving Spanish for her parents, particularly her father. The French language was associated with economic success and cultural prestige in Tangier, as French bourgeois residents were generally wealthier than local Spaniards, many of whom were poor.[21]

Historian Mimoun Azziza deemed Spanish colonialism "a poor man's version of colonialism."[22] Still, Bendelac recalls that the typical mixture of languages spoken among Jews in northern Morocco was nicknamed "Judeo-Frañol."[23]

This mixture can be explained by looking at the prominence of Spanish in the daily lives of many Jews in colonial northern Morocco, including many prominent members of the community. Considered alongside Morocco's other centers of European influence, there appears to be nothing unique about the spread of French in Tangier at the beginning of the twentieth century. But the development of French education could not overtake the concurrent, rapid spread of Spanish in the urban environments of northern Morocco during the first half of the twentieth century. There, modern Spanish became the most widely spoken European language among both local Jews and Muslims, even as many among the latter barely spoke any French. In 1952, for example, philologist Rom Landau wrote that "the better-class Moor may speak French as well, but your servant, grocer, shoeblack, or waiter will have a smattering of Spanish."[24]

There were significant differences between Jews and Muslims in this respect. For many Muslims, unlike their Jewish counterparts, Spanish seemed to represent a foreign medium of communication utilized by the colonial bureaucracy and certain economic and public agencies that in fact excluded them as non-native speakers of Spanish. Data gathered by the Biblioteca Pública Española in Tangier gives one a sense of the relative accessibility of modern Spanish to Jews and Muslims. In 1946, Muslims who subscribed to the library numbered 1,931 as compared to 3,491 Jewish subscribers.[25] These numbers suggest that while Muslims were the single largest religious group, only a limited number were interested in Spanish or would meaningfully access it. The Spanish policy of religiously based divisions in education contributed to this gap as well as to low overall rates of schooling among the Muslim population.[26]

Conversely, Spanish was more accessible for the Jews in the north. Already in 1903, a report by the AIU on the Jews of Tangier mentioned how "the Judeo-Hispanic-Arabic language [Haketia] is spoken by more than two-thirds of the entire community."[27] Using data on religion and linguistic stratification, historian Maite Oujda Mata estimates that in 1914, 80 percent of the Jews in Tetouan used Spanish as their primary language at home, as compared to the extensive use of Arabic by the approximately 12,000 Muslims then living in the city.[28]

Another indication of the influence of the proximity between Spanish settlers and local Jews was the latter's increased exposure to Spanish culture, and their development of a taste for Spanish high culture, including literature and history. For example, in the mid-twentieth century, the most widely read periodicals in the city were Spanish, including *El Heraldo de Marruecos*, which was published in Tangier between 1925 and 1932 by the Hispanist Manuel Ortega with the aim of defending the interests of Spain in Africa. The most popular

Spanish daily, *España*, was established in October 1938 by Alto Comisario (High Commission) of the Spanish colonial authorities and distributed in Tangier until October 1967. As the primary Spanish newspaper in Africa, *España* had a daily circulation of 50,000 and was read by a great many Jews and Spanish-speaking Catholics alike.[29] Not only did local Jewish intellectuals begin to privately write in Spanish, they also became the editors and promoters of some of Morocco's earliest periodicals, most of which also appeared in Spanish.[30]

Despite the prestige of French and the circulation of many French-language newsletters and periodicals, the Spanish press seems to have played an increasingly significant role in the integration of wider sectors of the northern Moroccan Jewish society into the colonial world. According to Yvette Bürki, seven of the eleven newspapers published in Morocco were partly or fully in Spanish. Jewish ethnic newspapers exhibit similar proportions: out of eleven periodicals, only three were published in Arabic with Hebrew script.[31] Moisés Garzón Serfaty, editor of *Or-Luz*, attended the Spanish high school La Academia la General during his teenage years. There, he became enamored with modern Spanish poetry and literature, which he associated with high Spanish culture and influenced his relationship with the non-Jewish environment in Morocco. He mingled with Spanish poets such as Trina Mercader as well as with Arab Moroccan poets who wrote in Spanish, such as Mohamed Sabak.[32] He published some of his own Spanish-language literary efforts in *Or-Luz* in order to reach a Jewish audience.[33]

In 1956, the Tangier Jewish community club, colloquially known as the Casino Israelita, hosted Gerardo Diego, one of the most famous and beloved Spanish writers and poets of the time. A large crowd attended this event, as reported in *Or-Luz*.[34] Such events shed light on an elite class of local leaders, and the growing audiences that followed them, who attached their personal development to the Spanish language and culture. Most striking, however, is how this attachment would manifest as new habits adopted in day-to-day life.

ROUTINELY HISPANIC

In Tangier, one of the most important cultural spaces frequented by Spanish settlers at the time was the Gran Teatro Cervantes, officially inaugurated on December 12, 1913. With a capacity of 1,400, it aimed to promote Spanish culture to the growing Spanish-speaking population of the city. In this famous theater, notable Spanish companies performed many dramatic works, such as *La Barraca* by Federico García Lorca in 1934. The Cervantes theater hosted renowned Spanish artists like singer-actresses Estrellita Castro, Lola Flores, and Carmen Sevilla, and flamenco musicians Manolo Caracol and Juanito Valderrama. Valderrama's most important piece was "El Emigrante," a ballad for the millions of displaced Spaniards who fled the country in the years after the Spanish Civil War.[35] Though the theater featured other international artists, it focused on the Hispanophone world, hosting Latin American artists like Cuban musician Antonio Machín; Mexican singer Jorge Negrete; Argentina's most famous tango crooner Carlos Gardel; and Imperio Argentina, the stage name of Argentinean singer and actress Magdalena Nile del Río.[36] Through these and other traveling singers, the rising popularity of tango in Europe in the 1920s also reached Morocco and its Jewish community. This popularity was so influential that boys practicing for their bar mitzvahs, wanting to make their study for the ceremony more enjoyable, used to place the Torah intonation signs on lyrics of popular tango songs.[37]

A memorable event in the early 1960s was Imperio Argentina's performance at a *verbena*, a Spanish summer night fiesta, held at the Casino Israelita in Tangier. Imperio Argentina was accompanied by the famous Spanish pianist Gerardo Gombau. Among those responsible for organizing that verbena were Benjamin Benarroch, president of the Benchimol Jewish hospital in Tangier.[38] Jews like Alberto España engaged with Spanish cultural forms such as the *zarzuela*, a traditional Spanish musical genre.[39] Jacques Muyal, a Tangier Jew, became one of the famous jazz artists of that time. As a student at the Lycée Regnault, Muyal was influenced by the performances his parents would take him to at the Cervantes. He was later recruited to produce translations of jazz lyrics from English to Spanish for the *Jazz Hour* show on Radio Tánger. When flutist Herbie Mann performed in the city in March 1959 with Carlos "Patato" Valdez and Jose Mangual, Muyal was tasked with introducing their concert at the Cinema Alhambra.[40] Though the Hispanophone diaspora lacked a clear center, as we will see in chapter 3, exposure to Spanish culture helped connect Jews in northern Morocco to Latin American cultures.

Due to their great numbers and political influence, Spanish settlers played a significant role in shaping such local leisure activities that dominated the public sphere. In 1950, la Plaza de Toros, the bullring of Tangier, was inaugurated. Hosting the most important bullfighters from Spain, it had thirteen thousand seats and became a landmark that reflected the Spanish influence on Tangier's cultural life after the city regained its international status. In addition to the bullring, the following incomplete list of football (soccer) clubs established by Spanish settlers in Morocco illustrates to some extent the importance of football to the settlers' leisure culture: the regional Club Atlético de

Tetuán (founded in 1922); the Alfonso XIII Fútbol Club (1929); the Federación Hispano-Marroquí de Fútbol and Campeonato Hispano-Marroquí (1931); and la Sociedad Deportiva Tánger Club de Fútbol (1941).[41]

In the early 1930s, European sports culture was unpopular in the Jewish community, as evidenced by growing concern about the matter in the local Jewish press. Alberto Berdugo, the editor in chief of *Adelante*, one of the prominent Jewish newspapers in northern Morocco at the time, wrote in a report, "With the exception of football, Tangerine youth in general are not well acquainted with sports like cycling or pedestrian races."[42] Grassroots organizations soon began to fill that vacuum. Jewish and Muslim youths frequently played football together on the beaches of Larache, but soon some Jews began to organize themselves into teams based on neighborhoods or even streets. Their patterns of organization resembled the patterns common among non-Jewish football clubs.[43]

The criticism in *Adelante* about the lack of sporting activities in fact reflected a growing desire for recreational institutions that would demarcate the Jewish identity of their members against the backdrop of proliferating sport clubs and activities sponsored by Spanish settlers. The first explicitly Jewish local football club was Juventud Judía Deportiva (JID), followed by Macabenos—both founded in Larache in 1930. The Maguen David and Ideal football clubs were established the same year in Alcazarquivir.[44] In 1930, *Adelante* reported on the reunion of a group of Spanish Catholic scouts with their Jewish counterparts from Tangier and Larache as part of a festival held in Larache that year. The event started on Saturday afternoon with the arrival of the Spanish group to Larache and included a party on Saturday night and a football match on Sunday.[45] These teams did not play against Jewish groups in the French protectorate zone but forged a regional network in northern Morocco.

During the 1951–52 season, the Club Atlético de Tetuán football team even managed to compete in Spain's top league, the Campeonato Nacional de Liga de Primera División, alongside world-class clubs like Atlético Madrid. In the 1950s, in Tetouan's Varela stadium (named in 1950 after General José Varela, Franco's high commissioner in Morocco), Jews and Muslims played together as part of Club Atlético de Tetuán.[46] Football was not the only sport developed in northern Morocco by Spanish settlers. In 1956, *Or-Luz*, the Jewish periodical edited by Moisés Garzón Serfaty, published an interview with Samuel Serfaty, a Jew who coached Atlético de Tetuán's local basketball team. Starting out with El Rayo C.B. (El Rayo basketball club) in 1943, he passed through a number of Spanish basketball teams in Africa, among them Atlético y Union Africa Ceuta, which under his tutelage became Morocco's leading team in 1950–51.[47] Two decades later, Samuel Serfaty would become a leader of the new Jewish community in Valencia, Spain.

With the widespread acquisition of modern Spanish by northern Moroccan Jews and the growing dominance of Spanish culture in the public sphere, daily contact with non-Jewish Spanish speakers increased. Casual encounters between children in the street, interactions with neighbors in shared apartment buildings, and other forms of social mingling became habitual in a way that shaped the "re-Hispanization" of local Jews in northern Morocco from the bottom up, rather than just by means of direct colonial impositions.[48]

One of the prominent symbols of the re-Hispanization of local Jewish culture is the Hispanization of typical Jewish names since the mid-twentieth century. These names were often spelled, pronounced, or translated into non-Hebraic forms: Abraham frequently became Alberto, Yehuda was Leon, Baruch was Beniro, and other Jewish names simply adapted Spanish sounds; Moshe was Moisés, and Shlomo was converted into Salomón.[49] In addition, local Jews began to adopt the Spanish custom of using two surnames, those of the paternal and the maternal sides. Dual versions of prenames, both Hebraic and Hispanic and used by the same individuals, were no less emblematic of cultural transformation, representing a parallel need to define the boundaries of Spanish and other sources of European influence.[50]

SETTING COMMUNITY BOUNDARIES

The new lifestyles that arose out of daily interactions and engagement in leisure activities alongside the settler populations did not necessarily contradict traditional Judaism and its behavioral codes.[51] Since Judaism as it existed in colonial northern Morocco was an orthopraxy, it attached importance to the daily observance of religious laws in a way that could promote communal segregation for various community members. Already in the early 1930s, *Adelante*, the top Jewish newspaper circulating in northern Morocco at the time, reflected concern among local Jewish community leaders about the lack of Sabbath observance on the part of the younger generation of Tangier's Jews, some of who chose to work and send their children to school on the Jewish day of rest.[52]

Beyond the lack of religious observance, the Jewish landscape was also characterized by new practices alien to the traditional Jewish religious habitus. Calle Sevilla in the heart of Tangier was the main site of Christmas and New Year's celebrations among Spanish immigrants in the 1940s and 1950s.[53] The participation of Jews in such popular Spanish public celebrations of Christmas clashed with Jewish religious etiquette in the eyes of many. Simi, who grew up in the Judería of Tetouan, recalled a dispute with her father over her desire to attend a popular street parade (La Comparsa) on New Year's Eve. During our interview, she showed me a picture of her young uncle at such a festival, stating: "He was not like my father.... My father did not even allow me to eat a grape [referring to the Spanish custom of eating twelve grapes at midnight on New Year's Eve]."[54] This remark echoes ongoing notions about a new generation of Jews who felt more attached to colonial culture in northern Morocco and associated their attachment with intergenerational gaps.

Another custom that some Jews embraced was the Noche de Reyes, observed on January 6 to mark the Epiphany. On this night, children throughout the Spanish-speaking world expect to receive gifts delivered by the Three Kings who visited Jesus just after his birth.[55] In her 1987 memoir, Alegría Bendelac recalls how this custom penetrated her own Jewish home.[56] The widespread exposure to Christian customs among local Jews was indicated in a tape recording from a group trip by Tangier natives residing in Israel to their hometown in 1987. While sitting in a café in the heart of Tangier, the travelers spontaneously and joyfully began to sing Spanish Christmas songs. The performance erupted in response to an offhand remark by one of the participants about romantic relationships between Jews and Christians.[57]

As Nina Pinto Abecasis has shown, the phenomenon of *piropo*, the Spanish equivalent of catcalling, was also commonplace in northern Morocco. She notes that the piropo had sexual overtones, indicating a close observation of the female body that, to some extent, violated the norms of respect and honor that were the customary attitudes toward Jewish women.[58] The performance of piropo, at least as reflected in the oral traditions that Pinto Abecasis studied, may suggest to some extent intimate relationships between Jews and Spaniards—relationships that were not acceptable in the more formal discourse of the community. An indication of other sorts of informal relationships between Jews and Christians comes from the circumcision notebook of Rabbi Yamín, who operated in Tangier: 24 out of the 543 Jewish boys circumcised between 1929 and 1950 were born to a mother who had converted to Judaism from Christianity. Remarkably, four children had a Christian mother who had *not* converted, a fact that Rabbi Yamín did not attempt to conceal when he documented their circumcision.

More frequently, Jews would attend local bars and eat nonkosher food in violation of Jewish dietary laws that were otherwise usually obeyed.[59] An unexpected indication of the demand for nonkosher foods, typically Spanish dishes, appeared in the northern Morocco Jewish periodical *Or-Luz*. It was an advertisement for Bar Sevilla, an establishment in Tetouan, which clearly stated that it specialized in *gambas pil pil*—Spanish-style prawns. The fact that the editors

 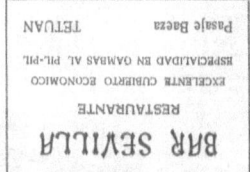 

Figure 1.1. Advertisement for Bar Sevilla published upside-down (*Or-Luz*, May 15, 1956). Courtesy of the Garzon Family. Stored at BZLPC.

had agreed to publish the advertisement, or that Bar Sevilla's owners thought to appeal to a Jewish audience through *Or-Luz*, suggests that nonkosher dining was probably not a rare occurrence among local Jews in Tetouan. The advertisement nonetheless seems to have been met with ambivalence among *Or-Luz*'s editors, as evidenced by their repeated decision to publish it upside down.[60] While it is hard to know the true intention behind the decision to publish the ad upside down, one reasonable interpretation is that it reflected the gap between the day-to-day lifestyles and religious ethics of Jews in Tetouan—both key aspects of their unique ethnicity in Morocco.

To understand how cultural boundaries worked, we also need to consider that by the early 1900s Jewish society in northern Morocco had become almost entirely urban, with rising numbers of immigrants coming into the larger urban centers of Tangier and Tetouan from smaller towns and villages in the Spanish protectorate zone and French-ruled southern Morocco. By the 1930s, Tangier's urban space was divided into two zones representing the "old" and "new" parts of the city. The old medina, situated on a hilltop next to the port in the northeast corner, overlooked the Bay of Tangier and was protected by a city wall. The newly built European section extended westward and southward from the medina. The layout of its broad commercial boulevards suggested a strong element of urban planning. Plaza de Francia, situated just a few minutes' walk south of the medina, marked the heart of the European area and the cosmopolitan cultural traits it represented. An impressive villa situated within the plaza and occupied by the French consulate symbolized the dominance of the European presence over the townscape. The Marchán, a luxurious suburban zone that extended westward from the medina, constituted another such cosmopolitan symbol. On the other hand, the Emsalleh area, referred to on the British admiralty map of 1942 as the "native quarter" within the new European city, resembled the medina with its large concentration of Muslims.

Figure 1.2. Le Grand Socco (Zoco Grande), Tangier, 1937. © Courtesy of CCJM, item 18981.

A central border zone architecturally separating the medina from the newer parts of European Tangier was nicknamed the Zoco de Fuera or Zoco Grande in Spanish—literally, "outer market" or "big market"—and colloquially was referred to as the Souk el-Kbir in Arabic or Le Grand Socco in French. From there, one would enter the old medina through the Beni Idar quarter, home to a concentration of historic Jewish institutions: ten synagogues, a yeshiva (religious seminary), and other communal facilities including a relatively large cemetery. Established in the nineteenth century, these institutions were still functioning as late as the 1950s.

By the mid-twentieth century, the linguistic shift from Haketia to Spanish that characterized most of the generation born around the early 1900s, was integrated into a socio-spatial divide between residents of newer and older parts of the city. Hélène recalled how her parents would berate her when she used Haketia words she had picked up from members of the community who still spoke it. Often when she used a word or an intonation that sounded like Haketia, her parents would say, "Stop! You speak like a girl from the 'Fuente Nueva'"—a site in the Jewish district of the medina.[61] The archaic way of speaking Spanish among the generation born in the nineteenth century was by and large interpreted by their children, Hélène's parents for example, as a sign of underdevelopment and even lack of urban mobility.

But the medina and the cultural world it represented in fact played a meaningful role in shaping communal heritage in the modernizing urban setting. For example, marriage ceremonies took place under the traditional chuppah, or wedding canopy, and were usually performed in one of the small synagogues there, followed by a celebration at home. In Tangier, the congregation occasionally accompanied the bride in a traditional parade through the streets of Beni Idar on their way to the synagogue ceremony.[62] Even though the Jewish part of Beni Idar had long ceased to function as the city's major Jewish population center, it nonetheless became a spatial emblem of Jewish heritage amid dramatic changes in the cityscape and their day-to-day routine.

In fact, demographically, the Beni Idar quarter was far from predominantly Jewish and was anything but ghetto-like. Writing in 1947, Onieva characterized the medina as a mosaic of ethnicities: a Spanish café next to a mosque, a Catholic church or a synagogue next to an Arab bazaar, a Jewish moneychanger's hut next to a shipping company.[63] Tangier, however, did not have many of the distinct religious or colonial divisions found elsewhere in Morocco.[64] The Jewish quarter, therefore, was no different from the entire medina as far as demographic diversity was concerned. In fact, the Jewish quarter bordered the area that the Spanish community considered its own historical site in the medina, where the Spanish Catholic Cathedral was located. The Spanish community in the 1940s and 1950s concentrated itself around the Calle Sevilla neighborhood, and the Gran Teatro Cervantes was a major meeting place for Jews and Spaniards there.[65]

This description demonstrates that dialectical and contextual mental transitions between the oppositional experiences of *modern-colonial* and *traditional-communal* spaces mutually shape modern Jewish life across their real and imagined townscapes. The establishment and active engagement with these boundaries became a defining practice of modernity for Jews in the region, more so than concepts like assimilation, integration, or tradition adherence. These boundaries were also crucial to facilitate coexistence between Spanish-speaking Jews and Catholics. Despite certain cultural commonalities, these two groups maintained their distinct identities, delineated by contrasting practices and beliefs, whose significance was amplified in the context of the actual reencounter.

Figure 1.3 illustrates how sites like the Gran Teatro Cervantes, which were otherwise associated with modern Spanish culture, could be repurposed and invested with traditional Jewish meanings in certain temporal contexts. It shows Jewish women dressed in *traje de berberisca* ("Berber dress") in a scenic representation of the *alheña* (henna) ceremony, associated with their Jewish

Figure 1.3. Jewish women dressed as berberiscas in a scenic representation of the henna ceremony. Gran Teatro Cervantes in Tangier, 1950s. © Courtesy of Ana Benarroch de Bensadon, Madrid. The author is grateful to Angy Cohen and Mercedes Guenun for their assistance in locating this photograph and acquiring the permission to use it.

ancestry in Spain. On the night before a wedding, celebrants would mark Noche de Berberisca (literally "Night of the Berber," also known as Noche de Novia)—the night of the henna ceremony, as it is better known among other communities in Morocco. The traditional *traje de berberisca* worn by northern Moroccan Jewish brides had equivalents in the Sephardi communities of Turkey, Greece, Algeria, and Bulgaria, with roots reaching back to fifteenth-century Spain.[66]

Images of wedding parades in the Alley of the Synagogues in Tangier or chuppah ceremonies at local synagogues across northern Morocco or even in private homes can stimulate our historical imagination regarding the sense of such semi-public spaces and the kinship networks they could generate. Participants exchanged their everyday social practices—dress codes, verbal mannerisms, and patterns of food and musical consumption—for new ones that would associate them more closely with their community. Matrimonial ceremonies constituted emblematic moments in which Jewish culture took on new meanings in the changing urban setting of colonial northern Morocco.[67]

This sensitivity to community time and space help to contextualize the emergence of institutionalized practices of community building that, in the context of Spanish colonialism, were mediated both by the state through Spanish schools and by the community through organized social activities and changing everyday habits. While Haketia and the culture it began to represent in the early 1900s was deemed archaic by the modernizing elite, it is important to highlight that the Spanish spoken by the mobile Jewish middle-class in the northern Morocco urban spaces was not uniform, and it retained Haketia influence depending on the social, temporal, and geographic contexts of speech. Relatedly, members of the Jewish elite also thought to leverage this language for modern ethnographic projects, which became essential to community building in light of major cultural shifts in colonial northern Morocco after 1912 and even more so after World War II, as the next chapter further explores.

TWO

IN (RE)SEARCH OF ORIGINS

"THE COLLECTION OF ROMANCES [IN HAKETIA] in this study was really begun long before I was aware of it. As a girl in Tangier . . . I heard many of them from my mother, singing them as they had been passed from generation to generation since the Jews were driven from Spain. . . . It was only during visits to Tangier, after I graduated Columbia [University], where I had done work in Romance philology, that I understood what Haketia was."[1] These words come from the prologue to an ethnographic work by Zarita Nahón, a native of Tangier who was one of the first Moroccans to graduate from Columbia University in 1929, as a student of the "father of American anthropology," Franz Boas. Studying in the department of anthropology, Nahón was a pioneer in conducting ethnographic fieldwork in Tangier and recorded Judeo-Spanish ballad songs.[2] Returning to her community in 1929, Nahón not only documented the ethnic heritage of the community; she also evoked it in a meaningful way. As she wrote in the prologue to her study: "Only by becoming one of them, could I get an old member of a family to talk, to reminisce, to open wide old archives. . . . They entrusted to me the romances that are no longer heard, in a language no longer spoken. . . . Their legacy lives again in these pages."[3]

I return here to Brian Keith Axel's wise questions: "Who in the most quotidian of ways, claims to be the subject of diaspora? [And] what are the everyday conditions for the identification of a subject of diaspora?"[4] This chapter draws on Axel's elemental questions in an attempt to explain how the diaspora of Hispanic Moroccan Jews, with their narrative of ancestry in Iberia, took shape amid the dramatic cultural changes that emerged from the encounter between Jews and Spanish settlers in northern Morocco from the outset of colonialism until its end in 1956.

My focus on northern Morocco in the first half of the twentieth century in this chapter has implications for the broader scholarship on ethnic heritage formation among diaspora groups, which is typically conceived of as a process that emerges in response to their emigration and displacement.[5] Understood as a "border line" between "pre-migration" and "post-migration" histories, migration among Jews from Islamic countries in the second half of the twentieth century is particularly considered to have brought about the "silencing" of pre-immigration traditions in new lands, followed, after a generation or two, by their "revival."[6]

Nahón's work and biography as an ethnographer offer a different view on ethnic heritage formation prior to the mass departure of Jews from Morocco and other Middle East and North Africa (MENA) countries in the mid-twentieth century. Her work demonstrates how those processes developed among a population that remained in its place of origin while interacting with both local and global trends of heritage preserving. The chapter explores an impulse to document the community's origins in Spain, as it developed not only against the backdrop of Spanish colonialism but also through scholarly ties between northern Morocco and the Americas, and the development of Jewish cultural ethnography in Europe and North America at the beginning of the twentieth century.

THE FORMALIZATION OF SEPHARDI HERITAGE

In the previous chapter, I described how the berberisca became an emblem of community life in an urban society that experienced strong outside influences on its culture. In fact, the tradition of wearing the berberisca dress on the night before the wedding was popular among Jews elsewhere in Morocco, where it was more typically known as *keswa el-kbira*, the Great Dress. Still, the community in northern Morocco stood at the heart of ethnographic works regarding this custom. Already from the mid-eighteenth century, Jewish weddings in Tangier and the musical traditions that accompanied them began to fuel the ethnographic imagination of European travelers, writers, and artists such as Samuel Aaron Romanelli, Eugène Delacroix, and Alexandre Dumas, whose 1849 book, *Le Veloce en Tanger, Alger et Tunis*, was perhaps the first literary work to rely on members of the northern Moroccan community to collect information about the wedding ceremony and interpret it.[7] Later, in his 1919 book *Los Hebreos en Marruecos* (*The Hebrews of Morocco*), Hispanicist Manuel L. Ortega mentions a traditional wedding parade that was accompanied by the singing of Sephardi ballad songs and religious *piyyutim*.[8] Other Hispanists, such as

Jan Jouin, attributed the berberisca dress to the pre-expulsion traditions that Jews had brought with them from Iberia. The curiosity about the berberisca constitutes only one example of how ethnographic intellectual networks began to feed a process of community building by integrating new imaginaries of Jewish origins in Spain.[9]

At the beginning of the twentieth century, a few local Jews in northern Morocco began to adhere to the Philo-Sephardi ideas developed by liberal Spanish intellectuals and politicians a few decades earlier. Among the few pioneers was Pinhas Asayag, a Jewish journalist from Tangier and former member of the junta, the local Jewish community council. In July 1904, he sent Senator Ángel Pulido a letter praising the role of the Royal Spanish Academy, which since 1917 had aimed to ensure the stability of the Spanish language, in bringing Jews closer to their Spanish "fatherland."[10] In his book *The Spanish Israelites and the Spanish Language*, Pulido acknowledges Asayag as a central figure in the promotion of Philo-Sephardi ideas among the Jewish community in northern Morocco and describes Asayag's connection with other enthusiastic supporters of the Philo-Sephardi campaign, among them Rabbi Mordojay Bengio, Tangier's chief rabbi at the time.[11]

To be sure, this kind of collaboration with the Philo-Sephardi campaign was not limited to Sephardi intellectuals in northern Morocco. The Philo-Sephardi movement aspired to promote the concept of an affinity with Spain across the Sephardi Mediterranean diaspora, including the substantial Ladino-speaking communities in the Ottoman Empire.[12] Nonetheless, the reaction of native Spanish-speaking Jews in northern Morocco to the Philo-Sephardi atmosphere differed from that of Ladino-speaking Ottoman Jews in one major aspect: their direct experience of Spanish colonialism and its tremendous cultural, economic, and political impact on their day-to-day lives, as we saw in the previous chapter.[13] In the context of early Spanish colonialism, the growing perception of Spain as a Jewish fatherland in fact reflected the adaptation of Jewish community leaders to the changing imperial setting that saw the rise of Spain as the dominant power in northern Morocco.

Already at the outset of the twentieth century, intellectual writing about the origins of the Jews in pre-1492 Iberia had begun to enrich and motivate Jewish communal gatherings and organizations in northern Morocco. On May 11, 1912, just a few months before the establishment of the Spanish protectorate in Morocco on November 27, a group of Moroccan Jews and Philo-Sephardi Christians in Tangier established the first Asociación Hispano-Hebrea, or the Hispanic-Hebrew Association, during a meeting at the Spanish Chamber of Commerce Hall. In the following months, similar associations were established

Figure 2.1. Pinhas Asayag. © Courtesy of CCJM, item 25056.

in Tetouan, Ceuta, Larache, and Alcazarquivir. Though not officially a Spanish governmental initiative, the main goal of these institutions was to promote identification with Spain among Jews in northern Morocco by dwelling on the common linguistic denominator.

From a community leadership perspective, expressed nostalgia for Spain also entailed some very concrete advantages, as the associations were designed to promote commercial ties and charity projects while Spain was cementing its political and economic influence in northern Morocco. As part of the ongoing struggle between France and Spain over the influence on the communities of the north, the Hispanic-Hebrew associations lobbied for the creation of libraries, organized conferences, and awarded academic prizes to those promoting knowledge of Spanish among Jews in Morocco.[14] This activity aimed to disseminate Philo-Sephardi discourse among the grassroots of the community, particularly among the local Jews who preferred to identify with French colonialism.

Consider, for example, the lectures of Dr. Avraham Shalom Yahuda (1877–1951), delivered in Tangier during that early period under the sponsorship of the local branch of the Hispanic-Hebrew Association. Yahuda was a biblical scholar appointed Special Numerary Chair of Rabbinical Hebrew Language and Literature at the University of Madrid. Yuval Evri, Allyson Gonzalez, and Michal Rose Friedman each explain Yahuda's motivations for engaging in this activity locally and globally, as an emissary from Palestine.[15] Less explored are the motivations of community leaders for hosting him and the impact of his mission on community building in northern Morocco. In 1914, according to one report, a crowd of more than 1,500 Spanish settlers and Jews gathered in Tangier to hear Yahuda lecture on the Jewish past in Spain.[16] While the associations had delegates throughout the Americas as well as in Paris, London, Vienna, Amsterdam, and Berlin, according to Ortega's 1919 book, only in northern Morocco did the brunches of the Hispano-Hebrew Association attract hundreds of affiliated associates who saw the immediate benefit of expressing affinity with imperial Spain after it had become a colonial power in the region.[17] Philo-Sephardi activities in northern Morocco further developed where Spanish colonialism met local Jewish community building. It is in this context that the linguistic revival of Haketia, and the intensifying interest in documenting literary and oral traditions that attached Jews in northern Morocco to pre-1492 Iberia, needs to be analyzed.

As mentioned earlier, following the establishment of the Spanish protectorate in 1912, the rapid transformation of Haketia into modern Spanish precipitated the disappearance of Haketia as a vernacular. This transformation was viewed by Jewish intellectuals in the community as the re-Hispanicization of Haketia: the purification of a Spanish idiom that had been degraded by the admixture of Arabic (and Tamazigh) words over the years. Others, however, came to perceive Haketia, and particularly its Arabic elements, as the most authentic indication of Jews' primordial origins in Iberia, requiring preservation through the mediation of the older generation of native speakers. These advocates constituted a dense network of Haketia speakers who would soon become ethnographic subjects for those seeking to document the community's dying linguistic (and musical) heritage. The fact that the entomology of the name Haketia was explained by some scholars at the time as stemming from the Arabic root Kh.K.Y (referring to speech) helped imbue it with a sense of precolonial Iberian coexistence between Jews, Muslims, and Christians in Al-Andalus/Sepharad.[18]

According to Gladys Pimienta, the first intellectual work to mention the word Haketia was Manuel L. Ortega's 1919 book *Los Hebreos en Marruecos* (*The Hebrews of Morocco*). Prior to that work, the Jewish-Spanish dialect was simply referenced in communal sources as Español—Spanish—which was perceived as a Jewish Moroccan language.[19] The academic definition of the dialect as Haketia in ethnography helped demarcate it as a "private" communal asset in contrast with Spanish, which represented the colonial sphere that seemingly threatened Haketia's survival in the modern urban context. This dynamic in fact began to elevate the academic status of Haketia, which had until then been regarded as a low status, incorrect, and colloquial form of Spanish spoken by the older generation of the Judería.

A central community figure promoting the preservation of Haketia was José Benoliel, a philologist, poet, and teacher from Tangier, who was nicknamed *el sabio* (the wiseman) by members of the community elite. Developing an academic career as a professor of Romance philology in Lisbon in 1881, Benoliel was one of the mobile individuals from the northern Moroccan Jewish elite who helped renew the Jewish community in Portugal in the late nineteenth century, several decades before a community was officially established in Spain. While serving as leader of Tangier's Jewish community between 1921 and 1929, following his return from Portugal, he became one of the first academics in the world to publish scientific articles on Haketia, many of which appeared in the bulletin of the Spanish Royal Academy.[20] José Benoliel's correspondence with Ángel Pulido played a pivotal role in shaping the field of Philo-Sephardi scholarship. Angel Pulido, in his letter to Benoliel, requested materials to be sent to the renowned philologist Ramón Menéndez Pidal. These materials, composed of Sephardi romances from Tangier, were instrumental in Menéndez Pidal's compilation of Moroccan Judeo-Spanish repertoire, and this collaboration marked the beginning of a much more comprehensive and enduring relationship between Spanish scholars and Moroccan Judeo-Spanish culture throughout the twentieth century.[21]

The dynamics that helped the Jewish communities of northern Morocco reaffirm their collective primordial attachment to Spain as part of the unique precolonial amalgam constituting their northern Moroccan identity were not detached from broader developments in world academia. This is also implied by Zarita Nahón's graduation from Columbia University, referenced at the beginning of this chapter. Nahón's interest in the Hispanic musical traditions of Jews in northern Morocco developed amid the growth of broader scholarly interest in Hispanic culture on the other side of the Atlantic, detached from the local context of Spanish colonialism in Morocco. For example, in 1920,

Maír José Benardete, professor in the newly established Spanish and Sephardi studies program at Brooklyn College in New York City, engaged in scholarly collaboration with Federico de Onís, the founder (also in 1920) of the Hispanic studies program, Casa Hispánica, at Columbia University.[22]

As a student at Columbia, Nahón became part of an international academic network whose work bridged Jewish studies, African studies, and Hispanic studies by adopting ethnographic techniques, long before the hybrid or transnational turn in the humanities. As Nahón testified in the prologue to her work, it was Professor Franz Boas—the leading figure in the development of cultural anthropology and the concept of cultural relativism—who called her into his office to explain the "urgency" of her return to Tangier to conduct ethnography, as long as the romances "still existed" there among the people.[23]

While Boas's cultural approach to anthropology was not necessarily rooted in his own Jewish origins, he did indeed work with many Jewish students at a time when Jewish studies was infused with an "ethnographic impulse," to use Jeffrey Veidlinger's phrase. That period was characterized by a growing number of "salvage ethnography," missions undertaken by Jewish intellectuals hoping to study and document the Jewish heritage of "the people" living in the Russian Pale of Settlement. These missions shaped the broader field of ethnography and later cultural anthropology. In Kiev, for example, Moyshe Beregovski and Zalmen Skuditski performed ethnographic fieldwork on Jewish musical traditions, just as Nahón's work did.[24]

Nahón's pioneering ethnographic fieldwork in northern Morocco introduced Tangier to that burgeoning scholarly network, especially after Columbia's Federico de Onís followed in her footsteps with his own fieldwork in Tangier. Initiated in 1930 and lasting eight years, de Onís's fieldwork hinged on his connection to Suzanne (Simy) Nahón de Toledano, a relative of Zarita Nahón. While it took Nahón months to "induce a significant part of the community to participate" in her project, many eventually collaborated; some even continued to send her material in New York after her return to Columbia.[25] Despite the generally philological orientation of (mostly German Jewish) scholars of the pre-1492 Sephardi heritage, Nahón reflected a trend among Sephardi intellectual and community leaders who began to apply ethnographic methods in their search for the "remnants" or "living roots" of Jews in pre-expulsion Iberia, rather than searching for them in texts.[26] Luna Benaim Boaknin, for example, compiled a series of local Judeo-Spanish melodies from 1919 to 1959. Her daughter recalled assisting Boaknin with her compilation work during the month of Ramadan, transcribing the lyrics her mother would sing in the community's age-old vernacular.[27]

The impulse to document the community's linguistic and folkloric practices would play an important role in defining the community's boundaries vis-à-vis Spanish colonialism while passing along uniform images of its precolonial origins in Spain. To further explain how this process developed, a survey of the emergence of a local Hispanophone Jewish press in the late 1920s and early 1930s is essential.

NEW MEANS OF DISSEMINATION

The local Jewish press was one of the most effective and practical tools for disseminating standardized intellectual concepts of the community's past to a broad audience. Toward the end of the nineteenth century and in the early decades of the twentieth, Tangier Jews played a significant role in the establishment of the first newspapers in Morocco, including *Le Reveil du Maroc*, *El Diario de Tánger*, and others. The first Jewish Moroccan newspapers appeared in reaction to the growing European presence and represented an attempt to differentiate the community's unique Jewish characteristics from the rest of Moroccan Jewry. These included *Le Mebasser Tob* (1894–95), *Kol Israel* (1914), and *El Horria* (1915–17), which appeared in Judeo-Arabic, and *La Liberté* (1915–22), published in French, prior to the creation of the international administrative zone of Tangier in late 1924.

Under Spanish colonial rule over much of the rest of northern Morocco after 1912, seven new Jewish newspapers were published in Spanish, including *El Eco Israelita* (1915), *Renacimiento de Israel* (1924–33), *Kol Hanoar: Órgano de la Unión Universal de Juventudes Judías* (1927), *Adelante* (1929–31/32), *Crisol Judío* (1931), and *Or/Or-Luz* (1956).[28] To this we can add the community's *Boletín Oficial* (1949–52). The prominence of the Spanish language reflects the community's increasing tendency to hispanize community documents following Spanish colonization, both in the protectorate region and in Tangier.[29]

The bimonthly Spanish-language publication *Renacimiento de Israel* (or *Hatehiya*, the word for "revival" in its Hebrew name) was one of the prominent ones.[30] But it was issued by Asher Perl, a Polish Jew who moved to Palestine and then resettled in Algeciras, Spain. Despite being printed in mainland Spain, the paper presented itself as the "defender of the political and national interests of the Jewish collectivity in Morocco." While Perl single-handedly wrote and edited all the articles, he relied on a network of collaborators to distribute the journal, not only in Tangier but in other towns in both Spanish and French Morocco as well as in Gibraltar, Buenos Aires, and Salonica.[31]

Unlike *Renacimiento*, *Adelante* was issued by a group of young local Jews who aspired to revitalize Jewish cultural and spiritual life in northern Morocco in the context of growing European cultural influence, as discussed in the previous chapter. The paper came into being primarily at the initiative of Jack (Jacobo) Sabáh Nahón, its managing director and main founding editor. Isaac Bendayan Benayoun was its first editor in chief and was replaced after about a year, in October 1929, by Alberto Berdugo. Isaac Elbaz served as honorary president. *Adelante* was in fact bilingual, integrating some French articles that enabled a wide range of intellectuals to read and contribute to it. However, *Adelante*'s founders and writers, many of whom graduated from Alliance Israélite Universelle (AIU) schools, still represented a generation of Sephardi leaders who welcomed stronger ties between Spain and northern Moroccan Jews. Consequently, they did not necessarily conceive their adoption of the modern Spanish language as contradictory to their French orientation.

The Spanish-language press exemplifies the way community narratives of ancestry in Spain were shaped in conversation with developments in Spanish colonialism and its reception in the late 1920s and early 1930s. While disseminating information to the community in a novel way and reflecting the smooth adoption of modern Spanish by local Jews and their more general upward social mobility, these newspapers worked simultaneously to strengthen the impulse to locate Sephardi origins in medieval Spain that helped generate a notion of long-lasting attachment already from the fifteenth century.

In January 1931, for example, selected students from the Hispano-Israelite and Hispano-Arab schools participated in an annual trip to mainland Spain under the sponsorship of the Spanish government. One of them was Alberto Lascar, a student from the Seminario Rabínico, a religious school in Tangier established by the Hispanicist and community leader José Benoliel. Lascar's impressions from his visit were published in *Adelante* as part of the newspaper's effort to encourage readers to contribute letters to the editor. In his report, he described the trip as a dream come true, one that allowed him to experience, on Spanish soil, the ancestral connection to Spain that his parents had long spoken about. Lascar opened his article by describing how the idea of visiting Spain came about: "I am a Jew, and considering this, gentlemen, [you may] appreciate the joy that filled me when the venerable Father Antonio communicated the good news [about the upcoming trip] to us . . . : 'Boys, the Honorable Mr. Manuel Aguirre de Cárcer [de Tejada], has obtained for you, from the Spanish government, that a trip be made annually to our beloved homeland, so that in this way, you, Spaniards of Morocco, awaken your affection for that homeland that you do not know and that was the cradle of your parents and grandparents.'"[32] While we do not know the specific motivations for Lascar's descriptions, its publication indicated the existence of initiatives by the Spanish government to appeal to Tangier's Jews as well as the positive reaction those initiatives occasioned in Tangier's Jewish press, which, as mentioned, was not subject to the direct censorship of the Spanish state.

The framing of communal genealogy and history around the community's shared roots in pre-1492 Spain helped strengthen the community's collective story in a way that also aligned with community leaders' political aspirations of remaining loyal to the Spanish colonial campaign. While similar ways of imagining the Sephardi past characterized some of the venerable families in central Morocco—especially in Fez and Meknes—the north's geographical proximity to Spain helped Jews in that region connect this mythical imagination of pre-1492 Spain with the modern Spanish state and its colonial project.[33] A visit to modern Spain was the ultimate opportunity to experience the connection between the old and new Spains—or at least to start expressing such a connection in the community press.

Despite the occasional polemics that *Adelante*'s writers directed against Perl's outsider meddling through his foreign newspaper, *Renacimeinto*, and his criticisms of Tangier's Jewish community leaders and the AIU school system (which Perl saw as impeding Zionism), *Adelante*'s editors praised Perl for two reasons: the latter's enthusiastic support of the Zionist cause (discussed in chap. 4) and the Jewish community's growing affinity with Spain. Even as *Adelante*'s editors viewed *Renacimiento* as a competitor, they announced with a certain degree of pride that it was the first and only Jewish newspaper in modern mainland Spain, a fact that marked the revival of Spanish Jewish life following centuries of absence. *Adelante*'s editors were proud of their success in becoming, over a period of just half a year, one of "Africa's top Spanish newspapers" and appealing to a readership of hundreds of Jewish and non-Jewish subscribers (including Muslims), thereby serving the "reencounter." They decided to celebrate the accomplishment with a festive banquet in February 1930 at Hotel La Palmera.[34] *Adelante*'s editors also described how *Dépêche Marocaine*, one of Morocco's most prominent periodicals at the time, put its printing press at their disposal.[35] Furthermore, a series of non-Jewish periodicals in northern Morocco, including *El Porvenir de Tánger*, *L'Echo de Tánger*, *El Eco Mauritano de Tánger Heraldo de Marruecos*, *El Estatuto de Tánger*, *El Popular de Larache*, and *Diario Marroquí de Larache* acknowledged *Adelante*'s importance in reviving the connection between Moroccan Jews and Spain in a series of letters sent to its editorial board on the occasion of its first anniversary.[36]

Adelante's editors described their goal as relieving the "pain of the misunderstanding and separation between peninsular Spaniards and Sephardi Spaniards." Some of the newspaper's articles thus reflected an inherited tension between nostalgia for and alienation from pre-1492 Spain, the fatherland that had expelled them. However, they also reflected the active desire to heal that painful wound through calls—often with a highly critical tone—to repeal the Alhambra edict of 1492.[37] The appeal of narratives of Spanish ancestry among northern Moroccan Jews would be put to one of its biggest tests from the mid-1930s until the mid-1940s.

SEPHARDISM UNDER FASCISM

The political situation in the years when Pulido, Ortega, or the editors and contributors of *Adelante* and *Renacimieneto* spread their Philo-Sephardi narrative drastically changed by the mid-1930s and 1940s. The early 1930s saw the rise of Pan-Arab and Jewish nationalism in Morocco in light of Jewish-Arab clashes in Palestine, first in 1929 and then in the Arab Revolt of 1936, which inspired regional turmoil reaching as far as Morocco. A series of anti-French strikes were also sparked by the Berber Dahir, or Berber Edict of May 16, 1930, which sought to separate the Arabic- and Tamazight-speaking Muslim groups in French colonial Morocco into distinct legal systems.[38] These and other, related events taking place across the Middle East and North Africa manifested locally in northern Morocco in the mid-1930s.

To strengthen his hold on Spanish Morocco, Franco disseminated what Eric Calderwood calls "the Andalus-centric narrative of Moroccan history" as a strategy to strengthen his colonial hold. Franco's conservative Catholic regime somewhat paradoxically promoted the discourse of "Hispano-Moroccan brotherhood"—the idea that North Africa was a historic extension of Spain and the aspiration of returning Spain to the age of the Convivencia. According to this narrative, the culture of Al-Andalus did not disappear in 1492 with the Christian reconquest of Muslim Granada; rather, it migrated to Morocco, where it continued to thrive until the present day. This discourse was promoted not only by the Francoist regime but also by Muslim nationalists, as in the case of M'hammad Binnuna, who nicknamed Tetouan "the daughter of Granada." But this discourse only reflected Franco's efforts to maintain peaceful relations with the Moroccan Muslim elite. Relying on that narrative, Franco managed to recruit some seventy thousand Moroccan troops in his rebellion against Spain's second republic.[39]

Double standards were no less apparent in the case of Jews. Amid the antisemitic winds blowing from Eastern Europe in the pre-Holocaust years, antisemitic expression in Spain took the form of accusations that Jews sought to stir disorder. Franco and his nationalist supporters railed against the so-called

Jewish-Bolshevik-Masonic conspiracy, blaming world Jewry for Spain's deterioration into civil war.[40] Franco's anti-Jewish expressions contradicted his regime's declared commitment to Philo-Sephardi objectives and revealed how cynical his discourse was. In Franco's mind, a cultural separation between Sephardim and Ashkenazim became essential for colonizing the Jewish communities of Morocco. With the victory of Franco's nationalist military regime in northern Morocco in July 1936, the Andalus-centric narrative of Moroccan history became entwined with Philo-Sephardism, fueling the emergence of new local institutions that helped further disseminate the idea with Franco's support. The founding in 1938 of the General Franco Institute for Hispano-Arab Research was a landmark event in that regard. The institute published dozens of works emphasizing the historical and cultural connections between Al-Andalus, Morocco, and Francoist Spain.

Moreover, some community leaders and members of the Jewish intellectual and economic elites continued to support the Philo-Sephardi philosophy even when it was imbued with strong fascist spirits. These supporters recognized that as long as Franco's fascist aspirations did not result in tangible and direct anti-Jewish violence, collaborating with his Philo-Sephardi narrative about the distinctiveness of Sephardi Jews in fact remained a valuable source of stability, both for individuals and the community. The motivations behind their stance remain a subject of ongoing debate and speculation, but the financial support extended to Franco by Jewish bankers like the Hassán family in Tangier and Jacob Benmamán in Tetouan serves as a clear example of the existence of such a collaboration.[41] No less evident is the influence of Franco on the development of the communal narrative of ancestry in Spain.

Franco's cultural campaign unexpectedly bolstered the community's ancestral narrative through the institutions it established. In January 1938, Jewish leaders from Tetouan sent a letter to Juan Beigbeder, the high commissioner of the Spanish protectorate in Morocco. The letter expressed support for a proposal to establish a center for Talmudic studies in Tetouan, which would eventually be known as the Maimonides Institute. A year later, *Sefarad* was established as the mouthpiece of the Instituto Arias Montano de Estudios Árabes y Hebreos (Arias Montano Institute for Arabic and Hebraic Studies), established by the Francoist regime in 1939 and named after Benito Arias Montano, the sixteenth-century Spanish Bible scholar.

Jewish leaders and intellectuals from the community used these Francoist-funded institutions to advance and disseminate literary knowledge of the community's origins, ranging from biblical studies to Sephardi culture and linguistics. *Sefarad* ran articles by the writer Abraham Isaac Laredo with titles like "El nombre de Sefarad" ("The Name Sepharad," 1944), "Sefarad en la literatura hebraica" ("Sepharad in Hebraic Literature," 1944), and "Las Taqanot de los Expulsados de Castilta: Marruecos y su matrimonial and sucesorial regimen" ("The *Taqanot* [Halakhic enactments] of the [Jews] Expelled from Castilla: Morocco and Its Matrimonial and Successor Regime," 1948). Laredo was among the Arias Montano Institute's first collaborators.[42] Another prominent figure in that regard was Rabbi Salomon Benshabat Benarroch, the head of the Maimonides Institute in the 1940s. He published a variety of articles and books that were designed to draw a connection between rabbinical studies in Morocco and the study of biblical literature in medieval Spain.[43]

The notion of Sephardi exclusivity extended beyond the confines of the Spanish colonial perspective on Sephardi Jews. In the late 1930s, a few thousand Jewish refugees arrived from Europe and settled in Tangier. Although this influx constituted a financial drain on the Jewish community council, from 1939 local leadership worked closely with world Jewish organizations, such as the American Joint Distribution Committee (JDC), to provide them with asylum. While expressing solidarity, the encounter with Ashkenazi refugees also provoked a sense of estrangement that strengthened Sephardi identities. Exemplifying this sense of intra-Jewish estrangement upon the intensifying encounter with European Jewish refugees, Carlos de Nesry, a local lawyer and member of the Junta of Tangier, wrote, "Never has the Jew of Tangier felt more Spanish, more Sephardi. Never has he so much felt so strongly the powerful lifeblood of his heredity."[44]

As in the late 1920s and early 1930s, when the Philo-Sephardi discourse was disseminated to the broader community, in the 1940s and early 1950s too, Jewish institutions continued to bring the ideas about Jewish roots in Spain to lay community members. The Círculo Recreativo Israelita, known colloquially as the Casino Israelita, regularly hosted series of lectures on Jewish affairs.[45] Using the space of Tetouan's Casino Israelita in 1948, Rabbi Salomon Benshabat Benarroch explained to a large audience the connection between Jewish life in tenth-century Córdoba and their own present lives as Sephardi Jews in twentieth-century Morocco, declaring that for Moroccan Sephardi Jews, medieval liturgy from Iberia is almost as sacred as the Bible.[46] In this vein, an overview of communal life in Tetouan subtitled "A Brief Historical and Sentimental Overview of the Jewish Community of Tetouan," published in 1954 by León Coriat, started its narrative in the year 1492, right after the expulsion.[47]

IN LIGHT OF POSTCOLONIALISM

World War II sparked a wave of nationalist activity across the European colonies in Africa and Asia. On the one hand, this period of growing expressions of global Jewish solidarity manifested in the work of world Jewish bodies such as the JDC. On the other, it increased a sense of disparity among Jews and Muslims based on separate national aspirations (see chap. 4). In Morocco, 1943 saw the founding of the Istiqlal Party, the principal Moroccan nationalist movement. In April 1947, the Sultan of Morocco, Mohamed ben-Yousef, visited Tangier and delivered a speech that would become a landmark in the Moroccan struggle for independence. Four years later, in April 1951, the Istiqlal Party joined forces with two other local nationalist parties operating in northern Morocco: the Parti Démocratique de l'Independence (PDI) and the Moroccan National Front in Tangier. Amid this proliferation of nationalist movements, segments of Moroccan society were becoming alien in the eyes of local Jews, most of whom had developed a pro-European orientation during the colonial era.

On March 2, 1956, the French protectorate came to an end, and Morocco became an independent constitutional monarchy. On April 7, the Spanish protectorate ended as well, and in October Tangier was integrated into the new monarchy. With the formal end of the Spanish and French protectorates in Morocco, the year 1956 marked a major shift in the political situation of the Hispanic Moroccan Jewish diaspora. As Chris Silver has noted, the scholarly emphasis on Jewish Moroccan outmigration after 1956 has pushed aside research on forms of continuity in Jewish lives in the postcolonial context.[48]

Relatedly, Jewish solidarity on the one hand and postcolonial struggle against Spain on the other did not put an end to local Sephardi cultural activism. *Or-Luz*, a newspaper published in 1956 in northern Morocco, continued to serve as a mouthpiece for Philo-Sephardi discourse even after the Spanish protectorate was coming to an end as Morocco's independence was achieved in February 1956. In the volume that appeared that month, Yosef D. Benmaman published an article about the "symbol of Sefardism, the man who is known and appreciated in every Jewish home: Doctor Pulido."[49] The narrative was also fed by articles about the "Chuetas en Mallorca" (on the history of Majorcan Crypto-Jews and Conversos); by an article from Dr. Medina Wahnon about Maimonides; and by an article entitled "Imágenes de Sefarad" ("Images of Sepharad"), all published in May 1956, two months after Spain's protectorate ended in the region.[50]

Concrete encounters with the physical space of modern Spain, which became more frequent as the postcolonial twentieth century unfolded, combined with the imagination of Spain as a Jewish place of origin to engender some fascinating literary constructions of northern Moroccan urban space. One example is an article from *Or-Luz* entitled "Añoranzas de un Sabbat" ("Longing for a Sabbath"), in which the author, Salomon Medina, a Jewish physician from Tetouan who resided in Seville in 1956, fused his yearning for the Sabbath atmosphere of his childhood in Tetouan with a description of the alleys of the ancient Judería of Seville.[51] He wrote, "I daydreamed of those alleys [in Seville] that [resemble the ones] my eyes saw as a child [in] the Jewish quarter of Tetouan."[52] "Remembering" or referring to that section of the city helped evoke a nostalgic narrative that detached the narrators as well as the readers from their concrete spatial and temporary contexts, attaching spatial meaning to tradition.

Writing under the pen name MOGAR some twenty-five years after Alberto Lascar's 1931 description of his journey to Spain in *Adelanate*, and only two months after Morocco's independence from France and Spain, the editor of *Or-Luz*, Moisés Garzón Serfaty, described his own impressions from a visit to the Spanish city of Cadiz—a city where "there is no reminder left of the existence of Spanish Hebrews" but to which a new wave of immigrants from Tetouan was then arriving to study. He started his account with an allusion to the major change that had occurred in the ability of Jews to settle in Spain since 1492, comparing the medieval expulsion with the more pleasant and exciting contemporary journey in the opposite direction, from Morocco back to Spain, as colonialism ended. More importantly, MOGAR expressed his great curiosity about the Jewish past in Cadiz and how, during his trip, that curiosity led him to the local library and into conversations with local people who he suspected might "remember" Jewish life in Spain.[53]

The academic and cultural production of communal origin stories continued during and long after most Jews had begun to emigrate. Jews in Morocco and beyond continued to consume and create a discourse that connected them to Spain, whether in independent Morocco, in Israel, or in Spain itself. Ethnographic projects focusing on the Hispanic roots and language of the northern Moroccan community, such as Manuel Alvar's field study in Tetouan, Larache, and Melilla in the period from 1949 to 1959, and the fieldwork undertaken by Samuel G. Armistead, Joseph H. Silverman, and Israel J. Katz across northern Morocco in 1962–63, testifies to a cooperation among researchers and local residents, or at least an awareness of a powerful narrative of shared communal heritage.[54]

Figure 2.2. Author's relatives (from Tangier) dressed up to emulate the Andalusian past in an instance of "reenactment tourism." Photography studio in the Alhambra compound, Spain 1953. © Courtesy of Daniel Moreno.

Alberto Pimienta, a Tangier Jewish musician, remarked in a 1987 interview conducted in Tangier, "I have a lot of respect for all these scholars who worked hard to record and document the *romancero* or Spanish ballad songs, but for me, as a musician in Tangier, it wasn't a major part of my musical repertoire." Pimienta asserted that Spanish ballad songs were stylistically foreign to the space of Tangier. However, while sharing his experience, Pimienta also recalled how he had engaged in documenting Spanish ballad songs in Tangier in 1959, as it was part of his community's spirit.[55] This anecdote helps reframe my discussion in the context of Axel's questions: "Who in the most quotidian of ways, claims to be the subject of diaspora? [And] what are the everyday conditions for the identification of a subject of diaspora?"[56] This chapter has revealed a network of heritage commemorators who helped produce a standardized story of Jewish ancestry in Spain that made sense of community renewal under colonialism and the vast Hispanicization of the Jewish communities in northern Morocco. This story of shared origins in Iberia would further extend its reach through transnational migration and rising Jewish and Moroccan nationalisms. While the intensifying impulse to document Jewish ancestry in Spain was a result of Spanish colonialism, it would survive regime changes, decolonization, and migration, as we shall see in the following chapters.

THREE

MOROCCO IN LATIN AMERICA, LATIN AMERICA IN MOROCCO

BY THE EARLY NINETEENTH CENTURY, INTERNATIONAL migration had become an important feature of Jewish life in Morocco. Jewish immigrants from northern Morocco were recorded during that period in mainland England, Bukhara, Sudan, Palestine, the Azores, the Canary Islands, and other more distant destinations, including parts of the United States, the Caribbean Basin, and the Brazilian and Peruvian Amazon basin.[1] Moroccan migration unfolded against the backdrop of intensifying international migration in the nineteenth century, including from the Middle East and North Africa. For example, in Syria and Lebanon, both wellsprings of emigration from the Ottoman Empire at the time, we observe the tendency of various non-Muslim minorities—Maronites, Catholics, Greek Orthodox, Druze, and Jews—to migrate to the Americas.[2] However, in Morocco, emigration to Latin America, which was associated with the Spanish-speaking Jews of northern Morocco, was generally a Jewish phenomenon.[3]

The first periodicals in northern Morocco to discuss Jewish migration to South America were associated with the Alliance Israélite Universelle (AIU) and appeared in the second half of the nineteenth and the early twentieth centuries, serving as functional reports on its development in real time. Such sources have been widely employed by scholars since the 1980s to characterize this migration as a form of Jewish emancipation, distinguished from other forms of international migration among Moroccan Muslims and the circular patterns that characterized it.[4] To offer a different view, in this chapter I examine how Jewish migration to Latin America came to shape one of the first transnational Moroccan communities at the beginning of the twentieth century, one dominated by Hispanic Moroccan Jews. I demonstrate how in the first half of the twentieth century, migration began to shape the diasporic consciousness of Hispanic Moroccan Jews living in northern Morocco. Crucially, through transregional links with Latin America, these Jews began to evince a sense of collective belonging to the Hispanophone world and used it as a source of local empowerment. Beyond the specific questions of community formation in Latin America, this chapter speaks to the broader question of how international migration affects identities among populations that do not themselves emigrate—in this case, the majority of Hispanic Moroccan Jews who remained in northern Morocco until the mid-1900s.

EARLY ROOTS, GLOBAL ROUTES

In the seventeenth and more extensively in the eighteenth century, a handful of Jewish Moroccan merchants played significant intermediary roles in trade between Morocco and Europe.[5] Some Moroccan trade networks, mostly based in Tetouan, were part of a broader Sephardi trade diaspora across much of the western Mediterranean until the nineteenth century. In the mid-eighteenth century, Jews from Tetouan settled in London and Amsterdam, for example.[6] In 1729, a British-Moroccan treaty provided for the tax-free import of water, food, and other goods into Gibraltar by Moroccan Jews. Consequently, during the eighteenth and early nineteenth centuries, Moroccan Jews, mainly from the north of the country, established immigrant colonies in Gibraltar, situated only a few miles from Tangier. Close rabbinical ties were maintained between Tetouan and Gibraltar, as evidenced, for example, by Yitzhak Ben-Gaulid's responsa with the community in Gibraltar. In 1843, Moroccan Jews in the British colony issued *Esperanza* (also known as *Tikvat Israel*), among the oldest newspapers in the Jewish world. Portugal and its Atlantic colonies also attracted Jewish merchants, who established their communities in the late nineteenth and early twentieth centuries.[7] At the beginning of the nineteenth century, Oran, in French-occupied Algeria, was a significant immigration destination for Moroccan Jews, again mostly from the north. In Oran, Jewish immigrants from Tetouan established one of the first Moroccan newspapers to appear outside of Morocco, *Maguid Micharim* (Heb., *The Preacher of Righteousness*). Edited and published by Eliyahu (Eli) Karsenty, it was initially called *Le Tétouanais* and appeared in Judeo-Arabic between 1895 and 1896.[8]

Emigration from Morocco to the Mediterranean colonies in Gibraltar and Algeria at the time can by no means be understood as a strictly Jewish phenomenon. In the first half of the nineteenth century, Muslim merchants from Fez, for example, also moved to West Africa and Egypt-Sudan, mostly to

Cairo. Others resettled in Manchester and Marseille. Oran also became a site of significant Moroccan Muslim immigration around that time, largely from neighboring northern Morocco. The immigrants were natives of the Rif area who moved to work on French colonial projects in Algeria.[9]

International labor migration, both to and from Morocco, was deeply rooted in the country's changing bilateral relations with colonial European powers. Following Spain's defeat of Morocco during the Spanish-Moroccan War of 1859–60, Moroccan policymakers implemented a set of military, economic, and political reforms that, among other things, led to rapid urbanization. These included the opening of the country's coastal towns to European immigration. A central case in point was the city of Tangier, which, as we have seen, became one of the main European concentrations in Africa at the time, situated just a few miles from European shores. Tangier's urbanization in the mid-nineteenth century brought large waves of internal Muslim migration into the city, from the inland and the surrounding rural Rif area. The latter was among the poorest parts of Morocco. Waves of Jewish immigration to Tangier also began with the arrival of politically and economically notable families from nearby Tetouan and from Meknes and Sale in Morocco's interior.[10]

From the second half of the nineteenth century until the outbreak of World War I in 1914, emigration from Morocco entered a new phase. In those years, tens of millions of people moved within Europe and, from there, to Africa, Asia, the Americas, and Oceania. On the eve of World War I, some thirty thousand North Africans, many of whom were Moroccan Muslims, were working in the metallurgical industries and the mines of mainland France.[11]

Dramatic political, social, and economic changes were taking place simultaneously in different parts of the world, leading to a global rather than exclusively European age of mass migration. Brazil and Argentina, two major immigration destinations in Latin America, as well as Venezuela had recently gained independence from Portugal and Spain. In the course of developing national aspirations for economic expansion, coupled with the need for a steady labor supply, these countries and others adopted liberal immigration policies. Some of them set up immigration agencies in Europe for the express purpose of achieving their economic aims.[12]

The end of the nineteenth century was also marked by the "rubber boom" in the Brazilian Amazon. The Brazilian government published pro-immigration propaganda in Europe and offered foreigners government labor contracts with benefits, including free transportation and often free land. The Amazon River and its tributaries were opened to foreign shipping, attracting a variety of European-owned shipping companies such as the Red Cross Line and

Hamburg-America. These companies would link Belém do Pará and Manaus with Lisbon, and Barcelona with the Azores, Marseille, Genoa, and Tangier.[13]

THE TRANSATLANTIC MOROCCAN JEW

The emigration of Moroccan Jews to Latin America began as early as 1810, when a few Jews from northern Morocco began to work as *regatões* (Amazonian River peddlers), traveling between towns and cities across the Brazilian Amazon. During the 1870s, after the demand for rubber from that region increased, Moroccan Jews, regardless of their relatively small numbers—just several hundred in the overall migratory process—became a significant element in the economic life of the Amazon. Joining European, Syrian, and Lebanese businessmen, they became rubber traders, regatões, and *aviadores* (owners of shipping houses and import-export traders) that scattered themselves across the Amazon until they reached its western terminus in the Peruvian city of Iquitos.[14] In 1910, Professor Isaac Pisa, a traveling teacher for the AIU schools in Morocco, visited Iquitos and reported that out of a population of about three hundred Jews, two hundred were former students of the AIU in Morocco. Typical names seen on storefronts along the city's main thoroughfare included, according to Pisa, "Cohen, Toledano, Benmergui, Delmar, Serfaty, Benassayag, Elaluf, Pinto, etc.; exactly as in Morocco."[15]

After sojourns in Brazil or the more established communities of the western Mediterranean, some Moroccan Jewish migrants began to regard Argentina as a viable alternative for establishing themselves in commerce. Moroccan Jews in Argentina started out as peddlers, and of these, some became *petits commerçants*, many of whom opened small shops specializing in clothing and fabrics, while others established large businesses, mainly as textile manufacturers. Whereas other Jewish immigrants to Argentina tended to concentrate in the capital city, Buenos Aires, Moroccan Jews spread across the country. As early as the 1880s, Moroccans were the first Jewish settlers in many interior cities. According to a census undertaken in 1909 by local authorities, the interior of Argentina was home to 358 Moroccans.[16] Moroccans in Argentina were scattered in one of the smallest Jewish hubs that even in 1900 was ranked twenty-fourth in size. As a place that had just begun to attract Jewish immigrants, Argentina lacked an established Jewish elite and much of the socioeconomic gaps and related paternalist and arrogant attitudes toward newcomers that might have placed Moroccans in the lower ranks of Jewish society.[17] For non-Jewish Argentinians, the "Spanish" appearances of Jewish immigrants from northern Morocco and their fluency in Spanish often masked their religious or ethnic origins in

Map 3.1. South America political map. © Bardocz Peter/ iStock Getty Images, ID:1147294164. https://www.istockphoto.com/portfolio/BardoczPeter?mediatype =illustration.

Morocco. The average Argentinian tended to associate them with non-Jewish Spaniards rather than with the two other communities of Jewish immigrants to the country—the *Turcos* (meaning "Turks," though in fact they were Arabic-speaking Jews) and the *Rusos* (Jews from Eastern Europe), who had become a main target for xenophobia in Argentina.[18]

In Venezuela, the first signs of a Jewish Moroccan presence date back to the 1880s.[19] Jews from northern Morocco, many of whom had resettled in southern Spain, joined larger waves of Spanish emigration to Venezuela from the provinces of Andalusia and Galicia, as well as the Canary Islands.[20] These pioneering individuals concentrated in the eastern part of the country, mainly in Barcelona, Carúpano, and Cumaná, while others settled in the center, in La Victoria and Villa de Cura. Nevertheless, the majority of Venezuelan Jews were concentrated in Caracas and surrounding areas like Los Teques and La Guaira. According to Carciente, by 1907 there were 207 Moroccan Jews living in Caracas alone.[21] As in other Latin American destinations, most Moroccan Jews in Venezuela started out as itinerant peddlers, moving up within a generation or two into the ranks of merchants and bankers. Many chose to work in the textile industry. Small wonder, then, that two of the six most important textile firms in the country, La Casa Benatar and Bendelac y Cía, were owned by Jews from northern Morocco. Northern Moroccan Jews even participated in the establishment of the first Commercial Bureau in the country.[22]

Despite the relatively small number of people who emigrated from northern Morocco, the influence of emigration on the region's small communities was disproportionately significant. As mentioned, the first branches of the AIU schools were opened in Tetouan and Tangier in the early 1860s. The worldwide AIU school system was a direct outcome of a refugee crisis in which displaced members of northern Morocco Jewish communities resettled among fellow community members in Gibraltar during the Spanish-Moroccan War of 1859–60. The AIU was seen by both local leadership and European philanthropists as part of the rehabilitation of these communities. The founding of the AIU represented a new hierarchization in which western European and North American Jews treated the Jewish communities of the east, including East European Jews and Maghrebi Jews, as Jewries in distress (see chap. 5 about this twentieth-century development). But this new global dynamic also gave rise to local community-building efforts in northern Morocco managed by the newly founded community council in Tangier that promoted the opening of the AIU schools.[23] The AIU network then became crucial to facilitating the incorporation of its hundreds of graduates from northern Morocco into the Hispanophone and Lusophone world.

In June 1879, the AIU board in Paris asked school directors to list all of the pupils who had passed through their schools since they opened. The list from the Tangier school, covering the period between 1864 and 1879, shows that out of 403 graduates, 143 (35 percent) indeed had emigrated.[24] In Tetouan, emigration rates were slightly higher: of 420 pupils who had graduated from the local AIU boys' school between 1862 and 1869, 162 (38.5 percent) had emigrated.[25] Over the following decade and a half, migration increased. In 1885, an inspector sent by the AIU in Paris reported that "the school in Tetouan produces [pupils] only for export... it supplies ninety-five percent of the students sitting on its benches to emigration... especially to Latin America."[26] Meir Levy, director of Tetouan's AIU school at the turn of the twentieth century, explained the change in migration destination preferences in a "Report Concerning Emigration": "With the progress that has been made in navigation, the distances have become shorter. One sets sail for Caracas as easily as one went to Gibraltar or Oran twenty-five years ago. I know some of these emigrants who have made the transatlantic crossing as many as six times."[27]

One might assume that their Sephardi origins eased the acceptance of Moroccan Jews in their Latin American destinations. Yet until 1912, Moroccan Jews traveling overseas usually did not declare their Jewish Moroccan origins and occasionally used European passports—typically Spanish, British, or French—upon entry.[28] Different from its policy toward Moroccans in the Spanish mainland, in 1875 Spain authorized the granting of Spanish citizenship to all Moroccans living in Venezuela, practically all of whom were Jews.[29] In the remote places where they scattered in search of livelihoods, the earliest pioneers found the maintenance of traditional Jewish communal practices almost unmanageable. Those individual migrants who worked the Amazon River in the mid-nineteenth century, for example, were not financed by any specific Jewish émigré organization, even less so by well-established Jewish communities. They were entrepreneurs mostly supported by interpersonal networks, including connections with local indigenous rubber tappers in the Amazon.[30]

These developments were not just an outcome of Jewish emigration from northern Morocco to far-flung destinations but also a product of the migrants' prior ties with non-Jews in their places of origin. Following the Spanish-Moroccan War of 1859–60, northern Moroccan coastal cities attracted a growing number of Europeans, Spaniards in particular.[31] Modern Castilian Spanish was then spoken by growing numbers of bourgeois Jews in northern Morocco, learned in the course of their evolving commercial and social connections with Spaniards, which rapidly multiplied following the Spanish-Moroccan War and were mediated by the AIU school system prior to the establishment of the protectorate in 1912 (see chap. 1). Globalization, which in this context involved Spanish settlement in both northern Morocco and Latin America, reduced to some extent the cultural, psychological, and physical distance between the two regions. Acquiring proficiency in Portuguese—linguistically similar to Spanish—was also manageable for many Spanish-speaking Jews.

Paradoxically, the establishment of the AIU, the groundbreaking Jewish-French educational project grounded in ethnic solidarity among Western European and "eastern" Jews, would in fact play a part in generating strong connections with non-Jews, and not necessarily Francophones. European languages, as well as the new professional skills and worldviews acquired or enriched at these schools, increased their graduates' mobility and tendency to form networks that went beyond their local communal circles.

In the late nineteenth and early twentieth centuries, an increasing number of Moroccan Jewish immigrants were engaging in community organization as a result of their migratory experiences. Some helped found communal infrastructure including synagogues, ethnic clubs, and other more global institutional structures. On November 5, 1891, the Sociedad Israelita según Ritual Sefardíta (Israelite Society according to the Sephardi Rite) was founded in Buenos Aires. Moroccan immigrants were concentrated in the southern part of the city (the San Telmo, Monserrat, and Constitución neighborhoods), where they established the synagogue Ets Haim. Another synagogue, Chaar Hashamayim, was built nearby.[32] Several other communal bodies were designed to serve the Moroccan Jewish community in the city: Guemilut Hasadim was founded in 1897 and then a new organization called Hesed ve-Emet in 1905, dedicated to "the proletariat class of Buenos Aires," which challenged the former organization's standing. Moroccans were not the only immigrant Jews to establish communal institutions at that time. In 1909, for example, Sociedad Israelita de Socorros Mutuos Varsovia (after 1927, the name was changed to Zwi Migdal after one of its founders) was established in Buenos Aires by Eastern European Jewish immigrants. A year later, they set up Hevra Kedusha Ashkenazi, the burial society for Ashkenazi Jews. Jews from Damascus established Bene Emet in 1915 and Hesed Shel Emet Sefaradit, the burial society for Jews from Aleppo, in 1929.

Adriana Brodsky has explained the sociopolitical dynamics that gave rise to multiple Jewish organizations in the city. The newly established communities did not come into being merely to fulfill religious or communal needs but also for the purposes of self-esteem and boundary maintenance between different ethnic groups that shared the same space. By 1905, there were three thousand non-Ashkenazi Jews in Argentina. Breaking with the earlier tendency of

Moroccans to scatter throughout the country, 750 Jewish immigrants now concentrated in Buenos Aires, almost all of them from northern Morocco, mostly from Tetouan. Preferring to socialize among their own, most immigrants from northern Morocco in Buenos Aires did not join the Congregación Israelita, the central official Jewish communal organization established by Jewish immigrants from Europe. Rather, they gathered for prayers in private homes.

The Sociedad Israelita según Ritual Sefardíta, established in 1891, became known as the Congregación Israelita Latina in the twentieth century. This designation lasted until 1976, when it changed its name to Asociación Comunidad Israelita Latina de Buenos Aires. For purposes of ethnic self-assertion, Moroccan Jews in Buenos Aires collectively described themselves as Latin. The choice was likely based on their imagined Hispanic origins and corresponding language and used to differentiate themselves from the ethnic cultures and languages of Ashkenazi Jews—but not only them. They also sought to differentiate themselves from Syrian and Ladino-speaking Jews from the Ottoman Empire, who used *Sefaradí* more frequently to describe their particularistic organizations.[33]

Although most Spanish-speaking Moroccan immigrants to Latin America were not strictly subordinated to ethnic communal frameworks in their daily lives, they, like many other groups of immigrants, began to develop nostalgic attachments to their places of origin, designating times and places at which they could express their unique connection to Morocco, and northern Morocco in particular. This hometown consciousness was based on their Sephardi and even more clearly on their Latin Jewish origins as symbols of their particularistic local Jewish identity. In Venezuela, too, the Centro Hispano-Israelita (Hispanic Israelite Center) recreational club, operated by Moroccan Jews in Caracas between 1931 and 1935, identified as Hispanic, whereas the Eastern European community adopted the name Sociedad Israelita *Ashkenazit* de Venezuela to indicate its own distinctiveness.[34]

This process of community differentiation in Argentina and Venezuela began to shape the way Latin America was perceived in the Jewish communities of northern Morocco, where, by the end of the nineteenth century, a new sort of ethnic migration agency had emerged. Leon Serfaty, a Tetouan native, was nominated by the director of the AIU school in Tetouan to promote the work of the AIU among his fellow immigrants in Buenos Aires, where a branch of the AIU had been established in 1892. In 1899, for the first time, the AIU Graduates Association in Tangier subsidized the emigration of twelve recent graduates to Latin America, marking a break from the recent past, when migration was facilitated by less formal ties among graduates.[35] By 1899, the AIU in northern Morocco had taken on an active role as an agency of specifically

Jewish migration to Latin America. The Jewish Colonization Association (JCA), based in Argentina, provided the social framework for Jews wishing to migrate to Latin America.[36] The AIU promoted the relocation of teachers from northern Morocco to JCA colonies in Argentina. By the end of the nineteenth century, there were twenty schools operating in these colonies, all directed by AIU graduates.[37] The character of the networks facilitating Jewish emigration from northern Morocco to Latin America thus changed as the identities of the migrants changed. Through these evolving ethnic networks, teachers sent to work in Jewish schools, rather than just recent AIU graduates and their friends, began to join the migratory trend.

Subsequently, transnational connections between home and abroad were strengthened on the basis of remittances that helped establish new institutions in Morocco. In the late nineteenth century, the AIU Alumni Association in Tangier, established in 1893, made special appeals to its overseas graduates, who would respond with generosity that far outweighed their numbers. For example, as Susan Gilson Miller has shown, the contribution of overseas alumni for the period 1895–1900 totaled 30 percent of all donations, even as they comprised only 13 percent of the AIU graduates. In 1898 alone, émigrés contributed 40 percent of the total while comprising only 16 percent of donors.[38]

Once the benefits of maintaining ties with émigrés became understood, the Jewish community council of Tangier established an Emigration Fund "to assist in the emigration of youth who have an aptitude for salesmanship, or who know a trade." The fund was announced in local synagogues, along with the application criteria: applicants aged eighteen to twenty-two years old had to submit a letter of recommendation and promise to use the money for passage only. Once the announcement was made, a steady stream of requests began.[39] Synagogues in Tangier and Tetouan thus became places where local Jews learned to attach their understandings of migration and their migratory aspirations to their religious Jewish background, and where they could access the resources needed to realize those aspirations.

THE BIRTH OF A LEGEND IN MOROCCO

A report in 1901 noted how the "Americans" (referring to Moroccan émigrés in the Americas) offered proof to their compatriots back home that hard work in one's AIU studies paid off.[40] Later that year, Isaac Pisa, deputy of the AIU in Morocco, traveled to Iquitos and wrote, "In Tangier, they speak of Iquitos as if [it were] a fabulous city with streets of gold. It is typical of [a] Tangierian to make his fortune in Iquitos. That is the vision and the dream of young people.

[Yet] you must know without doubt that the road is long and [the] climate is harsh.... The first years for immigrants are terrible. They have to adapt to climate, customs, and commerce."[41] Pisa's words reflect a legend in the making among Jews in northern Morocco, one in which migration was seen as a process of deliverance from poverty and a passage to paradise.

Migration had a tremendous influence on economic life back home as hundreds of families in Tangier and Tetouan relied on remittances for their livelihood. The standards of living of the families of expats were impacted not only by remittances from Latin America but also by the new businesses opened in northern Morocco by prosperous returnees. One of these businesses was La Grand Bazar La Caraqueña, or The Caracas Native's Grand Bazaar, which operated on La Luneta Street, adjacent to Tetouan's poor Jewish neighborhood.[42]

The outbreak of World War I in 1914 interrupted this relative prosperity and the age of migration. Beginning in the 1920s, many countries throughout the world witnessed high rates of inflation followed by a severe economic downturn in the 1930s—the Great Depression. Consequently, two of the three million immigrants who had settled in Argentina and Brazil during the 1920s would return to their places of origin. Immigration to Argentina between 1914 and 1929 fell by about half compared to the period between 1900 and 1914.[43] In Venezuela, the economic hardships of that era also negatively influenced immigration policy. As a result, Jewish emigration from northern Morocco to Latin America dwindled.[44]

The circumcision notebook kept by Rabbi Vidal, who worked in Tetouan from 1880 to 1940, illustrates the dramatic decrease in Jewish emigration from Tetouan to Latin America following the war. Between 1888 and 1897, an average of around one father each year was recorded in Rabbi Vidal's notebook as residing abroad (and thus possibly returning to Tetouan for the circumcision ceremony). Reports of migratory flow for those years reveal an average of 2.2 emigrants per year. In the subsequent period, from 1900 to 1912, migration continued at a slightly increased but still modest pace, boosting the annual number of emigrant fathers who sought Rabbi Vidal's services to 3.15. However, the period between 1913 and 1940 marked a clear decline, with the total number of emigrants over this twenty-eight-year period totaling only eleven and producing an annual average of just 0.4 emigrants who availed themselves of Rabbi Vidal's services.[45]

The change in migration trends is indicated by the number of returnees. Records show that in 1912, there were 161 Argentine nationals in Morocco, all of whom were returning Jewish expatriates: sixty-one of them returned to Tetouan, twenty to Tangier, and twenty-one to Larache, and forty-eight resided in Casablanca. In 1927, the Argentine consulate in Rabat reported that seventy-nine Argentinean nationals then living in Morocco were naturalized Moroccan natives who had returned to their homeland that year.[46]

In addition, many members of the freemason lodges of the Gran Logia Regional de Marruecos were returnees from Argentina, Brazil, and Venezuela; they belonged to Latin American lodges before joining the Moroccan ones and many were in fact Jews, including Samuel M. Nahón, member of Harmonía y Fraternidad de Brasil, and Leon Cohen Sedero, the founder of freemasonry in Tetouan who had begun his fraternal activity in Brazil. A. Samuel Chocrón and David Wahnon, from the Victoria Lodge No. 9 in Caracas, also visited the Melilla lodge in 1934.[47]

The returnees, as well as those who stayed in Latin America, soon became objects of communal pride and a reliable source of moral support. For example, the Hahnasat Orhim (Welcoming Guests) society was a communal institution originally established in 1911 in Tangier for the purpose of lodging visiting rabbis and communal figures. The society's existence depended upon the flow of charitable donations, including those from overseas. In its first three years of operation (1911–13), the society derived its income from members in Tangier and representatives abroad, the latter spread across some seventeen cities throughout the world, among them Iquitos, Caracas, Buenos Aires, and the three Brazilian cities of Itacoatiará, Manicoré, and Parintins.[48] The total contributions collected from overseas during the Jewish calendar year 5672 (1911–12) nearly equaled the amount collected in Tangier itself.[49]

Over the following eight-year period (1913–21), the welcoming society ceased to meet and publish bulletins due to the political and economic hardships caused by World War I. Remarkably, however, the influx of donations from abroad did not stop.[50] The society was even able to purchase land in Cuesta de Marchán, a luxurious part of Tangier, where forty guest cabins for use by out-of-town visitors were built.[51] When publication of its bulletin resumed in 1921, the society's first issue indicated that "various donations" had been collected abroad.[52] It was even possible to establish a special fund for the construction of a new hostel and synagogue solely from the contributions of the Moroccan émigré community in Caracas, which raised the significant sum of 3,011.50 francs.[53]

Overall, the number of donors living abroad was not much larger than the number living in Tangier. But the former seems to have been comprised of businesspeople who were more active in the communal life of their country of residence. In this period of global depression and declining migration, their participation distinguished their names in the history of their communities. As part of the rising hometown consciousness of Moroccan Jews living in Argentina, those in the province of Córdoba campaigned to raise significant amounts to help the poor in Tetouan and for the Benchimol Hospital in Tangier. In 1926, they raised funds to help build the walls of the Jewish cemetery in Alcazarquivir. In 1931, the Jewish community of Tetouan requested that money be raised to build the walls of the Jewish cemetery in that city. To that end, commissions were formed in Buenos Aires and the interior provinces of Argentina.[54]

In 1930, an announcement in *Adelante* greeted the "Peruvians in Morocco" on the anniversary of Peru's Independence Day (June 21, 1821). The message is one among many that attests to the fact that, after World War I, with transatlantic migration on the wane globally, communities in Morocco had among them Jews of Latin American origin who continued to maintain a sense of attachment to their former countries of residence in the New World, even after their return.[55]

An examination of the few available issues of *Renacimiento de Israel* reveals evidence of expatriate remittances in the local discourse on Latin America as a source of local empowerment. In an article entitled "Our Compatriots in Buenos Aires: Philanthropic Gestures," the author wrote, "Not a single year passes without clear proof of their [that is, the Moroccan Jewish community in Buenos Aires's] immense kindness, and their profound and nostalgic love for their city of birth: Tetouan.... These beloved sons... do not merely remember their [biological] fathers and brothers, but the entire population, especially the poor and the needy [of the community in northern Morocco]. Do we have in Tetouan a philanthropic society or institute that is not lavished upon and generously assisted by these very noble compatriots?"[56]

A report in *Adelante* referred to a significant donation by Léon Taurel, a wealthy businessman and one of the leaders of the Moroccan community in Venezuela, who had visited Tetouan around the time of the 1929 report, which recounted Taurel's impression that the synagogues of the city were not spacious enough and not suitable to modern needs. He thus decided to donate money to build a large synagogue for Tetouan. The report ended with a question from the paper's editor as to whether something similar might happen in Tangier.[57] In another article, the newspaper announced the publication of a new book by Samuel J. Benchetrit, a young man from a poor Tangierian family who had moved to Argentina, describing him as an intellectual source of pride for the entire community.[58]

The editorial boards of both *Adelante* and *Renacimiento* covered trips to northern Morocco by eminent Jewish visitors from Latin America, such as Don Savador Essayag and Don Samuel Benattar from Venezuela, Ramón Benchaya and Isaac García from Argentina, and many others.[59] These Spanish Moroccan émigrés became subjects of interest in the pages of Jewish periodicals, and their visits helped to perpetuate the discourse on migration to Latin America as a financial asset and a source of pride long after transatlantic migration had declined, even among those local Jews who had no direct connections with émigré businesspeople.

As we saw in the chapter 2, in the 1920s the emerging scholarly interest of Hispanists and Philo-Sephardi advocates in the Iberian roots of the Jewish population of northern Morocco led to the development and dissemination of a communal narrative of ancestry. One of the first Philo-Sephardi advocates to draw cultural connections between the immigrants' roots in pre-1492 Spain and their migration to Spain's former colonies was in fact Ángel Pulido in his famous book *Stateless Spaniards*. There, he stressed that, being part of the "Spanish race," Jews were in fact part of a global Hispanophone diaspora. He reproached the AIU leadership for prioritizing the study of French over Spanish among the Jews in northern Morocco, arguing that AIU was missing an opportunity to use their natural proficiency in Spanish, which would also prove more useful for successful migration. Pulido compared the then fifty-eight million native French speakers worldwide with the eighty-five million Spanish speakers to make his point about the advantages of investing in Spanish-language education for Jews.[60]

Advancing a similar argument, Hispanicist Manuel L. Ortega claimed in his book *Los Hebreos en Marruecos* that the journey to Spanish America so improved the command of modern Spanish among Jewish immigrants from northern Morocco that the locals mistakenly saw them as Spaniards rather than Jews.[61] Pulido and Ortega were followed by Robert Ricard (1900–84), who wrote one of the earliest academic essays on the migration of Jews from northern Morocco to Latin America in 1928.[62] Born in Paris, Ricard completed his PhD at the Sorbonne in 1933, focusing on the Spanish religious influence on Mexico in the sixteenth century. A 1926 visit to Morocco, where he delivered a series of lectures, made him aware of the connection between Morocco and his scholarly interest in Spanish Central America.[63] Two years later, in a pioneering article, he described the success of Hispanophone Moroccan Jewish émigrés in Argentina and Brazil and the wealth that some of them had brought back to their Moroccan hometowns.[64]

Ricard's academic work came at a time when the Jewish community in northern Morocco was increasingly emphasizing its communal connections to Latin America, and it is reasonable to believe that he was influenced by his encounter with community members during his 1926 visit to Morocco. Indeed, in his 1928 article, Ricard thanked Mr. Y. D. Semach, secretary general of the

AIU in Morocco, for sharing with him information about Jewish migration to Latin America. While Semach wrote and compiled those reports for the practical use of the AIU rather than for ethnographic purposes, the Philo-Sephardi campaign used them for their own purpose of expanding Spanish influence.

Pulido's, Ortega's, and Ricard's interests in the connection between Spanish Latin America and the post-1492 Jewish diaspora in the Mediterranean did not develop in a vacuum and in fact reflected broader contemporary efforts to draw such connections. Rodolfo Gil Torres-Benumeya, one of the most enthusiastic advocates of Andalusian nationalism, is a good example. He used the Africanist periodical *La Revista de Tropas Coloniales* (known since 1926 as *África: Revista de Tropas Coloniales*), which circulated in Morocco, mainland Spain, and Buenos Aires, to issue a call for the Spanish authorities to reach out to the (mostly Christian) Arab Siro-Lebanese communities in Latin America—which he saw as part of Spain's historic Andalusi diaspora—in order to promote Spain's mission to spread its influence worldwide.[65] However, Spain's influence on the eastern parts of the Mediterranean were limited, unlike its colonial influence in northern Morocco. As almost all North African immigrants in Latin America were Jews, the mission to spread Spain's culture and commercial influence in the diaspora became associated with the Jewish communities in northern Morocco. The connections to Latin American destinations were mediated by evolving self-perceptions about their roots in Iberia. Small surprise, then, that one *Adelante* article, for example, drew an explicit connection between the "discovery of America" and the Jewish community's roots in Spain.[66]

A TRANSATLANTIC COMMUNITY, A PROLONGING PRIDE

The relationship between Morocco and Latin America extended beyond the mere literary constructions of Jewish origins in Iberia and in fact shaped living connections with those who had undertaken the transatlantic journey. Given the extent of the almost half-century-old migration from Morocco to Latin America by the mid-twentieth century, many Jews in northern Morocco had acquaintances or family members living in the New World. Beyond any shared ancient histories, their connections to Latin America were fueled by the legends they would hear in their family circles about relatives living abroad and sometimes leading adventure-filled lives in the Americas. One example is the story by Abraham Pinto, who had returned to Tangier from the Amazon rubber trade (probably around the turn of the twentieth century) and finally agreed, at the age of 83, to share his adventures with his closest family members. These memories were written down by Pinto's nephews at his request in Tangier on November 12, 1945.[67]

Here again, however, the scholarly institutions developed by Spanish colonialism in Morocco, particularly by the Francoist regime (see chap. 2) facilitated the transmission of these stories and their standardization as part of a collective communal narrative. For instance, the General Franco Institute for Hispano-Arab Studies published *Indianos Tetouaníes* in Tetouan in 1951. The book was part of a trilogy, *El Indiano, al Kadi y la Luna*, authored by Isaac Benarroch Pinto, the son of a returning migrant from Latin America.[68] In his novel, Benarroch Pinto recounts the thrilling story of a young man from the lower classes of Tetouan's Jewish society who immigrates to Argentina in 1867 with the aim of alleviating his family's economic burdens. His success overseas changes the economic destiny of his family, enabling his father to quit his job as a tinsmith and "live as the father of a rich trader from overseas." The novel ends with the protagonist returning to his hometown to attend his sister's wedding and donating money to the needy of the Jewish community there.[69] Benarroch Pinto's narrative processed historical events into a story to which Jews could relate based on their understandings of Latin American migration as they were conveyed in popular communal narratives and family stories.

These ties were reflected in a few contemporaneous publications. In Venezuela, still one of the major migratory destinations for Jews in the Spanish protectorate in the 1940s, *El Mundo*, a recent but important Jewish periodical edited by Jews from Tetouan, published material indicative of the ties between Jewish communities in northern Morocco and Venezuela. It published the first chapters of *Indianos Tetouaníes* in 1949, even prior to the novel's appearance in Tetouan.[70] That same year, it also published a report on the establishment of Or Hayeladim, an educational institution in Tetouan, noting that the Moroccan community in Caracas had financed its inauguration. The authors sent a copy of the article for republication in the northern Moroccan journal *España*, a Spanish-language newspaper read by northern Moroccan Jews and non-Jews alike.[71] In her report about Spanish Morocco for the 1953 edition of the American Jewish Yearbook, Hélène Cazes Bénatar described Or Hayeladim as the principal charitable institution of the Jewish community of Tetouan.[72]

In 1949, the official bulletin of the Tetouan Jewish community reported on a ball organized by Jacobo Bentata, a wealthy Jew from Venezuela. In 1956, two months after Morocco's independence, *Or-Luz* published an interview with a descendant of the community living in Argentina who had visited Tetouan for the first time in his life that year. The main impression conveyed by the interview was that "Tetouan preserves most purely its traditions and costumes." The interviewee was presented as a successful pediatrician who never forgot his ancestral origins in Tetouan.[73]

Remarkably, Moroccan Jews in Venezuela started to organize themselves communally only in the early twentieth century. They were scattered across towns such as La Guaira, Puerto Cabello, Maracaibo, and Los Teques, where they gathered in private homes for weekly Sabbath prayers and other religious obligations.[74] It was only in 1907, in Caracas, that a group of immigrants from Morocco founded the Sociedad Sefardí de Beneficencia, a Sephardi welfare society with 178 members. The organization lasted for only two years. Another attempt was made in 1919 with the Sociedad Israelita de Venezuela, which aimed "to improve the moral and intellectual level of Jews in Caracas" and lasted until 1923.[75] Then, in 1930, a group of prominent Moroccan immigrants founded the Asociación Israelita de Venezuela (AIV), the central communal organization of Sephardi Jews in that country. Its goal, to establish a central Sephardi synagogue to replace the numerous small private ones, was finally realized in 1939, when members inaugurated the El Conde synagogue in Caracas.

The legendary quality of early migration to Latin America continued to reverberate in the stories of northern Moroccan Jews throughout the twentieth century and beyond. In her memoir, published in the US in 1987, Alegría Bendelac describes her father's migration to Venezuela as an adolescent, recalling how, unlike those who had preceded him, he had returned home with a little bundle of gold coins.[76] Bendelac's description echoes the way migratory experiences to "America" were typically narrated to the younger generation, whether in the first or third person, thus fueling the imaginations of many youngsters in Tangier and Tetouan, their family circles, and their Jewish friends. These and other narratives were alive in Tangier in the 1980s, in Venezuela in the 1990s, in the United Stated in the first decade of the twenty-first century, and in Israel as late as 2010, continuing to shape the collective story of dispersion among Hispanic Moroccan Jews well into the twenty-first century.[77]

In an interview I conducted in 2009, Perla, then in her seventies, recalled hearing Brazilian songs in her grandmother's house growing up and recounted anecdotes about the Amazonian way of life that she had heard about from her husband's family.[78] Daniel, whom I interviewed in Israel around the same time, shared memories of a visit by his Argentinian aunt to Tangier in the 1950s. For him, then only ten years old, her visit produced an exciting encounter with the "Americas" and its "aristocratic lifestyle," at least as he recounted it in the interview.[79] In another interview, Clarice reminisced about her relatives' earlier migration to Latin America and recalled a story about "Los Peruanos" (the

Peruvians), a Jewish family who returned to Tangier from Iquitos in the Peruvian Amazon. This story triggered her memories of additional stories about another uncle who had emigrated to the Amazon and made a fortune. In the following chapters, I will discuss how this prolonging legacy of migration, and the affinities to the broader Hispanophone world it created, interacted with the development of Zionism in northern Morocco and Latin America from the early through the mid-twentieth century.

FOUR

ZIONISM AND THE HISPANIC MOROCCAN DIASPORA

IN 1951, A SPANISH-LANGUAGE ARTICLE ENTITLED "Folklore" appeared in *Noar*, the newspaper published in Casablanca between 1945 and 1952 by a group of Jews originating in northern Morocco. *Noar* was one of the most prominent Jewish newspapers in Morocco at the time, and probably the most widely circulated Zionist newspaper in North Africa.[1] The author of the article, Joseph Tapiero, shared with *Noar*'s readers some Spanish *romances*, or folk ballad songs that his mother had taught him as a child in Tangier. Tapiero was one of the readers who had responded to a call issued by the paper's editors to share such romances in "ancient Spanish"—that is, in Haketia.[2] The next issue of *Noar* included a call to assist scholars investigating the Judeo-Spanish dialect of Morocco, which, despite being "the closest to Spanish among all Judeo-Spanish dialects," was the most understudied, according to the author.[3] These articles were published in a small Spanish-language section in *Noar* called "El Mundo Sefardí" ("The Sephardi World"). As noted in the announcement that preceded the initiation of this section, one of its purposes was to demonstrate the loyalty of Sephardi Jews worldwide to their "ancient patria," Spain.[4]

While this connection between Spain and Jews from northern Morocco should come, by now, as no surprise, its expression in *Noar* should not be taken for granted. The initiative to publish *Noar* came from the ranks of the Charles Netter Zionist youth movement, whose leaders—Alfonso Sabah, Daniel Levy, Maurice Timsit, Raphaël Benacerraf, and Joe Lasry—belonged to the religious conservative camp of Zionism that strongly supported the immigration of Jews to Israel after 1948.[5]

Moreover, the use of Spanish in this otherwise Francophone newspaper had no practical linguistic rationale, as its readers were typically fluent in French.

In fact, it is reasonable to assume that many of its readers, coming from the interior communities of Morocco, did not even read Spanish fluently, if at all. Shortly after the establishment of the protectorate in 1912, Casablanca evolved from a small fishing village into a commercial metropolis, attracting waves of internal migration from across the country that included all ethnoreligious groups. In some respects, Casablanca surpassed Tangier as the main commercial center in Morocco. Against this backdrop, a large number of Jews from northern Morocco moved southward in search of new economic opportunities as northern Morocco entered a period of internal warfare and saw an influx of refugees from the Spanish Civil War.[6] Jews from all over the country and not just from northern Morocco increasingly made "Casa" their home, and the Jewish population numbered around eighty thousand in 1950, around a third of the country's Jews.[7]

A good explanation for *Noar*'s call to embrace a Spanish identity would thus have to consider the way Jews from the north formed their own ethnolinguistic community in Casablanca while capitalizing on their editorship of this prominent Zionist periodical. For example, the "Sephardi World" section of this newspaper published in Casablanca occasionally ran news from northern Morocco. Attachment to the "Sephardi World," then, served the self-affirmation of Spanish-speaking Jewish immigrant communities from the north who resettled in Morocco's biggest city, Casablanca.

In this context, nostalgia for the mythological Spanish "fatherland" among *Noar*'s editors did not contradict their devotion to the Zionist cause, even when it reflected more concrete ties with the Spanish state and the Francoist colonial regime after 1948. In 1952, *Noar*'s editors reproduced an article published earlier in the Francoist periodical *España* detailing Spanish Senator Ángel Pulido's Philo-Sephardi activity on behalf of the world's Sephardim, which it referred to as his "admirable endeavor for the Jewish people."[8] The author, Rahma Toledano, a well-known journalist from Tangier and a former president of the Alliance Israélite Universelle (AIU) Alumni Association, maintained regular contact with Pulido. In 1955, she joined a delegation headed by S. D. Lévy, the representative of the Jewish National Fund (JNF) in Casablanca, that traveled to Madrid to commemorate Pulido's death some twenty-three years earlier. On that occasion, Lévy expressed his dual devotion to the Zionist cause and to the Philo-Sephardi campaign when offering to commemorate Pulido by planting trees in the Haruvit Forest in the Lachish area of southern Israel. The idea was realized a year later, on June 1, 1956, in the midst of the Moroccan struggle for independence. The JNF invited official guests from Spain to Israel for the first time, and the Spanish flag was flown in Israel.[9]

The link between Jewish affinities for Spain and activities to promote Zionism in Morocco by a network of devoted Zionist leaders in the early 1950s is striking, especially given the state of diplomatic relations between Israel and Spain at the time. In 1948 and 1949, Franco attempted to establish ties with Israel, but Israel demurred, mainly due to the Spanish regime's relationship with Nazi Germany. This incident in turn shaped Spain's engagement with the Arab world in the 1950s and the declaration of a "Spanish-Arab friendship"; however, in 1956, Spain rejected Israel's request to establish full diplomatic relations.[10] None of this changed prominent Moroccan Zionist activists like S. D. Lévy's affinity with Spain, or its deployment by community leaders in the course of building Zionist institutions in Morocco.

Looking at such developments, this chapter explores the way community-building processes among the leadership elite of Hispanic Moroccan Jews were intertwined with their growing identification with Zionism, Israel (after 1948), Spain, and Latin America, as well as independent Morocco. While diversity within the modern Zionist project is often attributed to regionally based differences—such as between North African and Eastern European Zionism—in this chapter I argue that to understand the complexities of the Hispanic Moroccan case, greater attention to transregional communal networks that served as tools for community building and empowerment is essential.[11] Highlighting forms of interconnectivity as a way to understand the reception and interpretation of Zionism across Hispanophone and Hispanophile networks from the early 1900s through 1956 helps us rethink scholarly descriptions of Morocco exclusively in terms of national or regional analyses.

A NEW ZIONIST DIASPORA

To understand the dynamics that fueled the enmeshment of Zionism and Sephardi attachment to Spain in the mid-twentieth century, we must first examine the regional and global development of the community from the turn of the century, when Zionism in northern Morocco was a weak idea with few adherents. In the late nineteenth century, Argentina became a hub for Jewish immigrants from Eastern Europe, some of whom brought with them Zionist ideas. Through their activities, Argentina soon became a prominent center for Zionism in Latin America and the broader Hispanophone world. In 1897, Argentina was home to a local branch of Hovevei Zion (The Lovers of Zion), an early Zionist group first established in Eastern Europe in 1881. While Moroccan Jews in Argentina were not among the forerunners of Zionism, they would soon integrate Zionism into their organizational strategies. In 1904, some individuals of Moroccan descent participated in Argentina's first Zionist Congress, and in 1907 Moroccan immigrants founded their own Zionist groups in Vila Mercedes, Margarita, and Rosario.[12]

Through new émigré newspapers, Moroccan Jews came to play a role in a spread of Zionist ideas across Latin America that was disproportionate to their relatively small representation in local Zionist organizations. Established in Buenos Aires in 1917 by Jacobo and Samuel A. Levy, two immigrants from Tetouan, *Israel* was the first Spanish-language Zionist newspaper worldwide. Its appearance in Spanish—unlike most Zionist periodicals at the time, which were in Yiddish—was motivated by its Moroccan founders' alienation from the local Zionist scene. This scene was then dominated by networks connecting Eastern European immigrants with their hometowns. *Israel*'s presentation of Zionist ideas facilitated the integration of the small Moroccan Jewish community into Argentina's Jewish immigrant society by helping readers sharpen their identification with a shared country of identification that helped unite them.[13] In its first year, *Israel* had about ten thousand subscribers from across Latin America, including individuals who were not necessarily of a Moroccan Jewish background or Jewish altogether. According to its first issue, it also maintained twenty correspondents in seven Argentinean provinces, six in Morocco, two in Brazil, and one each in Paraguay, Uruguay, Chile, the US, and Spain.[14]

The founding of *Israel* reflected the more globalized character of Moroccan Zionism that began to emerge out of the hubs of Jewish immigrants from northern Morocco, similar to other Zionist organizations in the twentieth century but with its own distinctions. In Brazil, as in Argentina, Zionism helped Moroccan Jews integrate into both the local Jewish and broader Brazilian societies. In 1916, David Jose Peréz, a Moroccan Jew from Tangier whose family settled in northern Brazil, joined with Alvaro Castilho, a non-Jewish Zionist sympathizer, to found the first local Zionist newspaper in the country, *A Columna* (*The Column*). Like *Israel* in Argentina, *A Columna* was the first Jewish Brazilian newspaper to appear in Portuguese, the national language. Unlike other Zionist activities taking shape in the country among Eastern European Jews, *A Columna* targeted Jews who were scattered across Brazil.[15]

The rise of Zionist activity in Latin America paralleled that in Morocco. Eretz Israel (the Land of Israel) had long been a point of reference in Jewish liturgy, and the Jewish communities in northern Morocco were no exception. This traditional connection manifested as established networks of fundraising, correspondence between rabbis, and even travel to Palestine.[16] The characteristics of traditional attachment to Eretz Israel, however, changed dramatically with the growing influence of European Zionism at the outset of the twentieth century. Influenced by the same spread of European Zionism, just three years after the establishment of Hovevei Zion in Argentina, the first modern Zionist group in Morocco appeared in Tetouan, in September 1900. Rabbi Yehuda León Jalfón (also spelled Halfon), president of the High Rabbinic Tribunal of Tetouan, together with Dr. Y. Berliavski, a Jewish Russian physician who had immigrated to Morocco, started in Tetouan a small Hebrew-language study club called Shivat Zion (Return to Zion). Shaarei Zion, or Gates of Zion, was established the same month in the southern port city of Mogador. A decade later, new clubs appeared throughout Morocco, including Havaad Hazioni in Tangier, Shaare Zion in Ceuta, Bonei Yerushalaim in Larache, and Magen David in Casablanca. At the time of their establishment, these institutions were too small and marginal to stir opposition in and beyond the community. If anything, they had to combat the vast majority of northern Moroccan Jews' apathy toward the Zionist movement, as they saw it.[17]

ZIONISM AND SEPHARDI ANCESTRY, A PRACTICAL MARRIAGE

It may seem remarkable that Zionist activism among Hispanic Moroccan Jews took place almost concurrently with the "reencounter" between Spain and Morocco, but in fact, as already shown above, these two processes were often promoted by the same individuals as a joint project of communal revitalization. Rabbi Jalfón, one of the staunchest supporters of the Philo-Sephardi movement, is a prime example, as evidenced by a series of eighty-nine letters he exchanged early in the twentieth century with Manuel Ortega, the aforementioned enthusiastic proponent of the Philo-Sephardi movement in Spain and editor of the Philo-Sephardi bulletin *La Revista de la Raza*.[18]

In response to his link with Jalfón, Ortega himself mentioned Zionism, as a momentous movement of Jewish renewal, in the same book in which he discussed the role of Sephardi Jews as Spain's most loyal diasporic agents.[19] Earlier, in his canonical 1905 book *Stateless Spaniards*, Ángel Pulido, the forefather of the Spanish Philo-Sephardi movement, declared Spain "a second Zion" for Sephardi Jews.[20] While seemingly contradictory, there was a wider intellectual basis for this intertwining of Zionism and affinity to Spain. In the aesthetics of nineteenth-century Jewish life, pre-1492 Spain was deemed a model for maintaining Jewish particularism beyond the confines of the ghetto. That idealized image of Sepharad shaped the reclaiming of Hebrew and biblical texts as much as they shaped the appeal of Judeo-Spanish literature.[21]

Beyond any literary imagination, in colonial northern Morocco the entwining of Sephardi and Zionist identities also had political and pragmatic added value. The fact that European Zionism was embraced and developed by enthusiastic followers of Philo-Sephardism like Jalfón may have softened the attitude of Spanish colonial authorities after 1912 or diminished suspicion about possible disloyalties to Spain, contrary to the French colonial context. The Balfour Declaration of 1917 significantly aroused the French colonial authorities' suspicions about Zionist activities, fearing that they might stir disloyalty to French rule and evoke nationalist spirits. In this atmosphere, the intertwining of Philo-Sephardism and Zionism as two forms of Jewish renewal in northern Morocco continued to develop in the 1920s, as a sign of dual loyalty.

In the context of early Spanish colonialism, claiming a connection to Spain also had a practical organizational motivation. As his correspondence demonstrates, Rabbi Jalfón, for example, received Zionist material from Avraham Shalom Yahuda, the (then) Madrid-based biblical scholar, and from Ignacio Brauner, the head of Spain's Jewish community. In 1920, Zionist activists in northern Morocco had institutionalized transregional networks by incorporating themselves into the Spanish Zionist Federation established in Madrid that year. In 1922, to mark the collaboration, the federation changed its name to Federación Hispano-Marroquí Sionista and summoned representatives from both locations, including Spanish-speaking Moroccan Jews residing in Casablanca, to join this transregional Zionist federation that connected Spain and Morocco.[22]

In the 1920s and early 1930s, when Zionism became more acceptable among community leaders to promote international Jewish solidarity, it was not rare for Zionist activists to openly show strong affection for the Spanish state as a practical tool for promoting the global spread of modern Zionism. Dr. Ariel Bension is a case in point. As the son of a Moroccan immigrant to Palestine in the nineteenth century, he became a delegate of the JNF, for which he hoped to collect funds from the less active Sephardi communities worldwide. After serving as a JNF representative in Latin America, in 1932, just before his untimely death, Bension became a member of the Royal Spanish Academy. He had started his journey in 1921 in Spain and continued on to Portugal and Gibraltar, meeting a number of leaders from the globalizing community of northern Moroccan Jews. According to Bension, in Spain, the "Casa Sefarad" (the Sepharad House), an association initially established to promote the "reencounter" and return of Sephardi Jews to Spain, also became a base for promoting Zionist activity in the country.[23] Rabbi Jalfón was in touch with Bension prior to his trip to Argentina, where he would encourage the local Moroccan community to found local branches of the Zionist group Bene Kedem.[24] While on the eve of colonialism foreign European Zionist ideas were not embraced by the elite of the Jewish communities as smoothly as the Philo-Sephardi campaign, already by the 1920s the two projects were complementing one another.

Small wonder, then, that in the late 1920s the periodicals *El Renacimiento de Israel* and *Adelante*, despite their different orientations, both represented the interests of the Philo-Sephardi campaign while simultaneously including Zionist content. *Adelante*, which presented itself as "Africa's top Spanish newspaper,"[25] even marked its own first anniversary with a special issue in honor of Theodor Herzl. In that issue, next to a photo of Herzl and Chaim Weizmann, then president of the World Zionist Organization, the editors placed a photograph of José Benoliel, the well-known philologist of Haketia, and of M. André Pierre, president of the Press Association of the High Commissioner of Spain in Morocco.[26]

While the intertwining of Sephardi and Zionist identities became acceptable, they did not advance without difficulties. In 1929, the community council of Tetouan subscribed to the Tangier-based *Renacimiento de Israel*. In 1931, four out of six members of that council voted in favor of canceling that subscription due to financial issues, causing Jaime Vidal Israel, one of the enthusiastic supporters of Zionism in the council, to quit his membership in protest.[27]

Moreover, the marriage between Zionism and Sephardi identities must be further contextualized in terms of the emerging ethnic rift between Sephardi and Ashkenazi Jews over the influence—or lack thereof—of Sephardim in the Zionist movement, as it gained further momentum after the Balfour Declaration. In general, many Sephardi advocates of Zionism, including Moroccans, felt excluded from the more comprehensive, Yiddish-speaking networks of the Zionist movement. The *Israel* and *A Columna* newspapers, established by Moroccan Jews, ought to be understood as essential vehicles for empowering Sephardim in the global institutions of the Zionist movement, as explicitly described in a 1917 article in *A Columna*.[28] The establishment of the World Sephardi Federation (WSF) in 1925 marked the culmination of that tension as well as a shift in the ability of Sephardi communities to organize separately within the global Zionist movement. This initiative arose out of the Jerusalem-based Sephardi Community Council (SCC) in its struggle for the equal representation of Sephardim in the World Zionist Organization.[29]

One of the advantages of gathering a variety of communities, ranging from Ladino-speaking Jews from Turkey to Arabic-speaking Jews from Syria, under the Sephardi-Zionism banner was the ability to create umbrella organizations that empowered each community. In Argentina, for example, immigrants from across the Middle East and North Africa (MENA) region and Ladino-speaking world began to unify in the 1920s under the framework of Sephardi Zionism and, as Adriana Brodsky has shown, to highlight the status of Spain as a secondary Jewish homeland alongside Israel.[30] The pragmatic organizational benefits afforded by unification can be distinguished from the ideological Philo-Sephardi discourses taking shape elsewhere throughout the Sephardi world. Samuel A. Levy, editor of *Israel* in Buenos Aires, used the Zionist periodical to promote attachment to Spain. In one article he even refers to Senator Ángel Pulido as a "Second Herzl." Pulido himself mentions Levy in *Stateless Spaniards*, referring to him as a prominent agent of Philo-Sephardi ideas worldwide.[31] On the other side of the Atlantic Ocean, the editorial board of *El Renacimiento de Israel* in northern Morocco suggested honoring Pulido in the JNF's "golden book." In a follow-up article, noting that the idea to recognize Pulido had come from the Moroccan community in Argentina, the editors included a copy of a report on the subject that had been previously published in *Israel* in Buenos Aires.[32]

HISPANIC ZIONISM AND COMMUNITY EMPOWERMENT IN CASABLANCA

In the early twentieth century, new forms of communal organization among Jews in Latin America paralleled community-building processes among Hispanic Moroccan Jews—not only in northern Morocco but also in the country's rapidly developing commercial center, Casablanca. In the nineteenth century, several Spanish-speaking Jewish families from northern Morocco had been among the first Jews to settle in Casablanca. In 1880, they established the Junta, a community council that resembled in its name and organizational codes the modern Jewish community councils in their northern Moroccan hometowns. This Spanish-speaking leadership also lobbied for the founding of a Casablanca branch of the AIU, which would eventually open in 1897.[33] In 1898, Jewish immigrants from Tangier in Casablanca established their own synagogue, Shevet Achim, at 8 Dar el-Makhzen Street, in front of the Great Mosque. The synagogue was located in the heart of Casablanca's commercial district, where a number of northern Moroccan families had settled. By 1912, and until its closure in 1940, Shevet Achim served a nearby community center for immigrants.[34] As a minority group, northern Moroccan immigrants to Casablanca continued to use Spanish as their internal language of communication.[35]

As in Argentina and Brazil, Zionist activism played a strategic role for the leaders of the Jewish community in Casablanca. One of the major figures in the local Zionist scene, who would soon become a leader in the broader nationwide Zionist movement in Morocco, was S. D. Lévy, who appeared at the beginning of this chapter as the Zionist leader promoting ties between Israel and Spain in 1955. An AIU graduate, Lévy developed his teaching career at various branches of the AIU school system—first in Tunisia in 1894, then from 1894 to 1900 in Tangier, and finally as principal of the Casablanca branch from 1900 to 1902. In 1903, Lévy joined the Jewish Colonization Association (JCA) and spent the next ten years as principal of the school at the JCA's colony in Mauricio, Argentina. As an AIU representative, he helped recruit students from North Africa to the JCA. In Argentina, he worked closely with refugees from Russia until 1913, when he returned to Morocco and resettled in Casablanca. Lévy engaged in all of these activities despite the fact that the AIU and JCA maintained a general opposition to immigration to Palestine.[36]

In Argentina, Lévy was exposed to Zionist organizational practices, as recounted above. After his return to Casablanca in 1913, he imported some of those ideas back to Morocco and became a pioneering Zionist organizer together with Spanish-speaking émigrés from northern Morocco like Yaacov Raphaël Benacerraf, a wealthy tea merchant with whom Lévy established the first Zionist group in the city. In 1927, Lévy was elected president of both the Jewish National Fund (JNF) and the Magen David association. He later became the president of the Moroccan branch of the French Zionist Federation. In 1926, Lévy was among the most prominent writers for *L'Avenir Illustrée* (1926–40), a Zionist periodical founded by Jonathan Thurscz, a Polish Jewish immigrant to Casablanca with strong ties to European Jewish communities and a command of French, German, Polish, and Yiddish.[37] *L'Avenir Illustrée* would prove to be one of Morocco's longest-standing Jewish publications. Zionist activity in Morocco in the 1920s and 1930s was largely characterized by the tight collaboration between Lévy, his colleagues in Casablanca, and other European Jews like the Polish-born Solomon Cagan.

This group represented a small network who struggled to bring Zionist ideas to North Africa against the resistance of local Jewish leaders. In 1932, Elie Nataf, former principal of the Alliance Israélite Universelle and secretary of the Jewish community of Casablanca, established the Jewish newspaper *L'Union Marocaine* to counteract the Zionist-oriented *L'Avenir Illustrée*. He represented an educated elite of "integrationist" Moroccan Jews who were influenced by the Jewish-Arab riots in Palestine in 1929, rising Arab nationalism in the 1930s, and the Berber Dahir of 1930. Beyond Zionism, *L'Union Marocaine* countered *L'Avenir Illustrée* on many other issues, including, for example, education, communal administration, and the legal status of Moroccan Jews. *L'Avenir Illustrée* ceased publication in 1940 after the French authorities deported Thurscz due to his illegal Zionist activity.[38]

The remaining Zionist activists who had founded *L'Avenir Illustrée* went on to establish a successor publication, *Noar*, which appeared from 1945 until 1952. The new newspaper reflected a major shift in attitudes toward Zionism in Casablanca and across the country. Still, as demonstrated at the beginning of this chapter, despite its appeal to the local Francophone audience in Morocco, *Noar* mirrored the transregional network that its founders had initiated in the late nineteenth century with the establishment of the global Spanish-speaking Moroccan community and its affinity for Spain.

POST-1948 DEVELOPMENTS

Despite their global reach, until the mid-1940s, Zionist networks in Morocco were small and monitored by the authorities, and exerted only minor influence on the majority of Moroccan Jews. Zionism in that period was not oriented toward emigration to Palestine as much as it was toward fundraising and providing an intellectual-organizational framework for Jewish communities worldwide. Even as late as 1944, S. D. Lévy, one of the most prominent leaders of Moroccan Zionism, did not see emigration as a fruitful solution for Moroccan Jews, preferring to invest in community developments in his Moroccan homeland.[39] But due to the momentous impact of events after World War II—most prominently the founding of the State of Israel in 1948—Zionist migration subsequently became far more influential among a much wider swath of the Jewish population and leadership. Between 1948 and 1956, 98,243 Jews, more than a third of the country's entire Jewish population in 1948, left for Israel.[40] This came at a time when, paradoxically, the State of Israel determined that Jewish immigration from North Africa was not a matter of urgency, prioritizing other communities in Iraq, Yemen, and Libya that became independent earlier than Morocco, Tunisia, and Algeria. In November 1951, Israel even approved a "selection" policy that limited Jewish immigration based on age and medical condition as well as their ability and willingness to work in agricultural settlements.[41]

Israel's restriction on Jewish immigration from North Africa, effective since November 1951, began to loosen in light of the local struggle for Moroccan independence, which became increasingly violent in the summer of 1954. Though Jews were not often explicitly targeted in the struggle, they sometimes fell victim to the rising violence, as when seven Jews in the town of Petitjean were killed by a mob on August 3, 1954. The situation further deteriorated with anti-French riots in the summer of 1955 after Sultan Mohammed V was exiled to Madagascar by the colonial administration. The number of immigrants to Israel increased from 2,996 in 1953 to 8,171 in 1954 before soaring to 24,994 in 1955. That year, the Mossad founded Hamisgeret ("The Framework" in Hebrew), an organization responsible for recruiting and training agents to undertake secret emigration operations in Morocco.[42]

On January 10, 1961, a smuggling ship carrying forty-three illegal Jewish Moroccan migrants sank alongside the northern shores of Morocco. All on board drowned. This unfortunate incident sparked a sequence of events, which together led local Jewish leaders, Israel, and world Jewish organizations to pressure the Moroccan government to alleviate the 1956 emigration ban on its Jewish citizens. In May 1961, Abd-el-Kader Benjelloun and Moulay Ali Alaoui, representatives of the recently crowned King Hassan II, and Alex Gatmon, the top envoy of the Misgeret, held secret negotiations in Europe concerning that issue. By July that year, they reached an agreement. According to the agreement, the Jewish humanitarian association United Hebrew Immigration Aid Society (HIAS) would open offices in Morocco, and under its patronage Israel would organize migration. Morocco was required to issue collective passports to Jews wishing to leave the country. In return, Morocco would receive a down payment of $500,000 and indemnities of $100 per capita for the first fifty thousand Jews choosing to depart, and then $250 per capita for the rest. The implementation of this agreement came to be known as Operation Yakhin. From November 28, 1961, through December 31, 1964, planes and ships from Casablanca and Tangier transferred olim, via southern Europe, to Israel.[43] During the operation, 89,742 Jews immigrated to Israel from Morocco. By the end of 1971, 114,158 people, 70 percent of the Jewish population in Morocco in 1961, would eventually immigrate to Israel as result of this undertaking.[44]

To understand how this development, from 1948 to 1961, strengthened the link between immigration to Israel and Zionist activities, we need to consider developments outside of Morocco, among European Jews, from the early 1940s. As mentioned, at the outbreak of World War II, a few thousand Jewish refugees arrived from Europe and settled in Tangier. Although this influx constituted a financial drain on the Jewish community council, it still evoked a spirit of Jewish solidarity. After the war, this spirit did not come to an end but intensified. For instance, in December 1947, Tangier's Jewish community, as an independent entity within Morocco (due to Tangier's international status), joined as the sixty-first member country affiliated with the World Jewish Congress (WJC). The collaboration would take place in the context of expanding local and global Zionist networks. At the time, new international Jewish organizations had begun to express a growing interest in the Jewish communities of Asia and Africa, whose relative demographic significance had been augmented because of the destruction of European Jewry during the Holocaust.

In 1948, several such organizations, which had initially been established to assist European Jews during wartime, sensed they had accomplished their original missions and began searching for new "Jewries in distress," mostly in Africa and Asia. In this context, a few of the major Jewish bodies operating in Morocco, most prominently the AIU and the American Joint Distribution Committee (JDC), began to change their pre-1945 orientations. Though they did not always outwardly acknowledge it, they began to imbue their philanthropic and educational activities with Zionist activism as a way of preparing the ground for mass immigration to Israel.[45]

These events on the global Jewish diaspora front coincided with a significant wave of Jewish migration to Tangier, taking place against the backdrop of more localized post–World War II developments. The Tangier International Zone, which returned in 1945 after five years of annexation by Franco's Spain, rejuvenated the city's appeal among immigrants. Representatives of the JDC in Tangier reported to the Casablanca office in November 1954: "It is believed that more and more children will come to the Jewish schools, because, as you know, more and more people come from the Spanish Zone to Tangier, or at least send their children, even if they cannot come themselves yet."[46] The same report indicated that some 60 percent of those joining the new Association for Professional Training, organized in postwar Tangier by the JDC, came from the Spanish protectorate zone, rather than from Tangier itself.[47]

Together with the demographic shift, a new political reality began to set the ground for a new form of Zionist activity designed to promote immigration to Israel. During the Spanish annexation of Tangier by Franco between 1940 and 1945, Zionist activities were restricted as, in contrast to earlier Spanish attitudes, Franco associated European Zionism with alien socialist ideas. However, when the international administration resumed between 1945 and 1956, Zionist groups and activities revitalized themselves, enabling the world Jewish organizations and, after 1948, the new State of Israel to invest in Zionist institutions. In the late 1940s, there emerged various Zionist-oriented youth movements, including Bnei Akiva and Bachad (the Alliance of Religious Pioneers), which had a religious orientation; Dror and Hashomer Hatzair, which had a socialist orientation; and Habonim, Gordonia, and the scouts group Éclaireurs Israelites (also known as the Charles Netter youth group), which was more oriented toward France—all of which provided new frameworks for Zionist activities among the Jewish youth of Tangier and its environs. The

Youth Department of the Jewish Agency took advantage of these groups to recruit suitable youngsters for immigration to Israel.[48]

An increasing number of high school students from local middle-class families in northern Morocco were affiliated, at least formally, with Zionist youth movements.[49] The local Zionist Federation viewed the Lycée Français, which represented the successful incorporation of local Jews into the non-Jewish educational environment, as an institution where potential immigrants to Israel should be sought.[50] Similarly, the list of donations to Magbit, a Zionist fundraising organization supporting immigration to Israel, included a sizable amount donated by individuals from Tangier. Some donors were affiliated with the Casino Israelita, a cornerstone of local Jewish life that was strongly associated with the wealthier, pro-European elements of Tangier's Jewish society. Notably, they donated even though they themselves would probably never seriously consider immigrating to Israel.[51]

Emigration was also grounded in political changes on the domestic Moroccan front. In May 1955, by which time the local Aliyah Office, serving Jews who wished to immigrate to Israel, had been forced to shut down by the Tangier International Zone administration, an exhibition of Jewish books, including books in the Hebrew language, took place at the Casino Israelita. A report by the Jewish Agency's Department of Education and Culture in Exile described how the organizers could "barely shut the doors of the hall," as it was packed with curious people. Over the course of the exhibition, the Zionist Federation of Tangier racked up numerous new subscriptions. Radio Tangier, a popular local radio station in Spanish, promoted the event, and it was even covered in the most widely circulated local newspaper in Spanish, *España*, whose reporters made no reference to the exhibit's Zionist character.[52]

At the time, Zionist activities were not defined as such, but new terminology, including *Jerez*, emerged. *Jerez* (pronounced "Kheres," in a way that resembled the pronunciation of the Spanish city Jerez) became a well-known abbreviation for Eretz Yisrael (the Land of Israel) and was commonly used in an attempt to avoid using the word *Israel*, so as not to attract unwanted attention.[53]

Despite the growing interest in Zionism, northern Morocco produced among the smallest numbers of immigrants to Israel. During Operation Yakhin, only 17.9 percent of the Jewish population of Tangier emigrated to Israel. In neighboring Tetouan—the second largest city in northern Morocco—only 20.5 percent of Jews left for Israel. These relatively low percentages contrast sharply with the 77.2 percent of Jews who left Marrakech and the 54.5 percent who left Casablanca for Israel. By the end of 1972, when 70 percent of Moroccan Jews had immigrated to Israel, only 30.4 percent of the local Jewish population of northern Morocco had done the same.⁵⁴ To understand this gap between Moroccan communities, we need to consider developments in the Hispanic Moroccan Jewish diaspora after 1945, which channeled migration aspirations and even Zionist activism elsewhere than Israel.

THE OLD/NEW LATIN AMERICAN CONNECTION

As in the earlier stages of the twentieth century, dramatic developments on the domestic front coincided with changes in migration policy elsewhere in ways that significantly influenced the community of Spanish-speaking Jews.⁵⁵ During the 1940s and 1950s, Venezuela experienced an unprecedented economic boom, mostly due to its flourishing petroleum industry. Venezuela's economic and political stability contrasted starkly with the insecurity and unrest in much of the rest of South and Central America to such an extent that its national discourse described the country's economic progress as "magical." Channeling this economic success to industrialization, between 1949 and 1958, when many Jews from northern Morocco immigrated to Israel, Venezuelan authorities began to encourage the permanent settlement of Europeans. Laborers from southern Europe flooded the country under Venezuela's bilateral agreements with Spain (its former colonizer), Italy, and Portugal.

Between 1951 and 1959, some 131,995 Spanish immigrants settled in Venezuela, constituting the single largest ethnic group among the 318,959 immigrants who entered the country during that period. These events coincided with Franco's policy to promote emigration as a means for reducing social turmoil in Spain after 1956. By 1961, Spanish nationals comprised some 31.4 percent of the entire population of foreigners in Venezuela, where immigration authorities facilitated family reunification and the permanent settlement of new immigrants. To that end, they required that migrants' relatives already living in the country confirm that their own economic situation was stable and that they were willing and able to assist their immigrant relatives.⁵⁶

These shifts in Venezuela's immigration policy, which paralleled dramatic events in Israel and Morocco, were recognized by world Jewish organizations operating in Morocco as providing momentum to the promotion of Jewish emigration. In October 1955, Raphael Spanien, co-director of the European headquarters office of HIAS, prepared a report on Morocco's Jewish society with the aim of assisting Jewish emigration from the country as it approached decolonization. After wrapping up its operations among Jewish refugees in Europe, HIAS's focus shifted to North Africa, which was deemed a place from which Jews needed to be rescued in light of rising Arab nationalism. The main concern of HIAS as the struggle for independence from Spain and France was gaining momentum in the 1950s, as we saw earlier, was to find alternative migration routes for North African Jews, other than the Israeli option, as a way of avoiding clashes with Moroccan and colonial authorities. A search for alternative destinations also came as result of HIAS's view that middle-class or Westernized Jews from northern Morocco and Casablanca were not suitable for immigration to the young and underdeveloped State of Israel.

Spanien's work in Morocco began in 1941 when he worked for HICEM, a body created through the merger of three Jewish migration societies: the New York-based Hebrew Immigrant Aid Society (HIAS), the Jewish Colonization Association (JCA), and Emigdirect, based in Berlin. HICEM's acronym reflected this institutional merger. As the head of the HICEM's Marseille headquarters, Spanien helped organize the escape of Jewish refugees from Europe to the Americas through Casablanca.[57] Thirteen years later, his conclusion after visiting Tangier and Casablanca, and after looking into various migration alternatives including Chile, Brazil, Venezuela, Colombia, Australia, and Canada, was that Venezuela would be the most suitable destination for Spanish-speaking Moroccan Jews. In his report to the main HIAS office following his visit, he explained his choice of Venezuela by pointing out that, in the north of the country, many Jews already had kinship links to the country and thereby better than average chances of receiving visas to settle in Venezuela. Spanien wrote, "My belief is that we should avail ourselves of the good will gesture shown by the Sephardi community of South America for the salvation of part of the Jewish population, closer to them [in terms of kinship and culture] than were the victims of European events since 1933."[58]

Spanien's conclusion should come as no surprise given the scale of migration from Morocco to Latin America over the previous century. Spanien was aware of the historic connections between the communities in northern Morocco and Latin America and wanted his organization to leverage them to facilitate migration at a time when organizing Jewish emigration from the MENA region was a top priority.

A bigger surprise is the group of people Spanien planned to enlist for support—namely, prominent Zionist activists who had set up bases in Tangier and Casablanca early in the century with the aim of bringing Zionist activities to lower-class Moroccan Jews. These leaders included Alfonso Sabah, a major figure leading the AIU's softening position toward Zionism after World War II, and Paul Calamaro, the former president of the Zionist Federation in Morocco, who replaced S. D. Lévy after his resignation in 1944 and who continued to serve as a prominent leader of Moroccan Zionism well into the 1950s. By 1955, these prominent Zionists were deeply involved in facilitating immigration to Israel and forging connections with emissaries from the Jewish state.[59] Spanien first worked with Calamaro, who, according to Spanien, realized in 1954 that putting all his efforts into promoting Jewish emigration to Israel would not prove feasible due to Israel's selective immigration policy, which had been in effect since late 1951. Calamaro's modus operandi matched that of Spanien and HIAS: to help any Jew get out of Morocco, regardless of his or her final destination. Supportive of this agenda, Calamaro gladly referred to Spanien a number of candidates for whom the process of emigration to Latin America would run smoothly due to their kinship ties to Venezuela.

As mentioned earlier, the number of Jewish immigrants to Israel increased significantly in the summer of 1954 and soared in 1955, due to changing immigration policies in Israel. Spanien and his Zionist collaborators in Morocco were still determined to work on the Venezuelan option even as Israel had become a favorable destination for Moroccan Jewish migrants, since they saw the local Jewish population as culturally unsuited for and uninterested in immigration to Israel. For example, Alfonso Sabah, the prominent Zionist leader mentioned earlier, had considered joining his brother, Leopoldo Sabah, who had recently settled in Venezuela. The siblings had another brother, Jack (a former editor of *Adelante*), who moved to Argentina in the 1940s.[60] Alfonso's brother-in-law, Jacobo Bentata, had also recently left for Venezuela. As mentioned in Spanien's report, Sabah was in favor of emigration to Venezuela as long as it did not "counteract the Zionist ideal and, in his mind, the religious one." Sabah endorsed Spanien's idea of prioritizing Venezuela as a destination for Spanish-speaking Jews and referred potential immigrants to Spanien in Tangier and Casablanca. According to Spanien, through his kinship networks, Sabah maintained good contacts in Venezuela, in particular his relative Léon Taurel, a wealthy businessman who headed the country's Moroccan-led Sephardi community.

In Tangier, Spanien also met with Carlos Albo, the Moroccan-descended Venezuelan ambassador to Tangier who, as honorary consul of Venezuela, had the legal capacity to issue immigration visas. Albo helped simplify the legal procedures for Jewish Moroccans seeking to immigrate to Venezuela.[61] To facilitate immigration to Venezuela, Calamaro put Spanien in touch with a lawyer and human rights activist named Nelly (Helen) Cazes Bénatar, a Tangier native who resided in Casablanca, where she organized relief plans for Jewish refugees in Morocco who had fled Nazi Germany. In 1944, Bénatar was chosen as one of Morocco's representatives for the WJC meeting in Atlantic City. Seeing itself as responsible for relieving the torment of world Jewry after the Holocaust, the WJC assumed the task of resettling displaced Jews. After the war, Cazes Bénatar worked with the JDC to prepare Jews for emigration to Israel.[62] With her help, Spanien used the JDC offices in Tangier and Casablanca to interview candidates, and their completed files were sent by Albo to the Moroccan community in Venezuela, since most had relatives there or were simply "of the same origin as Jews at the head of the Sephardi community of that country."[63] Remarkably, Spanien notes at the end of his report that not only did his suggestion of promoting Jewish immigration to Venezuela not create hostility among prominent Zionists in Morocco, but they in fact fully collaborated with him.[64]

The described incident demonstrates an interpretation of Zionism as a tool for global networks among Zionist leaders of a highly mobile Hispanic Moroccan diaspora that had an established transnational awareness already in the early twentieth century. Yet, it may also reflect a more lenient approach toward the incorporation of Jews as minorities in postcolonial Morocco.

REAFFIRMING MOROCCO AS A HOMELAND

With the formal end of the Spanish and French protectorates in Morocco, the year 1956 marked a major shift in the political situation of the Hispanic Moroccan Jewish diaspora. Moroccan independence was followed by about eighteen years of political and economic turmoil and then a series of coups and conspiracies in the early 1970s that ended with the 1973 constitutional revolution. During those years, national considerations led to the neglect of the northern region, a relatively poorer territory than the ex-French zone. Foreign embassies were moved to Rabat, the new national capital. Many of the buildings erected in the north during the construction boom of the 1940s were left empty. The fledging nationalist regime saw Tangier, in particular, as the symbol of the old colonial order and worked to change its character. Subsequently, the city began to attract large numbers of Muslim peasants from the Rif area, a migration that, over the next five years from Morocco's independence, changed what had been Tangier's strong European character.

From 1956 to 1961, the Moroccan government enforced a ban on the emigration of Jewish Moroccan citizens. Liberal circles within the Moroccan leadership feared that if Jews left the country, the nation's economy would suffer. Pan-Arabists in the nationalist Istiqlal Party, for their part, feared the possible contributions of Jewish immigrants of Israel at a time when this country was at war with its Arab neighbors. However, the catastrophic forecasts made by Israeli and world Jewish organizations in in the early 1950s as to the future physical, political, and economic security of Jews in independent Morocco failed to materialize.[65] Immediately following Moroccan independence in March 1956, many Jews received Moroccan citizenship, and the process of their incorporation into the new nation-state soon began. An emerging elite within Jewish society in Morocco enjoyed the new atmosphere, which promoted incorporation of Jews into the Moroccan state, some even ascending to positions in the new government. This included Jewish communists, who already in 1947 considered anti-Zionism an expression of their Moroccan patriotism. In 1956, Jewish militants in the Parti Communiste Marocain (the Communist Party of Morocco, or PCM) maintained this strong rejection of Zionism and especially of those who worked with the Jewish Agency to promote migration to Israel. Among these activists was Abraham Serfaty, a Marxist political activist whose family was from Tangier. Nonetheless, identification with the Moroccan nationalist movement did not always preclude additional national affinities. Léon Benzaquen, a Tangier native, had served as the Moroccan president of Keren Hayesod in the 1940s and also became the first Jewish minister to serve in Morocco's independent government in 1956.[66]

Alongside Casablanca, Tangier became a major hub for such Jewish integrationist activities and aspirations. Abraham Laredo, an enthusiastic Hispanophile mentioned in chapter 2, is a prominent example. In 1956, he was appointed president of the Junta of Tangier and took on other communal positions as well, such as president of the local branch of the Oeuvre de Secours aux Enfants, a humanitarian Jewish organization. Concurrently, Laredo was one of the most enthusiastic activists in al-Wifaq, an association of Muslims and Jews founded in February 1956. This association aimed to promote interfaith coexistence based on ideals of equal citizenship and civic participation in the public affairs of what they envisioned as secular and democratic Morocco. Al-Wifaq organized numerous events with the goal of fostering an interfaith foundation for Moroccan national solidarity. Alongside al-Wifaq, another initiative called Les Amitiés Marocaines (1950–1956), a multifaith association encompassing Christians, Jews, and Muslims, emerged as an early endeavor to reshape the Moroccan state. It's goal was to extend the benefits of Morocco's independence to the Jewish and Muslim communities, advocating for innovative legal approaches to integrate Europeans who opted to stay in postcolonial Morocco.[67]

As the political developments were taking place in the aftermath of World War II and the decolonization of Africa and Asia, the affinity for Spain that had flourished under Spanish colonialism did not decline and in fact contributed to the enrichment of postcolonial Zionist and local Moroccan identities in a unique way. As noted by Alma Rachel Heckman, the 1956 edition of al-Wifaq's magazine featured photographs of its interfaith events as well as full-page images of the Sultan Mohamed V and the Crown Prince Mulay Hassan. The article included some content in praise of the Convivencia, interfaith coexistence in Al-Andalus, as a model for the new Jewish-Muslim relations under the Moroccan national banner. This perspective, at least during the initial months of Morocco's independence, resonated with the notion of a Hispano-Arab brotherhood developed by Spanish colonialists.[68]

Carlos de Nesry, the famous Jewish intellectual, lawyer, and member of the Junta of Tangier, who also became a senior activist in the nationalist Parti Démocratique de l'Independence (PDI), provides insights into the discourse of the city's integrationist elite. In his book *Le Juif de Tanger et le Maroc*, published in 1956, de Nesry maintained that the feeling of Jews for Israel was not a problem of dual loyalty but rather an expression of historic attachment.[69] Moreover, as Brahim El Guabli showed, as part of his reenvisioning of the new postcolonial Moroccan state, "He [de Nesry] argued in the clearest terms that it was possible for Moroccan Jews to remain Westernized culturally and linguistically while also participating fully in the new state."[70] As historian Maite Ojeda Mata has described, de Nesry made clear through his actions that, in addition to his affinities for Morocco and Israel, Spain was also close to his heart. His incorporation into the Hispanophone elite of northern Morocco in the 1940s and 1950s is evidenced also by his hispanized first name and surname: de Nesry was the son of Rabbi Yahia Nezry, who came to Tangier from the southern parts of Morocco. In a pivotal role, in 1948, he mediated between the newly formed Israeli government and the Francoist regime, making sure that Spanish interests in Jerusalem were maintained.[71] His multifaceted identity and diplomatic efforts further illuminate the intricate dynamics of this historical period.

While Moroccan Jewish participation in the anticolonial movement coalesced around antifascist activism, the anti-Zionist tendencies in al-Wifaq and assertions of Moroccan nationalism, for the community leadership in northern Morocco they did not seem to sharply contrast with their pro-Zionist expressions nor with affinities toward Spain, the former colonizer of northern Morocco.[72] As the political status of Jews in independent Morocco became a topic of interest in the local Jewish press, the Hispanic-oriented and pro-Zionist periodical *Or-Luz* was no exception.[73] On the occasion of Moroccan independence, Sidi Embarek Bekkai, the Moroccan prime minister, sent a telegram to the American Jewish Committee (AJC) in New York. In the telegram, issued after Bekkai's meeting in November 1954 with representatives of the AJC, he declared the commitment of the Moroccan authorities to equality of rights for all Moroccan Jews. *Or-Luz*'s editorial board reprinted the telegram on the front page of its February 1956 issue.[74]

In April 1956, Sultan Mohammed V (appointed king in 1957) and two of his sons paid a historic visit to northern Morocco, attending one of the galas organized by Al-Wifaq at the Casino Israelita in Tetouan. The main aim of their visit was to promote the reunification of the two formerly separated French- and Spanish-dominated regions of the country. *Or-Luz* covered the visit in detail and attached great significance to the event, which it marked by placing a full-page portrait of the Sultan and the Crown Prince Mulay Hassan on the cover of the magazine.[75] *Or-Luz* covered the gala in detail and noted that it was attended by Mulay Hassan; the deputy prime minister; and five other ministers, including Dr. Leon Benzaquen. As the report related, members of the Istiqlal Party stood as guards of honor at the entrance. Mulay Hassan emphasized in his speech, according to the report, his father's commitment to equality of rights for Muslims and Jews. The report added that, later in the evening, many Muslim and Jewish men and women joined the festivities. As late as four in the morning, "no one hastened to leave the club."[76] *Or-Luz* ran photographs from the event and described a group of Muslim and Jewish women awaiting the landing of the sultan's airplane at the local Sania-Ramel Airport.[77]

Or-Luz reflected a tripartite attachment that dwelled strongly on the romanticized refences to the Convivencia in al-Wifaq's magazine. In 1956, the year of Moroccan independence, it was the only Spanish-language Jewish newspaper that appeared in Morocco and thus provided the main platform for promoting Jewish affinity with Spain and its culture. Like many of its predecessors in the 1920s and 1930s, *Or-Luz* did not miss the opportunity to promote the legendary image of Senator Ángel Pulido, describing him in 1956 as "a famous and venerated Gentleman in all Jewish homes."[78] Another example is an *Or-Luz* article entitled "Let's Get Familiar with Our Past," which praised the tenth-century revival of Hebrew poetry (*piyyut*) and philological and literary traditions in Iberia, focusing on two tenth-century Jewish writers, Menahem Ben Saruk and Dunash Ben Labrat. The author, Solomon Bensabat, posited a continuity between the Jews of medieval Iberia and contemporary Jewish life in northern Morocco, envisioning "a Moroccan Jewish cultural renaissance grounded in the revival of the heritage of medieval Sepharad," as Eric Calderwood put it. Bensabat described pre-1492 Jewish history in Sepharad as no less important for Jewish life than Jewish history in the holy land at the time of the Bible.[79]

Bensabat was a rabbinic scholar who helped spread these ideas in a number of lectures and articles, particularly after 1948, when he was appointed as the academic director of the Maimonides Institute in Tetouan (see chap. 2).

While his Philo-Sephardism comes as no surprise, a less acknowledged fact in the relevant literature about Bensabat's biography is his concurrent nomination as one of the five Jewish members of the Moroccan National Assembly in November 1956. Another lesser-known fact, highlighted by the historian Yigal Bin-Nun, is that Bensabat also provided assistance to the clandestine Israeli immigration organization Hamisgeret after it was established in 1956 to help Jews leave the country illegally for Israel.[80]

Bensabat, like de Nesry and other Jewish figures from northern Morocco, represented a complex amalgam of national affinities and their associated communal and intellectual networks, even during a period of heightened nationalist sentiments, Zionism included. Alongside Moroccan, Spanish, Sephardi, colonial, and other global affairs, *Or-Luz* covered Zionist affairs and even Ashkenazi Jewish history. It reported on a scholarly lecture about the lives of Jews in Europe, held at the Casino Israelita in Tetouan, the same place Bensabat delivered his talk about the Jewish past in Iberia, and where al-Wifaq organized its gala. This lecture was seemingly formulated to evoke feelings of Jewish national solidarity in the audience. As at the al-Wifaq's gala, here too the reporter pointed out that the hall was packed with locals, mainly women. *Or-Luz* ran an article entitled "Great Jewish Figures," which dealt with nineteenth-century Jewish painters, among them Mark Chagall.[81] Another article dealt with Albert Einstein as a subject of national Jewish pride.[82]

Among the diversifying local and global identities, *Or-Luz* included Zionist-oriented articles among its wide range of topics, despite the clandestine nature of Zionist activity in 1956, the year that *Or-Luz* first appeared. Many articles reflected a clear interest in the newly formed State of Israel.[83] For instance, to celebrate the Jewish holiday of Tu Bishvat, its cover page included an illustration of young field workers wearing round, brimless hats in what appeared to be a typical Israeli countryside landscape (fig. 4.1).[84] Some of the "great Jewish figures" mentioned above were figures from modern Hebrew culture, such as Hana Szenes, Hayim Nahman Bialik, and Shaul Gutmanovich Tchernichovsky. The last two were famous national Hebrew poets.

In the same month as Moroccan independence, *Or-Luz* published a love song dedicated to the gulf of Eilat composed by Solomon Medina, who had expressed his yearning for the Judería of Toledo in a previous issue. The song was a promotion for Medina's forthcoming book, *The Yearnings of a Jew*. It was followed by an article about fishermen in the Sea of Galilee, and the subsequent issue featured a piece about the actor Danny Kaye's visit to Israel.[85]

As Moroccan Jewish identity diversified, *Or-Luz*'s cover pages marking Tu Bishvat stood in seeming contradiction to other cover images that expressed

Figure 4.1. *Or-Luz*'s cover on the occasion of Tu BiShvat (*Or-Luz*, February 2, 1956). Courtesy of the Garzon Family. Stored at BZLPC.

Figure 4.2. *Or-Luz*'s cover on the occasion of Prince Muley Hassan's visit to Tetouan (*Or-Luz*, April 18, 1956). Courtesy of the Garzon Family. Stored at BZLPC.

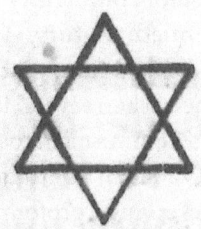

LUZ circula por:
MARRUECOS, ESPAÑA, VENEZUELA Y NORTEAMERICA

Año I - Número 5

Figure 4.3. Information regarding *Or-Luz*'s circulation (*Or-Luz*, May 15, 1956). Courtesy of the Garzon Family. Stored at BZLPC.

an integrationist orientation, such as an image depicting the Grand Mosque that the sultan had begun constructing in Casablanca, or a photograph of Sultan Mohamed V with Prince Muley Hassan during their visit to Tetouan (see fig. 4.2).[86] Rather, both Moroccan and Zionist issues represented aspects of Moroccan Jews' diversifying Jewish lives—lives that had both local and global dimensions and that featured a mixture of affinities with Spain, Latin America, and now, in the context of rising nationalisms, the new states of Morocco and Israel.

These seemingly contradictory nationalist expressions could coexist because, in the eyes of the editors and perhaps many readers, they were more closely associated with an enduring globalization of communal culture than with emigration to Israel and related calls to negate their "exilic" past, as some political Zionists would advocate for Jewish life in Morocco. In the end, many of the Zionist activists mentioned in this chapter did not emigrate to Israel, even if they were often active in facilitating the emigration of other members of the community.

S. D. Lévy, one of the earliest advocates of the Zionist project and who, after 1948, called for Jews to emigrate to Israel, died in Casablanca at the age of ninety-five in 1960, twelve years after the founding of Israel. Lévy was conceivably too old to emigrate, but other activists like Rahma Toledano moved to Spain, where she lived until her death in 1971.[87] Moisés Garzón, *Or-Luz*'s founding editor, ended up in Venezuela in 1958, where he continued to promote Zionist ideas in the evolving Hispanophone diaspora late into the twentieth century (see chap. 5).

Looking at the perspective of community actors, the critical conclusion of this chapter—which has explored interconnectivity between the hubs of the Hispanic Moroccan Jewish diaspora as a major factor in the development of Zionism among this community—also lies in the argument that the pre-1948 mode of Zionism as a tool for community empowerment developed well into the second half of the twentieth century, even when Israel's state agencies worked to leverage Zionism for mass immigration projects. Even in 1956, the year of Moroccan independence, when several leaders of the Hispanic Moroccan community expressed their commitment to the Moroccan national project, this earlier mode of pre-1948 Zionism continued to evolve and coexist with new nationalist ideas while preserving a profound and enduring connection to Spain as a historical Jewish center. This attachment to Spain played a pivotal role in shaping the perception of Zionism as an integral part of a mosaic of ethnonational identities rather than a monolithic one. In chapter 5, I look at how the immigration of most Moroccan Jews to Israel in the 1960s and 1970s continued to shape the Hispanic Moroccan Jewish community's attitude toward Israel and Zionism and integrate it into their amalgam of identities in Venezuela.

FIVE

MOROCCANS IN VENEZUELA: A NEW GLOBAL HIERARCHY

BETWEEN 1948 AND 1970, ISRAEL TRANSFORMED from a small demographic hub with approximately 650,000 Jews—out of a total world population of 11.5 million—into a significant demographic center of Jewish life, with a total population of more than 2.5 million Jews out of a global 12.6 million Jews. By 1968, some 71 percent of the Jews who had immigrated from Asia and Africa had migrated to Israel. In the post-Holocaust era, about 80 percent of the immigrants from Eastern European countries, excluding Jews from the Soviet Union, also made Israel their new home. Jewish immigrants from Muslim countries and their descendants came to constitute about half of the Jewish population of Israel in the 1950s, even when Israel was home to only about a fifth of world Jewry, and regardless of the small fraction they composed of the total estimated population of Jews worldwide.[1] In the 1970s and in the aftermath of Operation Yakhin, during which most remaining Moroccan Jews immigrated to Israel, Moroccan Jews and their descendants came to constitute the largest country-of-origin group in Israel until the mass migration of Jews from the former Soviet Union in the 1990s.[2]

In the nineteenth century, mainstream narratives of Jewish solidarity, like the one introduced by the Alliance Israélite Universelle (AIU), began to divide the world into Jewries "in distress," residing in countries or regions characterized by anti-Jewish persecution, and Jewries in the "developed" world, charged with responsibility for the well-being of their persecuted brethren. In fact, organized transnational Jewish solidarity networks have long existed, but in the nineteenth century these networks became inextricably intertwined with modern colonial regimes.[3] In the postwar period, after Israel and the Americas had replaced Eastern European, Asian, and African countries as the demographic and cultural centers of world Jewry, these new centers of Jewish existence were invested with responsibility for new "Jewries in distress," even as Israel itself relied heavily on external support. This imagined hierarchy of the Jewish world led to efforts by Hebrew Immigration Aid Society (HIAS), the American Joint Distribution Committee (JDC), and other Jewish organizations, some of them Zionist and others not, to "rescue" Jews from Morocco as French and Spanish colonialism drew to a close by facilitating their migration to Israel and the West, as noted in the previous chapter.

Against the backdrop of this turn of events, in the 1960s Israel became a prominent point of reference in shaping modern concepts of Jewish migration and solidarity worldwide. Long-existing hierarchies between "Eastern" (Asian, African, and East European) and "Western" (American and Western European) Jews informed the Zionist project with an old-new purpose that saw Israel and Zionist activities as responsible for the fate of world Jewry who remained in the diaspora. In this context, Israeli leaders such as David Ben-Gurion divided world Jewish populations between "Jewries in distress," who conceivably or visibly required the immediate assistance of the Jewish state, and Jews in "affluent countries," whose migration to Israel was not expected to occur in the foreseeable future, due to the comfort and stability of their communities. "Western aliyah," including the Jews from Latin America, was perceived by prominent Zionist leaders as an "Aliyah of choice." Unlike the rescue Aliyah designed for Jewries in distress, immigration from the West required more investments in easing the economic and social integration of migrants to make the process cost-effective. Western Jews—first and foremost US Jews, then the largest Jewish demographic concentration—were expected, at the very least, to support the Zionist project from afar. Considering their perceived assimilation into their broader non-Jewish societies, a main concern in the efforts to convince these affluent Jews to immigrate entailed, according to Ben-Gurion's strategy, the development of their Jewish identity and a sufficient knowledge of Hebrew.[4]

In the early 1970s, the approximately 2.2 million Soviet Jews came to the forefront of this global salvation narrative as representatives of the largest immobile Jewish hub behind the Iron Curtain and outside Israel. An international solidarity campaign on their behalf was sparked by the 1970 Leningrad trials, at which nine defendants, seven of whom were Jews, were convicted of attempting to hijack a Soviet airliner. Under the banner of "let my people go," many Jews worldwide called on the Soviet Union to grant Jews equal civil rights and religious freedom or allow them to leave the country, while lobbying the US government to pressure the Soviet Union. This call for freedom was influenced by contemporary political realities, such as American sparring with the Soviet

Union during the Cold War, in which the treatment of Soviet Jews became a symbol of Communism's "moral bankruptcy."[5]

The strategy of rescuing Soviet Jews by encouraging American intervention was developed from 1953 through the 1970s, when the Israel-based Zionist Nativ office worked with Jewish organizations in the US to lobby for the emigration of Soviet Jews to Israel and North America.[6] Transnational collaboration between Israel and other influential Jewish hubs on behalf of oppressed Jewries was not limited to Soviet Jews. Syrian Jews, for example, were acknowledged in 1971 by the World Jewish Congress, headquartered in Paris, as "our No. 2 problem." In Canada, for instance, the country's Zionist Federation, the National Council of Jewish Women, and Hadassah-Women's International Zionist Organization (WIZO) sent resolutions, statements of concern, and telegrams to Canadian, United Nations, and Syrian officials.[7]

By the 1970s, Venezuela constituted one of the prominent hubs of the global diaspora of Hispanic Moroccan Jews after 1948, numbering, according to some estimates, around 6,000 immigrants and their descendants, and around 12,000 by the early 1990s.[8] Between the early 1970s and the 1990s, the ratio of Sephardim (most of whom were Moroccans) to Ashkenazim gradually increased among Venezuela's Jews. In 1998–99, the Asociación Israelita de Venezuela (AIV) and its Ashkenazi equivalent, the Unión Israelita de Caracas (UIC), recorded an almost equal number of registered members: 2,160 Sephardim as compared to 2,493 Ashkenazim. The Sephardim in Venezuela, mostly immigrants from northern Morocco and their descendants, were slowly becoming more prominent among Venezuelan Jewry.[9] As a community, the social and economic situation of Moroccan Jews in Venezuela was far better than the situation of most newcomers in Israel at the time.

How, then, did the community of Moroccan Jews in Venezuela fit into the described global dynamics and Jewish hierarchies after 1948? What meaning did Hispanic Moroccan Jewish leaders in Venezuela attach to their Moroccan identity in this context? To answer these questions, this chapter shows how an attachment to multiple hubs, as well as new interpretations of Zionism, served as a discursive tool for empowering the Venezuelan Hispanic Moroccan Jewish community in the 1960s and early 1970s vis-à-vis Jews in distress. My analysis also builds on the previous chapter to demonstrate how the evolving character of Zionism as a segment of the broader Hispanic Moroccan Jewish mosaic and as an organizational framework for community-building not only survived the post-1948 process of migration to Israel but in fact played a role in consolidating new global power dynamics among Hispanic Moroccan Jews in the 1960s and 1970s.

A TROPICAL "MELTING POT"

As described in chapter four, the large waves of Jewish emigration from Morocco to Israel in the 1960s were relatively small in northern Morocco compared to the rest of the country. Whereas for less mobile communities Israel was often the only migratory option, for a community that had established international hubs already in the nineteenth century, Israel was a less attractive migration destination. This general observation needs to be examined against Venezuela's post-1948 national immigration policies and the local conditions of integration experienced by Moroccan Jews.

Due to Venezuela's relative prosperity in the aftermath of World War II and the new open-door policy adopted by dictator Marcos Evangelista Pérez Jiménez (1952–1958), this country increasingly began to receive a more diverse set of immigrants, most prominently from Europe.[10] The Jewish population of Venezuela was a marginal minority, amounting to some twelve thousand in a total population of approximately eight million in the 1960s. Venezuela's most prominent and visible cultural and economic elite came from Europe, particularly Spain. At the national level, since Venezuela's independence from Spain in 1810, and even before, "modernization" was strongly associated with the cultural and racialized "blending" of the creole, mestizo, and indigenous people with the population of Europeans. New immigration policies preferred European immigration as a way to whiten the country's already mixed population, thereby "cleansing" the negative influence of non-white traits.[11]

By virtue of their native tongue, Spanish-speaking Jewish immigrants from northern Morocco had a historic advantage over other immigrants from Europe and the Middle East in their smooth assimilation in the country, which continued into the mid-twentieth century. Unlike in France, where the North African population comprised a large Muslim immigrant society and a smaller but diverse Jewish one, Spanish-speaking Jews from northern Morocco comprised the majority of the Moroccan group in Venezuela. In their attempts to assimilate, they could make themselves ethnically or racially invisible among Venezuela's large Catholic Spanish population. Like Spaniards, they were southern European in appearance, and despite some differences in dialect they spoke Castilian Spanish fluently both within and outside of their ethnic immigrant community. By contrast, Jews from Eastern Europe tended to maintain their native languages—usually Yiddish, Hungarian, or German—for the purposes of internal communication.[12]

Spanish-speaking Moroccan Jews in Venezuela also took advantage of their connections to a community of trailblazers who had successfully adapted to the local economy. Visitors' accounts recall that among Moroccan descendants, there were several bankers, import-export agents, and insurance agents as well as representatives of other independent professions, and a report by Israeli officials lists the names of some Jewish Moroccan millionaires in Caracas in the early 1950s.[13] By the 1960s and 1970s, a number of Moroccan immigrants and their descendants had successfully incorporated themselves into local politics, journalism, intellectual life, and industry. One outstanding example was Gustavo Pinto Cohen, the country's minister of agriculture from 1975 to 1979. Another example is Dr. Alfonso Benzecri Benmergui, minister of health and social assistance from 1978 to 1981.[14] Moroccan Jews were also present in Venezuelan academia.[15]

The history of relatively smooth integration, which had helped to fuel Jewish immigration to Venezuela from northern Morocco beginning in the late nineteenth century, had the paradoxical effect of diminishing efforts at communal organization until the 1960s. Despite significant immigration from Morocco during the 1950s, by 1959 the AIV—the country's main Jewish communal organization, founded in 1930 by Moroccan immigrants and dominated by them ever since (see chap. 3)—claimed only around fifty members.[16] A general atmosphere of apathy toward Israel and even to larger questions of Jewish identity more broadly characterized Venezuelan Jewish society as other forms of ethnic affirmation became prominent.

Neither this reality nor the fact that most Jews from northern Morocco in Venezuela had not immigrated to Israel meant that their histories were completely detached from the rising global influences of Zionism and related forms of Jewish solidarity after 1948. In November 1947, Venezuela voted in favor of UN Resolution 181, which approved the partition of Mandatory Palestine into Jewish and Arab states. This support can be attributed to the work of the Comité Venezolano pro-Palestina Judía (the Venezuelan Committee for Jewish Palestine), established earlier that year by eighteen Venezuelan intellectuals and writers, among them the poet Andrés Eloy Blanco, the diplomats Mario Briceño Iragorry and José Nucete Sardi, and the novelists Antonio Arraiz, Lucila Palacio, and Miguel Otero Silva. The "Jewish ambassador" to the committee's meetings was Moisés Sananes, a Jew of Tetouani origins who was well known as the founding editor of *El Mundo Israelita*, a mainstream Jewish Venezuelan weekly at the time.[17]

As in Morocco, the utilization of Zionism as a means for increasing Jewish solidarity in Venezuela significantly proliferated after the founding of Israel, as world Zionist organizations transmitted Zionist ideas to the grassroots of the community and became prominent on the local Jewish scene. Only through the increasing intervention of Israeli diplomats and Zionist emissaries would Zionism establish a durable base in Venezuela. As in many countries, Israeli emissaries tied the revitalization of Jewish communal life to the community's general identification with Israel and Zionism. Unlike in Morocco, they could even use leftist values like socialism, common to both modern socialist Zionism and the local Venezuelan political arena in the 1960s, to convince local Jews to connect to the political Zionist cause.[18]

Within the Zionist Federation of Venezuela (FSV), several branches of international Zionist organizations—including the local Jewish National Fund (JNF), the United Israel Appeal (UIA, or Keren Hayesod in Hebrew), WIZO, and the Unión de Jóvenes Hebreos youth movement—cooperated with one another. Hashomer Hatzair, Maccabi, Bnei Akiva, and B'nai B'rith América, with their 150 registered members as of 1966, composed the Zionist youth network operating in Caracas.[19] In 1961, some seventy young members between the ages of twelve and seventeen joined the Hashomer Hatzair Zionist youth movement.[20]

A shared pro-Zionist approach and Zionist-oriented activities soon became a prominent glue holding together the local multiethnic Jewish community, including the large Moroccan segment. In 1961, an Israeli envoy to Caracas reported that the number of Jewish students in the Herzl-Bialik School, whose Zionist orientation is already embedded in its name, was constantly on the rise, and it was becoming the central Jewish institution in Caracas.[21] In fact, by 1969, some 95 percent of local Jews had enrolled their children in the school. Herzl-Bialik offered sixteen instructional levels, or grades, beginning with kindergarten and continuing through high school. Classes were made up of pupils from a variety of Jewish ethnic backgrounds, Moroccan Jews included.[22] While not officially part of a Zionist organization, in practice, any local Jew who wanted to enroll his children in the Herzl-Bialik School had to contribute dues to the UIA fund, reflecting an intertwining of communal and Zionist activities.[23]

A few attempts to launch extramural, Moroccan-oriented Jewish educational initiatives fell short, including the Cultura-Tarbut School and the Bambi private kindergarten, both of which operated in the Maripérez neighborhood, home to many Moroccan immigrants to Caracas.[24] Beside the Herzl-Bialik School, the Club Hebraica, a social, recreational, and cultural center, encompassed the vast majority of Jewish activities. Hebraica was the initiative of two siblings of Moroccan descent, John and Gonzalo Benaím Pinto, the latter then serving as vice president of the AIV.[25]

This organizational unification in the 1960s reflected a major shift in the general attitude of the community toward Zionism as a tool for Jewish unification. While earlier attempts to unite the Jewish community under umbrella organizations in the 1940s fell short, in the 1960s and 1970s they succeeded thanks to the engagement of local branches of global Zionist organizations.[26] In this context, in 1966, all of the small local Jewish organizations, including the AIV, the Ashkenazi UIC, and the country's Zionist organization, united under a single umbrella known as La Confederación de Asociaciónes Israelitas de Venezuela (CAIV), the Confederation of Jewish Associations of Venezuela. The CAIV's official mouthpiece was the *Nuevo Mundo Israelita*, which openly declared its Zionist orientation. This weekly was founded by Rubén Mérenfeld and the Tetouan-born Moisés Garzón Serfaty, the aforementioned editor of *Or-Luz* also serving as the CAIV's president. *Nuevo Mundo Israelita* was distributed door to door for free to registered Venezuelan Jews.[27]

SEPHARDI ZIONISM IN MOTION

Despite the prominence of a national Jewish "melting pot" strategy that aimed to homogenize Jewish cultural life in Venezuela, the Moroccan-led Sephardi organizations were not weakened or negatively affected. In fact, they used the momentum of the country's revitalized Jewish life to develop their own particularistic activities like never before. In the AIV's bulletin of April 1967, the group's leadership congratulated some sixty new members who had recently joined the organization. The leaders expressed satisfaction with the fact that, prior to becoming members, several had been among "those who remain at the margins of communal activities."[28]

Joining the AIV was an act of ethnic identification that not only boosted membership numbers but also validated the importance of its work. The AIV sent two subscription forms to each of its members, hoping they would spread the word about the social benefits of joining the association. This effort lasted well into the late 1960s. By May 1971, the one-thousandth member had subscribed, and by September 1972 nearly a hundred children were attending a variety of courses offered by the AIV. The organization, of course, hoped to continue expanding.[29]

While joining Jewish institutions cannot be inherently considered proof of Zionist solidarity, Zionist affiliation and organizations facilitated and enriched social activity among Moroccan Jews in Venezuela, as well as their connections with Moroccan Jews elsewhere. Such was the case with the AIV's El Grupo Herzl, founded in 1970, and the private Hebrew lessons that the AIV designed for children who had difficulties acquiring the language or wished to advance further.[30] These activities supplemented normal recreation on Saturdays and the more traditional historical rituals that Moroccan Jews observed through the AIV, such as the *hilula* (public commemoration of a saintly rabbi) of Rebbi Shimon Bar Yochai in the Moroccan synagogue Tiferet Israel and the hilula of Rebbi Meir Baal Hanes in the Club Israelita—both well-known annual gatherings for Moroccans Jews.[31] On another occasion, the Zionist Federation of Venezuela invited Jo Amar, a popular Moroccan musician in Israel, to sing in the Moroccan synagogue on the anniversary of Israel's independence on May 7, 1971.[32] Zionism and community development among Sephardi Jews went hand in hand also in the establishment of transnational ties between Moroccan Jews in Caracas and in Israel, as well as with their reference to their roots in Morocco and the creation of an amalgam of historic and contemporary identities.

These developments on the local Venezuelan front were connected to a broader shift in Sephardi Zionist activism occurring around the 1960s and 1970s. Already in the early twentieth century in Argentina (see chap. 4), Zionism was used as a pragmatic tool for consolidating Moroccan leadership and as a source for empowering their agency in global Jewish activism. Immigrants from a variety of Middle East and North Africa (MENA) countries also began to unify under the framework of Sephardi Zionism and to lobby for a stronger position in the World Zionist Organization. Unlike earlier in the century, however, the 1960s and 1970s had a different political and demographic context. By the mid-1960s, as mentioned, most Jews from Muslim majority countries and groups of Jews from Eastern Europe had moved to Israel, while Soviet Jews were largely immobile behind the Iron Curtain. Many of the remaining Jews in the world had concentrated in the Americas and Western Europe, considered to be relatively welcoming environments.

In Venezuela, Moroccan Jews were building a community that in general identified with Israel and collaborated rather smoothly with Ashkenazi immigrants in their shared efforts to invigorate Jewish life in the tropical country. In Israel, however, Moroccan Jews were having a very different migration experience as they attempted to integrate into the Jewish state. Many Jewish immigrants from Muslim countries encountered significant hardship integrating into the Ashkenazi-dominated Israeli society. After their arrival to Israel, many Moroccan Jews were placed in impoverished urban areas and later in "development towns" in the geographical periphery of the country (see chap. 7). Memorable events that shaped a shared sense of marginalization in Israel include the shooting in July 1959 of a Jewish Moroccan resident of the Haifa neighborhood of Wadi Salib, which sparked a series of ethnic demonstrations across Israel; and the 1971 Black Panthers protests, in which working-class Jewish immigrants from Morocco attempted to draw attention to their economic distress.[33]

Aligning with the perceptions of world Jewish hierarchies between affluent Jews and Jewries in distress, the earlier form of Zionist Sephardi solidarity widened the perceived global hierarchies within the world Sephardi diaspora. In 1958, the Sephardi Community Council (SCC) in Jerusalem established a new periodical titled *BaMa'aracha* (Hebrew for *In the Battle*), which focused on ethnic discrimination in Israel. *BaMa'aracha* brought to the awareness of its Israeli Mizrahi and Sephardi readerships the communal development of Sephardi centers in the Americas and Western Europe as a way of calling upon them to join forces with their more economically affluent brethren abroad.[34] Reports on these communities increased at the beginning of 1971 against the backdrop of the Black Panthers demonstrations in Israel, which demanded an end to government's social and economic marginalization of *Mizrahim*. The common belief was that by drawing the attention of these affluent communities to the "social problems" in Israel—namely ethnic discrimination against MENA Jews—a new "Sephardi" solution would emerge.[35]

In their narratives about Jews from MENA countries, the World Sephardi Federation (WSF) and other world Sephardi bodies distinguished between the different regional situation of MENA Jews: those who remained in the "old world"—that is, in Muslim countries—and therefore might experience physical danger; those who moved to Israel and experienced economic distress and cultural marginalization; and those who immigrated to the West and therefore might experience the "spiritual danger" of assimilation.[36] On May 25, 1972, as a response to the Israeli Black Panther protests, the World Zionist Organization formally included the WSF in its organizational framework for the first time. As a result, the Department for Zionist and Social Activity among Sephardi and Mizrahi Communities was established. In 1974, this department created the journal *Hedim: Kehilot Sefaradiyot Ba'Olam* (*Echoes: Sephardi Communities of the World*) to familiarize Israeli readers with the growing interest of Sephardi communities worldwide in Israeli affairs—itself an outgrowth of the department's activities.[37]

In February 1972, the WSF gathered together 280 representatives from Sephardi communities across the US in the Shearith Israel synagogue in New York City to establish the American Sephardi Federation (ASF). Later, on October 26, La Federación Sefaradí Latinoamericana (the Latin American Sephardi Federation, or FeSeLA) was founded in Lima, Peru, as an umbrella organization for the Sephardi communities in Latin America within the WZO.[38]

The main objective of FeSeLA in Latin America, the Jewish Agency's Sephardi affairs department, and the other newly established branches of the WSF was to strengthen Sephardi communities facing "spiritual danger" while incorporating their communal activity and leadership into the global decision-making body of the Zionist movement. It also sought to enrich and transmit Sephardi culture as a way of raising the self-esteem of Sephardim as a group and strengthening their contributions to Jewish life in Israel and elsewhere. Struggling against discrimination in Israel and "rescuing" Jews from Muslim lands were thus seen as ways of contributing to the unity of the Jewish people and strengthening the Zionist cause.[39] This interpretation of Zionist activism by Sephardi leaders worldwide in the second half of the twentieth century reverberated in the local perceptions of Hispanic Moroccan Jews in Venezuela as they came to establish their own separate institutions.

BECOMING VENEZUELAN MOROCCANS

Despite the relatively smooth integration of both Ashkenazim and Sephardim, and the overall community's integration in Venezuela more broadly, Moroccan Jews in Venezuela increasingly participated in the global trend of reclaiming Sephardi origins in Spain as a political and organizational tool. Just two years before the founding of FeSeLA, a new Moroccan-run periodical marked the first step in an awakening of Sephardi consciousness in Venezuela that coupled Sephardi identity with northern Moroccan hometown nostalgia. It was *Maguén-Escudo* (hereafter *Maguén*), a combination of the Hebrew word *maguén* (shield) and its Spanish equivalent, *escudo*. In the early 1970s, *Nuevo Mundo Israelita*, a newer edition of *Mundo Israelita*, began to appear as a joint venture of the AIV, UIC, and, later, B'nai B'rith. The editors of *Maguén*, Moisés Garzón Serfaty and Rubén Mérenfeld, both fervent Zionists, were also the founding editors of *Nuevo Mundo Israelita*. The latter was a unification project that integrated into its editorial board a representative from the FSV, B'nai B'rith, and the CAIV. The mouthpiece of the AIV, *Maguén* came into being at Garzón Serfaty's initiative in January 1970.[40]

Garzón Serfaty became one of the most prominent figures promoting a global Sephardi consciousness, even as he coedited *Nuevo Mundo Israelita*, which represented a united Venezuelan Jewish community. Previously the editor of *El Diario de Africa*, a Spanish-language newspaper in Morocco, and of *Or-Luz*, Garzón Serfaty's biography following his immigration to Venezuela reflects a rather smooth assimilation into the national environment. Garzón Serfaty graduated from the Central University of Venezuela with a degree in economics and continued his education at the Catholic University of Caracas. In 1980, he was a staff member at two local colleges. However, his integration into Venezuela's labor market did not diminish the active role he had been playing in the local Moroccan Jewish community almost since the time of his arrival.[41] Garzón Serfaty dedicated much of his activity in the new country to promoting *Maguén* as a Sephardi periodical with strong connections to Morocco, Israel, Spain, and Venezuela, just as he had with *Or-Luz* but in a different context.

Maguén's very first editorial remarks, which laid out the publication's raison d'être, identified loyalty to both Venezuela and Israel as major factors comprising their identities as Moroccan Jews in Venezuela: "We wish to deliver a fraternal greeting to all our co-religionists in Venezuela and to our sister [mainly Ashkenazi] organization, who, in one way or another, are guided by the same noble purposes . . . [namely,] working for the aggrandizement of Venezuelan Jewry and for this broad, open, honest, and generous homeland [Venezuela] in which many of us were born and to whose historic hospitality we are all witnesses. We also want to express our salutation to the dignified diplomatic representative of the State of Israel, with which we undoubtedly identify."[42] Many of *Maguén*'s numerous articles dealing with Israeli history and culture focused on Latin American connections and the role of Hispanic Moroccan Jews in mediating them. For example, one such article touted the respectable place of Latin American Jewry in donating to the JNF and reported the long list of forests in Israel named after Latin American figures like Simón Bolívar from Venezuela, as well as early nineteenth-century figures from Colombia, Peru, Bolivia, Ecuador, and Panama.[43] Another article mentioned the AIV's efforts to publish a book in Hebrew about Bolívar to spread his legacy in Israeli academic and public discourse.[44]

The Sephardi community of Venezuela, comprised mainly of northern Moroccan Jews, maintained a collective memory of its status as pioneers among the country's Jewish settlers, arriving long before the Ashkenazim.[45] This narrative framed the history of Jewish migration by focusing on early Sephardi history in Latin America and integrated numerous archival documents from the founding of the AIV in 1930.[46] The overall tendency to focus on earlier Sephardi migration to Venezuela characterized references to the emigration of Moroccan Jews in *Maguén*.[47] While this framing had additional motivations related to the integration of Sephardi Jews into Venezuelan society, as I will show in the next chapter, it was also useful in structuring a unified communal narrative that connected them to the historical Sephardi diaspora. By employing this narrative, Moroccan Jews in Venezuela could position themselves differently from the way they conceived of Moroccan Jews who migrated to Israel or even Jewish societies in Eastern Europe. They viewed and represented themselves not as Jews in distress or physical danger but instead as part of the empowered segment of world Jewry that bore responsibility for aiding those in need.

...Het gebeurde in Bagdad deze week...

Figure 5.1. An illustration of persecuted Jews wearing yellow stars, said to represent "The Situation of Jews in Arab Countries" (reproduced from *Maguén* 10, March, 1971, 21). © Courtesy of CESC. Available at https://cesc.com.ve/files/magazine/010.pdf.

The global proliferation of Jewish narratives of distress and solidarity in the aftermath of the Holocaust strongly reverberated through *Maguén*. From its earliest issues, the periodical's calls to "free" Jewries in distress included references to Jews in Iran and Arab countries, as well as the Soviet Union, that were all placed under the same banner.[48] The "let my people go" slogan appeared in a number of reports on Iranian and Syrian Jews in the early 1970s.[49] One such report graphically tied the destiny of these distressed Jewries in Morocco to the recent memory of Jews in Nazi occupied Europe, as figure 5.1 shows.

Coinciding with the final stages of Jewish migration from Muslim majority countries, the Israeli-based World Organization of Jews from Arab Countries (WOJAC) was established in 1975 by the then–vice chair of the Knesset,

Mordechai Ben-Porat, to promote the legal right to restitution of Jews from Arab countries. Supported by the Jewish Agency and Israel's Foreign Ministry, WOJAC established branches in New York, London, Rome, and Zurich.[50] The organization promoted the idea that Jews in Arab countries shared a unified destiny in the mid-twentieth century: distress and expulsion.

In the backdrop of this atmosphere of activism, one of the first articles in *Maguén* about the history of Moroccan Jews appeared under the title "An Unknown Future for Moroccan Jewry" in the winter of 1972. It depicted an atmosphere of anxiety among the Jews of Morocco in light of the recent political instability in the country following attempts to assassinate King Hassan II.[51] This story and the discourse that framed it did not originate in *Maguén*'s pages, which merely replicated the more general discourse of the AIV regarding the precarious situations of Jewish communities in Muslim majority countries like Morocco, which were generally deemed hostile to Jews. This narrative enabled the community of northern Moroccan Jews in Venezuela to define their new status also vis-à-vis Jews who still lived in Morocco, many of whom were their relatives.

Earlier, in 1966, the Club a de Venezuela organized a Purim Festival and dedicated all of the proceeds to the communities of northern Morocco. The invitation explained this act of generosity by stating that "as you [local Jews] know ... they [the communities in northern Morocco] are in an extremely precarious situation. ... We need to tie our community organization to the imperative goal of supporting these brethren."[52]

In February 1969, Gonzalo Benaím Pinto, the president of the AIV, sent several dispatches to the leaders of the Jewish communities in Tangier and Tetouan with an offer to purchase religious artifacts from the synagogues and transfer them to Caracas for safekeeping.[53] By these acts and statements, northern Moroccan Jews in Venezuela positioned themselves as the elite of their diaspora, responsible for the well-being not only of their compatriots in Israel but of those who stayed in Morocco.[54]

This paternalistic approach to Morocco and other Jews in distress on the part of Venezuelan Jews mixed with nostalgic representations of their Moroccan hometowns to forge a complex perspective on their vanished histories in Morocco in the early 1970s. In fact, alongside the small number of references to the contemporary Moroccan nation-state that appeared in *Maguén*, a different kind of reference began to appear around that time, imbuing the connection to Morocco with a strong sense of nostalgia for a Jewish hometown life that had come to an end with Morocco's independence. For instance, one of the first articles in *Maguén* to reference Morocco was entitled "Memories from

Tangier." It included nostalgic musings by Isaac R. Toledano, who mentioned that he had spent most of his life in Morocco, particularly in Tangier.[55] This short essay began with a "reminiscence" about Jewish Tangier at the beginning of the nineteenth century, long before Toledano was born, in which he described the origins of the Jewish communal leadership and the foundation of local synagogues "before the declaration of independence in Morocco, which put an end to the protectorate."[56]

The final words of Toledano's essay support the idea that many Jews experienced alienation following Moroccan independence, when immigration began, and the nostalgic narrative came to an end: "These memories always result in melancholia for those who lived in the city. . . . *That* [i.e., Jewish] Tangier permanently disappeared [after Moroccan independence]."[57] Toledano's focus on Jewish *lieu de memoir* prior to 1956 helped him shape his memories to fit the narrative of immigration from Muslim countries to the safe haven in Venezuela as a way of reaffirming his new status as a Moroccan Venezuelan Jew. In a subsequent article entitled "What I Have Done for Israel," Toledano also tied this notion to his local Zionist identity, noting that, due to his advanced age, he could not join the large number of Tangier Jews who had fulfilled their duty by returning to Israel. He maintained, however, that his inability to immigrate to Israel in no way diminished his lifelong support for the State of Israel from afar, which was part and parcel of his commitment to the Jewish people.[58]

Against the backdrop of postcolonial Jewish migration to Israel, such narratives of Jewish persecution expressed nostalgia for a lost Moroccan golden age, as well as a sense of pride in being affluent Jews in the new Venezuelan homeland. Both homelands were linked in the collective story of Hispanic Moroccan Jews as international developments shifted their Jewish affinities. It was against the backdrop of mass immigration to Israel in the 1960s, the geographical distancing from their place of origin, and the buzz created by Zionist organizations and Israeli emissaries worldwide around immigration to Israel that Zionist affinities and attachments to Morocco, Spain, and Venezuela coalesced more harmoniously than ever before, changing the connotations of these places in the communal narrative as it developed in Venezuela in the 1960 and 1970s.

Writing about Tangier as a Jewish lieu de memoir whose history ended in the mid-twentieth century facilitated the inclusion of elements from medieval Spain. Toledano even dedicated one of his two nostalgic accounts of his city of origin, Tangier, to the Spanish senator Ángel Pulido and his campaign to revive Spain's Jewish past.[59] The link between nostalgia for Morocco and the Iberian past is at the heart of the next chapter.

SIX

SPAIN AND THE POSTCOLONIAL DIASPORA

IN THE EARLY 1970S, SEPHARDI COMMUNITIES across Europe and the Americas joined the WSF and launched a number of local branches, including the ASF in New York City, FeSeLa in Latin America, and the Canadian Sephardi Federation. About three years later, on January 23–25, 1976, representatives from across Spain were summoned by the WSF to a summit in Málaga, where the country's Jewish community joined the WSF. Sephardi representatives from across Spain signed the branch's founding document, including David Ventura from Barcelona, Philippe Halioua from Madrid, Menáhem Gabizón from Ceuta, Simón Hassan from Seville, León Shriqui from Málaga, Leon Levy from Melilla, and Samuel Serfaty from Valencia.[1] Mauricio Hatchuel Toledano was nominated chair of the Spanish branch, Samuel Toledano became one of its senior executive board members, and Rabbi Baruj (Benito) Garzón Serfaty was its secretary. Later, Serfaty became Spain's chief rabbi.[2] A native of Tetouan, Rabbi Garzón Serfaty collaborated with his brother Moisés Garzón Serfaty in Venezuela who had participated in the creation of FeSeLa a few years earlier.[3] Almost all of the members of this new community leadership in Spain were originally from northern Morocco.[4] From May 23 to 27, 1979, the WSF held a world summit in Madrid, attended by two hundred representatives, including some from Tangier and Israel.[5]

These events in the mid- through late 1970s represent a milestone in the overall transformation from the colonial context in which Hispanic Moroccan Jewish identities developed and thrived to a new postcolonial reality that endowed these identities with new national and transnational meanings. Originally developed by Philo-Sephardi advocates and Spanish colonialists to promote colonial expansion, as shown in chapter 2, the notion of ancestry in Spain among the community leadership not only survived postcolonial migration to Spain, as I argue in this chapter, but even intensified as Hispanic Moroccan Jews made Spain their new principal hub. As it made new organizational sense in multiple additional hubs from the late 1960s through the 1990s, the notion of ancestry continued traveling across the diaspora, strengthening the ties between its hubs.

To explore how the notion of ancestry in Spain buttressed community formation after most Jews had left northern Morocco in the last third of the twentieth century, I will begin by setting a historical background for understanding Spain's changing attitude toward the Sephardi diaspora, including that of northern Moroccan Jews, in the new postcolonial context. I will then address how this shift manifested in transnational ties forged by the Hispanic Moroccan community in Spain, with additional hubs in the US and Israel. Finally, paying special attention to the global community's most prominent center in the Americas, Venezuela, I will show how postcolonial attitudes toward Spain and the ties they generated from afar helped Moroccan Jews integrate into Venezuelan society by virtue of their globalizing community.

A REVIVAL FROM ABOVE

Usually, scholars of migration identify collective nostalgia and ethnic preserving among a diaspora as an outcome of physical distancing from their imagined or real homelands.[6] Adopting a more transregional network approach to analyze diaspora-making, my discussion in the following section demonstrates how a nostalgic approach for Spain, and a related salvage ethnographic discourse toward its past, from the late 1960s, intertwined with the building of a new geographic base in that country.

Despite the centrality of Spain to nineteenth- and twentieth-century narratives about the shared origins of Hispanic Moroccan Jews, it was not until the 1960s that mainland Spain became a prominent base for Jews from northern Morocco. Spain differed in that regard from the other hubs of Jews from northern Morocco in the Iberian Peninsula, British-ruled Gibraltar and Portugal. Cities in southern Spain like Seville, Málaga, Tarifa, Cadiz, and Algeciras indeed attracted, among other sorts of migrants, refugees from the 1859–60 war, but Spanish authorities at the time encouraged their return to Morocco rather than their permanent settlement in the region.[7] From the perspective of the Jewish communities, a *herem*, or a rabbinical ban placed on Spain for expelling Jews in 1492, also set back immigration for religious reasons.[8]

The concept of Hispano-Moroccan brotherhood, which portrayed Jewish and Muslim North Africans as part of the Spanish family, was primarily employed to justify colonialism rather than to encourage the immigration of Muslims and Jews from these territories to Spain or to foster genuine interfaith coexistence within mainland Spain (see chap. 2). Despite a series of legislative changes, including the abolition of inquisition tribunals in 1834, the repeal of "purity of blood" statutes in 1837, and the enshrinement of religious freedom in the 1869 constitution, the Spanish government continued to perceive Spain as a predominantly Catholic nation while regarding religious minorities within its territories as foreigners.

While Jews from northern Morocco did migrate to mainland Spain in the early decades of the twentieth century, the country witnessed more significant waves of Jewish migration from elsewhere. The Balkan Wars (1912–13) and the disintegration of the Ottoman, Austro–Hungarian, and Russian Empires following World War I provoked the immigration of both Ashkenazi and Sephardi Jews to mainland Spain. Moroccan Jews were barely represented in these waves. During World War II, Spain allowed only a few thousand Jewish refugees from Eastern and Southeastern Europe to pass into its territory. In an attempt to distance itself from Nazi Europe and appeal to the Western Bloc after the defeat of Italian and German fascism, the Spanish government sought to more meaningfully contribute to the rescue of Jews during the remainder of the war. After the war, the Francoist regime justified these efforts to influential Catholic conservatives through an appeal to the Christian value of "love for all the races," as argued by a 1949 pamphlet produced by the government.[9]

By its own declaration, post–World War II Franco's Spain also shared with Israel the post-Holocaust aspiration to "rescue" Jews from the Muslim world, placing a special emphasis on Sephardi Jews in Egypt. Between the Arab-Israeli War of 1948, Gamal Abd al-Nasser's rise to power in 1952, and the 1956 Suez crisis, the prospects of Jews in Egypt were worsening. Wishing to portray itself as a savior of the Jews as a means of warming relations with the West, Spanish diplomats denied Egyptian national narratives about Jewish-Muslim fraternal relations. They did so even at the expense of their relations with Egypt and other Arab countries that developed narratives regarding Jewish emigration as an outcome of Zionist manipulation. Spain also enabled the world bodies that organized Operation Yakhin in the 1960s to use its territories in Africa. Spain never held a clear policy to organize the emigration of Moroccan or Egyptian Jews but rather engaged in sporadic initiatives by diplomats who collaborated with American-based Jewish organizations and Jewish leaders.[10]

Against this backdrop, in the mid-1950s, Moroccan Jews appeared in greater numbers than ever before in several cities in southern Spain—cities like Málaga, Seville, and Valencia. A few thousand Moroccan Jews—most from middle-class families—were estimated to have been living in Spain by the 1960s, usually in Madrid, comprising some 65 percent of the country's small Jewish population. Although Spain did not automatically offer nationality to citizens of the protectorate, the populations from northern Morocco were among the foreigners who gained easiest access as a result of prior residency in the Spanish territories of Ceuta and Melilla, or through ad hoc letters of naturalization that Spain granted individuals who served its interests.[11] The majority of Moroccan Jews in Spain originated from northern Morocco, as Spain was more accessible to them both geographically and, as indicated in chapter 1, culturally. For example, the *Or-Luz* Jewish newspaper, which announced the weddings of local Jews in Tetouan, noted in 1956 that Spain was a popular destination for Jewish honeymooners from northern Morocco.[12]

The migration of Jews from Morocco to Spain took shape against the backdrop of the postcolonial atmosphere that spurred migration from Morocco in the 1950s. Not only Jews but also Muslims—particularly those from northern Moroccan cities and towns, including Tetouan, Nador, Huceima, Larache, and Chefchaouen—began to immigrate to Spain in increasing numbers by the 1960s.[13] However, beyond the relatively higher percentage of Jews among the several thousand Moroccan immigrants in Spain, Moroccan Jews were distinct from their Muslim immigrant counterparts in other ways. Forty percent of Moroccan Muslim immigrants in Madrid were registered as laborers, whereas Moroccan Jews dominated the field of administration, which their Muslim counterparts rarely entered.

Conversely, the field of nonprofessional *petits commerçants* and artisans was dominated by Moroccan Muslims and included hardly any Jews. Differences in the age of immigrants were also evident. While many Muslims were in their thirties, the Jewish migrant population was more multigenerational.[14]

Still, the migration of Moroccan Jews to Spain up until the late 1960s was not organized, and the Jewish institutions remained underdeveloped by the immigrant community. For example, Jews who kept kosher relied on the supply of kosher meat from nearby Gibraltar. Spain's Jewish communal organization at the time was in fact dominated by Ashkenazi Jews. Max Mazin, a Lithuanian Jew, was the president of the Jewish communities of Spain from 1961 to 1970. The lack of official Sephardi organization can be attributed to the general aspiration of the fascist regime to build the Spanish nation around Catholic values.

Unlike in other countries of Moroccan Jewish immigration, the major shift that drove the Hispanic Moroccan Jewish community to organize in Spain came from above, through unprecedented efforts by the Spanish government to restore the country's Jewish communal life in the context of the withdrawal from Morocco, and even more so following Franco's death in 1975.

To understand this shift, we need to consider that the late 1950s saw a change in Franco's overall economic policy, marked by dramatic social and cultural transitions. Responding to a severe economic crisis and worker and student strikes in 1956—partly resulting from Spain's unsuccessful colonial campaign in Morocco—Franco issued a series of plans designed to modernize the economy. Consequently, Spain entered its *desarollismo*, or "development" years, from 1960 to 1975, marked by considerable urbanization, economic mobility, the expansion of the industrial and service sectors, and a major increase in secondary and higher education attendance. The number of students in Spanish universities for example, grew from sixty thousand in 1961 to about four hundred thousand in 1976.[15]

The social changes reflect Spain's emerging strategy in the 1950s to integrate into the Western Bloc without renouncing the principals of its authoritarian regime. Granting credibility to a national elite of technocrats who acquired their training from abroad, Franco sought to modernize the economy by investing in human capital and education. World organizations such as the International Monetary Fund, the World Bank, the Organization for European Economic Cooperation, UNESCO, and the US government collaborated, as this model of authoritarian modernization was designed to prevent communist influence on the economy. It was argued that developing a consumer society and a business sector and training skilled workers would improve living conditions and help the regime survive without leaving room for social protest. Spain's economic opening to the West was met with global recognition and accompanied by new pedagogical methodologies that replaced the prevailing nationalist and Catholic ways of teaching.[16]

Spain's opening to the West coincided with the development of world Sephardi organizations and cultural activism in the 1960s through the 1980s. In 1968, Yeshiva University was the first American academic institution of higher education to incorporate a Sephardi studies program, which began to issue a new journal called *The American Sephardi*.[17] These developments were part of a trend in American Jewish studies toward integrating Sephardi studies in broader curriculums.[18]

Influenced by its strengthening ties with—and pressure from—world Jewish organizations and world Sephardi communities, the Francoist regime in the late 1960s began to change its earlier attitude toward Jewish minorities on the ground.[19] In 1967, a new "religious freedom" law was passed by the Spanish parliament, marking a separation of church and state after more than thirty years of dependence on the Roman Catholic Church. A year later, Jews in various Spanish cities were officially permitted by the government to organize into local communities that would be recognized as official representatives of the country's Jews.

On December 16, 1968, the Beth Yaacov Sephardi synagogue was inaugurated by Moroccan immigrants on Balmes St. 3 in Madrid and became the first synagogue to be officially recognized by the Spanish monarchy since the Alhambra Decree. That same year, a Sephardi Museum was created by royal decree at the ancient Samuel Halevi synagogue in Toledo's Judería. The late 1960s and early 1970s also saw the emergence of a new Jewish leadership in Spain dominated by immigrants from northern Morocco. Born in Tangier on August 15, 1929, Samuel Toledano graduated from the law faculty at the University of Paris and moved to Spain in 1959. In 1968, Toledano received from Spain's Minister of Justice Antonio Oriol a proclamation formally revoking the Catholic monarchs' Expulsion Decree of March 31, 1492.[20]

Even with these significant milestones, it was only with the death of Francisco Franco on November 20, 1975 that Spain truly entered a new political era characterized by more tolerance for democratic and pluralistic rhetoric. Unlike the weak tone that characterized the opening of new institutions in Franco's late years, following his death the new government wished to rebrand Spain by distancing itself, de facto and de jure, from the former authoritarian regime. For example, in an important symbolic move in 1976, Spain's Queen Sofía attended a Friday night service in Madrid's new main synagogue, Beth Yaacov. As noted in the opening paragraphs of this chapter, the momentous political events in Spain coincided with major events on the global Sephardi-Zionist front in the 1970s, which further shaped the characteristics of the Moroccan-led Jewish community in Venezuela and in Spain.

The representation of the Moroccan-led Jewish community in Spain in those global Sephardi networks coincided with a change in local Jewish demography. The year 1973 saw the establishment of a military dictatorship in Argentina, an event that encouraged emigration from that country to Spain. This led to joint communal activities between old and new immigrants. For example, in 1986, a group of immigrants from northern Morocco and Latin America came together in Madrid to establish a new periodical called *Raíces: Revista Judía de Cultura* (*Roots: A Jewish Review of Culture*). *Raíces* became the forerunner of a range of organizations that produced intellectual writing about Sephardi Judaism in

Spain. The periodical's director was Jacobo Israel Garzón, who immigrated from Tetouan to Madrid in 1959, and among the founding members was the Ceuta-born Moroccan Jewish philologist Iacov Hassán.[21] They collaborated with other immigrants from Latin America, many of whom were of Ashkenazi origin, including Horacio Kohan, Esther Gordon, Liliana Kohan, Uriel Macías, Manuel Aguilar, Arnold Liberman, and later Abrasha Rotenberg.

A survey of the early issues published between 1986 and 1992 reveals that they featured the writings of many world figures responsible for the revival of Jewish heritage in Spain: Marcos Ricardo, a Jew of Syrian descent who immigrated to Madrid from Buenos Aires; Shlomo Ben-Ami, Israel's ambassador to Spain; philologist Ana María López Álvarez, who worked at the Museo Sefaradí; and Rabbi Jacobo Israel Garzón. In the spirit of national reconciliation with the Jewish past, *Raíces* reached an audience far beyond the local community; its writers included Jews and Christians and hailed from a variety of countries and professional backgrounds. According to *Raíces*'s official website, as of 2011 it was distributed to all the Jewish communities of Spain, Portugal, and the Americas and had subscribers throughout Europe, much of Latin America, and the US. In Spain, subscriptions reached every province through bookstores.[22]

While local events in Spain aligned with the post–World War II trend of multiculturalism in Europe, Spain's approach was notably distinct. As Spain aimed to align itself with Western Europe, it also distanced itself from the historical narrative of Hispanic Moroccan brotherhood. This created a paradox, as Spain also sought to integrate Moroccan groups as immigrant minorities while considering the global discourse of postcolonial multiculturalism. Clearly, community building on the domestic Spanish political front was intertwined with the proliferation of global networks that worked to integrate narratives of Jewish ancestry in Spain. This process would also have implications for the globalizing Hispanic Moroccan community in Israel.

SPAIN, ISRAEL, AND THE EVOLVING SEPHARDI DIASPORA

During Franco's reign, there was a general political preference for establishing relations with world Jewry over Israel, for fear of ruining delicate relations with Arab countries. With the death of Franco, the new king of Spain, Juan Carlos I (reign 1975–2014), revised the country's diplomatic strategy and called for Spain to establish ties with "all nations."[23] This change seemingly set the ground for official relations with Israel. On December 21, 1977, Rabbi Ovadia Yosef (1920–2013), then the Sephardi Chief Rabbi of Israel (also known as the

Rishon LeZion), met with the king of Spain and Cardinal Marcelo González in the royal palace.[24] In 1979, Spain was incorporated into the World Jewish Congress, and an Israel-Spain Friendship Association was established in Spain to promote collaboration with the State of Israel.[25] Spain soon began to recognize the advantages of reaching out directly to the population of Judeo-Spanish speakers in Israel as cultural proxies. In 1985, Spain's royal radio granted "Kol Yisrael in Ladino," the Judeo-Spanish section of Israel's national radio service, an award for its activity.[26]

Almost a decade later, in 1986, formal bilateral ties between Spain and Israel were finally established. In the 1980s, Spain reassessed its reliance on the Muslim world at the expense of ties with Israel. As it completed its incorporation into the international community by joining NATO in May 1982 and the European Economic Community in January 1986, ties with Israel served the goal of rebranding Spain as a Western European power.[27] In this process of reconciliation with Israel, Spain also relied on cultural affiliation that relied on Hispanic Moroccan Jewish agents (see chap. 7). One of the prominent figures who helped establish the new relationship was the Tangier native Shlomo Ben-Ami (formerly Benabú), who immigrated to Israel in 1955 and eventually joined the faculty of Tel Aviv University as an expert on Spanish history. He would serve as Israel's ambassador to Spain from 1987 to 1991, the most momentous years in the budding diplomatic relationship between the two countries.[28]

The cultural ties that resulted from the warming relations between Israel and Spain culminated in the year 1992 with the marking of the quincentenary of the Alhambra Decree. The international ties of Spain's Jewish community, already expanding in the 1980s, further expanded in that context. In 1990, a Spanish-language radio program called *Aadas y Adafinas*, produced by immigrants from northern Morocco in Paris for the Radio de la Communauté Juive, hosted Ben-Ami. The show concentrated on the preparation for the upcoming quincentenary. Ben-Ami used the occasion to explain, from his own perspective, how Spain viewed the celebration as a way to reconcile with the Jewish people rather than to just promote diplomatic ties with the State of Israel. He specifically declared that Israel would feature in the global celebration only as a hub for a significant Sephardi "community," rather than as the Jewish nation-state. According to Ben-Ami, the prominent role of Yitzhak Navon, then Israel's minister of education and culture, in the preparations was due not to his position as an Israeli politician but rather to his identity as a Sephardi Jew.[29]

This statement by an Israeli diplomat of Hispanic Moroccan origin in Spain suggests the complexities that characterized the emergence of bilateral relations between Spain and Israel as epicenters of the Sephardi diaspora, and as homes to new Sephardi communities. Spain continually saw itself as having major influence on the Jewish world, even as it forged ties with Israel. In 1990, Spain bestowed its highest honor, the Prince of Asturias Award for Concord, on Sephardi Jews worldwide. In the broader geopolitical context, 1992 marked the high point of Spain's democratization process in the years following Franco's dictatorship. With Madrid declared the cultural capital of Europe and Barcelona hosting the Olympics, Spain's international status and global recognition as a democratic state reached new heights. In addition, the Universal Exposition of Seville, or Expo '92, also held in 1992, was themed "The Age of Discovery." From the government's perspective, the quincentenary was indeed an opportunity to strengthen its ties with the power centers of the free world by demonstrating its tolerance for and connection to the Jews that resided there.[30]

On March 4, 1987, a working group called Sefarad '92: El Redescubrimiento de la España Judía (Sefarad '92: The Rediscovery of Jewish Spain) was established by Luis Yánez Barnuevo, the first person to be appointed as Spain's secretary of state for Iberia-America and the Caribbean International Cooperation. The working group was appointed directly by the king of Spain and constituted a section within the Spanish Ministry of Foreign Affairs and a unit within the larger National Commission for the Commemoration of the Fifth Century since the Discovery of America.[31]

Responsible for the commemoration of both the five hundred years since the "discovery" of America and the Alhambra Decree, Barnuevo worked with the Tangier-born Samuel Toledano, then president of the Federation of Jewish Communities in Spain. On December 2, 1990, the Jewish community of Spain launched the Comisión Nacional Judía Sefarad '92, a separate international Jewish body designed to work with the state-led Sefarad '92 committee. This Jewish body was headed by Mauricio Hatchel and included additional members such as the aforementioned Samuel Toledano, Isaac Querub, and David Grebler, president of the Jewish community of Barcelona. Their main international collaborators were Israel's Yizhak Navon, who represented the Jerusalem-based Sephardi Community Council (SCC) and the New York City–based ASF.[32] The US was also represented among the leaders promoting the Spanish government's Sefarad '92 program worldwide. Hal Lewis of the ASF was appointed as the project's international director general.[33] The 1992 quincentennial commemoration, which coincided with a new kind of attention to Spain's multicultural past, led to a torrent of new publications and served community leaders' and intellectuals' calls for greater pluralism.[34]

But while the Sefarad '92 project embodied the spirit of multiculturalism and reconciliation, it was not untouched by intercommunal politics and global hierarchies within the Jewish world. Though led in Spain by many Jews of northern Moroccan origin, the influence of community organizations representing the Hispanic Moroccan Jewish diaspora elsewhere was relatively minor. In an interview for the radio show *Aadas y Adafinas*, Solomon Momy Benayoun, president of Mifgash Benei Tanjir (MABAT, Reunion of Tangier's Natives), the main body representing Jews from northern Morocco in Israel (the focus of the next chapter), described how his organization was excluded from planning the quincentennial due to Israeli domestic politics. Benayoun accused Yitzhak Navon of disconnecting the Hispanic Moroccan Jewish community from the larger Sephardi diaspora due to its background in an "Arab country," Morocco. Benayoun's comments reveal the complexity of adding Jews from northern Morocco (in Israel) as a hub to the global effort to link a Sephardi diaspora that increasingly branded its Iberian past as a patrimony that separated them from Mizrahi and Arabophobe Jewish communities in the Middle East and North Africa (MENA) region.[35] Shlomo Ben-Ami, as an Israeli representative, encapsulated this imagined separation in his radio interview for *Aadas y Adafinas*, marking the difference between the revival of Sephardi Jewish and Andalusi-Muslim revivals, deliberately disassociating the new community in Israel from the Andalusi-Muslim world. He deemed Toledo the capital city of Sefarad, whereas Granada was the capital of Al-Andalus.[36]

MOROCCO AS SPAIN IN VENEZUELA

The struggle for the inclusion of Israeli Hispanic Moroccan Jews in the Sephardi revival of the 1990s is only one example of how the global community sought to merge their Moroccan past with their notion of being a Sephardi diaspora and take advantage of the international ties this union would offer. In the 1970s, amid a significant postcolonial migration that had weakened concrete ties between Hispanic Moroccan Jews in Morocco and their worldwide hubs, a different form of blending Moroccan and Hispanic identities had emerged. In that process, references to modern colonial encounters between Hispanic Moroccan Jews and colonial Spain were minimized to make more room for mythologies of Iberian ancestry.

In Venezuela, a new cultural boom in the 1970s marked this process. From the earliest issues of *Maguén* in 1970, its editor and contributors pursued a tendency to selectively reconstruct the image of northern Moroccan townscapes as Jewish-Sephardi *lieux de memoir*. They very often attempted to impart academic validity to their constructions by supplementing them with scholarly essays reproduced from academic journals in the field of Hispanic and Sephardi studies. One article in *Maguén*, entitled "Romanceros de Marruecos," offered readers select passages from an academic study by Harvard University's Paul Bénichou (see chap. 2), who had collected the romances during his field work in Morocco.[37] Remarkably, out of seventy romances, the romance chosen to represent Morocco in *Maguén* was "El Sevillano" ("The Man from Seville"). A number of other articles in *Maguén* likewise conveyed to the paper's Moroccan Jewish readers that Spanish romances had been a significant part of their collective past.[38] Another article in *Maguén*, one of the publication's first, dealt with the etymology of Jewish surnames in northern Morocco, asserting that even those with "Berber and Arabic roots" were no less Sephardi due to the coexistence of Arab and Hispanic cultures in pre-1492 Iberia.

The idea derived from academic research published in *The American Sephardi*, which had begun to appear a few years earlier.[39] The US-based publication gave *Maguén* editors access to valuable historical narratives that they could utilize for their own purpose of establishing a unified communal narrative in Venezuela. It also served their declared objective of constructing a narrative that would appeal to a wider Sephardi audience. In the 1970s, world centers of Sephardi studies in US academia limited their attention either to the study of Jewish roots in Iberia or to the early modern Sephardi diaspora elites whose presence in the West stretched from Amsterdam and Hamburg to colonial America.[40] Scholars became attracted by the ancient texts, liturgy, and linguistic heritage of Sephardi Jews in Sepharad as well as the experiences of early modern Marranos, whose hybrid religious character in fact connected the Jewish with the non-Jewish.[41]

In Venezuela, where Moroccan Jews were the most prominent component of the local Sephardi community, nostalgia for northern Moroccan hometowns was slowly becoming intertwined with their appeal to their collective past in medieval Spain, as exemplified by many of *Maguén*'s articles. For instance, the framing of the history of Morocco as linked to premodern Iberian history helped develop the idea that a shared Hispanic civilization historically, rather than just culturally, united Spain and the Americas. At the same time, it also helped reshape nostalgia for Morocco and reframe Moroccan Jews' collective migration story as it was still unfolding.

Recent postcolonial migration from Morocco was seen as less relevant than the narrative of displacement from Iberia in 1492. One article by Abraham Botbol Hatchuel focused on "The Sephardim and their contribution to the economic and cultural development of Venezuela." It was based on a lecture he delivered on September 22, 1992, at an event marking the eightieth anniversary since the founding of the Venezuelan Spanish Chamber of Industry and

Commerce. The event included an exhibition of photographs titled "Jewish Roots in Spain," sponsored by Iberia Airlines. Botbol Hatchuel, who attended as a representative of the Asociación Israelita de Venezuela (AIV) and the Centro de Estudios Sefradíes de Caracas (CESC, Center for Sephardi Studies of Caracas), noted, "Today when the barriers of religious intolerance have finally been lifted, in democratic Spain, one cannot seriously talk about the history of that nation . . . without seriously taking into account the contribution of Sephardi Jews. . . . Similarly, even today in Venezuela, it is impossible to study the history of its independence and the evolution of its development as a free nation, without the names of Jews who came to these Caribbean lands, with the desire to give the best of each of them in favor of this country."[42] A notion of "Sephardi supremacy" in pre-expulsion Iberia dominated his account, which credited Jews with carrying the intellectual spirit from medieval Baghdad to golden age Córdoba and focused on well-known Jewish figures who had contributed to the development of Spain: Ibn-Gabirol, Maimonides, Yehuda Halevy, Benjamín de Tudela, and many others.[43] Remarkably, Botbol Hatchuel tied his narrative about the Sephardi ancestry in Spain to academic research and provided further support through the Bible. He wrote, "Spanish historians, such as the Jesuíta Juan de Mariana, among others, confirm that the Jews arrived in Spain for the first time with King Nebuchadnezzar on one of the trips he made to the (Iberian) peninsula. . . . This chronicle should not be very far from reality, since in the Bible, in the book of Obadiah . . . the name of Sepharad [indeed] appears. . . . There we may read *verbatim* (textualmente) one of the prophecies: the exiles of Jerusalem who are in Sepharad will possess the cities of the Negev."[44] Later, Botbol Hatchuel turned to the Dutch Jews of the Western Sephardi diaspora as a driving force behind financial and commercial development from Brazil to New England. He described their settlement in the Caribbean Island of Curaçao as a momentous event in Venezuela's economic history due the thriving community of merchants and bankers these migrants established before many of them relocated to mainland Venezuela. He concluded by referencing the "no less important" branch of Sephardim who had recently arrived in Venezuela from North Africa, as if this was a coherent continuation of previous Sephardi migration to the Caribbean.

Against the backdrop of the growing global awareness of Sephardi issues, the early 1970s witnessed the publication of major works on the Judeo-Spanish dialect of northern Morocco by Hispanic Moroccan Jewish leaders in Venezuela, which lucidly associated local Moroccan Jews to premodern Iberia and entwined this attachment with their Moroccan background. Isaac Chocrón's novel *Rómpase en Caso de Incendio (Break in Case of Fire)*, published in 1975, included a chapter written entirely in Haketia, marking the first time the Judeo-Spanish dialect was presented to the wider Venezuelan public.[45] The following year saw the release of the novel *La Vida Perra de Juanita Narboni* by the non-Jewish Tangier native Ángel Vázquez (1929–80), in which he uses Haketia to describe his childhood memories of living alongside Jews in northern Morocco.

In 1977, a new edition of José Benoliel's landmark dictionary of Haketia was published by the CESC. The main goals of the CESC, according to its founders, were (and still are) to recover, research, preserve, and transmit the heritage of Sephardi Jews. Alegría Bendelac, a native of Venezuela who spent most of her childhood in Tangier, began her academic career at Pennsylvania State University after moving to the US with her family in 1963. A specialist in French literature, she began to focus on her ethnic background only in the 1980s, writing about the Jews of northern Morocco as part of a fellowship she received from the National Endowment for the Humanities.[46] In 1989, the AIV and CESC helped publish her first monograph in Spanish, *Voces Jaquetiescas*, which was dedicated to preserving the community's cultural and spiritual life. The following years saw renewed interest in the role of Haketia as the unique spoken language of Hispanic Moroccan Jews, a testimony to their long-lasting attachment to Spain, as they saw it. The CESC became at the time the most prominent communal institute publishing new works on Haketia worldwide.[47]

In 1995, Manuel Alvar of the Royal Spanish Academy was invited to attend the Semana Sefardí, or Sephardi Week, in Caracas, where he presented the dictionary of Haketia.[48] In a piece for *Maguén* on the occasion of the book's release, the New York-based Alvar explained the importance of investing in research about Haketia. According to him, the common practice of agglomerating any Judeo-Spanish dialect under the umbrella term *Ladino* is a modern (post-1940) innovation. It captures only its historical usage in religious practice but misses regional diversities among the Judeo-Spanish-speaking communities. Haketia thus offers a gaze into the historical and regional varieties of everyday speech in the North African Judeo-Spanish world that disappeared in the aftermath of mass emigration.[49]

The academic project of salvaging Haketia was encouraged during the seventh annual Semana Sefardí event in Caracas by a conversation that took place in Haketia between several prominent members of the community, including Moisés Garzón Serfaty, Sara Fereres de Moryoussef, León Bengio, Isaac Benjamín Nahón, Aharón Cohén Serfaty, and Lucy Garzón de Benarroch. The report in *Maguén* mentioned that several hundred people had attended the event at the AIV building.[50]

This network of scholars and community leaders who have been working globally to revive Haketia since the late 1970s contributed much to the tendency of Jews from northern Morocco in Venezuela to merge their identification with Morocco with their identification with Spain. However, they often did this while pushing aside many of their modern experiences, particularly those under Franco and experiences related to the twentieth-century colonialization of Morocco and particularly their postcolonial migration.

During the first Semana Sefardí event in Caracas in June 1982, Abraham Botbol Hatchuel made one of the very first academic references to Haketia.[51] Botbol Hatchuel also authored one of the first volumes issued under the imprint of the CESC's Biblioteca Popular Sefardí. Published in 1989, the book was titled *El Desván de los Recuerdos: Cuadros de una Judería Marroquí* (*The Attic of Memories: Pictures from a Moroccan Jewish Neighborhood*). Its first chapter, "Judaism in Sepharad," included a map of the Jewish communities of the medieval Iberian Peninsula, clearly illustrating, from the outset, Botbol Hatchuel's propensity to entwine the geographical borders of his hometown in colonial Morocco with the imagined borders of medieval Spain. In this way, nostalgia for the physical space that he had, in fact, left in the twentieth century was reduced to a mythological space that helped generate a collective story. Along these same lines of mythologizing Morocco's space, a chapter entitled "La Judería Encantada" ("The Enchanted Judería") focused on events in the nineteenth century.

In fact, Botbol Hatchuel referenced Vilar's book, *Tetuán, en el Resurgimiento Judío Contemporáneo (1850–1870)*, as a means of imparting validity to his own descriptions of Jewish life in Tetouan prior to his birth. Vilar's book, published with the sponsorship of the AIV four years earlier, helped Botbol Hatchuel reconstruct the geographical boundaries of Jewish life in the Judería of Tetouan, where he had spent his childhood years. Botbol Hatchuel was an economist, insurance agent, poet, and journalist who was born in 1935 in the Spanish enclave of Ceuta on Morocco's Mediterranean coast. He moved to nearby Tetouan with his family when he was still a toddler and spent most of his youth there. He moved to Caracas in 1964 after earning a graduate degree in economics from the University of Geneva in Switzerland.[52] These sights and memories from Morocco prior to his emigration to Switzerland—for example, how and why he decided to study in this country—were effaced or deemed irrelevant to his efforts to advance the integration of Moroccan Jewish immigrants into the broader Venezuelan community.

Following his arrival in Venezuela in 1964, Botbol Hatchuel took on several communal roles, including secretary of the AIV, founder and director of the Hebraica Club, and general secretary and later director of the Confederación de Asociaciones Israelitas de Venezuela, the framework that unified Venezuela's Ashkenazi and Sephardi communities. In 1984, Botbol Hatchuel was appointed president of the new Comité Venezolano de Asociación Sefarad-España, an association established to strengthen the cultural ties between Sephardi Jews in Venezuela and modern Spain in light of the Sephardi revival promoted by the latter. In a 1987 issue of *Maguén*, Botbol Hatchuel described to Venezuelan readers the efforts by the Spanish government and its Jewish community to promote the commemoration of the Sephardi past through worldwide events, mentioning the advocacy of Rabbi Baruj Garzón, Mauricio Hatchuel Toledano, Moisés J. Bendahán Israel, and Saadía Benhamú Guanich.[53] To further understand how and why Sephardi activists in Venezuela worked to infuse their Moroccan identities with a strong reference to premodern Iberia, let us turn to how the Sephardi diaspora came to impact Venezuela's cultural elite in the 1970s through the 1990s.

DIASPORA FORMATION AS A MEANS FOR INTEGRATION

In 1970, the year of its founding, *Maguén* brought to its Venezuelan readers a number of articles by Moroccan Jews in Spain. One of these seminal articles was "La Real Academia Española y Los Judíos" by Carlos Benarroch, president of *Amistad* magazine in Barcelona (Spain), in which he discussed the newly positive attitude of Hispanic studies scholars toward Jewish subject matter.[54] Beyond curating content, the AIV disseminated the story of the community's Spanish origins through public events that made use of its global networks. In June 1972, the AIV in Caracas invited Rabbi Benito (Baruj) Garzón, a leader of northern Moroccan Jews in Spain and the brother of Moisés Garzón Sefarty, to deliver a series of lectures to the city's Sephardi community. He lectured on political aspects of Jewish life in Spain, and his talk was followed by another lecture by Elías Benaím from the AIV, entitled "Judaism in Spain: Past, Present, and Future." The events were well attended and made a positive impression on the audience, according to *Maguén*'s reports.[55]

Interest in the history of the Hispanic Moroccan Jewish origins in Iberia culminated in the 1980s with the establishment of landmark institutions for the study of Sephardi Jews in both Venezuela and Spain. For example, *Maguén* reappeared in 1981 after a seven-year hiatus.[56] June 1982 witnessed the celebration of the first Sephardi Week, an event designed to spread the communal narrative within and beyond the Jewish community, even at the national level in Venezuela. The AIV organized the event in collaboration with the Venezuela committee of FeSeLa, the regional network of Sephardi Jews that was affiliated with the WSF.[57]

The summer of 1982 was a milestone in that regard, as it also witnessed the grand opening of the CESC, founded two years earlier in June 1980 as part of the AIV's fiftieth anniversary celebration. Dr. Jacob Carciente, a historian of northern Moroccan descent, was the Center's chairman and served in that capacity from its establishment until the year 2000.[58] The president at the time was Moisés Garzón Serfaty, founder of *Maguén*, and the vice president was Amram Cohén Pariente.[59] The CESC organized academic seminars, including in the classrooms of Universidad Central de Venezuela after the former was able to reach an agreement with the university to offer courses in Sephardi studies. The CESC collaborated with other academic institutions worldwide, efforts that were reflected to some extent in *Maguén* and other publications.[60]

In the Caracas-based CESC's charter, its founders announced their desire to develop Sephardi culture as a way of strengthening ties between Jewish communities worldwide, "as well as with the peoples with whom we largely share a common cultural heritage, [such as] the peoples of Spain, Latin America, and Portugal." The academic institutions mentioned in the document were the Hebrew University of Jerusalem, Tel Aviv University, Yeshiva University of New York, the Sephardic Educational Center of Jerusalem, the Arias Montano Institute in Spain, and the Center for Research and Dissemination of Sephardi Culture of the FeSeLa, based in Buenos Aires. In these institutions, scholars of Latin America and Iberian Studies could serve their goal of strengthening their international Hispanic network.[61] Given this global reach, it is not surprising that the CESC ended up funding and publishing a Spanish version of Rabbi Mitchell Serels's book in 1996, the same year he was knighted by the king of Spain. Rabbi Serels, born in Tangier, was one of the leading advocates for the Spanish-speaking Moroccan community in New York and then in Ontario, Canada, in the 1980s and 1990s.[62]

In fact, much of the CESC's activity was oriented toward the construction of nostalgic connections to Jewish Iberia that also strengthened the attachment of Sephardi Jews to their new country of residence, Venezuela. Along these lines, in 1985 Moisés Garzón Serfaty, then the president of FeSeLa, encouraged communities across Latin America to appeal to their governments to name urban sites after Maimonides, following Caracas's example. The AIV successfully requested that a new avenue and plaza in East Caracas be named after Maimonides, and the inauguration took place on June 10, 1990.[63]

This development should be understood against the backdrop of a variety of applications of "Sepharadism" to local and global contexts, ranging from nineteenth-century Germany to postmodern literary imaginings of Sepharad among MENA Jews worldwide, occasionally overshadowing their more recent histories and origins in the Arab and Islamic realms.[64] In Canada, for example, Francophone Moroccan Jews imagined their Sephardi origins as rooted in France and Francophone culture, a story that helped them identify with Quebec's Francophone Canadian "Quiet Revolution" in the late 1960s.[65] In contrast to the Canadian context, in which Francophone North African Jews were at a disadvantage in the Anglophone communal structures operated by Quebec's Ashkenazi Jewish community, in Venezuela, due to their larger numbers and early arrival in the country, Moroccans more rarely felt excluded from Jewish activities by the country's small Ashkenazi elite. As we saw in the previous chapter, Sephardi Jews from Morocco participated in all of Venezuela's mainstream Jewish organizations and even led them.

The creation of the CESC and the Sephardi revival it promoted saw Spain as a source of cultural empowerment and even Europeanization, and it was motivated by a process of self-representation vis-á-vis Venezuela's national (non-Jewish) elite more than vis-à-vis other Jews. As Edna Aizenberg has shown, the identification of Hispanic Jewish influence in Latin American literature by way of a focus on the Sephardi past served as a strategic tool that helped Jews integrate into Spanish-speaking Catholic countries despite religious differences.[66] Toward that end, the Moroccan community sought and received recognition from local national elites.

During the first Semana Sefardí in June 1982, the AIV headquarters was visited by well-known Venezuelan professors, intellectuals, writers, and artists, including, for example, the playwriter and novelist Isaac Chocrón, the director and actor Enrique Porte, the writers Fausto Masó and Salvador Garmendia Graterón, and the Italian Venezuelan novelist Victoria De Stefano. They all actively participated in an event celebrating the Sephardi roots of local Jews, which included, among other things, traditional *piyyutim*, a Sephardi food festival, television screenings, and even an Israeli folk-dancing performance. Isaac Chocrón was in fact among the leading writers in the country whose work Aizenbeg has identified as promoting the "re-Sepharadization" trend.[67]

Despite strategically using their Jewish roots in Spain as a means of Europeanization, an example of how the identification of Moroccan Jews as Sephardi served to distinguish them from Ashkenazi-European Jews comes from Isaac Chocrón's aforementioned 1975 novel *Rómpase en Caso de Incendio*. In this novel, he dedicated a chapter to Haketia, mediating this dialect to the Venezuelan reader and delving deep into the meaning of being a Venezuelan Jew of Moroccan descent. His character Daniel Benabel, an economist in the

Venezuelan Ministry of Foreign Affairs, decides to undertake a trip to his ancestral hometown of Melilla, and then to Tangier, after he loses his father, wife, and son in the earthquake that struck Caracas in 1967. In the novel, the protagonist writes to a friend in New York, "So you think it's funny that a Jew like me would want to live among the Moors? You forget that I am a Sephardi Jew: so African, so Spanish, and so Venezuelan that the Yiddish-speakers in Brooklyn would consider me a heretic."[68] Explicitly differentiating his hybrid identity from North American or other expectations of separation between Jews and Muslims, Chocrón appealed to Venezuela's national hybridization ethos, the *mestizaje*, which accepted the blending of African and European identities.

Recognition from the Venezuelan elite increased the motivation of many unaffiliated Moroccan Jews, as well as other Jewish groups, to join the global "Sepharadization" trend emerging in the US and Spain. A month after the Semana Sefardí in June 1982, Moisés Garzón attested that the event was among the first to truly attract "people who hardly ever attend community events" and that it yielded the first expressions of interest in the Spanish origins of the Venezuelan Jewish community at the national and international levels, including among the diplomatic representatives of Israel and Spain and the national Venezuelan press. As Garzón noted, more than 1,100 people signed the visitors book that the organizers made available to guests.[69]

This notable degree of interest in the event relates to the way Iberian origins contributed to the assimilation of Jews into the Venezuelan cultural elite. For example, a major topic of focus with respect to the Sephardi past was folklore, especially musical traditions. In 1985, an article in *Maguén* reproduced from the newsletter of the American Jewish Committee described how Spanish ballads from before "the Discovery of America" and "the Expulsion Edict of 1492" continued to appear in Latin American songbooks after the conquest of the Americas, as indigenous populations were influenced by Iberian Portuguese settlers. According to the author, "Much of the culture of medieval Spain would be carried from the Iberian Peninsula in two different directions: to the Near East by the Sephardim and to America by the conquerors, among whom it is very probable that there were Spanish Jews." The author went on to explain how the shared origins of Latin American Spaniards and Sephardi Jews eased the integration of the latter in Latin America.[70]

In 1987, *Maguén* opened its sixty-fourth issue with three essays that linked local Sephardi heritage with the Spanish ballad tradition. One article mentioned a cultural event dedicated to Hispanic romances that took place at the Caracas-based (non-Jewish) cultural center PRISMA from May 28 to June 7, 1987, in which Jewish and non-Jewish artists, intellectuals, and musicians participated, including singer Ana Fernaud, musicians Rafael Benatar and Fernando Silva, and actors José Serrano, Diana Peñalver, Marcos Moreno, and Alfredo Sandoval. On that occasion, Moisés Garzón Serfaty delivered a lecture on "Romancero Sefardí."

Another example of the forging of meaningful connections between a Venezuelan Jewish identity and the Sephardi past in Iberia comes from an essay by Eduardo Gil, a Venezuelan actor and theater director of national renown, who also participated in the event at PRISMA. Gil repeated a similar idea: "The romancero is like a bridge through which the old poetic essences of the Middle Ages traveled until the 16th and 17th centuries.... In its moment of greatest diffusion, it accompanied the conquerors on their journey to America ... and the Jews who were expelled from Spain to Asia Minor and to the coasts of Africa."[71]

Continuing along these lines, in another essay, Moisés Garzón Serfaty treated romances as a symbol of Spanish, Latin American, and Sephardi world heritage, a genre of folksong that celebrates the Hispanic-Jewish connection. He wrote, "In many places in Spain and even Latin America, but especially in Sephardi Jewish communities, little-known romances, or new versions of them, are collected and saved from oblivion through the enormous work carried out by scholars and researchers over the years." He then offered a list of Jewish and non-Jewish scholars who had contributed to that effort worldwide.[72] Documenting the affinity between the old and new worlds of Spanish influence served to incorporate northern Morocco into the Venezuelan narrative in a smooth way but also dwell on its connection to a global diaspora of Hispanic Moroccan Jews who had been investing in similar efforts of salvage ethnography.

In chapter 2, I showed how the developing field of Jewish studies in Spain, France, and the US came to shape the self-consciousness of the Jewish community in northern Morocco as a separate Moroccan community with origins in Iberia. Starting in the 1920s, scholars such as Zarita Nahón, Robert Ricard, Paul Bénichou, Iacov Hassán, José Benoliel, and others helped formulate this narrative with works on Haketia and the romanceros that came to influence and shape the community in colonial Morocco. By the late 1970s, these prolonged scholarly efforts had come to serve northern Moroccan Jews in their postcolonial hubs.[73] In those hubs, following the end of Spanish colonialism in Morocco, new ideas of affinity with Spain and their intertwining with Moroccan histories have emerged, as I will further show in the final two chapters of the book.

SEVEN

HISPANIC MOROCCANS IN ISRAEL

"WE CERTAINLY HAVE THE OBLIGATION TO increase the awareness of the Israeli public to the fact that not all Jews of Moroccan origin are of a *Magrebi* [North African] culture [as is typically thought in Israel]."[1] With these words, Dr. Amada Nahón Avital, one of the founders of Mifgash Benei Tanjir (MABAT, the Reunion of Tangier's Natives in Israel), mentioned in the introduction to this book, explained one of the principal motivations for the creation of this organization in Israel. Established in 1979 in collaboration with Yona Benchimol and Alfonso Sabah, a Moroccan Zionist leader (see chap. 4), MABAT would serve as the principal association of Jews from northern Morocco in Israel until it ceased activity in the mid-1990s.[2] At the time of MABAT's founding, Israel had already become a hub base for the global community of northern Moroccan Jews.[3]

As a self-defined Jewish nation-state and the mythic holy land of Jewish collective memory, Israel was distinguished from other hubs of Hispanic Moroccan Jews. The narrative of homecoming was embedded in the state's creation. Yet, the Israeli experience was also distinguished by the well-known hardships associated with the immigration and integration of its immigrant populations, particularly Moroccan Jews. By the 1970s, in the aftermath of Operation Yakhin, during which most remaining Moroccan Jews immigrated to Israel, Moroccan Jews and their descendants came to constitute the largest country-of-origin group in Israel, lasting until the mass migration of Jews from the former Soviet Union in the 1990s.[4]

Both terms that have served to categorize Moroccans as Jews from Muslim countries in Israel—"Mizrahim" (literally "Orientals") and the earlier "Edoth Ha-Mizrah" ("Communities of the East")—reflected and reinforced their experience of absorption in Israel as disadvantaged minorities. While Jews from northern Morocco and the rest of their Moroccan compatriots in Israel were generally treated by the Israeli establishment and the public as a unified group from a single country of origin, the community of Spanish-speaking Moroccan Jews came to constitute a separate cultural and linguistical minority within the population of Jewish Moroccan immigrants. MABAT's Spanish name, Asociación de Oriundos de Tánger, Tetuán y demás Ciudades de la ex-Zona Española de Marruecos, Ceuta, Melilla y Gibraltar, demonstrated the organization's aspiration of resisting the state classification by forming a separate Moroccan community based on shared Hispanic language, culture, and history in northern Morocco. The boundaries of the reimagined global community in fact exceeded Morocco, as Ceuta and Melilla were officially Spanish territories on African soil rather than parts of the Spanish protectorate. Similarly, Gibraltar was dominated by immigrants from northern Morocco and their descendants but was not itself part of the protectorate.

Looking at these occurrences, this chapter traces how northern Moroccan Jews in Israel separated themselves from other Moroccans and how they utilized their global networks to reinforce this separation. When taken at face value, Avital's attempt to negate the community's Maghrebi origins might be seen as a form of Europeanization. I argue that we might also interpret it as a way of bridging North African and Hispanic traditions as the community sought its rightful place within Israel's broader Mizrahi or, more specifically, North African cultures. To demonstrate why northern Moroccan Jews sought to conceptually differentiate themselves from the rest of Moroccan Jewry, I will explore their efforts to build a centralized communal body, preserve Haketia, and create connections to Spain and northern Morocco as a means for self-empowerment in Israel.

JEWISH COMMUNITY BUILDING IN ISRAEL

Jacobo Israel Garzón remarked that despite an elite of Zionist bourgeoisies from northern Morocco in Israel, this country attracted the "less accommodated" population from the Hispanic Moroccan Jewish community.[5] While this might reflect a broad division within the global diaspora, this data cannot sufficiently explain the internal divisions among Hispanic Moroccan Jews in Israel. Jewish Agency records from 1972 on the occupations of immigrants from northern Morocco to Israel prior to their immigration reported an extraordinary 28.6 percent as white collar or free professions. This was almost double the national percentage for all Moroccan Jewish immigrants, at a time when

Moroccans comprised 17.6 percent of all immigrants to Israel considered of "working age."[6] According to other figures, northern Morocco also produced the highest ratio of wage earners—one per every 4.5 immigrants. In Casablanca, the ratio was one to 5.6.[7]

While figures concerning pre-immigration background do not fully represent post-migration developments, some figures regarding their integration in Israel may explain the continuing gaps between the communities of the north and the national average for Moroccans. In the 1970s and 1980s, Moroccan Jews were concentrated in development towns on the geographical periphery of Israel or in particular neighborhoods in Israel's large cities. This distribution reflected the segregation of most Moroccan Jews in Israel's geographic and economic peripheries, often far from the country's major centers.[8] However, a 1985 MABAT membership roster listing some 769 individuals indicates that several cities were home to a relatively large proportion of immigrants from northern Morocco. The five cities with the largest populations of MABAT members were Jerusalem (seventy-two members), Netanya (forty-nine), Bat Yam (forty-two), Petah Tikvah (thirty-eight), and Ashdod (thirty-five), all located in central Israel. The latter four cities tended to be comprised of lower-middle class immigrants and became destinations for upwardly mobile immigrants from Muslim countries from the late 1960s, but more evidently in the 1990s.[9]

While this information might reflect representative concentrations, the remaining 533 registered MABAT members dwelled in sixty-five other Israeli cities, towns, villages, and kibbutzim. Considering the different neighborhoods within each locality, including the five large cities mentioned above, we can infer that the community was not concentrated in any single area. Some towns in Israel, including Azur, Or-Yehuda, Kfar Shmariyahu, Atlit, Netivot, Mizpe Ramon, and Sderot, had only one MABAT member each. The latter three communities were home to typical Moroccan concentrations, and the small number of members might indicate a tendency of Jews from northern Morocco to associate with the wider Moroccan population, dwelling on shared histories and Francophone and Arabophone backgrounds.[10]

The list of places of residence, ranging from the affluent town of Kfar Shmariyahu to the more impoverished town of Sderot, in fact reflected a more diverse socioeconomic structure characterizing the immigrants who arrived from northern Morocco and joined community organizations in Israel in the 1970s through the 1990s. Unlike many immigrants from the southern parts of Morocco, who in the 1950s were channeled by Israel's political establishment into the southern and northern peripheries according to development plans, the smaller number of Jews from northern Morocco immigrated to Israel later, beginning in the mid-1960s, and tended to spread throughout the country. Consequently, despite some concentrations, Jews from northern Morocco lacked a well-defined geographic center that would have enabled them to organize strong and stable communal bodies capable of influencing the daily lives of community members. In 1990, for example, there were only seven specifically northern Moroccan synagogues across the entire country.[11] MABAT's Hebrew name—which includes the word *Mifgash*, meaning encounter or reunion—demonstrates the desire of its founders and members to reunite the community dispersed across the country.

The experience of YOMAS, the Hebrew acronym for Yotsei Maroko ha-Sefaradit, or émigrés from Spanish Morocco—a short-lived organization founded in 1993—reveals the difficulties imposed by the demographic reality on organizational capabilities. The founder, Dr. Joseph Bengio, who served as president of MABAT in the mid-1980s, designed YOMAS to serve as an organization for northern Moroccans from southern Israel. Members came from Ashdod, Ashkelon, Dimona, Eilat, Kiryat Malachi, and Sderot, among other places. In 1993, YOMAS had 298 registered members.[12] There were also more localized attempts to gather Jews from northern Morocco in the cities where they comprised larger communities, as in the case of the Colonia Española de Ashdod.[13]

These organizational dynamics were not unusual in an immigrant-absorbing country like Israel. From the 1970s through the 1990s, newly formed immigrant organizations of Middle East and North African MENA Jews in Israel thrived. Some patterns of gathering were characterized by differentiation based on town of origin, as indicated by the hometown newsletters that immigrants circulated, such as *Minhat Ashur* for Jews from Mosul, Iraq; *Neharde'a* for Baghdadis; and *Brit* for Jews from Mogador, Morocco. Beyond groups based on immigrants' hometowns, new forms of cultural and regional identification less common in their countries of origin helped set the stage for novel partnerships in Israel. For example, a common denominator of ethnic bulletins was their editors' and readers' place of residence in Israel such as the Yemenite community bulletins *Hadre Teman* in Nahariya and *Mipa'ate Teman* in Kedummim. Like YOMAS, which split from MABAT, groups like the Alliance of Tunisian Immigrants in Beersheba and the South (1990) and MATAN—Netanya Tunisian Club (1995) indicated similar patterns of local organization in the 1990s.[14]

Linguistic background also formed the basis for new partnerships. Unlike in the major demographic hubs emerging in Latin America and Spain, in Israel, Spanish-speaking Jews from northern Morocco encountered a new linguistic milieu in which their native Spanish language was marginal and associated at the time with Latin American immigration rather than their North African heritage. While most Jews from northern Morocco commanded French and occasionally Arabic, their Moroccan origins could go unnoticed. On the institutional level, MABAT organizers sought to partner in Israel with the larger Organización Latinoamericana en Israel (OLEI), an umbrella organization intended to unite Spanish-speaking Jewish immigrants from Latin America and Spain scattered throughout Israel.[15] According to Salomon Benhayon, MABAT's president in 1989, OLEI, which included mainly Ashkenazim from Latin America, was a natural ally due to the two organizations' shared linguistic Hispanic heritage. For example, in expressing solidarity with MABAT, the chair of OLEI's Committee for Aliyah and Absorption referred to the expulsion of Jews from Spain in 1492 as a "second Holocaust," painting a shared history of suffering experienced by Sephardi and Ashkenazi Jews alike.[16]

MABAT's collaboration with OLEI, however, was based on more practical motivations: OLEI's country-wide branches in Israel, which were more developed than its own, could help MABAT disseminate "Haketia culture" and the northern Moroccan narrative of ancestry in Spain.[17] MABAT hardly aspired to become Latin American or even Spanish but rather to underscore its members' unique Moroccan traditions through networks accessible to them.

MOROCCANS, BUT DISTINCT

Given the organizational particularities of northern Moroccan Jews, the establishment of MABAT needs to be understood as part of a boundary work taking shape in Israel vis-à-vis Jewish communities that came from southern Morocco, deemed by MABAT's founders as "forasteros," foreigners, or simply "Moroccans from the south." From the 1970s through the 1990s, in addition to the social protests organized along ethnic lines by Israel's Black Panthers movement (see chap. 5), other expressions of cultural identity emerged via popular music, public assertions of ethnicity, and intellectual debates. Poets, musicians, and writers deployed a vocal ethnic discourse that accentuated the uniqueness of the Moroccan experience and became one of the most recognizable features of the cultural conflict between "European" Ashkenazi Jews and "Oriental" Mizrahi Jews.[18]

Notably, the Mimouna celebration, a religious and communal ritual marking the end of Passover among Jews in Morocco, gained a high public and political profile in Israel. Already in the mid-1960s, Shaul Ben-Simhon, a native of Fez who became a member of the Mifleget Poalei Eretz Yisrael (MAPAI, translated as Workers' Party of the Land of Israel) party, helped raise that profile by organizing a public Mimouna event in his capacity as a leader of Brit Yotsei

Maroko—the Alliance of Moroccan Jews in Israel. What started as a small gathering of some three hundred Jews from Fez in a public park in Jerusalem became, from the 1970s onward, a massive, carnivalesque celebration with tens of thousands of participants. The raucous style of the Mimouna celebration in Israel in those years led to increased stereotyping of North African cultures by the rest of the Israeli public and drew criticism from the ranks of the Sephardi and Moroccan intellectual elite for how it flattened the diversity of the Moroccan community and its pre-immigration history.[19]

MABAT's founder made a clear effort to distinguish the Spanish-speaking community of northern Moroccans in Israel from the negative image of Moroccans that dominated the Israeli discourse, joining in the criticism of the boisterous atmosphere of the Mimouna celebration. In *MABAT Revista*, a booklet summarizing the association's activities during the 1980s, Avital openly acknowledged that her decision to found MABAT was in part a reaction to the Mimouna phenomenon and her resulting "dissatisfaction" with the emerging stereotype of Moroccan culture in Israel. The new type of Mimouna celebration was, according to Avital, a "pseudo-folkloric tradition [that had] little in common with our [Hispanic Moroccan] tradition."[20] MABAT consequently set out to preserve the community's unique cultural, religious, and folkloric patrimony. This involved collecting cultural material from the community and working for the preservation of Haketia and other traditions as distinctly more authentic, and thus more valuable, North African patrimony.[21]

During the 1980s, MABAT circulated among its members a number of brochures and letters containing announcements, articles, and summaries of its cultural activities, such as the aforementioned *MABAT Revista* on the occasion of its tenth anniversary (1989–90). Through its publications, MABAT presented itself as the most relevant framework for organizing a unified and separate Hispanic Moroccan community in Israel. A circular summoning people to participate in a hilula included the slogan "MABAT is the hyphen uniting past and present; MABAT is you!"[22] In one case, the hilula of Rabbi Mordejai Bengio—the legendary Great Rabbi of Tangier's community toward the end of the nineteenth century—was broadcast on a national radio program narrated by Moshe Shaul, the head of the Ladino Section of the Israel Broadcasting Authority.[23]

The hilula was a typical North African tradition involving a pilgrimage to the tomb of a saint on the anniversary of their death, an occasion on which miracles were said to occur. Ironically, this tradition was distinct from and irrelevant to the preservation of Ladino, as would be any tradition associated with North Africans.[24] Nonetheless, drawing on the cultural and linguistic connections between Haketia and the wider Judeo-Spanish domain, MABAT organized activities that bridged North African and Ladino cultural traditions for their own organizational benefits. To further understand these dynamics, we need to consider how academic studies of Jews from the Islamic world, including Ladino studies, gained momentum in Israel at that time.

THE ROLE OF ACADEMIA

Researching the evolution of the study of Moroccan Jewish history and culture in Israel, Daniel Schroeter has concluded that until the late 1970s, the subject remained largely outside secular academia and was confined to the domain of rabbinical scholars.[25] In the early 1970s, when Israel witnessed an ethnic revival, a momentous change occurred in domestic attitudes toward the study of Jewish history and culture in Muslim countries. In tandem with the global rise of Sephardi studies and the founding of local and international Sephardi studies centers, in 1972, Misgav Yerushalayim, the Centre for Research and Study of Sephardi and Oriental Jewish Heritage, was founded through a joint initiative of the Hebrew University, the Zionist-oriented World Sephardi Federation (WSF), and the Sephardi Community Council (SCC) in Jerusalem. Viewing the study of the Sephardi past as a national priority, in 1977 Israel's Ministry of Education created the Center for Incorporating the Heritage of Sephardi and Mizrahi Jewries and allocated unprecedented funds for scholarly research on the topic. The year 1979 witnessed a number of pioneering academic conferences in Israel, as well as the appearance of the journal *Pe'amim*.[26] In this context, Ladino and Moroccan cultural traditions both became hot topics of investigation in the humanities in Israel.

Unlike elsewhere, in Israel there was a significant population of Jewish immigrants from Muslim countries who prioritized this topic. The increased prominence of Mimouna and other North African celebrations in Israel in the 1970s and 1980s motivated top anthropologists and folklorists to research their origins through fieldwork, prioritizing ethnography over textual scholarship.[27] Many of these studies noted either directly or indirectly how dramatically Israeli Mimouna celebrations differed from the traditional rituals that took place in Morocco. Many of the scholars who devoted their careers to the study of Jewish communities in Muslim countries were themselves immigrants from those countries, combining their newfound interest in their own ethnic identities with the rise of this new scholarly field.[28] The appeal to the Jewish past in Morocco and its binding with the present had a similar objective to efforts expended elsewhere in the Hispanic Moroccan Jewish diaspora (see chap. 6). It reflected a cultural resistance designed to help the community reclaim its own history while still adjusting to the Israeli national discourse.

MABAT's founding came about during that academic revival, and it too invested in academic research. In *MABAT Revista*, it hailed the activity of the Folklore Research Center at the Hebrew University, which offered a course on the affection for saintly rabbis among North African Jews.[29] On the same page as this announcement, MABAT published a "traditional story," written in Tangier in 1964 by Sarita Benzaquen, that recounted a miracle performed by a local saint. According to the writer, the story represented the unique heritage of the north.[30] At the initiative of one of its founders, Alfonso Sabah, MABAT created the Yona Benchimol Scholarship at Bar-Ilan University for the study of the cultural heritage of northern Moroccan Jewries.[31] MABAT later established two additional scholarship funds specifically earmarked for students of northern Moroccan origin and funded by Agudat Sabah, the Sabah family's foundation.[32] These projects became part of a well-established network that could efficiently and systematically disseminate shared narratives and guarantee proactive individuals the resources to produce them.

For MABAT, scientific support for the communal narrative and their dissemination was one of the principal roles of academia. In Israel, Gladys Pimienta, a prominent member of MABAT, started a project to preserve Haketia at the Ma'ale Adumim Institute for the Documentation of Judeo-Spanish Language and Its Culture, affiliated within the Sefarad Society. In 1982, using this academic infrastructure, she called on other MABAT members to submit photographs and essays in order to create an archive of historical sources and testimonies about Jewish life in northern Morocco. MABAT announced an essay contest whose winner would be determined by an academic jury and then published.[33] In 1983, Beit Hatfutsot organized an exhibition of photographs in association with several of MABAT's most prominent members: Amada Avital, Gladys Pimienta, and Joseph Bengio. The exhibition, which traveled across Israel for the next two years, was also sponsored by the Center for the Integration of the Oriental Jewish Heritage, an affiliate of the Ministry of Education and Culture.[34]

Scholars who conducted field research, regardless of their ethnic origins, helped revive MABAT's ethnic networks. For instance, MABAT collaborated with the scholar Shoshana Weich Shahak, who since 1973 has been recording and studying Sephardi musical traditions at the Jewish Music Research Centre of the Hebrew University. Weich Shahak used *MABAT Revista* to call on members to collaborate with her research on northern Moroccan Jewish melodies.[35] Her eventual fieldwork took place in Tel Aviv, Bat Yam, Holon, Ashdod,

Ashkelon, Jerusalem, and Ramat Eliyahu in Rishon le-Tzion throughout the 1980s and 1990s, enabling MABAT's members to experience and act on their ethnicity, and to forge or strengthen communal networks—all as the result of growing scholarly efforts.[36] Weich Shahak's research yielded several academic publications.[37] She also participated in several academic conferences at the time, where she presented her work on Hispanic Moroccan musical traditions. Her academic activities sought to cultivate—mostly among established Hispanic Moroccan Jewish community members—a sense that northern Moroccans in Israel comprise a singular ethnicity. Weich Shahak helped women from northern Morocco express their ethnic voice—literally—through an audio cassette recording of life cycle songs.[38]

MABAT encouraged the use of different media to commemorate the ethnic past within academic circles. In September 1985, the organization called for video recordings of testimonies about the Jewish community in Morocco. The announcement emphasized that the testimonies would be evaluated by an academic team.[39] In 1986, MABAT collaborated with Beit Hatfutsot at Tel Aviv University to present *Florilegio*, a collection of recorded romances from northern Morocco, some of which were later broadcast by Kol Yisrael. MABAT also issued an audio cassette containing twenty-five of these romances.[40]

These projects and their participants understood themselves as playing a proactive role in promoting a united communal narrative that still needed further exploration. As mentioned in the introduction and in chapter 2, the Haketia dialect had been declared a "dead idiom" by Spanish and French philologists who came to Morocco to document what remained of it in light of modernization and the adoption of modern Spanish since the 1920s. In Israel, MABAT was one of the main body that triggered Haketia's revival in a postcolonial context. It has since been followed by other initiatives, including academics who have sustained the revival project over the past decade.

Significantly, the Haketia revival project tended to mask the fact that modern Spanish was more commonly spoken in pre-migration Morocco. Prof. Yaakov Bentolila, a Tetouan native who became the leading scholar in the field, asserted that he began thinking about Haketia only in the 1980s, when he launched his research into the idiom.[41] Remarkably, the trigger for his academic interest in Haketia was MABAT's gathering in 1983, to which he had been invited to lecture on the dialect as a philologist who was also a Tetouan native.[42] As in pre-migration colonial northern Morocco, the Haketia idiom was then still perceived by many immigrants from northern Morocco and their descendants as an inferior and archaic form of Spanish. It was thus treated with a certain ambiguity; most identified Haketia with a collective past rather than with their own personal history. Nevertheless, the idiom eventually took on a more unifying role for Hispanic Moroccan Jews in the process of defining their unique Hispanic identity during Israel's ethnic revival and distinguishing themselves vis-à-vis other Moroccans whose European—mainly French—identity was allegedly more recent and thus more artificial.

This reclaiming of Haketia required the suspension of memories from colonial spaces in northern Morocco, as was the case in Venezuela, but with nuances specific to the Israeli context. For example, the *MABAT Revista* published an article by Gladys Pimienta, a Tangier native, concerning a "traditional" custom among the Jews of Tetouan to place a *matesha*, a swing, on their patios after Passover. According to the article, the custom had a social function, enabling young, unmarried girls to meet potential husbands. The article was accompanied by the publication of romances, known as "the matesha songs," which, according to MABAT's article, were commonly sung in Tetouan.[43] In an interview with Gladys Pimienta, she remarked that "many of the songs I have collected here [namely, in Israel], including this one, I had never heard of in Morocco, nor did my mother, I think [smiling]."[44] Like many of her proactive counterparts, she learned about many traditions through her participation in academic activity. Clearly, the "Matesha" and other romances were not fictional, yet they represented marginal aspects of the memories of middle-class immigrants who had integrated into the colonial scene, held over from previous generations in Morocco. In another interview with Pimienta, she mentioned how, as a teenager in Tangier, she had attended the Lycée Français, the non-Jewish French schools in Tangier, and that she had dwelled in the city's western neighborhood, densely populated with Spaniards and Frenchmen, and with relatively few Jewish inhabitants. In 1968 she left Tangier to study psychology at the Sorbonne in Paris, from where she eventually immigrated to Israel in 1977.[45]

MABAT's founders, regardless of their diverse personal experiences with Haketia before and after their immigration to Israel, described its preservation as one of their central goals, alongside its aspiration to reunite the community in Israel. It encouraged immigrants from northern Morocco to recall and document memories involving Haketia. For example, during a recipe contest, MABAT specifically asked the participants to recount anecdotes about the dish using Haketia, rather than "modernized" Spanish variants.[46] The focus on Haketia also meant that MABAT began to incorporate the other North African, including the Arabic, components of Haketia into the broader field of Ladino studies, bridging what until then had been two separate entities.

Viewing these developments from a broader perspective, it becomes clear that a new global network has emerged since the 1970s to connect Israeli academia with institutions at the forefront of Sephardi studies elsewhere in the world, a process mediated in no small part by the northern Moroccan community elite in Israel.[47] As discussed in previous chapters, the tendency had long existed to separate the study of Judeo-Spanish philology from the more recent history of MENA communities. The focus on premodern traditions helped reaffirm the myth of pre-1492 "Sephardi supremacy" over post-1492 MENA cultures. This distinction remains crucial to a formerly Haketia-speaking community that asserted their own cultural distance from the bulk of Moroccan Jews, perceived as Arab Jews or more commonly Mizrahim, who cannot claim the same linguistic pedigree.[48]

Such ideas shaped MABAT's ties with the emerging field of Ladino studies in Israel, even as they maintained their Moroccan origins. Moshe Shaul, chair of the Sefarad Society and former head of the Ladino Section of Kol Yisrael, praised MABAT's mission of spreading their unique Moroccan Judeo-Spanish culture.[49] The partnership with Ladino study networks has helped MABAT members shape their unique identity as Hispanic Moroccans separate from the broader North African population, while still emphasizing a distinct identity rooted in the historic North African Arabic milieu.

Several academic or semi-academic Sephardi studies journals helped disseminate the ethnic narrative in Israel. One example is *Aki Yerushalayim*, issued since 1979 by the Sefarad Society for Preserving and Cultivating the Judeo-Spanish Heritage, which has dedicated, from time to time, a special section to articles on Haketia and northern Morocco.[50] At the turn of the twenty-first century, after MABAT had ceased its activities, other academic institutions continued its mission of maintaining the ethnic narrative. Since 1997, the National Authority for Ladino has provided academic support for the Sefarad Society in light of a new law aimed at promoting the preservation of Judeo-Spanish culture in Israel.[51]

Another example is the *El-Prezente* journal, issued by the Moshe David Gaon Center for Ladino Culture at Ben-Gurion University.[52] Founded in 2004, the Gaon Center, headed by Professors Tamar Alexander and Yaakov Bentolila, both members of the National Authority for Ladino, is one of the most prominent institutions dedicated to the preservation of Haketia. A few of the Gaon Center's academic events have been dedicated to northern Moroccan culture and history (often nicknamed *Haketia Evenings*). A list of invitees to an event celebrating the issuing of the second volume of *El-Prezente* in March 2009 reveals that the 179 invitees came from thirty-eight cities, towns, and villages throughout Israel.[53] The word *Haketia* itself has continued to be an emblem of the broader ethnic narrative connecting North Africa to Spain via shared origins, as the name of the Gaon Center's Haketia Evenings indicates.[54]

The siblings Sidney and Gladys Pimienta continued to dedicate time to the collection of documents and artifacts related to the Jewish community in Morocco. The Pimientas eventually created a private collection of material in their home, which has attracted researchers such as the author.[55] Sidney's projects included transliterations of manuscripts in *Solitreo* (traditional Sephardi handwriting), photographing and mapping the Jewish cemetery in Tangier, and genealogical surveys. With the assistance of another sibling, their brother Jimmy in Belgium, one major project to which Sidney and Gladys were especially dedicated was the transliteration of the minutes of the Junta—a thick manuscript compiled into a book, the work of more than two decades from the late 1980s until 2010.[56]

A RETURN TO TWO HOMELANDS

While Hispanic Moroccan identity was constructed through an attachment to historic representations of the past, more concrete transnational ties connecting modern-day Spain, Israel, and Morocco also helped define the community vis-à-vis "other Moroccans," or the forasteros from the south. A thorough discussion of the phenomenon requires an examination of MABAT's peak period of activity in the mid-1980s.

The year 1986 was a momentous one in the history of bilateral relations between Israel and Morocco, and between Israel and Spain. In July 1986, Israeli prime minister Shimon Pères visited Morocco for the first time to meet with King Hassan II. One of Pères's achievements during this visit was winning the Moroccan government's agreement to allow Israeli passport holders to enter the country. That agreement led to visits by organized tour groups from Israel, usually composed of close friends or family members who visited typical tourist sites as well as family graves, saints' tombs, and other Jewish sites in Morocco.[57] In July 1987, MABAT members in Israel organized their own group trip to their Moroccan cities of origin, taking advantage of the new agreement.

The MABAT trip included, in addition to the usual shopping and entertainment, encounters with Jewish community leaders, prayers, visits to Jewish cemeteries and synagogues, tours of the former Jewish neighborhoods of Tangier, Tetouan, and other cities in the north, and brief stops in Casablanca and Rabat. In attendance was musicologist Shoshana Weich Shahak, who used the trip as an ethnographic opportunity to record participants outside of Israel—for example, at the Casino Israelita in Tangier (see fig. 7.1).

This return trip in July 1987 resembled many of the "heritage trips" undertaken by Moroccan Israelis at the time, and yet it was one of a kind, since it served in practice to combine both nostalgia and contemporary attachment to

Figure 7.1. Shoasha Weich Shahak records romances sung by the trip's participants at Tangier's Casino Israelita, 1987. © Courtesy of Rina Ben-Abu.

two home countries: Spain and Morocco. The unique encounter was enabled not only by the geographical proximity of Spain and Morocco but also by recent diplomatic developments in the bilateral relationship between Israel and Spain. In the 1980s, as post-Franco Spain struggled to rebrand itself as a liberal democracy, tourism was seen as a major means of promoting multiculturalism and marketing the country to the world. Policymakers invested in marketing medieval Spain as a paragon of interfaith coexistence.[58] These developments coincided with warming relations between Spain and Israel, which culminated in the establishment of official diplomatic ties in 1986, the same year as the agreement between Israel and Morocco. Given this confluence of events, it was only natural that Spain would arouse curiosity among Jewish Israelis, who hoped to explore the country's historic Jewish sites and visit the birthplace of the great Sephardi figures whose names appeared prominently in Israeli public discourse.

MABAT's tour lasted thirteen days, from July 13 to July 25. It began in Spain, in Torremolinos, where the participants met with members of the northern Moroccan Jewish community from Málaga and Marbella. For MABAT members from Israel, visiting Spain was not just a matter of searching for their Sephardi origins but also a momentous event that enabled them to reunite with their kin in one of the larger hubs of Hispanic Moroccan Jews at the time. The second day was dedicated to traveling from Spain to Morocco through Ceuta, where again the group met with local Jewish community members. Following a ten-day visit to Morocco, the final days of the trip were devoted to a visit to Gibraltar and its Jewish community, also of northern Moroccan descent, and then to historic sites in Seville, Cordoba, Toledo, and Madrid.

The practical logic behind the inclusion of Spain as part of a heritage tour to Morocco was that Spain was a convenient geographical entry point to Morocco, given the absence of direct flights between Israel and Morocco. Yet the historic sites they visited in Spain also encapsulated much about the way Hispanic Moroccan Jews understood their past in Morocco and as a global diaspora. This was particularly salient given the revival of interfaith discourses in Morocco in the 1980s. At the time, pilgrimages of former Jewish residents of Morocco to saintly tombs in their hometowns was propagated by the Moroccan state to argue for its historic inclusiveness of Jews and their loyalty to the Moroccan monarchy.[59]

Despite the pragmatic cause, Abraham Benabu, MABAT's treasurer, in fact described the visit to Spain in *MABAT Revista* as the beginning of "the encounter with our origins."[60] Reports about the trip and the return of Tangier's Jews to their motherland made it into the Spanish press. One report mentioned that in Torremolinos, forty-five Tangier Jews met with the Moroccan consul in Málaga and representatives of Moroccan Airlines and Morocco's Ministry of Tourism.[61] In the communal imagination, Spain seemingly served as a geographical extension of Morocco, even when Morocco had been an independent state for more than three decades in 1987.

The unusual entwining of Spain and Morocco was also a result of the unique geopolitical position of Ceuta and Melilla. While the major urban centers that had been home to Hispanic Moroccan Jews for centuries witnessed their almost complete disappearance of their Jewish communities, the same was not true for parts of the northern coastal region.

Unlike mainland Spain, the two Spanish enclaves on African soil, Ceuta and Melilla, have a different history of welcoming Jewish migration. During the Spanish-Moroccan War of 1859–60, Ceuta and Melilla served as military outposts for Spain's colonial expansion into Africa, and in 1863, right after the war ended, Spanish authorities declared them duty-free ports in order to populate them. In 1887, a customs office was established in Melilla, the new center of Spanish dominance in Africa, and all restrictions on the residence of foreigners, including Jews from nearby Moroccan cities, were revoked. By 1921, more the 3,000 Jews, most of them from nearby Tangier and Tetouan, had settled in Melilla alongside 300 Muslims and about 42,000 Catholic settlers who immigrated from mainland Spain.[62] In 1940, 2,410 Jews were still living in Melilla, and by 1991 their number declined to about 1,000. In 1991, Jews lives in that city together with 37,467 Spaniards and about 26,000 Moroccan Muslims.[63]

Melilla, one of the hometowns represented by MABAT, still had a thriving Jewish community at the turn of the twentieth century, which in fact constituted one of the largest urban concentrations of Jews on North African soil, albeit geopolitically a Spanish territory.[64] Though Melilla is an integral part of the Spanish state, the Moroccan Jews who live there are not recent immigrants but a community residing in its North African place of origin as full Spanish citizens.

This reality produced some vibrant transnational ties, forged as smoothly as with any other community in mainland Spain. On October 2, 1995, about 550 Jews from the city of Melilla reunited in the Ram Hotel in Jerusalem for the First Melillian Congress. Most of them were living in Israel, but some visited from Spain and Venezuela. The group was led by Rabbi Shlomo Wahnon and was distinguished from MABAT by its overtly religious orientation. At the gathering, they read a blessing sent by Ignacio Velázquez Riviera, the acting mayor of Melilla, and screened a video from the city. Three weeks later, on October 23, a similar rencounter of about forty Melilla natives took place in Madrid, inspired by the Israeli event. They met at the Madrid Bet Yaacov synagogue for a screening of the same video from Melilla, which they had received from the community in Jerusalem. A third such encounter took place on November 14 in Barcelona, where Rabbi Shlomo Wahnon again presented the video. Other events followed in Caracas and Melilla.[65] A weeklong visit to Melilla then took place in March 1996, including a seminar at a hotel and a visit to Rabbi Saadia Hadati's tomb in Nador in northern Morocco.

This unique transnational pattern challenges the traditional geopolitical dichotomy between Europe and North Africa and once again complicates the idea that nostalgia among Jewish immigrants from Morocco was formed through a process of distancing from one's homeland. In fact, it illustrates that movement between multiple homelands—places that were also geographic hubs for the northern Moroccan Jewish diaspora—was central to expressing and developing a communal nostalgia for a diasporic past. The next chapter will further explore the role of one of those hubs—Israel—in generating the global story of the community, with a specific focus on smaller hubs in France and North America.

EIGHT

A GLOBAL HISPANOPHONE DIASPORA

IN SEPTEMBER 1981, JUST TWO YEARS after the founding of Mifgash Benei Tanjir (MABAT, Reunion of Tangier's Natives) in 1979, its board declared its intention to launch an international congress in Tel Aviv that would bring together Jewish immigrants of northern Moroccan origin from across the world.[1] The congress, scheduled to take place in Tel Aviv in August 1983, carried such great importance in the eyes of MABAT's organizers that as early as January 1982 they circulated a call among Israeli members to hurry and register for the event. They wrote, "Our first affiliated [community] in the 'golah' [diaspora], as well as other interested individuals in Europe and America, insistently demand that our reunion take place."[2] A list included in one of the organization's internal unpublished documents reveals how MABAT planned to appeal to the worldwide diaspora, mentioning the major hubs where Jews from northern Morocco resided, such as Spain, Venezuela, Brazil, and Argentina, as well as the smaller hubs in France, the US, Switzerland, and Canada.[3]

As we saw in chapter 7, the emergence of a community organization among immigrants from northern Morocco in Israel must be understood within the context of Israel's domestic ethnic revival in the 1970s and 1980s. Representing a local branch of a transregional diaspora, however, the community's establishment in Israel was also influenced by the global Sephardi revivals and the interpretation of the community's Spanish origins in the new major hubs in Spain and Venezuela (see chap. 6). At the same time, MABAT's records reveal that the immigrant community in Israel actively worked to influence the global diaspora abroad by helping establish sister organizations in countries with smaller concentrations of Spanish-speaking Moroccan Jews in France, the US, and Canada. As the 1983 congress approached, MABAT established a committee for international affairs called the Comisión de Organización Internacional that was specifically designed to work toward that goal.

Important studies on the Moroccan-led Mizrahi ethnic revival and formation in Israel tend to view these phenomena as local manifestations of a broader minority rights protest movement that swept throughout the postcolonial world in the 1960s and 1970s (see Introduction).[4] However, these studies hardly address the global dynamics of ethnic formation among Sephardi and Middle East and North Africa (MENA) Jewish populations outside of Israel and how they engaged in conversation with events in Israel. In this chapter, I show how MABAT's global activities and the transnational connections it forged may help fill this methodological gap separating the study of MENA Jewish migration and Mizrahi ethnicity in Israel. Continuing the narrative developed throughout the previous chapters of this book, this chapter challenges the conventional understanding that postcolonial immigration to Israel from Morocco inevitably marks the endpoint of Jewish Moroccan global diaspora-making, or otherwise contradicts it.

To further analyze the postcolonial dynamics in the proliferation of the Hispanic Moroccan Jewish diaspora, here I suggest adapting a recent scholarly concept by proposing "the Global Hispanophone." This category of analysis echoes the more established concepts of the Global Lusophone, Francophone, and Anglophone. It incorporates regions of the world that were bound by the Spanish Empire beyond Latin America, the Caribbean, and the Iberian Peninsula itself—namely, North Africa, Equatorial Guinea, the Philippines, and other regions that scholars rarely study alongside one another. The Global Hispanophone paradigm advances the study of local contexts hitherto marginal to major historical centers, transcending existing boundaries and bringing the past and present of these far-flung regions into dialogue with each other.[5] I employ this concept to analyze the ties between hubs of the Hispanic Moroccan Jewish diaspora in non–Spanish-speaking countries in which Hispanic Moroccan Jewish communities were established in the 1970s through the 1990s. I show how through this process the preservation of Haketia and other Hispanic patrimonies came to be a synergic source of empowerment for smaller hubs, Israel included.

ZIONISM IN ISRAEL, A CONTINUING DIASPORIC HERITAGE

A first step toward understanding MABAT's motivation in its global outreach, as well as the dynamics of trinational ties between Israel and other hubs, is to discuss the way they formulated their Zionist identities. As we saw in chapters 4 and 5, the endorsement of pro-Zionist ideas by community leaders in Morocco and Latin America did not necessarily lead to their immigration to Israel, partly because some interpreted Zionism as a cultural movement that served to help define and strengthen local Jewish communities, along with other affinities. This function of Zionism as an ethnic diaspora movement continued to shape the community in Venezuela as late as the 1970s, when immigration from Morocco to Israel reached its final stages. As Zionism blended with community building in Latin America, similar cultural-organizational dynamics characterized MABAT in Israel when it began to incorporate Zionist ideas into its shared origin story.

MABAT Revista provides evidence for that process. The first essay that appeared in that bulletin was a love song for the State of Israel composed by MABAT's founder Amada Avital. Its cover page was dedicated to announcing that "MABAT salutes the State of Israel."[6] This should come as no surprise considering that one of MABAT's founders, Alfonso Sabah, was a prominent Zionist activist in Morocco (see chap. 4). *MABAT Revista* reproduced a series of documents—including reports from *Adelante, La Liberté,* and *El Eco Israelita,* periodicals that had appeared in northern Morocco in the early twentieth century—to reassure readers that Zionism was part of MABAT's identity as a community. Alongside references to the participation of Jews in northern Morocco in Zionist youth movements and Zionist clubs like Maguen David, MABAT emphasized the generous financial contributions of the northern Moroccan community to the *shekel* (originally a biblical Hebrew coin) enterprise.[7] In this context, purchasing a shekel was the practice of paying membership dues to the World Zionist Organization (WZO), which since 1897 conferred the right to elect delegates or be elected to the World Zionist Congress. In practice, the shekel served as a donation to the WZO.

The connection that MABAT drew between the material wealth of the community and its devotion to Zionism was not incidental. This connection served to develop a broader sense of pride among MABAT members as part of a Moroccan group that could actually enrich the Zionist project through its historical and contemporary prosperity in the diaspora. In other words, the founders of MABAT maintained that contemporary Zionism could benefit from the presence of northern Moroccan Jews in Israel, as a community that has been relatively prosperous outside of the country. Following the logic of this narrative, the first section in *MABAT Revista* was titled "What was our community like?" The title was followed by a subheading: "What were its concerns, and what have we been able to *reproduce, here* [in Israel], *today?*"[8] The next thirty-seven pages provided the anticipated answer to these questions. Among other things, MABAT included its plans to resume the tradition in northern Morocco of donating to the Jewish National Fund by planting a forest in Israel in MABAT's name during 1989.[9]

The next page listed the wealthiest local contributors to the Oeuvre de Nourriture et d'Habillement, the charitable Feeding and Clothing Project for the Alliance Israélite Universelle (AIU) schools in Tangier in 1931; and included an article concerning La Cantina Sarita Sagues, a soup kitchen founded in 1934 for the benefit of the needy in the community.[10] Seeking to demonstrate a continuation of communal wealth in Israel, Mosad Alazrachi (later known as Bet Elazraki), a home for children at risk, was inaugurated in Netanya in the 1960s through the generosity of Victor Alazrachi, a northern Moroccan donor. The Sabah family, to which the aforementioned cofounder of MABAT belonged, promoted this social welfare project in Israel.[11] MABAT presented the initiative as a clear continuation of the spirit of the Laredo-Sabah home, established with communal funds in Tangier in the early 1900s, and more generally of the overall generosity of the community. While philanthropy has been an important factor in the formation of ties between Jewish communities worldwide throughout the modern period, philanthropy was used here by MABAT to demonstrate the economic status of Hispanic Moroccan Jews in Israel.[12]

MABAT's invitation to its brethren abroad to come to Israel in the summer of 1983 and celebrate their Hispanic Moroccan Jewish identity was related to these dynamics of self-assertion in Israel. MABAT's publication reiterated the idea that Israel, as a developing country, relied on affluent Jews from around the world to assist it in becoming a strong nation. One essay in *MABAT Revista*, published in 1990, was headlined "Zionism in Transition—we cannot pretend that everything is working out well for our Israel this year."[13] The four-page essay concluded that "Israel needs [the diaspora's] assistance, and its Aliyah."[14] The same idea had appeared five years earlier in a circular that laid out MABAT's raison d'être as an organization, when MABAT presented itself as a diaspora group capable of improving the social status of Moroccan Jews in Israel.[15] MABAT's self-positioning echoed a similar discourse characterizing diaspora-based immigrant associations from "affluent countries" (to use the Zionist terminology, as presented in chap. 5) that claimed a philanthropic position in the Zionist project. These organizations included, for instance, the Association of Americans and Canadians in Israel.[16]

MABAT's interpretation of Zionism conjured a nostalgia for the perceived devotion of Jews in northern Morocco to the well-being of the state of Israel.

In support of its argument that MABAT was one in a line of northern Moroccan associations that had contributed to Israel's well-being, the organization offered biographical anecdotes about successful Jews from northern Morocco who, it claimed, played a role in Israel's establishment. These included, for example, biographies of Jacob Salama (who, after his immigration, changed his name to Yavin), an immigrant from Tetouan in 1956 who overcame harsh assimilation difficulties to become a thriving Israeli industrialist. Another example was a published interview with Knesset member Daniel Levy, a native of Ceuta. Newspaper items reproduced by MABAT confirmed his success in Israel. The editors of *MABAT Revista* evidently sought to highlight success stories to discredit the negative image of North African immigrants in Israel as underprivileged Mizrahim.[17]

As we saw in chapter 6, since the Israeli Black Panthers demonstrations of the 1970s, Zionist-oriented Sephardi organizations had paid greater attention to social problems in Israel and developed a global philanthropic system for supplying financial and moral support. They created a solution to what was seen by Israeli scholars and policymakers and the broader Israeli public as the "ethnic problem"—that is, the socioeconomic gaps separating Jews from Asian and African backgrounds and Jews from Europe, collectively "Ashkenazim." In that context, MABAT leaders saw a great advantage in partnering with their more affluent northern Moroccans abroad, who had already gained a different reputation in Israeli public discourse as better off but less organized (see chap. 5).

Beyond stimulating excitement at the opportunity to reunite with old friends and relatives from around the world, the 1983 congress was thus aimed at promoting awareness among MABAT's members that they were part of a global community, not just a small, marginalized Moroccan group in Israel. This can be seen as a response to world hierarchies between "affluent Jews in the West" and "Eastern Jews in distress." This attitude aligned with the view of critics who claimed that the raucous Israeli Mimouna celebrations disrespected the historical and present-day traditional practices of Moroccan Jews outside of Israel. A few years later, in his interview for the radio show *Aadas y Adafinas*, Shlomo Ben-Ami, then Israel's ambassador to Spain who was himself regarded as a success story of the Tangier Jewish community, explained the important role of Hispanic Moroccan communities outside of Israel in helping Moroccans in Israel take pride in their past. By enhancing international research into that past, the community could show that its Moroccan identity was not solely defined by, and in fact went far beyond, the Israeli context.[18]

MABAT'S GLOBALIZING NETWORK

The motivation for maintaining transnational collaboration can also be analyzed from the perspective of domestic organizations in the other destination countries that began to work with MABAT in the 1980s. Unlike in Israel, North African immigration to France was more diverse and included both Muslims and Jews. The May 1968 student riots across France brought new awareness and sensitivity to the diversity of ethnic and cultural groups in French society, as well as to political activism. One of the first associations established in France by Algerian Jews demanded rapid integration into French society. The same was not true, however, for the smaller groups of Jews from Tunisia and Morocco, among whom a large number of hometown associations arose after World War II. For example, among Tunisian Jews, former residents of Sousse (1979), Béja (1980), La Goulette (1984), Ariana (1985), Jerba (1986), Bizerte (1993), Le Kef (1994), Gabès (1994), Nabeul (1994), and Sfax (1995) established new organizations.[19]

In postcolonial Francophone communities, the term *Sephardi* was broadly defined to include the Judeo-Arab, Berber, and even Francophone colonial cultures of North African Jews as part of the construction of nostalgic narratives intended to unite these groups as a community. In Francophone communities, the term tended to include Sephardi rites and Mediterranean folkloric traditions such as the hilula that were seen as the post-1492 traditions of expelled Spanish Jews, as opposed to the concrete connection to contemporary Hispanic culture we have seen among northern Moroccans.[20] However, as early as the 1920s, French scholars had played a role in establishing the nostalgic attachment of Sephardi Jews in northern Morocco to Judeo-Spanish culture, despite French colonialism's competition with the Spanish colonial project in Morocco. As mentioned previously, Robert Ricard published one of the earliest works on the emigration of Jews from northern Morocco to Latin America in 1928,[21] and Paul Bénichou (1908–2001), a French writer, critic, and literary historian, studied Haketia among native speakers in the 1940s.[22] Other prominent scholars included Ladino studies scholar Haim Vidal Sphiha[23] and prominent members of the Hispanic Moroccan community including Philip Abensur; Sara Leibovici, a researcher of northern Moroccan oral traditions; and Raphaël Benazeraf, who had been a prominent Zionist leader in Morocco. These figures all continued to engage in academic activity in the aftermath of significant migration from northern Morocco to France.[24]

While the Sephardi revival in France was different from that in Israel and Spain, all three revivals occurred in a similar time frame and were unmistakably connected to one another. Founded two years earlier in Israel, MABAT served as the main inspiration for France-MABATT, which added a second *T* to demonstrate that their organization also represented Tetouan, the second largest urban center in northern Morocco. The French group hoped to strengthen the attachment to Spain, conceptually and concretely, and to promote social networking among northern Moroccan Jews. France-MABATT declared its aspiration to forge new contacts between the scattered Spanish-speaking Moroccan immigrants not only in France and the Iberian Peninsula but also in Israel.[25]

The link between France-MABATT and MABAT in Israel was based not only on the shared historical circumstances of ethnic revival in both countries but also on concrete transnational kinship ties that facilitated the connection and culminated in the founding of France-MABATT. France-MABATT's eventual creation in 1983 was also partly motivated by the Spanish language radio show *Aadas y Adafinas*, mentioned above. In 1981 the recently created RCJ, a Jewish radio station broadcasting in the Paris area, launched a program dedicated to Jewish languages. Aldo Altit, then a director for French national television and originally from the northern Moroccan city of Alcazarquivir, hosted a one-time program for the station dedicated to the community of Jews from northern Morocco. In planning the show, he reached out to Jimmy Pimienta, an immigrant from Tangier, for help collecting cultural material on the community. Based in Paris, Jimmy was strongly influenced by the work that his two siblings in Israel, Gladys and Sidney, were undertaking at the time. Gladys was then working on "Proyecto Folklor" for the Israeli national radio station Kol Yisrael, and Sidney was collecting material for a genealogical project. Jimmy took advantage of his occasional family and professional trips to Israel, Spain, and Morocco to conduct a series of interviews. His extraordinary endeavor eventually yielded almost 300 hours of unique recordings spanning, among other places, Paris, Madrid, Caracas, Tel Aviv, and even Tangier itself—the vast majority of them in Spanish (see Introduction).

France-MABATT was eventually established in 1983 by Aldo Altit, Philip Abensur, and Jimmy Pimienta as they headed to Israel to participate in MABAT's congress. In the same year, France-MABATT issued its first publication, the anthology *Nuestras Bodas en Tetuán*, edited by Sara Leibovici in the preparation for the 1983 congress in Tel Aviv. It is a compilation of historical essays, ranging over a century and a half, that treat the topic of wedding traditions celebrated in Tetouan.[26] While the founding of France-MABATT was explicitly dependent on the ethnic circumstances that led to the founding of MABAT in Israel, it also came to enrich the Israel-based organization through the transnational ties both organizations forged.

AS FAR AS THE NORTH AMERICAN EDGE

Though effectively functioning as hubs for world Jewry in the late twentieth century, Canada and the US were among the last countries incorporated into the global network of northern Moroccan Jewish activism. A relatively large population center began to take shape in Montreal against the backdrop of developments in Israel and France. In Montreal, Spanish-speaking Moroccan Jews were a smaller minority of only a few hundred families within a larger Sephardi community of almost twenty thousand Jews in the 1980s, still the largest concentration of MENA Jews in Canada, of which North African Jews comprised a majority. In the Francophone province of Quebec, the French rather than the Spanish component of North Africans' pre-immigration colonial history dominated their immigration and integration experiences.[27]

Like other Francophone immigrants, immigrants from northern Morocco found themselves participating in the local struggle between Anglophones and Francophones over the cultural identity of Quebec. Since the late nineteenth century, the Jewish community had been led by Yiddish-speaking Eastern European Jews, who adopted English as their main language of communication outside of the community. The arrival of Francophone Jews in the 1960s began to split the community on linguistic-cultural issues, in addition to intensifying the Sephardi-Ashkenazi divide. A minority of Francophone Jews began to share the views of Quebecois nationalists that saw Quebec as the home of a Francophone nation under British and American imperialism.[28] Most saw Quebec's nationalist Francization project as beneficial to them, even if they did not support the goal of Quebec's separation from Canada. The Moroccan communal institutions mostly used French as their language of communication, and Francophone culture was integrated into Sephardi identity.

Among postcolonial Francophone Jews, the term *Sephardi* was broadly defined to include the Judeo-Arab, Amazigh, and Francophone colonial cultures of North African Jews. For example, the local version of the Semana Sefardí developed by the Latin American branch of the World Sephardi Federation (WSF) was called Semaine Sépharade and later Quinzaine Sépharade, which, in Montreal, included a variety of cultural orientations that incorporated Sephardi traditions and Francophone culture. The Soirée Orientale, for example, was a gala benefit for a synagogue or community center that featured popular Middle Eastern music.[29]

It was in this diverse ethnic context that activities in Montreal emphasizing the separate Hispanic identity of Jewish immigrants from northern Morocco took shape. The native Spanish language of Jews from northern Morocco came to represent a unique *lieu de memoire* for hometown memories, often reverberating in the form of musical performance and intellectual inquiry into Hispanic-Iberian origins via the study of Haketia and Judeo-Spanish romances. *La Voix Sépharade* (known as *Présence* between 1969 and 1978), the main Sephardi publication in Canada since its inception, was issued in Montreal. The journal was intended for MENA Jews and the wider audience of Quebecois readers and was the only platform through which northern Moroccan Jews could reach the community.

As mentioned in chapter 2, Zarita Nahón was among the first to collect Spanish ballad songs from the community after graduating from Columbia in 1929. Some forty-six years later, another community member, Oro Anahory Librowicz, also a Columbia graduate, was doing the same thing, exemplifying the continuity of colonial practices of Sephardi revival well into the postcolonial era. Born in Tetouan in 1948, Anahory Librowicz enrolled at Columbia in 1970, where she received her PhD from the Spanish and Portuguese Department four years later. Supervised by Hispanist Samuel G. Armistead, her research focused on romances—much like the work of Zarita Nahón, who had made a similar journey to Columbia University in 1929. Between 1970 and 1973, Anahory Librowicz retraced the footsteps of Spanish Moroccan immigrants who had resettled in Caracas, Madrid, Málaga, Marbella, Montreal, and New York. This project yielded a collection of 292 texts. In 1973, Anahory Librowicz moved to Montreal, and from there she continued her fieldwork, collecting traditional Judeo-Spanish songs in Spain, Venezuela, Canada, New York, and Israel.[30]

Another prominent figure in the ethnic revival of Canada's Hispanic Moroccan Jews was Solly Lévy from Tangier, Anahory Librowicz's teacher from the AIU in Tetouan. Another mediator between academic research and community formation was Judith Cohen, an Ashkenazi Montrealer then working on a dissertation about Sephardi ballad songs. In 1981, Anahory Librowicz and Lévy teamed up in Montreal. Together with Cohen and Kelly Sultán Amar, originally from Melilla, they formed a musical group called Gerineldo. The name of the group came from the Sephardi version of a Carolingian ballad in which a royal page sleeps with the king's daughter. The page's good luck gives rise to the uniquely Moroccan Sephardi expression "El mazal de Gerineldo" ("The luck of Gerineldo"). In addition to playing music, Gerineldo staged original plays in Haketia written by Solly Lévy. In the 1980s and early 1990s, Gerineldo performed several times a year for community institutions and Hispanic studies departments in North America, Israel, Spain, France, and Latin America, coupling the performances with academic sessions led by Anahory Librowicz and Cohen.[31] The Hispanic dialect of Haketia was thus presented to the larger

Moroccan community even in Francophone environments where Spanish was not widely spoken. Lévy translated stories into a "Haketizied" French in order to capture the humorous characteristics of Haketia. A small but enthusiastic group worked to disseminate Haketia culture within Montreal's Sephardi community and beyond.

As in France, here too, local activities among the northern Moroccan community in the 1980s were influenced by global development abroad, primarily in Israel. One of few articles concerning the Hispanic Moroccan Jewish community in *La Voix Sépharade*'s addressed the establishment of a new organization of Spanish-speaking Moroccan Jews in Canada in preparation for the MABAT congress in August 1983. The author, Clémence Lévy, reported that 150 people from Argentina, Venezuela, Canada, France, Spain, and Switzerland, as well as some 400 Israelis, had gathered in Israel for an "unprecedented assembly" of Spanish-speaking Moroccan Jews. The event was described both as an emotional personal encounter with kinsmen who were now scattered across the globe and as an expression of the global strength of a unified Hispanic Moroccan community. Lévy summarized, "We gathered in Tel Aviv with the aim not only of maintaining and strengthening contact with friends and relatives scattered around the world, but also preserving and salvaging the beautiful linguistic, cultural, liturgical, and folk traditions of our ancestors; fighting together for the migration (of Spanish Moroccan Jews) to Israel; creating a MABAT House in Jerusalem; organizing a scholarship fund for students; [and] creating MABAT groups in different countries or cities worldwide."[32] Lévy then focused on the exhibition held at Beit Hatfutsot during the MABAT congress in Tel Aviv, recalling how it featured lectures on "Spanish romances of the golden age" and Haketia. She ended her essay by urging the Spanish-speaking Moroccan Jews from Toronto and Vancouver who had come together on Israeli soil to join with the Montreal group and form what she explicitly called "MABAT-Canada."[33]

An article in *La Voix Sépharade* titled "Gerineldo en Israël" reported on the group's performance during the MABAT congress. The concert took place at the Ramada Continental in Tel Aviv and was attended by a large audience that included the Canadian consul and his wife. Gerineldo also performed a farewell play at Tel Aviv University's Bar Shira Amphitheater. A letter in Haketia read by Solly Lévy brought forth fits of laughter, and the event concluded with an authentic Sephardi wedding. Lévy remarked that after performing in Tel Aviv, Gerineldo planned to continue to Madrid, Barcelona, Paris, and Geneva.[34] Visiting Israel for the 1983 congress, Anahory Librowicz used the time to conduct additional interviews in Israel, which became a node on her global fieldwork map. The community in Israel was influenced by the development in Canada but also had its own influence on the development of the activities among their brethren in Montreal.

A body called MABAT-Canada has never been officially established, but as in France, transnational ties with the Israeli group were established around the 1983 MABAT congress and continued well into the 1990s. Gerineldo returned to Israel in 1992, for example. The Sephardi Educational Center of Jerusalem, created by a Los Angeles–based businessman, sponsored another performance at Hebrew Union College in Jerusalem. This episode, just one among many, demonstrates how Sephardi songs traveled across the global diaspora and assumed a transnational quality even as their circulation was occasioned by activity in the Israeli hub.[35] The way that smaller organizations and individuals on the move transmitted the community's heritage across North America can be illustrated by developments in New York and in Toronto.

In Toronto, home to about five thousand Jews from Tangier, the northern Moroccan community revolved mainly around religious activities and less with other forms of folkloric practice, even though the number of Tangier natives in Ontario was greater than in Montreal. The Ontario Sephardi Association, in collaboration with the Canadian Sephardi Federation (Fédération Sépharde Canadienne), organized the first Ontario Sephardi Week in Toronto from June 18–24, 1984. A performance of Judeo-Spanish songs by the Montreal-based Gerineldo group was included alongside a variety of representations of other MENA cultures, together with a lecture by Sara Leibovoci on her 1983 book issued by France-MABATT.[36]

As for New York, one of the pioneering institutions promoting the incorporation of Sephardi studies into Jewish studies in the US during the 1960s was the Edmond Safra Institute of Sephardi Studies at Yeshiva University, directed by Rabbi Mitchell Serels, one of the leading advocates for the Spanish-speaking Moroccan community in New York. Originally from Tangier, Serels also became the founding rabbi in 1984 of the Magen David Sephardic Congregation in New York, a synagogue serving Tangier Jews.

In 1985, Serels teamed up with John Stern, a German Jew who had found refuge in Tangier as a child during World War II. Together they founded a small New York–based organization informally known as MABAT-USA (though officially it was called Aficoman).[37] Alia Stern, John's spouse and the daughter of Rebbí Moshé Azancot, who served the Jewish community of Tangier until the 1990s, produced nostalgic writing about her hometown.[38] MABAT-USA, as it was called in unpublished documents, held occasional meetings and followed in the footsteps of its Israeli and French counterparts by hosting academics like Susan Gilson Miller. Rabbi Serels then relocated to Toronto to serve as rabbi of Petah Tikvah Anshe Castilla Synagogue, a newly established Sephardi synagogue in the Downsview neighborhood that conducted services in both Spanish and English.

ENTWINED HOMELANDS

In 1986, amid the geopolitical developments that would enable the return trip undertaken by MABAT members in 1987, Gladys and Sidney Pimienta traveled back to their hometown of Tangier in preparation for their final immigration to Israel. They eventually decided to stay in Tangier until 1989, when they finally left for Israel.[39] Having already engaged in heritage preservation activities in Israel for MABAT and the Ladino section of Kol Yisrael they continued to work in Tangier for Beit Hatfutsot in Tel Aviv, collecting and preserving Spanish ballad songs, this time on Moroccan soil. Tourists from Israel and elsewhere who visited Tangier, since its opening to Israeli passport holders, and were interested in the Jewish community would pay them a visit, including scholars like Harvard's Susan Gilson Miller and Alegría Bendelac. In July 1987, when the MABAT group traveled to Morocco accompanied by musicologist Shoshana Weich Shahak, they reunited with the Pimientas. Weich Shahak used the trip as an ethnographic opportunity to record participants. Jimmy Pimienta, who at the time served as France-MABATT's vice president, also used his trips to Tangier to reunite with old friends and family and to conduct ethnographic fieldwork, producing hours upon hours of recordings.[40]

At the crossroads of global events during the 1992 quincentennial, Spanish diplomats helped disseminate the call for "reconciliation" to the small Jewish community that remained on Moroccan soil. A circular issued by the community council in 1991 announced that Spain's consulate in Tangier had reached out to the Jewish community to inform them that the Ministry of Foreign Affairs would provide fifteen scholarships to Sephardi individuals interested in pursuing advanced studies in the history of Spain. The circular instructed interested parties to obtain more information from the Jewish community's central office. Even in the absence of a youthful population and an actual congregation, Abraham Azencot, last president of the community, devoted himself to preserving the attachment to Spain as the global network of the community was gaining momentum elsewhere.[41]

By then, France-MABATT's place in the globalizing network of preservation organizations had become more prominent as it prepared to present an exhibit as part of the Sefarad '92 project, the event that opened this book. Planning to tour the exhibit throughout France and Switzerland, the organizers teamed up with Momy Levi. Jimmy Pimienta had moved to Brussels by then but continued to work closely with his partners in Israel to launch additional projects.[42] These and other active members of the diaspora were highly mobile individuals whose movement helped crystallize and fortify a communal network that transcended national and regional borders, as well as ethnic and linguistic contexts, using their Spanish background to define the uniqueness of their Moroccan Jewish identities.

In closing, let me refer to the words presented in the introduction to this book, by Abraham Hassan Cohen, France-MABATT's president, in his speech at the Spanish embassy in Paris on July 5, 1990. During a planning session for the upcoming Sefarad '92 conference, a part of the international quincentennial celebrations, he maintained that Jews from northern Morocco in their global diasporas are in "a better position than anyone else to promote this reunion." This twist to the overall tendency to romanticize the Jewish past in pre-1492 Iberia cannot be fully explained without considering the matrix of international links that shaped the new diaspora and the mutual influences of local and global developments through their hubs in the twentieth century.

We must consider additionally the Hispanic cultural traits and linguistic capabilities that enable Jews in Spain and Latin America, but also in Israel, Morocco, and the non–Spanish-speaking countries of North America and Europe, to build connections with contemporary Spain and utilize Spanish as a lingua franca to forge their distinct global network that connects them as Spanish-speaking Jews. At the same time, we must also consider Hassan Cohen's assertion that dwelling on their Hispanic identity did not mean they should shy away from their Moroccan background, but only imbue it with complexity—an amalgam of identities that transcended regional and national identities such as Israelis, Spaniards, or Moroccans.

EPILOGUE

ON THE MOVE AGAIN

The turn of the twenty-first century witnessed new developments that significantly influenced the environments in which major hubs of the global Hispanic Moroccan Jewish community appealed to their existing members and attempted to attract new ones. Following the election of Venezuelan president Hugo Chávez in 1998 and the inauguration of the Fifth Venezuelan Republic in December 1999, Venezuela witnessed what is considered one of the worst economic crises in modern Latin American history. According to the International Monetary Fund, local gross domestic product declined by 35 percent between 2013 and 2017. The economic crisis led to unprecedented political instability and a strong sense of personal insecurity, resulting in the emigration of millions of Venezuelans in the largest exodus South America has witnessed in the twenty-first century. According to the International Organization for Migration (IOM), between 2015 and 2017, the number of Venezuelan nationals living abroad increased by 900 percent.[1] The first to leave the country were the upper class, intellectuals, and professionals, followed by the middle class in the 2010s. Consequently, the number of Jews in Venezuela shrunk from around 22,000 in 1999 to roughly 9,500 in 2011, although exact figures are difficult to ascertain.[2]

Despite some variations in motivations for emigration, the exodus of Venezuelan Jews ought to be understood as part of the broader tragic exile of Venezuelans. Together with their fellow compatriots, Jews have been relocating to the US—mainly to the southern Floridian area, with its clear Hispanic presence—and to destinations in Europe and the Caribbean, most prominently Spain and Panama. Those who stayed on suffered from devaluated properties and often relentless fear from criminal attacks. In 2016 alone, tens of thousands of Venezuelans fled to Colombia, Brazil, Ecuador, and Peru; Peru even offered a special visa plan for Venezuelans. While most Venezuelan Jews who left at first preferred the US and Panama, Israel was a destination uniquely accessible to them via the country's Law of Return, which since 1950 has granted the right to immigrate and acquire Israeli citizenship to Jews worldwide. Those who moved to Israel were also entitled to financial assistance from the government for six months through an immigration "absorption package." In 2017, Israel began to treat Venezuelan Jews as a Jewry in distress (see chap. 5) and therefore sent emissaries to facilitate their immigration, though not without a tight background check of their Jewish origins.[3]

For those Hispanic Moroccan Jews who resided in Venezuela before leaving for the US and Israel, while more space has been made for their Venezuelan and Latin American identities, the Moroccan and Sephardi components of their identities have been reduced to the performance of religious rituals and the recounting of historical anecdotes. Hispanic Moroccan Jews immigrating from Venezuela are now being perceived and treated in their destination countries, by Jews and non-Jews alike, as ethnically *Latinx*.[4] Even in Israel, where a large Moroccan community exists, the community of Moroccan Jews from Venezuela is organized first and foremost around their shared experience of displacement from Venezuela and their concerns about the crisis in that country.[5]

In Miami-Dade County, Hispanic Moroccan Jews share space with thousands of other Moroccan Jews. Originally from the southern parts of Morocco, approximately ten thousand Moroccan Jews and their descendants migrated to Florida since the 1960s from Canada, France, Israel, and Morocco itself. Scattered across multiple sites in Miami-Dade and beyond, Moroccan Jews lack a central community body like the one they used to have in Venezuela, for example, and they tend to affiliate with one of the ten small Moroccan synagogues or with other synagogues nearby their place of residence. Some choose to affiliate with a synagogue based on the primary languages spoken by the majority of its members—French, English, Hebrew, or Spanish—rather than basing their choice on traditions or rites.[6]

In Miami, even the synagogue where older Moroccan rituals are usually preserved has become a "melting pot" for Latin American Jewish identities, including Venezuelans, Mexicans, Argentinians, Colombians, and Cubans, in a way that both sharpens national differences and highlights regional commonalities. Miami's Jewish Community Center and its Hispanophone Skylake Synagogue, a majority of whose members are Venezuelan Jews, are two prominent examples of sites where a variety of religious rituals originating in different

European and Middle Eastern communities of origin, including Morocco, are often melded into a single Latin American identity.[7]

While what it means to be Hispanic for Moroccan Jews in the US, Europe, and Israel has shifted at the turn of the century, the communal consciousness, organizations, and state-led projects that, since the early twentieth century, helped develop the unified story of origins in Spain still persist and evolve. As always, hypermobility can work both ways, strengthening one's northern Moroccan identity in a specific context and making it completely invisible in another. In 2018, for example, representatives from Sephardi communities in Argentina, Brazil, Canada, Chile, Colombia, Mexico, Miami, Peru, and Venezuela gathered for a FeSeLa reunion in Miami to pay tribute to Moisés Garzón Serfaty's activity on behalf of "Sephardi and Zionist" cultures in Latin America. Garzón Serfaty, the longtime leader of the Sephardi-Moroccan community in Venezuela, whose activities have been discussed throughout this book, resettled in Panama in 2016. At the FeSeLa meeting, Panama was added to the continental organization for the first time, in part because of his relocation there.[8] While the meeting focused on expressing solidarity with Venezuelan Jews, it also served as a platform to plan celebrations for the State of Israel's seventieth anniversary and the 120th anniversary of the first Zionist Congress, and to promote "heritage trips" to Morocco and the Iberian Peninsula.[9]

Moreover, even as new nodes in the diasporic network develop in Panama and Miami, Caracas has not become irrelevant. While many Venezuelan Jews have left their country, the Centro de Estudios Sefradíes de Caracas (Center for Sephardi Studies of Caracas) (CESC) is still producing an impressive amount of material on the history and culture of Hispanic Moroccan Jews and their attachments to Morocco, Spain, and Sepharad. In 2013, for instance, the Museo Sefardí de Caracas, established in 1999 with funds from Morris E. Curiel of Curaçao, held an exhibition entitled "De Noráfrica Venimos: Judíos de Marruecos en Tierra de Gracia" ("From North Africa We Came: Jews from Morocco in a Land of Grace") in collaboration with the CESC. The "land of grace" refers to Venezuela, as a country conceived in the collective narrative—from the early twentieth century onward—as a haven for Jews in distress (see chaps. 3, 5, and 6).

Unlike in previous decades, however, this exhibition was cosponsored by the Moroccan embassy in Caracas, which saw the Moroccan community in Venezuela, even as it was undergoing tremendous displacement, as one of its most significant diasporic agents in Latin America at the turn of the millennium. At an event held at the Maripérez Synagogue, the guest of honor was Ibrahim Musa, Morocco's ambassador to the Dominican Republic.

In the post-September 11, 2001, era, marked by increased discourse divisions between "Western" and "Islamic" civilizations, this new connection between the Moroccan kingdom and the Jewish Sephardi community in Venezuela emerged within the broader global trend of renewed fascination with the myth of interfaith coexistence in Al-Andalus as a form of resistance to Western, particularly American, imperialism. This revival gained popularity among marginalized groups in the West and across the postcolonial world, with Venezuela standing out as a particularly notable example. To demonstrate his solidarity with the modern Arab world in the aftermath of September 11, Chávez embraced the narrative of historical connections between indigenous Venezuelans, who fell under the dominion of white European Spanish colonialism, and the Andalusian Arabs expelled from Spain. This resonance extended beyond specific segments of Venezuelan society, including mestizos and Blacks, and allowed Chávez to establish stronger political and economic ties with non-Arab Middle East and North Africa (MENA) nations, such as Iran.[10]

However, it is essential to acknowledge that the political realities and interests in Latin America and the MENA region are far from homogeneous and simplistic, as exemplified by the strengthening ties between Morocco and the Venezuelan Jewish Sephardi community. In fact, Morocco had pulled out its ambassador to Caracas in 2009, after Venezuela's overt support for the Polisario's nationalist claims over the Western Sahara. Perhaps in reaction, cultural ties with the Moroccan monarchy were still considered significant in the eyes of the Hispanic Moroccan community's leadership in Caracas, who continuously claimed Jewish roots in Iberia (see chap. 6). Remarkably, they were also deemed valuable in the eyes on the Moroccan state, which sent its diplomatic representatives to an event preserving the culture of the Jewish community outside of Morocco and even helped sponsor the event in a country with which it had cut diplomatic ties.[11]

THE RETURN OF SPAIN, AGAIN

The persisting cultural production in the Caribbean region, even when circumstances of migration have been significantly altered by political and economic turmoil, ought to be explained by probing—once again—regional and global developments in the community network of Hispanic Moroccan Jews, both from diachronic and synchronic perspectives.

Concurrently with the mass emigration of Venezuelan Jews and the creation of new hubs, on the other side of the Atlantic, Spain underwent significant political changes that further enhanced the traditional role played by this country in the formation of the global Hispanic Moroccan Jewish community. A series of events following the election of Prime Minister José Luis Rodríguez Zapatero in April 2004 spotlighted Jews as emblematic of the country's post-Franco democratic and multicultural development since 1975. This was reflected in the emergence of a number of new Spanish publishing houses, including the Hebraica Madrid association, the Spinoza Foundation, and the Hebraica Bookshop-Editorial, among others.[12]

One of the most active participants in those developments was Jacobo Israel Garzón. Born in Tetouan in 1942, Garzón moved to Madrid in 1965, where he became a businessman. As the editor of *Raíces* from 1994 to 2005, and the president of la Federación de Comunidades Judías de España from 2003, he produced a great deal of material that was disseminated through the global network of scholars and community leaders. Between 2003 and 2018, he published some of the most important books on the history of Jews in Spain and northern Morocco.[13]

As Venezuela's role in the community's cultural production has declined over the past twenty years, Israel-based writers have, since the turn of the millennium, produced some of the most prominent literary and academic works on Hispanic Moroccan Jews, including but not limited to those of the Tetouan-born, Jerusalem-based writer Mois Benharroch and the folklorist Nina Pinto-Abecasis.[14] The work in Israel was directly connected to the founding of new institutions in Spain that were aimed at advancing collaboration on Sephardi matters between the countries. The 2006 founding of the Casa Sefarad-Israel (the Sepharad-Israel House) in Madrid by the Spanish Ministry of Foreign Affairs illustrates how the impetus for publishing in Spain coincided with the creation of new official institutions connecting the two major hubs of Hispanic Moroccan Jewry.[15] Beyond linking Spain and Israel, Casa Sefarad-Israel has promoted international initiatives to help maintain and disseminate the story of the Hispanic Moroccan Jewish diaspora through a global Sephardi network. The Erensya (Heritage) Summit, sponsored by Casa Sefarad-Israel and organized every two years in a different Sephardi hub—including Sophia, Istanbul, Madrid, Mexico City, Seattle, and Washington—has become an important new network in the twenty-first century. The Caracas-based Néstor Garrido, current editor of *Maguén*, and Solly Lévy from Montreal have taken on the role of representing Haketia and Hispanic Moroccan culture at the Erensya summits.[16]

Beyond the creation and dissemination of new material, the global reach of Spain's efforts to reinvigorate Sephardi culture has had an important influence on the community's ability to appeal to new members. In December 2015, the

Muslim population of Spain, many of whom were Moroccans, was 1,887,906 people, or 4 percent of the country's total population. The Jewish population was much smaller—somewhere between 12,000 and 40,000 people in 2011.[17] Jacobo Israel Garzón estimated that between 60 and 65 percent of Spanish Jews are of northern Moroccan heritage, and 30 percent have a Latin American background. Comprising a tiny fraction of Spain's roughly forty-seven million inhabitants, Hispanic Moroccan Jews as an ethnic-religious group in Spain are practically invisible, and, as Martina L. Weisz has noted, they are still typically viewed, as any other Jewish group in the country, as an "abstract element belonging to a distant past."[18]

This perception culminated in a 2015 nationality law that granted the right of full citizenship to Sephardi Jews worldwide as a means of "historical reconciliation." The same right was pointedly not granted to North African Muslim descendants of Iberian expellees.[19] Similar to Israel's Law of Return, the Spanish law took ethno-national background as a criterion for immigration and citizenship, which, in this case, also conferred European Union citizenship. Coinciding with the Venezuelan economic and political crisis and the mass departure of thousands of Venezuelan Jews, the 2015 law provided a practical impetus for "acting on" one's Sephardi roots in Iberia, just as the Israeli Law of Return motivated many unaffiliated Jewish Venezuelans to act on their Jewish backgrounds while considering migration.

In 2015, Venezuela, where most Sephardim were of Moroccan heritage, was second only to Mexico in the number of applications for Spanish citizenship under the new law (6,601 Venezuelans versus 6,975 Mexicans).[20] The pursuit of Spanish citizenship dominated the agenda of old Sephardi networks like FeSeLa, which now worked as avidly to help Moroccan and other Sephardi Jews acquire Spanish passports as it did to promote immigration to Israel.[21] Spain found itself again in the early twenty-first century in a position of casting its political authority to defend the interests of Sephardi Jews in the diaspora, and its agents for that matter were prominent members of the global Hispanic Moroccan Jewish community who helped individuals acquire Spanish nationality.

Back in Venezuela, new figures such as genealogist Blanca de Lima; José Chocrón Cohén, a lawyer of Moroccan descent; and Saadia Cohén Zrihen, a businessman of Hispanic Moroccan Jewish heritage, began to lay the groundwork for this new reaffirmation of Sephardi roots, even a few years before the 2015 law was passed. In 2009 and 2010, Casa Melilla (discussed in chap. 7) prepared Spanish naturalization charts for Hispanic Moroccans Jews. Around four hundred people received Spanish citizenship through its mediation.[22]

In Israel in particular, Sephardi origins were broadly defined for the purpose of the law. Jews whose lineage traced back to a variety of MENA countries, and who had maintained Sephardi rituals or surnames, including many from "southern Morocco," became eligible to apply. Thus, the law did not officially distinguish between Jews from northern Morocco and those from other parts of the country. It did, however, define Sephardi origins through cultural continuity, measured by proficiency in a (Judeo-)Spanish language. In Israel, then, many applicants from non–Spanish speaking backgrounds were required to pass a "Spanish test." For that reason, many who wished to apply only for the purpose of acquiring an EU passport pursued the "Portuguese alternative," which did not require any knowledge of Portuguese.[23] While passing the Spanish test was a nonissue for the first generation of Hispanic Moroccan Jews in Venezuela, many of whom had a non-Sephardi parent, it was more of an obstacle for the second and third generations in Israel and for Sephardim who did not come from a Hispanophone background.

The Federation of Jewish Communities in Spain eventually reached an agreement with certain activists and academic institutions in Israel to aid applicants looking to prove their Sephardi origins and acquire basic knowledge of Spanish (or Ladino or Haketia). Responsibility for teaching Haketia was assumed by academic centers that had long encouraged its study in Israel, including the Salty Center and the Gaon Center, whose Haketia programs predated the enactment of the law. The first Israeli recipient of Spanish citizenship was a descendant of Jewish immigrants from Tetouan.[24] In fact, the main person responsible for promoting and mediating applications was Rabbi Benito Garzón, a Tetouan native and the former chief rabbi of Spain (mentioned in chap. 6), who moved to Israel in 2013. From his new place of residence, Rabbi Garzón helped facilitate applications alongside other members of the Hispanic Moroccan Jewish community in Israel. In Jerusalem, the World Sephardi Congress, created and financed by a simultaneously Moroccan, Venezuelan, and Floridian donor, also processed applications.[25]

As the Hispanic Moroccan centers of global activity shifted at the turn of the millennium, the community in Brazil also began to play a growing role in preserving Hispanic Moroccan Jewish heritage. In April 2002, journalist and cantor David Salgado founded in Belém *Amazônia Judaica*, a community newsletter that transformed in 2010 into a mouthpiece of the Centro de Estudos Judaicos da Amazônia (CEJA). Run by Elias Salgado, David's brother, much of the center's activity is placed on setting archival collections for the histories of Jews in the Amazon basin, with a focus on northern Moroccan

Jews.²⁶ A specific focus is placed on Haketia preservation, as exemplified by the 2021 Haquitìa Festival, Zejút Abot, organized by the center. The twentieth anniversary of the foundation of *Amazônia Judaica* was marked by a special Haketia Corner, "El Rincón de la Haquitìa," led by Yehuda Benguigui, a physician who dedicates much of his time to Haketia preservation.²⁷ With the issuing of the 2015 laws, the CEJA became a small bridgehead for those Jews seeking to stress their Sephardi roots. Paulo Valadares, member of the CEJA committee and coauthor of the *Dictionary of Sephardi Surnames*, provides genealogical information that helps prove Sephardi origins for the purpose of the law.²⁸

In Morocco, the Cervantes Institute in Tangier has played a prominent role in the resurgence of Hispanized Haketia cultures since the 1990s, though not without local challenges. In 2014, in collaboration with the Centro Sefarad-Israel in Madrid, Cervantes in Tangier organized an exhibition titled "Los Hispano judíos de Marruecos." This event, intended to celebrate the cultural ties between Moroccan Jews and Spain, encountered protests. The central issue arose from the event's perceived pro-Israel sentiment, but also from the portrayal of Hispanic Moroccan Jews as being more akin to Europeanized Spaniards than North Africans. The latter categorization in particular was viewed by some Moroccan activists working to preserve Jewish Moroccan heritage as misplaced and an affront to these Jews' deeply rooted North African identities.²⁹ This evolving dispute over the (self-) categorization of Hispanic Moroccan Jews reveals the intricate interplay of identity, culture, and geopolitics at the turn of the millennium, and the persisting challenges in defining and preserving cultural identities in an increasingly interconnected world. The question of how this community is labeled within the context of Spanish cultural institutions not only influences the community's self-perception but also highlights the complex relationship between Moroccan and Spanish heritage as it has evolved in the twenty-first century.

Finally, on the cusp of concluding this book project, in the summer of 2022 I was invited by Paul Dahan, for decades an enthusiastic collector of archival material on Moroccan Jews, to participate in the creation of a new center for the research of northern Moroccan Jews, tentatively titled Centre de Recherche et Archives sur le Judaïsme du Nord du Maroc. Founded in Tangier with the explicit aim of making the city its primary hub, this center aims to forge a new network of Jewish and Muslim scholars and community leaders from various parts of the northern Moroccan Jewish diaspora. This project serves as another example of the evolving role of historical centers within this diaspora and its networks, continually generating new initiatives to foster stronger connections between the community and its Moroccan homeland in the twenty-first century.[30]

These developments on both the local and global scale, particularly the migration of Venezuelan Jews to Israel in recent decades (some of whom are my family members), and the growing academic interest in Haketia at the turn of the millennium—still strong at the moment of this book's completion—have played a role in shaping this book. They helped me appreciate how the local and the global, the individual and the macropolitical, research and community, are all concepts mediated by networks and practices that perpetually strive to make sense of modern diasporas. These ideas and their implications for scholarship will be addressed in the next section, Conclusions.

CONCLUSIONS

IN BOTH ACADEMIC AND POPULAR NARRATIVES, Jews, Armenians, and Greeks have long served as *archetypal* diasporic communities, characterized by the prevailing myth of returning to their ancestral homeland from various locations. Nevertheless, the contemporary histories of these diasporas, as of most modern diasporas, reveal significant phenomena of hybridization and internal divisions, shaped by the increasing interactions among different communities and underscored by their connections to multiple centers and global networks. Their processes of "homecoming" have also given rise to intricate intra-diaspora hierarchies, exemplified by instances such as the discrimination Mizrahi Jews faced in Israel or the challenges the *Akhpars* who were "repatriated" to Soviet Armenia experienced.[1]

Related key ideas shaping this book's analytical approach have been that increasing mobility and the related breaking of the "ghetto's walls" among organic communities who shared a common space brings about a propensity to reorganize based on nostalgic and romanticized appeals to a communal past, and that growing global solidarity and interconnectivity also create and foster new intra-diasporic hierarchies. As I have shown, these processes worked together to restructure the mechanism of diaspora-making among the small region-of-origin community of Hispanic Moroccan Jews in the eras of colonialism, increased migration, and nationalism.

As I argued, the *disadvantages* of being and becoming a small and distinct group in the context of colonialism and migration were proactively turned into *advantages* through the search for border-crossing comradeships and related narratives about shared pasts in multiple places. From this perspective, this study has attempted to advance a nuanced understanding of multilayered and multi-sited diasporas and their mechanism of mobilization, with specific implications for the research into Middle East and North Africa (MENA) Jewish and Sephardi diasporas.

Despite the vast and growing body of research on nineteenth- and twentieth-century MENA Jews, the relevant scholarship has not been oriented toward an understanding of MENA Jews as members of transregional diasporas, and even less as members of multi-sited diasporas that persisted beyond the middle of the twentieth century, with the evolving implications of nationalism and global migration. More specifically, Zionism and immigration to Israel are too often treated separately from analyses of the global Sephardi and MENA diaspora in their various regional hubs outside of Israel. Most studies that address the dynamics of diaspora-making and the related multiplicity of homelands look at the transformation of contemporary migrant flows into bipolar "transnational diasporas" that usually leave migrants suspended between two homelands, in the Zionist case as a result of homecoming to Israel.

Looking across time and space at a specific community of Moroccan Jews—the majority of whom once shared the same urban spaces in northern Morocco, and who distinguish themselves from the larger Moroccan Jewish community by adopting a Hispanic identity—the questions and critical approach of this book are different and more comprehensive as far as the search for a sound definition of diaspora is concerned. This book has demonstrated how this process of diaspora-making coalesced smoothly with the dual appeal of Israel and Spain as mythological centers. Community leaders even leveraged the support of both states from afar as a source of community empowerment in the various contexts where Hispanic Moroccan Jews constitute a demographic minority.

Chapters 1, 2, and 3 illustrated different aspects of Sephardi life under Spanish colonialism in North Africa up to the mid-twentieth century, and how the intense encounter with Spain, despite its threat to the Jewish community's precolonial, traditional habits, became a source of community empowerment. Focusing on Tangier and Tetouan, the major urban centers of most Hispanic Moroccan Jews in the first half of the twentieth century, chapter 1 delved deep into how Jews shaped their Hispanic identities through day-to-day interactions with Spaniards and the Hispanophone world. The Jews in the north thus reacted differently to the literary and colonial imagination developed in the Philo-Sephardi discourse than did Sephardi communities in the areas that did not come directly under Spanish colonialism, as in the Ottoman Empire. The intermingling with the Spaniard settler community exposed Jews to modern forms of Spanish, influencing their literary and cultural preferences and, in some cases, even what they ate, how they spent their leisure time, and with whom they engaged in romantic relations, among other aspects. While other European colonial traits, such as French, Italian, and English, were also influential, as a native Judeo-Spanish community, their collective attachment to the Hispanophone world was much simpler and helped them to differentiate themselves from non–Spanish speaking communities.

Nonetheless, colonialism among northern Moroccan Jews launched a dialectical process that helped reaffirm their Jewish Sephardi identities through a form of boundary setting and self-segregation from what was perceived as "too Spanish" or "too colonial." Matrimonies and Jewish dietary laws, for example, helped reaffirm community boundaries vis-à-vis an unprecedented exposure and strong association with Spanish society that, after all, was essentially non-Jewish and threatened Jewish communal traits. With regards to their increased awareness of Sephardi roots, this dialectic boundary-setting process came to reinforce older Hispanic Sephardi identities among northern Moroccan Jews in the context of Spanish colonialism. Looking at developments from the inception of colonialism through Franco's era of fascism and Morocco's independence in 1956, chapter 2 explored the motivations for an associated impulse to document Jewish ancestry in Spain. This process created the notion of a genuine Hispanic Jewish identity that was separate from the non-Jewish Hispanic world and yet celebrated interfaith coexistence. This process was not purely local. Rather, it was instigated by a global network of active community members, ethnographers, and philologists of Haketia invested in these Jews' past in pre-1492 Iberia.

Adopting a global network approach to heritage formation, chapter 3 explored how Jewish migration between northern Morocco and Latin America, beginning in the early nineteenth century, shaped a transregional hometown awareness among Hispanic Moroccan Jews. The first section of the chapter explored nostalgic attachment among Hispanic Moroccan Jews abroad to their hometown communities in northern Morocco and simultaneously their developing of a sense of Moroccaness vis-à-vis other immigrant communities. The next section then offered a new perspective on the way this migration increased the prominence of Latin America in the formation of local Hispanic Jewish identities in northern Morocco from the 1920s through the 1950s. Shaped by transnational ties with the hubs in Venezuela, Argentina, Brazil, and Peru, the notion of a successful migration increased the unique connection of the community to Latin America as a source for local empowerment. Influencing community memory in northern Morocco, "Spanish America" soon become a mythical reference point and a source of pride among Hispanic Moroccan Jews in Morocco. The proliferation of networks between Morocco and Latin

America, also became a factor influencing the self-understanding of communities in northern Morocco, as Jews with "ancestry" in Spain and as agents in the modern Hispanophone world, as discussed in chapters 1 and 2.

By uncovering such developments, this book is among the first to explore the globalization of Moroccan Jews in the context of the Global Hispanophone rather than in the more familiar context of postcolonial migrations from MENA countries to Israel, Western Europe, and North America. With this approach, chapters 4, 5, and 6 continued to challenge the trend in studies of Jewish migration from the MENA region to view as opposed processes the development of Zionism and immigration to Israel on the one hand and the construction of Sephardi diaspora networks and non-Israeli national identities on the other.

In chapter 4, I showed how the rise of Zionism in northern Morocco, beginning in 1900, was consistent with the global dispersion of Hispanic community networks between Morocco and Latin America, as well as in the new hub of Hispanic Moroccan Jews in Casablanca. In all those places, embracing Zionism helped Hispanic Moroccan Jewish leaders consolidate their leadership and empower themselves within global Jewish activism. In northern Morocco under early Spanish colonialism in the 1920s, the entwining of Hispanic identities, including the notion of Sephardi ancestry in Spain, had additional pragmatical motivations: it improved organizational ties with mainland Spain, expanded intracommunal networks of support, and even softened resistance by the colonial regime who, otherwise, like in the French zone, might have treated Zionism as a source for ethnonational disloyalty.

While the first section explored pre-1948 developments, the second part of the chapter turned to forms of continuity. Even when Israel's state agencies worked to leverage Zionism for mass homecoming projects, northern Moroccans left for Israel in the smallest numbers in Morocco, less than a third in the 1960s. As I explained, the long-established interconnectivity between the hubs of the Hispanic Moroccan Jewish diaspora continued to characterize the development of Zionism as a source for community empowerment and connectivity as late as the 1970s. Moreover, in 1956, the year of Moroccan independence, many leaders of the Hispanic Moroccan community who stayed in Morocco expressed their commitment to the Moroccan national project, further stressing in practice how their commitment to Zionism coexisted with other national loyalties, as well as with Philo-Sephardism and affinity to Spain. Crucially, entwining these national identities together helped affirm a sense of continuity in community organization.

In the 1950s through the 1970s, Israel and the Americas had gradually replaced Eastern European, Asian, and African countries as the most prominent demographic and cultural centers of world Jewry. An imagined hierarchy of the Jewish world—built on nineteenth-century divisions of the Jewish (colonial) world into affluent philanthropic Western Jews on the one hand and Eastern Jewries in distress on the other—led to efforts by Israel and North American organizations to "rescue" Jews from Morocco as French and Spanish colonialism drew to a close. The Zionist project at the time was increasingly informed by this ethos that saw Israel as responsible for the fate of world Jewry who "remained" in the diaspora.

Chapter 5 looked at Venezuela, the most prominent postcolonial hub of the Hispanic Moroccan Jewish community in the 1960s and 1970s, to understand how that process affected global northern Moroccan community solidarity. The chapter showed how a new Venezuelan Hispanic Moroccan Jewish narrative placed Venezuela Moroccans higher on the imagined hierarchy, ranking them vis-à-vis Moroccans in Israel and those who stayed in Morocco. Earlier narratives of nineteenth-century economic migration to Latin America and the successful integration of Moroccan Jews in Venezuela continued to serve late twentieth-century intra-diaspora politics and practices of local empowerment. This process also evoked nostalgia for Jewish life in northern Morocco prior to the country's independence and the mass departure of Jews in the aftermath of colonialism. The focus on Venezuela also helped me elucidate how the evolving character of Zionism at the time did not run counter to migration to destinations other than Israel, and to Jewish community building worldwide.

Chapter 6 looked at how the notion of the community's ancestry in Spain permeated these processes of identity construction and globalizing hierarchies in the 1970s through the 1990s. My analyses began by showing how narratives of ancestry in Spain, originally created to serve Spanish colonialism in the late nineteenth through the mid-twentieth centuries, were continuously used by Franco and the post-Francoist Spanish state, from the late 1960s to the 1990s, to rebrand Spain as democratic and thus historically tolerant to Jews (and Muslims). This rebranding helped the Spanish state to strengthen its cultural influence on the Sephardi diaspora outside of Spain—Israel included. The local Jewish leadership in Spain, dominated by northern Moroccans, capitalized on that narrative maintained by the state to smoothen their integration into a new Spanish national discourse but also to reach out to the global community.

At the same time in Venezuela, this updated narrative of Sephardi ancestry in Spain incorporated into Moroccan identities, helping the local Moroccan-led community integrate into the Venezuelan cultural elite who dwelled on related narratives that bridged Latin American and Spanish histories. Altogether the chapter showed how notions of ancestry in Spain continued to interconnect the diaspora, even when the local meanings of being Hispanic Moroccan changed dramatically after most Jews and Spanish settlers had left northern Morocco following independence.

This interconnectivity proved essential for community empowerment, not only among Hispanic Moroccan Jews in Spain and Venezuela but in additional hubs where Spanish culture was less prominent. Chapter 7 was dedicated to the several thousand Spanish Moroccan Jews who emigrated to Israel, where Judeo-Arabic, Judeo-Amazigh, and Maghrebi Francophone cultural traits were far more prominent. While the cultural divides between Hispanic Moroccan Jews and southern Moroccan Jewish communities had roots in pre-immigration Morocco, the fact that the Israeli establishment stereotyped Moroccans as culturally backward intensified the construction of a separate narrative emphasizing ancestral connection to Spain among the Jews of the north.

In Israel, immigrants from northern Morocco were not concentrated in any single location. Scattered throughout the country in dozens of urban and rural sites, leaders of the community appealed to academic institutions to help organize communal events. Through this process, Haketia, with its Arabic, Spanish, and Hebrew components, was employed to portray the community as authentically Moroccan with Spanish traits. It also served to argue that, unlike their southern counterparts, Hispanic Moroccan Jews' European roots had not been artificially imposed by modern French colonialism. As the last section of the chapter showed, this amalgam of identities created a unique transnational tie to contemporary northern Morocco. For instance, the return trip to their hometowns in 1986, as well as projects of preservation undertaken between members of the communities in Israel and those who stayed in Tangier and Spanish-ruled Melilla, all included clear references to modern and pre-1492 Spain as their additional homeland.

While influenced by developments on the global diasporic front, as recounted in chapters 6 and 7, local developments in Israel came to influence the smaller hubs of the Hispanic Moroccan Jewish diaspora as well. Chapter 8 recounted how the Israeli group of community leaders directly influenced the creation of sister organizations in smaller hubs in France, the US, and Canada. Considering transregional hierarchies between the hubs, as exemplified in chapter 5, international collaborations could help the community show that its Moroccan identity was not solely defined by, and in fact went far beyond, the Israeli context.

This chapter also addressed globalizing ties from the perspectives of smaller communities in Europe and North America, stressing how connections between communities in the non–Spanish speaking world benefited the communities in Europe and North America locally. Building on chapter 5, chapter 8 illustrated how a continuous interpretation of Zionism as a global network that benefited community construction also affected MABAT's activity to forge ties with the non-Israeli hubs. By viewing Israel as just one of many prominent nodes on the dynamic map of the globalizing Hispanic Moroccan Jewish diaspora, chapters 7 and 8 add to the literature on transnational Jewish communities in Israel and places them in a closer conversation with Sephardi and diaspora studies alike, rather than exclusively with Jewish and Israel studies.

Altogether, *Entwined Homelands, Empowered Diasporas* has challenged the conventional wisdom that distinguishes the Sephardi diaspora in the Americas from the immigration of North African Jews to Israel, and the related separations between Sephardi (Judeo-Spanish) studies and Mizrahi (including North African) studies, and between modern colonialism and pre-1492 histories in Iberia. In examining the benefits in the multiplicity of homelands for a small, dispersed group, this book advances scholarship on ethnic diasporas. By offering a nuanced perspective on an organic community on the move, particularly in the modern Jewish context, it is among the first studies to draw connections between synchronic and diachronic developments affecting the hubs of micro (hometown) diasporas across a range of sites across the world.

Finally, as many diaspora scholars have argued in recent years, diaspora formation and maintenance require a significant number of scattered participants who adhere to particular logic, even if situationally or in an ad hoc manner. It is through the adherence and devotion to proactive and often highly mobile individuals who assume the task of producing and disseminating a collective story of shared origins that a diaspora is created and maintained.[2]

While looking at how the local hubs engaged with one another, this book's chapters also stress how those engagements were made possible thanks to mobile individuals who traveled between the hubs and to northern Morocco, helping disseminate the narrative about its past. In this book, I showed how multiple stories of shared origins in Israel, Spain, and Latin America, produced in various geographical hubs over the course of a century, became a crucial material that flew through global networks. While read differently across the various diasporic hubs and through the years, those stories served to empower and interconnect a global community and—no less important—differentiate it from others.

This book has focused on histories of the twentieth century and thus excludes many individuals who have taken on the role of generating and disseminating this shared story in the last two decades. However, composed in the twenty-first century, this book has crystalized against the backdrop of international developments and a worldwide communal network that have continued to reshape the global community of Hispanic Moroccan Jews and enhance its interconnectivity, as recounted in the epilogue. Those twenty-first century developments directly affected my own family members who emigrated from Venezuela to the US, as well as the professional networks I have participated in while working on this research since 2009 (see the acknowledgments). These ongoing developments in the new millennium would merit their own research.

ACKNOWLEDGMENTS

AS I CONCLUDE THIS BOOK, it is clearer now than when I first began my research how my work has been influenced by my own position in an increasingly globalized network of northern Moroccan Jews. I reached this conclusion partly while participating in a series of academic events about and for the Hispanic Moroccan Jewish community in Israel, some of which were organized by my late colleague and dear friend Nina Pinto Abecasis. As the daughter of immigrants from Tetouan, Pinto Abecasis had dedicated her academic career to the study and preservation of Haketia in academia and in popular media. "It would be wonderful if the whole world spoke Haketia," she once remarked during a 2015 interview with the Israeli *Haaretz* newspaper, which left an impression on me. "It's a blend of cultures—Jewish, Christian, Arab, Muslim, European and North African—that merge to create a unique harmony," she explained with enthusiasm to the average Israeli reader.[1]

As a third-generation member of the Moroccan Jewish diaspora myself—the son of an immigrant to Israel from Venezuela, whose close family members had left Morocco for Venezuela in the 1950s—I began to feel increasingly curious about this community that I had barely been exposed to as a child. My Venezuelan connection also helped me think about the local developments I witnessed in Israel in more globalized terms. These notions and other related ideas helped me reach the conclusions I have drawn from this study about diaspora-making as an ongoing process intertwined with evolving networks of devoted individuals, including academics and community leaders, who cultivate a diasporic consciousness among dispersed individuals.

As I complete this book, it gives me great pleasure to express my gratitude to the numerous scholars, colleagues, friends, family members, and other dear people, some of whom are vibrant members of the evolving Hispanic Moroccan community who, together and separately, made this almost decade-and-a-half-long research adventure possible.

The seeds for this book were planted in 2008, when I was a PhD candidate in the Department of Middle Eastern Studies at Ben-Gurion University of the Negev (BGU). My PhD advisor, Relli Shechter, thoughtfully guided me as I was writing my work, titled *Ethnicity in Motion: Social Networks in the Emigration of Jews from Norther Morocco to Israel and Venezuela*—a project without which this book, even with its different archival work, inroads, and conclusions, would not have been born.

When I began thinking about a book, I had already left my academic cradle at BGU and gone to Tel Aviv University, where Yaron Tsur was incredibly generous, both intellectually and financially, in welcoming me into my postdoctoral world. His trust and continuous support have been crucial for my evolution as a researcher, and thus for this project too. At the Frankel Institute at University of Michigan, in the fall of 2016, members of the fellowship group Israeli Histories, Societies, and Cultures helped me tailor my work for an international audience while closely engaging with related works in the field. I am grateful to (in alphabetical order) Mostafa Hussein, Liora Halperin, Noah Hysler Rubin, Bryan Roby, Shachar Pinsker, Gavin Schaffer, Rachel Seelig, Ruth Tsoffar, Jeffrey Veidlinger, Shayna Zamkanei, Yael Zerubavel.

During 2018–19, the Jews in Islamic Contexts fellowship group assembled at the Katz Centre at UPENN helped me start thinking about the structure of this book. I am grateful to Esra Almas, Orit Bashkin, Nancy Berg, Chen Bram, Dina Danon, Keren Dotan, Yuval Evri, Hadar Feldman Samet, Michal Rose Friedman, Annie Greene, Alma Heckman, Kerstin Hünefeld, Arthur Kiron, Sifra Lentil, Lital Levy, Sarah Levin, Yoram Meital, Yigal S. Nizri, Natalie B. Dohrmann, Joseph Sassoon, Edwin Seroussi, Julia Philips Cohen, Heather J. Sharky, Reuven Snir, Deborah Star, Alon Tam, Alan Verskin, and Mark Wagner for their thoughtful remarks during the numerous opportunities I had to share my ideas with them on various levels of intensity.

My nomination as a faculty member at the Ben-Gurion Research Institute for the Study of Israel and Zionism in October 2019, and as the head of the research hubs, first for "Israel and the Jewish world" in 2020, and then for "Communities and Mobilities" in 2022, both at the Centre for the Study of Israel (MALI), constitute substantial milestones in organizing and finalizing this book. I am grateful to a list of people at the institute with whom I have shared my ideas while preparing this manuscript: Avi Bareli, Natan Aridan, Ben Herzog, Paula Kabalo, Gideon Katz, Esther Meir-Glitzenstein, Kobi Peled, Arieh Saposnik, Ofer Shiff, and Havatzelet Yahel. I am particularly grateful to Roy Shukrun, a visiting member of my research hubs in 2021–22, for reading the full draft of this book and making valuable comments. The BGRI also provided generous support on top of the funds I received as an Alon Fellow from the Israeli Council for Higher Education, which helped me finalize this project. I am also grateful to Matthew Berkman, Flora Pazerker and Yakir Goldfarb for their help in preparing the final manuscript of this book.

In addition, I owe thanks to a long list of friends, colleagues, and mentors who, at different stages of this long project, read and heard my ideas and shared some insightful comments and tips. They include, again in alphabetical order, Menashe Anzi, Gur Alroey, Omri Asscher, Ofir Abu, Samir Ben-Layashi, Michal Ben-Ya'akov, Yoram Bilu, Aomar Boum, Guy Bracha, Adriana M. Brodsky, William Clarence Smith, Yolande Cohen, Itzhak Dahan, Bat-Zion Eraqi Klorman, Noah Gerber, Silvina Schammah Gesser, Harvey Goldberg, Sasha Goldstein Sabah, Susan Gilson Miller, David Guedj, Tamir Karkason, Amos Noy, Yaron Harel, Ethan Katz, Malka Katz, Sebastian Klor, Nissim Leon, Matthias Lehmann, André Levy, Guy Miron, Jessica M. Marglin, Dario Micolli, Vanessa Paloma Elbaz, Alejandro Portes, Amnon Raz Karkozkin, Leonardo Senkman, Hadas Shabat Nadir, Hila Shalem Baharad, Batia Siebzehner, Paulette Kershenovich Schuster, Raanan Rein, Lior B. Sternfeld, Maite Ojeda Mata, Orit Ouaknine Yekutieli, Alex Valdman, Shoshana (Susana) Weich Shahak, Adi Sherzer, Emanuela Trevisan Semi, Piera Rossetto, and Rona Yona. I am particularly grateful to Daniel J. Schroeter, one of the most eminent scholars of North African Jewish history; at the stage of preparing the prospectus and structure for this book in 2019, Daniel read several draft versions and contributed important insights. I am also grateful to the two anonymous reviewers who read the original draft of my manuscript and contributed significantly to its improvement.

Luckily, the list of dear friends who helped this project mature includes, in addition, some of the scholars whose works focus on Hispanic Moroccan Jews: the Bentolilas, Yaakov and Yosi; David Benhamú Jiménez; Angy Cohen; Isaac Guershon; Nina Pinto Abecasis (Z"L); and Mitchell Serels. I also owe a major debt of gratitude to Oro Anahory Librowicz, Judith Cohen, Benito (Baruj) Garzon, Margalit Bejarano, Néstor Garrido, Jimmy Pimienta, and Elias Salgado, who read earlier versions of specific chapters of this book, shared their ideas, and helped make this book more accurate.

ACKNOWLEDGMENTS

THE COMMUNITY'S ARCHIVE

In this work, I construct what is essentially ethnohistoric research, and this work would never have been possible without my ties with prominent members of the Hispanic Moroccan community worldwide. My archival research included repeated visits to a few of my interviewees' homes, where I found valuable archival material. Though not organized according to any official archival standards, this material was essential for understanding the dynamics of the Hispanic Moroccan Jewish diaspora. Two remarkable examples are the rich collections of documents held by siblings Sidney and Gladys Pimienta and their brother, Jimmy Pimienta, who resided in Belgium at the time of this writing. These collections are the source of various documents used in this book and constitute objects of investigation in their own right.

The way in which I gained access to some of these sources and others revealed the truth of Axel's insight that a diaspora is defined by, among other factors, its "archive." The word *archive* itself comes from *arche*, Greek for origins, and from *arkheion*, Greek for a house where a publicly recognized authority keeps its documentation.[2] My ability to study the contents of such collections was made possible by the close connections between the topic of my research and my personal life—that is, my incorporation over the course of my study into the very web of ethnic knowledge production among the community and its prominent heritage preservers that this book documents.

I thus express my deep appreciation to many members of the Hispanic Moroccan Jewish community, first- and second-generation immigrants who, for almost a decade and a half, opened up their hearts and shared their life stories and perspectives. First and foremost, the Pimientas, Gladys, Sidney, and Jimmy; Soli Anidjar; David Benaish; Mois Benarroch; Lucy Benarroch; Simon Benoliel; Jacob Carciente; Sonia Cohen; Shlomo Dodo; Benito Garzón; Simone Melo Foinquinos (Z"L); Alicia Raz-Sicso; and many other dear people whom I interviewed, held conversations with, and exchanged correspondence with.

By introducing me to previously unfamiliar knowledge, thoughts, and life experiences, including those related to my own ethnic background, these individuals have significantly influenced my life and shaped my individuality as a researcher. These special people include some of my beloved family members: my grandmother Flora (Z"L), Alberto Mermelszteyn, Guila Moreno, Isaac Moreno, Jenny Mermelszteyn, and other more distant relatives, among them Rachel Israel, Lina Moreno, and Rebecca Serruya. Other contributors, no less valuable to this work, would rather remain anonymous, and I respect their wishes.

NOTES

INTRODUCTION

1. I thank Jimmy Pimienta, vice president of France-MABATT for kindly drawing my attention to the transcripts of that speech. The transcript of the French-language speech was published in the organization's mouthpiece (Hassan Cohen, "Los Judeo Españoles," 1–3.)

2. Muslims were expelled later than Jews, between 1609 and 1614. The commemoration of the 1492 events became a modern way of protesting self-pride among Sephardi Jews already in 1892, when Ottoman Jews, for example, sent delegates to Chicago for the four-hundred-year anniversary of Christopher Columbus's discovery of a "new world" (see Cohen, *Becoming Ottomans*, 45–73).

3. The French organization added a T to indicate the participation of Tetouan natives in addition to those of Tangier origins.

4. The expression *lo nuestro* differentiated the Spanish-speaking communities from the *forasteros*, literally foreigners—another common expression in the communal speech that referred to the *Toshavim* or the native Arabic- and Tamazight-speaking communities in the southern parts of Morocco (Moreno, *Europe from Morocco*, 35, 39, 43).

5. It should be noted that the word *Sephardim* in Hebrew in fact means both Sephardim and Spaniards.

6. Hassan Cohen, "Los Judeo Españoles," 1.

7. Hispanic is a term used in various historical and geographical contexts to mark linguistic and cultural ties with the Spanish-speaking world. Alexander and Bentolila, *La* (See Alexander and Bentolila, *La Palabra en su Hora*, 9–10).

8. Moreno, "Beyond the Nation-State," 1–21.

9. On Melilla, see Benhamú Jiménez, *La Jaquetía de la Comunidad Judía de Melilla*; on Casablanca, see Tsur, *A Torn Community*, 46–47, 171.

10. Ojeda Mata, *Modern Spain*, 45; see also Alarcón, *Diario de un Testigo*.

11. Pulido, *Españoles Sin Patria*.

12. In the final division of Morocco between France and Spain in November 1912, Tangier's future was left uncertain due to conflicting geopolitical interests between France

and Great Britain. For more on the colonial divisions of Morocco and the status of Tangier, see Gilson Miller, *A History*, 88.

13. Albet Mas, "Three Gods," 585, 595; 592, 598; Calderwood, *Colonial Al-Andalus*, 5; Campoy Cubillo, *Memories*, 91; Mateo-Dieste, *La 'hermandad' hispano-marroquí*, 25.

14. Gilson Miller, *A History*, 104–10.

15. Ojeda Mata, *Modern Spain*, 52; Schroeter, "Philo-Sephardism," 184.

16. Weisz, *Jews and Muslims*, 2; Ojeda Mata, *Modern Spain*, 45–53, 56–57; Campoy Cubillo, *Memories*, 7; Calderwood, *Colonial Al-Andalus*; Friedman, "Reconstructing," 65.

17. See, for example, Elbaz, "Looking at the 'Other'"; Rohr, "The Use of Antisemitism," 4.

18. Campoy Cubillo, *Memories*, 9; Mateo-Dieste, *La 'hermandad' hispano-marroquí*.

19. Chetrit, "Judeo-Arabic," 277; Rodrigue mentions, based on the AIU reports, that at least two-thirds of the communities in the north still spoke Haketia in 1903 (see Rodrigue, *Jews and Muslims*, 127–28.)

20. Bénichou, "Observaciones," 209–58.

21. Pinto Abecasis, *The Peacock*, xii.

22. For a more global perspective on the implications of that connection see Benmayor and Kandiyoti, "Ancestry," 219–25; Armistead, "Judeo-Spanish," 98–106; Zytnicki, *Les Juifs*; Schroeter, "The Shifting Boundaries," 145–164; Silverman et al., *Romances Judeo-Españoles*, 8.

23. Bernecker and Cook, "The Change in Mentalities," 67–68.

24. At the time, a new scholarship argued that clustering groups according to their geographic "origins" or "ancestries," and their traditional "local identities" before the advent of colonialism, was itself a discursive production of colonialism and nationalism (see, for example, Axel, "The Context of Diaspora," 31; Brubaker, "The 'Diaspora' Diaspora," 11.)

25. Bodenhamer, "Narrating Space," 7–27; Azaryahu and Alderman, "Historical Space," 179–94.

26. Gil, *The Disenchantment*, 12.

27. See, for example, Clifford, "Diasporas," 306, 325; Brubaker, "The 'Diaspora' Diaspora," 2. Scholars in the field began to interrogate the diaspora-homeland axis in the contexts of Jewish immigration to Israel, postcolonial migration, and globalization. André Levy's work is an important example of this new outlook as it has evolved since the 1990s, influencing the scholarship on MENA Jews. He criticizes what he calls the "solar-system model" of homeland-diaspora relations while exploring the Moroccan Jewish experience in Casablanca at the turn of the twenty-first century, a time when almost all local Jews had left for Israel and France, the primary centers of the emerging Jewish Moroccan diaspora (Levy, *Return to Casablanca*, 146–72). Other works examine the complexities of establishing new Jewish communities in Ottoman Palestine prior to the British Mandate (see, e.g., Lehmann, "Rethinking Sephardi Identity," 81–109; Bartal, *Galut in the Land*.)

28. Bahar and Halperin, "Diasporas from the Middle East," 215–21. Recent scholarship has begun to apply a more global lens to colonial histories of the Middle East (see, e.g., Kozma, Schayegh, and Wishnitzer, eds., *A Global Middle East*; Arsan, Karam, and Khater, "On Forgotten Shores," 6–7.)

29. Campos, Bashkin, and Sternfeld, "MENA Jewry after," 10-11.

30. Sperling, "Conceptualising 'Inter-Destination Transnationalism,'" 1097–115.

31. See, for example, Hissong, *Nationalism and Jewish Identity*; Sternfeld, *Between Iran and Zion*; Schulze, *The Jews of Lebanon*.

32. The ethnic assertion of MENA Jews in Israel is commonly labeled under the category *Mizrahim*. This is due to privileging universal models of ethnic, racial, and postcolonial

minority struggles that view them as a domestic development comparable to the Black civil rights movement in the US, or to struggles against postcolonial hierarchies in the Global South (see, for example, Roby, *The Mizrahi Era*, 10; Shalom Chetrit, *Intra-Jewish Conflict*.)

33. The post-1945 period in Jewish-Muslim relations is referred to by Meddeb and Stora as "the Great Rupture in the Middle East" (Meddeb and Stora, *A History of Jewish-Muslim Relations*, 375–444). See also Bensoussan, *Jews in Arab Countries*; Stillman, *The Jews of Arab*, 141–253; Abitbol and Astro, "The Integration," 248–61.

34. From the viewpoint of many sociologists, as well as critical theorists like Ella Shohat who were pioneers in offering a universalize analytical framework of Mizrahi studies, Sephardi and other MENA Jewish immigrant communities in France, Latin America, and the US have been seemingly regarded as too marginal, in terms of their political and demographic weigh, to be included in comparisons of the Israeli and non-Israeli cases. Shohat analyzed the more recent histories of twentieth-century displacements of Jews from MENA countries through the lens of Arab-Jewish/Palestinian-Israeli political tensions and the uprooting of communities by nationalist entities but rarely addressed the recent history of MENA Jewish communities in the Americas, even in studies that directly treat the topic of Arab-Muslim displacements in South America. Instead, her work examined the premodern experiences of both Jews and Muslims with Sepharad/Al-Andalus as the major frame of reference (see Alsultany and Shohat, eds., *Between the Middle East and the Americas*). See also Shohat, *Taboo Memories, Diasporic Voices*; *On the Arab-Jew*, 17–19; Shohat, "Sephardim in Israel," 1–35.)

35. Cohen and Schwartz, "Scholarship on Moroccan Jews," 592–612; Brodsky, *Sephardi, Jewish, Argentine*; Katz, *The Burdens of Brotherhood*. Interest in these communities as part of the Jewish diaspora arose in some works by demographer Sergio Della Pergola, who offered a quantitative demographic analysis (see Della Pergola, "'Sephardi and Oriental'").

36. Evri, *The Return to Al-Andalus*, 9, 48. Along these lines, a recent book by Alisa Meyuhas Ginio, a scholar of the Sephardi diaspora, dwells on the loss of identity among native Sephardi populations in Palestine following the establishment of Israel, marking that very separation in its analysis (see Meyuhas Ginio, *Between Sepharad and Jerusalem*); Schroeter, "From Sephardi to Oriental," 125–48.

37. For recent studies on Sephardi diasporas in a global Ottoman context, see Mays, *Forging Ties, Forging Passports*; Karkason, "The Iberian Diasporas," 319–51; Goldstein Sabah, *Baghdadi Jewish*, 55–56, 81–84, 101–02. See also Lehmann, *Emissaries from the Holy Land*; Philips Cohen and Abrevaya Stein, *Sephardi Lives*; Campos, *Ottoman Brothers*; Benbassa and Rodrigue, *Sephardi Jewry*. These seminal studies on the Sephardi diaspora do not breach the question of mass migration in the second half of the twentieth century. Consequently, much of the literature exploring the dispersion of MENA Jews in the second half of the twentieth century focuses on immigration to Israel, which it frames as a sui generis migration, unrelated to earlier and parallel Jewish and non-Jewish global migrations. Historians operating in this vein emphasize the role of (Ashkenazi) Israeli-directed initiatives to transport and absorb Jews from MENA countries and on (usually negative) experiences of immigration rather than exploring Israel as one important hub connected to many others (see, for example, Bashkin, *Impossible Exodus*, 23–28; Meir Glitzenstein, *The Magic Carpet*.)

38. See, for example, Chen Dekel, "Rethinking Boundaries," 77–88; Kobrin, *Jewish Bialystok*. In some correlation, there has been a conspicuous lack of work on immigration to Israel from places across the MENA region that produced only a small number of immigrants to Israel, such as northern Morocco, northern Tunisia, and Algeria, to name a few. One of the

only books dedicated to the history of the northern Moroccan Jewish community mentions immigration to Israel only briefly (see Serels, *A History*, 171–73). Most studies concerning the community in Israel focus on contemporary issues of memory construction and folklore (see Pinto Abecasis, *The Peacock*; Cohen, "Recordar, Resistir.")

39. Miccoli, ed., *Contemporary Sephardic and Mizrahi Literature*; Rossetto, "Mémoires de Diaspora"; Trevisan Semi, Miccoli, and Parfitt, eds., *Memory and Ethnicity*.

40. As was the case in Walter Zenner's pioneering book on Jewish migrant communities from Aleppo in Israel, New York, and elsewhere. Although embedded in a theoretical framework, Zenner's work does not deal with these communities as part of a diaspora, and the concept of homeland is underdiscussed (See: Zenner, *A Global Community*.)

41. Ojeda Mata, *Modern Spain*; Calderwood, *Colonial Al-Andalus*.

42. Quoted in Campoy Cubillo, *Memories*, 8.

43. Ennaji, *Muslim Moroccan Migrants*, 21; De Haas, "Morocco's Migration Experience," 47.

44. Bhatt, Goldberg, and Srivastava, "A Language-Based Method."

45. Campoy Cubillo and Vizcaya, "Entering the Global Hispanophone," 1–16.

46. Brubaker, "The 'Diaspora' Diaspora," 7; Alexander, "Beyond *The 'Diaspora' Diaspora*," 1546.

47. Cohen, *Global Diasporas*, 11.

48. See, for example, Tsuda, "Conclusion: Diasporic Homecomings," 325–50; Kasbarian, "The Myth and Reality of 'Return,'" 358–81; Triandafyllidou and Veikou, "The Hierarchy of Greekness," 189–208.

49. Ahrens and King, *Onward Migration and Multi-Sited Transnationalism*, v.

50. See Brubaker, "The 'Diaspora' Diaspora," 6; Miles and Sheffer, "Francophonie and Zionism," 119–48; Cohen, *Global Diasporas*, 13.

51. Axel, "The Context of Diaspora," 32. See also Brubaker's "The 'Diaspora' Diaspora" critique of identifying groups as diasporic entities without establishing whether its putative members identify as such.

52. Cohen, *Global Diasporas*, 13; Wessendorf, "Pioneer Migrants," 17–34.

53. Sheffer, *Diaspora Politics*, 26.

54. Weich-Shahak, *En Buen Siman!*, 192.

55. Jalfón de Bentolila, *Haketía: A Memoir*, 6.

56. Jimmy Pimienta's audio collection (hereafter PAC) includes more than 133 interviews, events, and radio shows recorded between 1986 and 1994 in multiple locations, including but not limited to Morocco, France, Canada, Venezuela, Spain, Israel, Portugal, and Switzerland. The collection is titled *Recueil audio: Témoignages, Entretiens et Documents Enregistrés sur le Terrain pour Diffusion dans le Programme Aadas y Adafinas de la Radio Juive de Paris, Radio Communauté (RCJ)*. Collections Famille Pimienta: Jimmy Pimienta, Les Judéo-Espagnols Du Maroc.

1. HISPANIC JEWS IN MOROCCO

1. Onieva, *Guía Turística*, 210.

2. One of the pioneering works in English that delved into this aspect is Cohen, "On Belonging and Other Dreams."

3. See Sandoica, *Pensamiento Burgués*, 569; Miège, *Le Maroc et l'Europe*, 120–123. The distinction between ethnoreligious groups in official statistics is based on a colonial,

sociolegal stratifications. Europeans were by and large Christians; yet this category may encompass several Jewish European nationals who were not registered as locals.

4. Jean Claude, "Les Europeens," 3.
5. López García, "Españoles de Marruecos," 17–48.
6. Gilson Miller, *Years of Glory*, 34.
7. For instance, the economic activity in Tangier's port dramatically increased from 8,905 tons of goods in 1945 to 175,225 tons in 1950 and 242,595 tons in 1952. The establishment of the General Employment Bureau around 1955 reflected the growing appeal of Tangier as an economic haven among lower-income migrants from Europe. Alamin Albazzaz, "Tangier," 21–22.
8. Adila, "Datos Para la Historia," 144.
9. Kutz, "State and Territorial Restructuring," 21.
10. La Porte, "Colonial Dreams," 821–844.
11. López García, "Españoles en el Marruecos Actual," 38–39.
12. Malo de Molina and Domínguez, *Tetuán: El Ensanche*.
13. Ojeda Mata, "Jewish Tetouan," 367.
14. Marglin, "Modernizing Moroccan Jews," 593, 601 n. 145; Laskier, *The Alliance Israelite*, 171–75.
15. González González, *Spanish Education*, 52–62; 76–77, 88-99; 168–72; González González, "Escuelas," 119–21, 128–30; Halstead, "A 'Somewhat Machiavellian' Face," 50. While "Jewish" is widely employed in this study as a socioreligious category, in historical Spanish sources, the use of *Jewish* often implies antisemitic sentiments, which is why the preference for "Hebrew" emerged in the Spanish Protectorate in Morocco as a replacement. Interestingly, many Jews in North Morocco also referred to themselves as Hebrews, influenced by the negative connotations associated with the term *Jewish* during the Spanish Protectorate. "Israelite," less commonly used in Spanish, is also widely used by local Jews and it is a result of French influence. (See, Ojeda Mata, *Modern Spain*, xv.)
16. See figures in Laskier, *The Alliance Israelite*, 311.
17. Cazes Bénatar, "Tangier," 453; Cazes Bénatar, "Spanish Morocco," 394–95.
18. González González, *"Spanish Education,"* 158; Laskier, *The Alliance Israelite*, 310.
19. Moreno, "De-Westernizing," 73.
20. A list of schools, youth monuments, and communal institutions in North Africa, CZA, File s5-12.177.
21. Bendelac, *Mosaics*, 15–16, 42–43.
22. Quoted in Campoy Cubillo, *Memories*, 8.
23. Bendelac, *Los Nuestros*, 133–36.
24. Sayahi, "Aqui Todo el Mundo," 42.
25. The Hispano-Franceca library in Tangier offered new books in French, Spanish, and English and published its services at the *Boletín Oficial*. See *Boletín Oficial* 1, October 1949, 12.
26. Sayahi, "Aqui Todo el Mundo," 41.
27. Y. Cohen, Tangiers, 1903, Archives of the AIU, Tunisia 1.D.1, [quoted in Rodrigue, *Jews and Muslims*, 127–128.]
28. Ojeda Mata, *Modern Spain*, 59–60.
29. For example, Isaac Toledano and Isaac Laredo from Tangier (together with Augustín Lugaro from Gibraltar) edited *El Eco Mauritano* (1886–1930); Yosef Hassán (from Tetouan) edited *El Magrebí* (1934); Samuel Cohen, who spent most of his life in Tangier, edited *España de Tánger* and was president of the International Press Association in Tangier. Cohen also edited a supplement to *España* called *España Semanal*—in which he adopted the pen name

of Claudio Laredo—and authored the Spanish-language novels *La Puerta Secreta* (Sevilla, 1953) and *Vacaciones en Europa* (Madrid, 1959). Al-Bazzaz, "Tangier During," 22; Crespo, *Les Espagnols au Maroc*, 90.

30. Rojas Marcos, "Literatura Española en Tánger," 80–83; Israel Garzón, *Los Judíos Hispano-Marroquíes*, 119.

31. Bürki, "Haketia in Morocco," 143.

32. Moisés Garzón Serfaty, interviewed by Leonardo Senkman, 1990 Venezuela, ICJ (213) 12.

33. See, for example, Garzón Serfaty, "Premio Gordo Numero," 14, 19.

34. "Gerardo Diego Triunfo en el Circulo a de Tetuán," 2.

35. "Juanito Valderrama," in *The Encyclopedia of Popular Music*, ed. Colin Larkin (New York: Oxford University Press, 2016). https://www.oxfordreference.com/display/10.1093/acref/9780195313734.001.0001/acref-9780195313734-e-74951.

36. For more information about these performances see Bendayan, *Une Jeunesse à Tanger*, 64–67.

37. For this testimony and additional observations on the reception of tango in the Jewish communities in northern Morocco, see "Tango Morocco," 2011, film by Martha Wolff, The Oster Visual Documentation Center, ANU—Museum of the Jewish People, courtesy of Martha Wolff.

38. Alberto Pimienta, "La Zarzuela y Los Judíos en el Teatro Cervantes de Tánger," interviewed by Jimmy and Gladys Pimienta, Tangier, PAC, call no. 106-CL.TG18.

39. Sr. Ahmed Goudian, "Un Musulmán Se Acuerda de los Antiguos Judíos Tangerinos," interviewed by Jimmy Pimienta, Tangier, PAC, call no. 13-LU.TG07.

40. Aidi, "Tangier's Jazzmen." Radio broadcasting across colonial North Africa, including in northern Morocco, was particularly multilingual. Christopher Silver notes, for example, that the Francoist Radio Sevilla started broadcasting in Arabic while searching for target audiences in North Africa, and that Italian radio broadcasting was particularly popular in the region before 1940. For more on the influence of radio broadcasting on the soundscape of North Africa in the late 1930s, see Silver, *Jews, Muslims and Music*, 106–107.

41. Adila, "Datos Para la Historia," 145–146.

42. Berdugo, "La Juventud Judía de Tánger y los Deportes," 6.

43. Such as La Santa Barbara (the Spanish military team), Radio Militar, F.T.F.D., the Prince of Asturias, the Lukus, the Liksus, and the Teja De Riali team. See also Beneish, "Los Macabeos."

44. Jacob Levy, "La Juventud Judía y los Deportes," 2.

45. "Larache en Fiesta," 2.

46. Based on information from the exhibition "Tetuán A Rayas, The Madroño (Bear) Became a Palm," featuring the history of the group held at the Cervates Institute in Tel Aviv, and later at the North Africa Jews Heritage Center on June 21. I am grateful to the late Nina Pinto Abecasis for kindly sharing this information with me and allowing me to use it for my research. Read more about the exhibition at "Un Atlético de Exposición," Marca Atlético, accessed June 20, 2020, https://www.marca.com/2015/10/15/futbol/equipos/atletico/1444894902.html.

47. "Samuel Serfaty," 15.

48. An interview with David (pseudonym), 2009, Israel; an interview with Nina (pseudonym), 2009, Israel; an interview with Perla (pseudonym), 2009, Israel; an interview with Benarroch Aquiba, 1990, ICJ (213)12.

49. See, for example, the list of names published in "Boletín de OSE, 1949–1950" (AR Geneva: Tangiers-OSE Bulletins, 1946–54) JDCA, Call No. 179.

50. The circumcision notebook of Rabbi Bar Vidal Haserfaty, composed between 1881 and 1940 in Tetuan, very frequently reflected typical biblical Hebrew names. Yishaq (301 out of 2,725), Abraham (277), and Moshe (231) were seen most frequently and were also the most common names among fathers (See López Álvarez, *La Comunidad Judía de Tetuán*, 314). A similar impression was given by Tangier's main circumcision notebooks (R. Habib Toledano, "Registo de Circunciones"; R. Samuel Benatar, "Registo de Circuncisiones"; R. Yamín Hacohen, "Cauderno de Circuncisiones"; R. Yehuda Ha-Cohen, "Cauderno de Circuncisiones," PPC).

51. The text from here to the end of the chapter is derived in part from Moreno, "Remapping 'Tradition,'" 378–400, https://doi.org/10.1080/1462169X.2021.1993542.

52. "Nuestras Doctrinas," 6; "Una Feliz Inciativa," 7.

53. Adila, "Datos Para la Historia," 143–44.

54. Simi (pseudonym), interviewed by Aviad Moreno, 2009, Israel.

55. Cohen, *Recordar, Resistir*, 461–62.

56. Bendelac, *Mosaics*, 43.

57. Songs in Judeo-Spanish, Tangier, 1987, SA-JUNL, Call No. Y-05669-f.

58. Pinto Abecasis, "The Piropo," 75–100.

59. Salomón (pseudonym), interviewed by the author, 2009, Israel. For additional indications see Cohen, "Recordar, Resistir," 163, 520–29.

60. Apparently, it is not a misprint since the practice repeated itself in other issues; see *Or-Luz*, May 15, 1956, 1; May 31, 1956, 16; June 15, 1956, 21.

61. An interview with Hélène (pseudonym), interviewed by the author, 2009, Israel; Pinto Abecasis, *The Peacock*, 229–41.

62. An interview with Hélène (pseudonym), 2009, Israel; an interview with Ruth (pseudonym), 2009, Israel. For the way weddings became emblematic of ethnic formation among Hispanic Moroccan Jews, see Pinto Abecasis, "Transformations in the Noche de Paños," 139–62; Pinto Abecasis, *The Peacock*, 4–8.

63. Onieva, *Guía Turística*, 320–22, 331.

64. In Tangier, therefore, a *Mellah* (Jewish quarter perceived by scholars as a local ghetto, designed to force the isolation of Jews by royal decree) in fact had never been created. Yet the concentration of Jewish facilities, as well as many Jewish domiciles and businesses in this area, left the impression of a segregated Mellah. See Kutz, "State and Territorial Restructuring," 22; Gilson Miller, "Apportioning Sacred Space," 57–60.

65. Adila, "Datos Para la Historia," 143–45.

66. Sánchez, "The Sephardi Berberisca," 37–38. Venessa Paloma Elbaz has recently identified transitional spaces like the Noche de Berberisca ceremony and musically oriented communal celebrations led by women (who supply essential information to the community as a whole) as "semi-public" spaces (Elbaz, "Jewish Music," 22.)

67. The endogamy in local Jewish society may explain why marriages were referred to, in many of my interviews, as symbolic ethnic traditions. An interview with Hélène (pseudonym), interviewed by the author, 2009, Israel; an interview with Ruth (pseudonym), interviewed by the author, 2009, Israel; an interview with David (pseudonym), interviewed by the author, 2009, Israel.

2. IN (RE)SEARCH OF ORIGINS

1. Silverman et al., *Romances Judeo-Españoles*, 7–8.
2. Armistad, "Judeo-Spanish Traditional," 335.

3. An annotated version of her work was eventually published in 1977. Silverman et al., *Romances Judeo-Españoles*, 8.

4. Axel, "The Context of Diaspora," 32; for Brubaker's problematization of clustering groups as diasporic entities without checking if members of those groups identify as such, see Brubaker, "The 'Diaspora' Diaspora," 11.

5. Chatty, *Displacement and Dispossession*, 34.

6. Moreno and Gerber, "Studying Jews from Muslims Countries in Israel," 7–39.

7. Shiloah, *Jewish Musical Traditions*, 48–53.

8. Ortega, *Los Hebreos en Marruecos*, 160.

9. Jouin, "Le Costume de la Femme Israélite," 167–86; See also Seroussi, *Sonic Ruins*, 82.

10. Pulido, *Españoles sin Patria*, 10, 61–62, 76, 159, 256.

11. Pulido, *Los Israelitas*, 180–90.

12. Danon, *The Jews of Ottoman Izmir*, 115; see also Danon, "Recueil de Romances Judeo-Espagnoles," 102–23, 263–75.

13. Meyuhas Ginio, *Between Sepharad and Jerusalem*, 286.

14. Guershon, "The Foundation of Hispano-Jewish Associations," 181–82, 186 ; Cohen, *Recordar, Resisitir*, 266.

15. Evri, *The Return to Al-Andalus*, 119–26; Gonzalez, "Abraham S. Yahuda," 406–33; Friedman, "Orientalism between Empires," 435–51.

16. "Spain,"10.

17. Ortega, *Los Hebreos*, 300. The short-lived *Kol Israel*, which appeared in Tangier in 1914, dedicated the front page of its fourteenth issue to the election held at the Spanish Chamber of Commerce for a new board of directors for the local Hispano-Hebrew Association. The reporter viewed the participation of a large number of members in the middle of a workday (Monday) as proof of that body's influence over Tangier's Jews. See "Elecciones de la Asociacion Hispano-Hebrea," 1.

18. Benoliel, "Dialecto Judeo-Hispano-Marroquí," 228–29.

19. Pimienta, *Un Aljófar y una Perla*, 25.

20. Benoliel, "Dialecto Judeo-Hispano-Marroquí (1926)," 209–33, 342–63, 507–38; 14 (1927), 137–68, 196–234, 357–73, 566–80; 15 (1928), 47–61, 188–223. See also Serels, *A History*, 267.

21. Elbaz, "Looking at the 'Other,'" 410–411, 416.

22. Hamilton, "Hispanism and Sephardic Studies," 182.

23. Silverman et al., *Romances Judeo-Españoles*, 7–8

24. See Veidlinger, ed., *Going to the People*, 7–8, 10.

25. Cited in Silverman et al., *Romances Judeo-Españoles*, 8.

26. Noy, *Experts or Witnesses*.

27. Seroussi, "Archivists of Memory," 199.

28. Bürki, "Haketia in Morocco," 121–55.

29. Serels, *A History*, 145–46; Ojeda Mata, "Jewish Tetouan," 371.

30. In the 1930s, the title was Romanized, and the subtitle *Revista Hispano-Sefarad (Hispanic-Sepharad Review)* was added.

31. Schroeter, "Renacimiento de Israel (Tangier)."

32. "El Viaje a España," 5.

33. Schroeter, "The Shifting Boundaries," 150.

34. "Indice de Revistas Ibéricas Sefaradíes," 5; see also "La Primera Etapa,"1-3. Among the articles in the newspaper's special first anniversary issue were "La Vuelta a España" ("Return

to Spain"), by Vicente Alvarez Buylla, and "Renacimiento de los Estudios Hispánicos en el Extranjero" ("The Revival of Hispanic Studies Abroad") by Alberto Cazés. Later issues ran articles titled "La España Que Fué" ("Spain, Once Upon a Time") and "Los Judíos Españoles Conservan Patrióticamente un Tesoro de la Raza" ("The Spanish Jews Patriotically Preserve a Treasure of The [Hispanic] Race"), among many others marking historic connections between the Jews of northern Morocco and pre-1492 Spain.

35. "L'edition de Notre Journal," 3.
36. "Juicios y Opinions," 3.
37. See, for example, Ich Yehudi, "Tolerancia No Es Ni Crea Derecho," 1-2; "Los Judíos de Lengua Española," 4.
38. Heckman, *The Sultan's Communists*, 50–51. Silver, *Jews, Muslims and Music*, 90.
39. Albet Mas, "Three Gods, Two Shores," 585, 595; 592, 598; Calderwood, *Colonial Al-Andalus*, 5–7, 170.
40. Rohr, "The Use of Antisemitism," 206–207.
41. Ojeda Mata, "Jewish Tetouan," 366–67; Israel Garzón, *Los Judíos*, 349.
42. Laredo, *Bereberes y Hebreos en Marruecos*; see also Laredo, "Lápidas Sepulcrales," 421–32; Vallicrosa, "Lápidas Sepulcrales," 63–72.
43. For more biographical details, see "Currículum Vitae de Salomon Bensabat Rédigé en 1962," stored at the Raphaël Benazeraf Collection, at the Yad Ben Zvi Institute, Jerusalem; for an online version, see https://www.judaisme-marocain.org/objets_popup.php?id=14150; see also Bensabat, "Hasdai Ben Chaprut," 115–23.
44. Cited in Gilson Miller, *Years of Glory*, 35.
45. "Tangier Budget for the First Half of 1955" (Morocco: budget-finance, 1947–1954), JDCA, Call No. C.56–706, 10.
46. Calderwood, "Moroccan Jews and the Spanish Colonial Imaginary," 1, 9, 13.
47. Coriat, "Mi Comunidad: Breve Reseña Histórica."
48. Silver, *Jews, Muslims and Music*, 143.
49. Benmaman, "El Símbolo del Sefaradísmo," 8–9.
50. "Los Cheutas y su Actual Situación," 3, 21; Wahnon, "Maimónides Profeta de la Medicina Contemporánea," 7–9; Santos de Carrion, "Imágenes de Sefarad," 9, 14.
51. Medina, "Añoranzas de un Sabbat," 12.
52. Ibid.; an earlier publication by that author appeared under the title *Latidos de Andalucía* in 1954.
53. Mogar, "Alegrías de Cádiz," 9, 20.
54. Silverman et al., *Romances Judeo-Españoles*, 17–22. See also Palacín, *Romances de Tetuán*; Palacín, *Cuentos Populares*; Bénichou, "Notas Sobre el Judeo-Español," 307–12.
55. "Alberto Pimienta, Su Acción de Recoger Cantos Judeoespañoles de Marruecos," interviewed by Jimmy Pimienta, Tangier, 1993, PAC, call no. 119-CL.MX13.
56. Axel, "The Context," 32.

3. MOROCCO IN LATIN AMERICA, LATIN AMERICA IN MOROCCO

1. Monaco, *Moses Levy of Florida*. About England, see, for example, Halliday, "The Millet of Manchester," 161; about the United States of America, see Leibovici, "La Emigración a América de los Sefardíes," 242; about Bukhara and Palestine, see Leibovici, "De Tetuán a

Bujara," 55–56; concerning Egypt, see Israel Garzón, *Los Judíos*, 212; about the Brazilian Amazon, see Benchimol, *Eretz Amazonia*, 79–104.

2. For instance, between 1908 and 1941, almost 65 percent of the Lebanese and Syrians entering Brazil through the port of Sao Paulo professed to be Catholics (Lesser, "From Pedlars," 396–97). See also Zenner, "Streams of Immigration," 146; Issawi, "The Historical Background of Lebanese Emigration," 30–31.

3. Mirelman, "Sephardic Immigration to Argentina," 13; Laskier, *The Alliance Israélite*, 311–12.

4. See Moreno, "Expanding the Dimensions," 5–6.

5. Schroeter, "Trade as a Mediator," 113–14; Lourido Díaz, "Los Judíos en Marruecos," 27–28.

6. Schroeter, "The Shifting Boundaries," 145–64.

7. Serels, *Jews of Cape Verde*, 53–55.

8. Haller, "Place and Ethnicity," 78; Miège, "L'activité Maritime a Tanger," 55–76. Copies of *Maguid Micharim* are digitized and available at https://www.nli.org.il/en/newspapers/tas.

9. Abu-Haidar, "La Coexistance Linguistique," 39.

10. Gilson Miller, "Kippur on the Amazon," 109; Bengio and Miège, "La Communauté Juive de Tanger," 152–54, 157.

11. Bennoune, "Maghribi Workers in France," 2.

12. Out of eleven million immigrants entering Latin America from 1851 to 1924, some 46 percent resettled in Argentina and 33 percent in Brazil (see Bejarano, "The Sephardic Communities," 26–29).

13. Liberman, "Moroccan Jews," 106.

14. In 1823, the first documented Jewish Moroccan name appeared in the license of commerce list issued by the Brazilian state of Para. In the ensuing years, several typical Jewish Moroccan names were documented. See Liberman, "Moroccan Jews," 107; Benchimol, *Eretz Amazonia*, 79–107; Blay, "Judeus na Amazônia," 43.

15. Segal, *Jews of the Amazon*, 51–52.

16. Mirelman, "Sephardic Immigration," 22.

17. Moya, "The Jewish Experience," 8–11.

18. Ibid., 16; Epstein, "Los Judeo-Marroquíes," 121; Bengio, "Juifs Marocains," 233–49.

19. Aizenberg, "Venezuela y los Judíos Curazoleños," 14.

20. Vilar, "La Emigración Judeo-Marroquí," 39–44.

21. Bejarano, "The Sephardic Communities," 25; Carciente, *Presencia Sefardí*, 158–60; Benoliel, "Présence Judéo-Marocaine," 220.

22. Carciente, *La Comunidad Judía de Venezuela*, 126; Vilar, "La Emigración Judeo-Marroquí," 47–49.

23. Moreno, *Europe from Morocco*.

24. Abensur, "Les Eleves," 6–10.

25. Laskier, *The Alliance Israelite*, 304–05.

26. Gilson Miller, "Kippur on the Amazon," 197.

27. Cited in Stillman, *The Jews of Arab Lands*, 205.

28. Vilar, "La Emigración," 12–13.

29. Blank, "The Integration," 213.

30. Bejarano, "The Sephardic Communities," 25; Gilson Miller, "Kippur on the Amazon," 204; Mirelman, "Sepharadim in Latin America," 242; Vilar, "La Emigración," 46; Mirelman, "Sephardic Immigration," 23.

31. López García, "Españoles de Marruecos," 20.
32. Epstein, "Instituciones y Liderazgo," 137.
33. Brodsky, *Sephardi, Jewish, Argentine*, 17–19, 22, 28, 61; Cohen, "Recordar," 412.
34. Levy Benshimol and Goldberg, *Diccionario de Cultura*, 118, 128; Goldberg and Hubschman, "Las Instituciones," 3.
35. Mirelman, "Sephardic Immigration," 17–21.
36. The JCA purchased land mostly in Argentina and Brazil, where Jews, mainly from Eastern Europe, were resettled for agricultural work (see Levin, "Labor and Land," 341–59; Falbel, "Jewish Agricultural," 325–40).
37. Epstein, "Los Judeo-Marroquíes," 114.
38. Gilson Miller, "Kippur on the Amazon," 199.
39. Serels, *A History*, 72.
40. Benchimol, "La Langue Espagnole," 128.
41. Quoted and translated in Segal, *Jews of the Amazon*, 52.
42. "Gran Bazar La Caraqueña," 22. See also Vilar, "La Emigración," 45; Bendelac, *Los Muestros*, 44.
43. Balán, "The Role of Migration Policies," 117.
44. About Venezuela's policy, see *Las Migraciones Laborales*, 11. A census taken in the city of Buenos Aires in 1936 indicated that by that year, out of the Jewish Moroccan community of a few thousand, only 420 had been born in Morocco; the majority were descendants of Moroccans. Furthermore, only five percent of Moroccan natives in 1936 were under the age of fifteen, meaning that most had probably arrived in earlier years (see Mirelman, "Sephardic Immigration," 21).
45. My own recapitulation, based on data provided by Álvarez, *La Comunidad Judía*.
46. Israel Garzón, "Destinos de Emigración," 114.
47. Vagni, "El Colonialismo Español."
48. "Delegados de Hajnasat Orhim," 11.
49. A total of 2490.20 Spanish pesetas (Ptas Esp.) and 30 pesetas Hassani (Ptas Hni) were collected abroad overall, compared to 3074.50 Ptas Hni and 170 Ptas Esp. (together totaling 2905.86 Spanish pesetas) collected in Tangier (see "Estado Financiero," 12–13; compare "Adherentes de Tánger," 16, with "Adherentes del Extranjero," 19–30).
50. Total contributions between 5673 (1913) and 5680 (1920) amounted to 28,083.57 Ptas Hni and 5232.50 Ptas Esp., out of which only 20,051.25 Ptas Hni and 482.50 Ptas Esp. were donated by local adherents (compare "Adherentes de Tánger," 10, 23 with "Adherentes del Extranjero," 13–16, 26–32).
51. Levy, "Informe del Secretario Contador," 2–3.
52. "Donativos Varios," 31; 14,565.64 Ptas Hni and 6879.70 Ptas Esp., out of which only 411.75 Ptas Hni and 508.15 Ptas Esp. were donated in Tangier. An additional list of "various donations" indicated another substantial amount of 9,773.89 Ptas Hni and 4,421.95 Ptas Esp., donated mainly by Moroccan émigrés, notably from Latin America.
53. A total of 3011.50 francs, with a value equivalent to 2,281.43 Ptas Esp. Each franc was converted into 1.32 Ptas Esp. ("Fondo Especial," 9, 32).
54. Brodsky, *Sephardi, Jewish, Argentine*, 85.
55. "La Proclamación de la Independencia del Perú," 3.
56. "Nuestro Compatriotas," 22.
57. "En Tetuán," 2.
58. "Un Libro de Samuel," 1.

59. "Notas de Tetuán," 12.
60. Pulido, *Españoles sin Patria*, 141, 161.
61. Ortega, *Los Hebreos*, 203, 275; the letter mentioned appears on page 349.
62. Ricard, "L'émigration [1932]," 259; Ricard, "L'émigration [1928]," 201–02; Ricard, "L'émigration [1932]," 427–29.
63. Ricard, *Diccionario Filosófico*.
64. Ricard "L'emigration [1932]," 427–29.
65. Benumeya, "El Futuro Problema," 2.
66. "El Discubrimiento de America," 5.
67. La Vida de Moyses y Abraham Pinto en el Bosque Amazon, "Memorias," accessed May 22, 2011, http://www.juifs-marocains-en-amazonie.com/
68. Benarroch Pinto, *Indianos Tetuaníes*, 9.
69. Ibid., 90.
70. Arques, "Indianos de Tetuán," 2–4; Arques, "Indianos de Tetuán" (December 17, 1949), 3–6; Arques, "Indianos de Tetuán" (December 24, 1949), 5–6; Arques, "Indianos de Tetuán" (December 31, 1949), 2–4.
71. "Or Hailadim," 3.
72. Cazes Bénatar, "Spanish Morocco."
73. Mogar, "Tetuán Conserva," 6.
74. Israel Garzón, *Los Judíos*, 218; Vilar, "La Emigración," 46; Carciente, *La Comunidad*, 128; Blank, "The Integration," 213; an interview with Gonzalo Benaím-Pinto, 1989, Venezuela, ICJ; an interview with Carlos Ben-Dahan, 1990, Venezuela, ICJ; an interview with Isaac Bendayán, 1990 (?), Venezuela, ICJ; an interview with Lea Almosny Mercedes, 1990, Venezuela, ICJ.
75. Levy Benshimol and Goldberg, *Diccionario*, 407–10; Blank, "The Integration," 213–14.
76. Bendelac, *Mosaics*, 13.
77. Alegría Bendelac's extensive fieldwork in northern Morocco during the mid-1980s evoked similar memories (Bendelac, *Los muestros*, 46–47).
78. An interview with Perla (pseudonym), interviewed by the author, 2009, Israel.
79. An interview with Daniel (pseudonym), interviewed by the author, 2010, Israel.

4. ZIONISM AND THE HISPANIC MOROCCAN DIASPORA

1. From 1949 onward, *Noar* was issued biweekly. Under the new editorship of Meyer Toledano, it aspired both to increase its circulation from two thousand to four thousand and to become the central journal for all Moroccan Jewry. From 1950 to 1952, despite its pro-Zionist orientation, the paper exposed Jews to political issues on the Moroccan national scene, such as the efforts to remove the Sultan (Tsur, *A Torn Community*, 97–98.)
2. Tapiero, "Folklore," 3; another person who responded to the call was Sara Leibovici, who brought to the awareness of *Noar*'s readers the recent publication of the anthology *Los 'Proverbios' de Sefaradítas Españoles* by Hispanist and philologist Mosco Galimir (Leibovici, "Refranes Judeo-Españoles," 3.)
3. Benarroch, "Necesidad de una Investigación," 2.
4. Ibid.
5. Tsur, *A Torn Community*, 97–98.
6. Gilson Miller, *A History*, 112; Israel Garzón, *Los Judíos*, 170, 176.

7. "Nos Echos- El Mundo Sefaradí," 3. About the size of the community, see Tsur, *A Torn Community*, 421.
8. "El Mundo Sefaradí," 2; see also Serels, *A History*, 294.
9. See also Meyuhas Ginio, *Between Sepharad and Jerusalem*, 225.
10. Weisz, *Jews and Muslims*, 40–41.
11. See Dubnov, "Zionism on the Diasporic Front," 211–212; Evri, *The Return to Al-Andalus*, 27; Boum, "From 'Little Jerusalem,'" 56.
12. Brodsky, *Sephardi, Jewish, Argentine*, 115–17. For a fresh network approach to the study of Hebrew culture and Zionism among Moroccan Jews in the first half of the twentieth century, see Guedj, *The Hebrew Culture*.
13. Rein and Lewis, "Complementary Identities," 99–116.
14. "Tomo 1"; see also Sieskel, "'El Jala,'" 84; Rein and Lewis, "Complementary Identities," 26.
15. Gherman, "The Beginnings of Brazilian Zionism," 164, 171, 173.
16. Ojeda Mata, "Jewish Tetouan," 363–64; Boum, "From 'Little Jerusalem.'"
17. Botbol Hatchuel, "La Comunidad Judía"; Yehuda, "Zionist Activity"; Cohen, "Spanish-Speaking."
18. Among a wider series of correspondence he held between March 1916 and January 1947 (Bentolila, "The Archive," 1–14.)
19. Ortega, *Los Hebreos*, 267.
20. Pulido, *Españoles sin Patria*, 184.
21. Schroeter, "From Sephardi to Oriental," 125–48; for how early Zionist orientalism incorporated Sephardi supremacy into its repertoire, see Saposnik, "Europe and its Orients," 1105–23.
22. Israel Garzón, *Los Judíos*, 21.
23. "Le Dr Bension," 3; "The National Movement in Spain and Morocco," 1–2.
24. Bejarano, "The Position of," 41–42.
25. "Índice de Revistas," 5.
26. "Jucios y Opinions," 3.
27. Ojeda Mata, "Jewish Tetouan," 365.
28. "Jornaes," 22.
29. Haim, *Particularity and Integration*, 183.
30. Brodsky, *Sephardi, Jewish, Argentine*, 115–22, 124, 643–44.
31. "El Apostolado de Nuestro Ilustre"; see also Meyuhas Ginio, *Between Sepharad and Jerusalem*, 254–55.
32. "El Dr. Pulido en el Libro," 5–6.
33. Cohen, "Spanish-Speaking," 262–63.
34. Pinto, "Recuerdos de Tangerinos en Casablanca, 1898–1940" (December 3, 1965), PPC. Also supported by the Minutes of the Junta of Tangier (see Serels, *A History*, 73, footnote 67).
35. Tsur, *A Torn Community*, 46–47, 171.
36. Laskier, "S. D. Lévy and Moïse Nahón," 51–86; Epstein, "Los Judeo-Marroquíes," 114; Levin, "From Tunisia to Argentina," 39–62.
37. For more on his activity and relationship with local and world Zionist leaders, see Gilson Miller, *Years of Glory*, 45.
38. Cohen, "Zionist Leaders," 265–66; Boum, "From 'Little Jerusalem,'" 58. For more on the development of Zionism in Morocco in the first half of the twentieth century, see Guedj, *The Hebrew Culture*, 47–51.
39. Gilson Miller, *Years of Glory*, 137.

40. Laskier, *North African Jewry*, 225.
41. Picard, *Cut to Measure*, 87–110.
42. Laskier, *North African Jewry*, 107.
43. Bin-Nun, "La Négociation," 303.
44. Aharoni, *The Aliyah, 1961–1964*, 2; Aharoni, *The Aliyah, 1961–1972*, 9.
45. Tsur, *A Torn Community*, 59–60, 197; Serels, *A History*, 157–59.
46. "Tangier Budget for the First Half of 1955" (Morocco: budget-finance, 1947–1954), JDCA, Call No. C56.301, 2.
47. Ibid.
48. Cohen, "The Jewish Scouts," 77, 91.
49. Laskier, *Israel and Jewish Immigration*, 257; Yossi Bentolila, "The Immgration," 82–83.
50. A list of schools, youth monuments, and communal institutions in North Africa, CZA, File s5-12.177.
51. See list of donations in *Boletín de Ose*, 1949–1950 (AR Geneva: Tangiers-OSE Bulletins, 1946–54 JDCA, Call no. 179).
52. A letter from Blumenthal to the Department of Education and Culture in Exile, June 24, 1955 (CZA, File s5-12.177); "Inauguración de Exposición de Libros Hebreos en el Casino a de Tánger," *España*, June 20, 1955 (found at the CZA, File s5-12.177).
53. Serels, *A History*, 163–64.
54. Aharoni, *The Aliyah, 1961–1964*, 2, 7, 9.
55. This section of chapter 4 (pp.82–85) is derived in part from an article published in *Journal of North African Studies*, June 30, 2022, copyright Taylor & Francis, available online: https://doi.org/10.1080/13629387.2022.2088522; for an extended discussion, see Moreno, "Expanding the Dimensions," 15–17.
56. *Las Migraciones Laborales*, 19–21.
57. Gilson Miller, *Years of Glory*, 61–62.
58. Report by Raphael Spanien concerning his visit to Morocco, March 1955. HIAS at Yivo, United HIAS Service Main Office, NY. Call no. RG 245.8, I-363, box 612. I thank Michal Ben-Ya'akov for drawing my attention to this document.
59. Tsur, *A Torn Community*, 190–96.
60. Serels, *A History*, 289.
61. See, for example, Birth certificate signed by Carlos Albo in Tangier, "Acta de Nacimiento, Estados Unidos de Venezuela-Consulado ad-Honorem de Venezuela Tánger," Tangier, July 11, 1952, MPC.
62. Ben-Ya'akov, "Cazès-Benathar"; Tsur, *A Torn Community*, 291. For more on her family and background as a member of the Hispanic Moroccan Jewish community, see Gilson Miller, *Years of Glory*, 9–23.
63. Report by Raphael Spanien, March 1955.
64. Ibid.
65. Laskier, *North African Jewry*, 186.
66. Heckman, *The Sultan's Communists*, 106–07, 117, 134–35.
67. Bin-Nun, "The Contribution of," 254; Bin-Nun, "The Movement," 236, 249; Serels, *A History*, 278–79; El Guabli, "Morocco Reimagined," 51–52.
68. Heckman, *The Sultan's Communists*, 136; Calderwood, *Colonial Al-Andalus*, 9.
69. Serels, "Nesry, Carlos De."
70. El Guabli, "Morocco Reimagined," 47.
71. Ojeda Mata, "The Sephardim," 9.

72. Heckman, *The Sultan's Communists*, 149–63.
73. Bin-Nun, "Moroccan Press Debate," 87–90.
74. Bin-Nun, "The Contribution," 263; "Telegrama Rabat-New York," 1.
75. Pouso Balleto, "S. M. Mohamed V en Tetuán," 4–5.
76. Ibid., 6.
77. Pouso Balleto, "El Príncipe Muley Hassan," 7; "Social: De la Llegada de," 9.
78. Benmaman, "Un Hombre Conocido," 7–8.
79. Bensabat, "Conozcamos Nuestro Pasado," 2, 10; see also Calderwood, "Moroccan Jews," 13–19.
80. Bin-Nun, "The Movement for," 235–84. See particularly page 257, note 58.
81. No title, *Or-Luz*, February 15, 1956, 4–6.
82. Kristol, "Einstein: Pasión de la Razón Pura," 4, 18–19.
83. See, for example, Blanc, "El Desarrollo del Idioma Hebreo," 5, 20; Borestein, "Noche de Pesca," 10–11.
84. "Cover page," *Or-Luz*, February 15, 1956.
85. Medina, "Bahia de Elath," 10; "Noche de Pesca," 11; Brender, "El Famoso," 10.
86. No title, cover page, *Or-Luz*, April 18, 1956; no title, cover page, May 31, 1956.
87. Benazeraf, "Episodes," 19, 25. Other advocates, like Alfonso Sabah, did emigrate to Israel, where they became community leaders and, as we shall see in chapter 7, sought to promote Hispanic Moroccan identity.

5. MOROCCANS IN VENEZUELA: A NEW GLOBAL HIERARCHY

1. DellaPergolla, "'Sephardic and Oriental,'" 12–14.
2. Schmelz, Della Pergola, and Avner, *Ethnic Differences among Israeli Jews*, 15.
3. Teller, *Rescue the Surviving Souls*.
4. Chazan, "Aliya From 'Affluent Countries,'" 405, 420; Livneh, "Does Zionism Have a Future?" 33; Herzog, "Symbolism and Policy," 49–64.
5. Troper, "The Canadian Jewish Polity," 237.
6. Peretz, *Let My People Go*, 2–4.
7. Troper, "The Canadian Jewish Polity," 245, 248–49.
8. Serels, *A History*, 180; Benoliel, "Présence Judéo-Marocaine," 227.
9. Della Pergola, "Jewish Out-Marriage," 156–57, 162–64.
10. De Haas, Catles, and Miller, *The Age of Migration*, 217.
11. Monk and Isaacson, *Comunidades Judías*, 95. Della Pergola, "Jewish Out-Marriage," 155. Concerning Venezuela's policies, see, for example, Padrón, "Whiteness in Latina Immigrants," 194–206.
12. Federbush, *World Jewry Today*, 462.
13. Wieland, "On a Remote Jewish Collective"; Even-Sapir, "Venezuela—a Land of Oil and Prosperity"; "Venezuela—the Sephardic Population" (found in the CZA, File S5-11.620).
14. Levy Benshimol and Goldberg, *Diccionario de Cultura*, 227–29.
15. An interview with Simi (pseudonym), interviewed by the author, 2009, Israel; an interview with Moisés Garzón Serfaty, 1990, Venezuela, ICJ; an interview with Carlos Gueron, 1991, Venezuela, ICJ; an interview with Perla Sultan, 1989, Venezuela, ICJ.
16. Federbush, *World Jewry Today*, 462.

17. El Khuffash Alvarez, "Venezuela, La Partición Del Mandato Británico," 29–37; Sananes Almoslinos and García Eugenio, *El Discurso*, 82–84; Belilty, "Nety Bargraser," 9–12; see also "Hace 26 años," 8.
18. Lejter, *Jewish Discourses*, 172, 273, 282–84.
19. Blank, "The Integration," 217; Monk and Isaacson, *Comunidades Judías*, 96–97.
20. A Dispatch from the Israeli Consul in Caracas to the Latin American Department in the Israeli Ministry of Foreign Affairs, January 26, 1961 (ISA, Call No. MFA, 3314 34.)
21. Ibid.
22. Kodesh, "A Great Lesson from a Small Mission," 459–66; Duvshani, "The Jewish School in Caracas," 3.
23. Blank, "The Integration," 210, 218, 220.
24. A letter from the board of directors to the AIV, February 28, 1963 (CAHJP, Call No. Ven/117); an interview with Gonzalo, 1989, Venezuela, ICJ.
25. Goldberg and Hubschman, "Los Pilares Fundacionales," 19–22.
26. Nassí, "La Comunidad Ashkeanzi," 5, 44.
27. Blank, "The Integration," 218; see also "Qué es CAIV," Confederación de Asociaciones as de Venezuela (CAIV), accessed January 25, 2011, https://www.caiv.org/quienes-somos/.
28. "Nuevos Socios," 1.
29. "La Asociacion Israelita de Venezuela Registra," 24; "Cerca de Cien Niños Asisten," 24.
30. "El Grupo Herzl," 11.
31. "Hilula de Rebbi Meir Baal HaNes," 18; "Hilula de Rebbi Shimon Bar Yohai," 19.
32. "La Visita de Jo Amar," 24.
33. Shalom Chetrit, *Intra-Jewish Conflict*, 43–140.
34. Such reports appeared frequently, mostly authored by David Sitton. See, for example, "BaMa'aracha's Editor Is Due to Visit the Sephardic Communities," 17.
35. "The Monthly News," 22 (appearing in an issue that devoted its cover page to a local housing crisis); Sofer, "Intensifying Activities by the WSF," 29, 31.
36. Sitton, *Sephardi Communities Today*, 176, 286.
37. See "Editor's Note," *Hedim* 1 (January 1974): 2.
38. Ronen, "The Founding Convention," 6; "In Latin America," 15; "Realizose con Éxito," 27. Mati Ronen was the WZO Sephardic Department's emissary to New York in 1973.
39. Garzón Serfaty, "FESELA a los 40 Años."
40. Guberek, *Crónica Testimonial*, 235–36. See also https://www.fesela.com/revista-maguen.
41. Ibid.; an interview with Moisés Garzón Serfaty, 1990, Venezuela, ICJ.
42. "Editorial-Deja Salir a Mi Pueblo," 3.
43. Benarroch, "Qué es y Qué," 11.
44. "Semana de Judaísmo Latinoamericano," 18.
45. See, for example, an interview with Daniel Bendahan, 1990, Venezuela, ICJ; an interview with Lea Almosny Mercedes, 1990, Venezuela, ICJ; an interview with Fortuna Bendayan de Furhman, 1989, Venezuela, ICJ; an interview with Mary Taurel, 1989, Venezuela, ICJ.
46. Aizenberg, "Judíos en la América," 11; Salama "El Yishuv Judio en Brasil," 8.
47. See, for example, Villar, "Primeros Emigrantes," 4; Villar, "Fernando VII," 10–13.
48. See, for example, "La Situación de los Judíos en los *Países Árabes*," 19–22. This report ends with the call "Let my people go" and demanding freedom of emigration for Jews of Arab

countries. The call for the "salvage" of Soviet Jews is repeated throughout 1971–72; "Editorial-Deja Salir a Mi Pueblo," 3.

49. Botbol, "Conferencia Mundial de las Comunidades," 8.

50. Shenhav, "World Organization of Jews from Arab Countries," 31.

51. "Futuro Incierto Para el Judaísmo Marroquí," 11–13.

52. An invitation by the Club a de Venezuela, February 23, 1966 (CAHJP, Call No. Ven/146).

53. A dispatch concerning the response of Jews from northern Morocco, May 14, 1969 (CAHJP, Call No. Ven/84); dispatches sent from Caracas to the Jewish communities of Tangier and Tetouan between February 18 and May 28, 1969 (CAHJP, Call No. Ven/84). The Moroccan community in Venezuela was not the only Moroccan community in the diaspora to adopt such a stance. The long-lasting Moroccan-led periodical *Israel* in Argentina featured many images of Moroccan Jews "in distress." At the outset of the 1970s, many of these concerns were directed to the communities in Israel.

54. See front-page photographs featuring the work of the JDC in, as the texts below explain, its "combat" against the terrible misery of Jews in Islamic countries (*Israel*, January 18, 1950; February 17, 1950) or efforts improve the economic conditions of Jews in North Africa (*Israel*, June 16, 1950; July 21, 1950). As for the situation in Israel, see, for example, a reprint of Albert Memmi's article expressing solidarity with Israel's Black Panthers (*Israel*, September 1973, 9).

55. Toledano, "Recuerdos de Tánger," *Maguén-Escudo*, September 1970, 17.

56. Ibid.

57. Ibid.

58. Toledano, "Recuerdos de Tánger," March 1971, 12.

59. Toledano, "Recuerdos de Tánger," December 1970, 29.

6. SPAIN AND THE POSTCOLONIAL DIASPORA

1. Narvoni, "The Jewish Communities in Spain," 5–6. Samuel Serfaty was mentioned in chapter 1 as the trainer of Atlético Tetouan's basketball team.

2. Avishai, "The Jews are Back in Madrid," 8–9.

3. The author's conversation with Rabbi Benito Garzón, September 8, 2020.

4. "The King of Spain Met," 18.

5. "Sephardi Roots and Public Activity," 8.

6. Duyvendak, *The Politics of Home*.

7. Vilar, *Tetuán*, 87–89.

8. Rohr, *The Spanish Right*, 12–14; Kerem, "Portugal's Citizenship for Sephardic Jewry," 6.

9. Gerber, *The Jews of Spain*, 264; Rein, "Diplomacy, Propaganda," 21; Schammah Gesser and Pinheiro, "Guest Editors' Introduction," 1–15.

10. Rein, "Diplomacy, Propaganda," 26–30.

11. Lisbona Martín, "La Especificidad," 75; on the process of Spanish naturalization, see Ojeda Mata, *Modern Spain*, 114–220.

12. See, for example, "Enlace," 5, 17.

13. Ennaji, *Moroccan Muslims*, 39.

14. Lisbona Martín, "La Especificidad," 74.

15. Bernecker and Cook, "The Change in Mentalities," 67–68.

16. Gómez Escalonilla, "Educación Para," 127–48; Gómez Escalonilla, "International Organizations," 73.

17. For more on the revival of Sephardic studies in the 1970s and early 1980s, see a summary of works and programs in *Jewish Folklore and Ethnology Newsletter* 5 (1982): 4–5.

18. Gerber, "Ingathering the Sephardic Experience," 32.

19. Rein, "Diplomacy, Propaganda," 21–33.

20. Israel Garzón, *Los Judíos*, 71, 73, 75–78; Lisbona, *Retorno*, 225. See also "Historia de La Federación," Federación de Comunidades Judías de España, accessed July 2020, http://www.fcje.org/historia.

21. Israel Garzón, *Los Judíos de Tetuán*, 121–22; Israel Garzón, *Los Judíos*, 81.

22. "Raíces Nos Invita a Cruzar un Puente Entre Dos Mundos." See also the editor's letter to the readers published in 2011, on the occasion of *Raíces*'s twenty-fifth anniversary (Israel Garzón, "Carta de un Caminante: Raíces y la Sociedad Civil Judía.")

23. Setton, *Spanish-Israeli Relations*, 78.

24. "Inauguration of First [Jewish] School in Spain," 8.

25. Israel Garzón, *Los Judíos*, 75, 77.

26. "Spanish Award for Radio Broadcasting," 18.

27. Lisbona, *Retorno*, 332; Setton, *Spanish-Israeli Relations*, 174–75.

28. He published the books Benami, *The Origins of the Second Republic*; Benami, *Fascism from Above*, and *Spain between Dictatorship and Democracy*.

29. Embajador de Israel en España-Shelomó Ben-Amí, "Patrimonio Judeoespañol, Marroquí de Habla Española-Interview for RCJ," interviewed by Jimmy Pimienta, Madrid (PAC, call no. 609-PE.IL03).

30. Lisbona, *Retorno*, 349–50.

31. "Sefarad '92: El Redecubrimiento de la España Judía, Grupo de Trabajo: Project Sepharad '92, Spain Visit, Major Jewish Organizations, 1988" (ASF IA, ASF AR6, CJH).

32. Lisbona, *Retorno*, 352, 358.

33. "ASF Hosts World Sephardi Meeting," cover page (found in Newsletters box, Sephardic Highlight, 1987–1990, ASF IA, ASF AR6, CJH).

34. Halevi Wise, "Through the Prism of Sepharad," 15.

35. Benayón, Presidente de Mabat Israel, "Entrevista sobre Mabat Israel," interviewed by the staff of Aadas y Adafinas de radio RCJ, Paris (PAC, 909– EX.IL03); Mauricio Hatchwell, "En Torno a Sefarad 92, an interview for RCJ," interviewed by Jimmy Pimienta, Paris, 1992 (PAC, call no. 807-EV.ES03).

36. For more on that separation between the Ladino scholarship and institutions in Israel at the time, see Refael, *Ladino, Here and Now*.

37. "Romancero Judeoespañol de Marruecos," 12.

38. See "Del Romancero Judeoespañol," January 1972, 9; "Morenica," 2; "Del Romancero Judeoespañol," August 1971, 9.

39. "Origen y Significado de Algunos Apellidos," 23.

40. Gerber, "Introduction," 11–12.

41. Efron, *German Jewry and the Allure*; Schorsch, "The Myth of Sephardi Supremacy," 47–66; Gerber, "Introduction," 11–12.

42. Botbol Hatchuel, "Los Sefardíes y Su Aporte," 50.

43. Ibid., 51–52.
44. Referring to the verse in the *Book of Ovadia* 1, 20.
45. Chocrón Serfaty, "Una Carta en Jaquetía," 35–37.
46. Bendelac, *Los Nuestros*, book cover.
47. Bendelac, *Diccionario del Judeoespañol*; Bendelac, *Voces Jaquetiescas*.
48. Alvar, "A Propósito del Diccionario de Jaquetía," 44–46.
49. Ibid.
50. "La Jaquetia Que Hablábamos," 46.
51. Botbol Hachuel, "El Judeo-Español," 58–62.
52. Heffes, "Botbol Hatchuel, Abraham."
53. "La Asociación Cultural Sefarad," 50–52.
54. Bearroch, "La Real Academia Española," 8–13.
55. "Conferencias de Rabi Baruj Garzón," 24.
56. Issue number 38 (January-March 1982).
57. "La I Semana Sefaradí de Caracas," 20–21.
58. In the 1990s, he published two books regarding the history of the Sephardi communities in Venezuela. See Carciente, *La Comunidad*, and Carciente, *Presencia Sefardí*; Carciente was also ex-president of the AIV (1970–74) and ex-chairman of the Executive Committee of the main Sephardi Synagogue, Tiferet Israel of Caracas (1978–80).
59. The board of directors included, in addition to Serfaty and Pariente, Amram Abraham Levy Benshimol, Abraham Botbol Hatchuel, Gonzalo Benaím Pinto, Pinhas Cohén Toledano, and Jaime Cohén Toledano—all immigrants from northern Morocco or their descendants.
60. Among the publications by the CESC that appeared in the 1980s, two particularly marked the growing interest in the Sephardi past. The first was *Cuentos Españoles, de Sefarad y los Sefardíes*, by Adela Alicia Requena (1984), and the second was *Romances de Ayer y de Hoy*, by Rabí Jacob Benadiba (1986).
61. "Documentos Que Hacen," 36.
62. Ames, "Spain's King Honors Sephardi Rabbi."
63. "Una Plaza y una Avenida," 12.
64. An overview of such cases is provided in Roumani, "'Le Juif Espagnol,'" 213–34; Evri, *The Return to Al-Andalus*.
65. Shukrun and Moreno, "Rethinking Moroccan Transnationalism."
66. Aizenberg, "Sephardim and Neo-Sephardim," 129–31.
67. Ibid., 131.
68. Nahón Serfaty, "Las Identidades," 32–34.
69. "La I Semana Sefaradí," July-September 1982, 20–21.
70. Kleinbort, "Romances Tradicionales," 18–25.
71. Gil, "El Romancero," 3.
72. Among them Don Ramón Menéndez Pidal, Manrique de Lara, Manuel Alvar, Samuel G. Armistead, Joseph H. Silverman, Elena Romero, Iacob M. Hassan, Oro Anahory Librowicz, Larrea Palacín, José Benoliel, Eleonora Noga Alberti-Kleinbort, J. Martínez Ruiz, P. Benichou, Moshé Attías, M. L. Ortega, and many others (see Garzón Serfaty, "El Romancero Sefaradí," 4).
73. Hassán, "Más Hebraísmos," 373–428; Benoliel, *Dialecto Judeo-Hispano-Marroquí*; Ricard, "Cartas de Ricardo Ruiz Orsatti," 99–115; Bénichou, *Romancero Judeo-Español*.

7. HISPANIC MOROCCANS IN ISRAEL

1. A circular distributed among MABAT's members, May 25, 1988, 5, PPC. I have touched upon the themes discussed in this chapter in a previous article published in *European Journal of Jewish Studies* (see Moreno, "Inappropriate Voices").
2. Prior to MABAT, Alfonso Sabah engaged in founding Agudat Sabah, a cultural society founded in Netanya.
3. Records from 1972 by the Jewish Agency documented at least 3,625 individuals who had utilized the agency's services to immigrate to Israel between 1961 and 1972 (Aharoni, *The Aliyah, 1961–1972*, 103).
4. Schmelz, Della Pergola, and Avner, *Ethnic Differences among Israeli Jews*, 15.
5. Israel Garzón, *Los Judíos*, 222.
6. The source refers to this group of occupations as necessitating education and training: clerks, teachers, lawyers, physicians, and the like. (See Aharoni, *The Aliyah of the Jews of Morocco, 1961–1972*, 34, 36, 113.) Since these figures encompass the population of immigrants to Israel from Arzila, Larache, Alcazarquivir, and Ouzane, small towns and villages that witnessed much smaller processes of burgounization, we may deduce that the relative number of such occupations was even higher in Tetouan and all the more so in Tangier.
7. Ibid., 69, 112.
8. Ben-Rafael and Sharot, *Ethnicity, Religion and Class*, 65, 71.
9. Leon and Cohen, "From the Mizrahi Middle Class Rehabilitation," 83.
10. A list of telephone numbers of MABAT members in Israel, 1985, PPC. The eventual number of subscribed members is probably higher, since the list did not indicate spouses that had similar phone numbers and address.
11. A. S., "Como Era Nuestra Comunidad?," 14.
12. A list of YOMAS members including their addresses, 1993, PPC.
13. See the newsletter *Comentario Español*, distributed and published by the Union de la Colonia Española de Ashdod. I thank David I. Beneish for sharing with me copies of that newsletter.
14. Ilan, "The Voice of the Mizrah," 213; Rosen Lapidot and Goldberg, "The Triple Loci," 116.
15. Babis, "The Paradox of Integration," 2226–43.
16. "Beit Hatfutsot-MABAT Israel, Fiesta de Hanukká-Live," Tel Aviv (PAC, call no. 804-EV.IL04).
17. Salomon Behayon, no title, *MABAT Revista* 1 (1989–90): 5.
18. Ouaknine Yekutieli and Nizri, "My Heart Is in the Maghrib," 165–94.
19. Levy, "Happy Mimouna," 11–13; Rosen Lapidot and Goldberg, *"The Triple Loci."*
20. Avital, "Porque MABAT," 105. A similar statement was made earlier in a circular distributed among MABAT's members dated May 25, 1988, 1, PPC.
21. Serels, *A History*, 177. In an interview for the radio show *Aadas y Adafinas* in 1987, Shlomo Ben-Ami affirmed this perspective while reflecting on his own childhood memories of Tangier. He argued that a focus on the "deeply rooted" Zionism among the Jews in northern Morocco would make the majority of the Israeli public respect North African Jewish culture more than would the contemporary Mimouna celebration, which he deemed "banal." (Embajador de Israel en España-Shelomó Ben-Amí, "Patrimonio Judeoespañol, Marroquí de Habla Española-Interview for RCJ," interviewed by Jimmy Pimienta, Madrid. PAC, call no. 609-PE.IL03.)

22. A circular sent to MABAT members, September 19, 1985, PPC, 2.
23. "Hilula," 55.
24. Refael, *Ladino Here and Now*, 76–77.
25. Shcroeter, "Moroccan Jewish Studies," 85, 89.
26. Tsur, "The Israeli Historiography," 236–38.
27. Using oral testimonies, Yissachar Ben Ami, for example, collected and complied in the early 1980s a corpus of popular traditions about hundreds of saints scattered throughout two hundred urban and rural Jewish communities in Morocco (see Shcroeter, "Moroccan Jewish Studies," 89–90).
28. Stillman, "The Academic Study of Islamicate Jewry," 36.
29. Ben-Ami, "Investigación del Folklore en Israel," 51–52.
30. Cimenti, "Sarita Benzquen: Cuento," 52.
31. "Yona Benshimol (z"l)," 15.
32. No author, no title, *MABAT Revista* 1 (1989–90): 14.
33. See "Concorso MABAT" in a circular sent to MABAT members, January 1982, PPC.
34. A circular sent to MABAT members summarizing the organization's activity from its founding in November 1979 to April 1988, dated December 13, 1988, PPC; a circular sent to *MABAT* members, dated September 19, 1985, PPC; Onne, *Jewish Communities in Spanish Morocco*.
35. Weich [Shahak], "Investigación de la Tradición," 61–62.
36. Weich Shahak, *En Buen Siman!*, 184–188.
37. Weich Shahak, "Riqueza Temática," 89–112; Weich Shahak and Díaz Más, *Romancero Sefardí de Marruecos*; Weich Shahak, *Cantares Y Romances*; Weich Shahak, "Passage-Rites in the Judeo-Spanish," 105–24.
38. Shoshana Weich [Shahak], "Investigación de la Tradición Musical." The performers were Alicia Bendayan, Ester Davida, Ginette Benabu, Jaky Benabu, Menashe Elbaz, Simi Suissa, Rahma Lucasi, Fortuna Mesas, Elvira Alfasi, Rachel Levy, Yitzhak Ben Ezra, and Floria Bengio. A second edition was issued as a CD in 2001 (Weich Shahak, *En Buen Siman!*, 184–88). An earlier scholarly project by Oro Anahory Librowicz was aimed at collecting ballad songs from northern Morocco among immigrants in US, Spain, Venezuela, Canada, Israel, and Morocco (Anahory Librowicz, *Florilegio de Romances*).
39. A circular sent to MABAT members, September 19, 1985, PPC.
40. "MABAT Realice Su Florilegio," 63.
41. Shabat, "Learning Is Never Boring."
42. An interview with Yaakov Bentolila (pseudonym), interviewed by the author, 2010, Israel.
43. Pimienta, "Los Cantes de Matesha." She worked on that article while conducting a project of preservation, mostly at the Ma'ale Adumim Institute for the Documentation of Judeo-Spanish Language and Its Culture affiliated within the Sefarad Society.
44. An interview with Gladys Pimienta, interviewed by the author, 2010, Israel.
45. An interview with Gladys Pimienta, interviewed by the author, 2009, Israel.
46. A letter entitled "Gran Concurso MABAT," circulated among MABAT members, 1988, PPC.
47. Later, in the early 1990s, the global interest in the Quincentennial and the related transnational collaborations in that regard included the Hebrew university. The Spanish National Committee set up to organize the event traveled to Israel to forge academic collaboration in this regard (presentation of Sefarad '92) in the Hebrew University of

Jerusalem by the president of the National Commission, 9.7.1987 (ASF archives, Projects, Sephard '92, Spain visit, major Jewish organizations, 1988).

48. Pinto Abecasis, "From Grandmother to Grandson," 100–18; Alexander and Bentolila, *La Palabra en su Hora*; Moreno, "De-Westernizing Morocco," 67–85.

49. Shaul, "Lingüística-La Haketia," 67.

50. See, for example, the following article appearing in Aki Yerushalayim: Pimienta, "Kantoniko de Haketia," 63–66.

51. See "La Pajina Djudeo-Espanyola de Aki Yerushalayim."

52. The Gaon Center dedicated the second volume of *El-Prezente* to the culture of northern Moroccan communities.

53. The list was kindly given to me by Prof. Tamar Alexander, the head of Gaon Center.

54. Additionally, a Journée Haketia (French for Haketia Day) was organized in Ashdod in 2008. The event attracted some fifty participants, gathering them in a hall to partake of a traditional meal. In fact, regardless of its name, the Journée Haketia was followed by an online discourse in French rather than Spanish, or Haketia. Dafina.net, le net des Juifs Marocains, "Forums Dafina - Les Juifs du Maroc - Darkoum- Journee Haketia a Ashdod," accessed November 11, 2010, http://dafina.net/forums/read.php?50,234289.

55. I can personally testify that, during my visit to their collection, their home would become transformed into an ethnic place, defined by their memories of pre-migration Morocco that dominated the discourse.

56. Pimienta, "Kantoniko de Haketia-La Kopla."

57. Levy, "Homecoming to the Diaspora," 98.

58. Schammah Gesser and Pinheiro, "Revisiting Isomorphism," 305.

59. Kosansky and Boum, "The 'Jewish Question' in Postcolonial," 432–33.

60. Benabu, "Notas de Viaje," 96.

61. "Congreso de Tangerinos en Terremolinos," no page number.

62. Ojeda Mata, *Modern Spain*, 77–78, 80–81.

63. Israel Garzón, *Los Judíos*, 172; Klecker de Elizalde, "Aspectos Demográficos," 54, 57.

64. Benhamú Jiménez, *La Jaquetía*, 24, 32.

65. Jadashot Melilla, *Publicación de Casa de Melilla en Jerusalen* 1 (January 1995).

8. A GLOBAL HISPANOPHONE DIASPORA

1. A letter circulated among *MABAT*'s members, September 1981, PPC.
I have touched on parts of the theme discussed in this chapter in my previous article (see Moreno, "The Ingathering," *European Judaism*). https://www.berghahnjournals.com/view/journals/european-judaism/52/2/ej520211.xml.

2. A letter circulated among *MABAT*'s members, January 1982, PPC.

3. Ibid.

4. Central and canonic studies in this regard were published by Ella Shohat, Yehuda Sehenav (see introduction).

5. Campoy Cubillo and Sampedro Vizcaya, "Entering the Global Hispanophone."

6. A. A., "Medinat Israel," no page number.

7. "La Preocupacion Sionista," 35–36; A. S., "Los Judíos de Tánger y Su Amor por Sion," 37–38.

8. A. S., "Como Era Nuestra Comunidad," 13.

9. "El Keren Kayemet Le-Israel," 18; "El Bosque de MABAT," 19.

10. Elbaz, "El Asilo Laredo-Sabah," 16; No author, no title, *MABAT Revista* 1 (1989–90): 17.
11. See "Our History," Bet Elazraki Children's Home, accessed May 5, 2014, https://elazraki.org/about/our-history/.
12. A. S., "Como Era Nuestra Comunidad," 13.
13. Avital, "Sionismo en Transición," 100.
14. Ibid., 104.
15. A letter circulated among MABAT's members, September 19, 1985, PPC.
16. Kahn, "They Came, They Saw," 41–54.
17. Avital, "A Boy from the Judería," 85.
18. Embajador de Israel en España-Shelomó Ben-Amí, "Patrimonio Judeoespañol, Marroquí de Habla Española-Interview for RCJ," interviewed by Jimmy Pimienta, Madrid (PAC, call no. 609-PE.IL03).
19. Rosen Lapidot and Goldberg, "The Triple Loci," 5, 9.
20. Roumani, "Le Juif Español," 233.
21. Ricard, "L'emigration (1932)," 427–29.
22. Bénichou, *Romanceros Judéo-Españoles*. Constituting an anthology, with variants and extensive scholarly commentary, of sixty-eight romanceros from Morocco. An earlier edition was published in Buenos Aires by the Instituto de Filología in 1946. See also Bénichou, *Creación Poética*.
23. Pimienta, "Espagnol et Haketía," 33–34; Sephiha, "Le Judéo-Espagnol du Maroc," 77–80; Benazeraf, *Refranero*; Sephiha, "Extinction du Judéo-Espagnol," 83–88.
24. See, for example, Benazeraf, *Refranero*.
25. "Vacaciones," 3.
26. Central works and figures are recapitulated in this volume, including essays by Isaac Benchimol, Manuel Ortega, Blanche Bendahan, Oro Anahory Librowicz, Jose Benoliel, Isaac Benarroch Pinto, and others. The earliest essay was originally composed in 1866 by the director of the AIU schools and addresses the practice among young Jewish émigrés in Latin America of returning to their communities in northern Morocco to marry within the community. For the statement on the influence of MABAT's congress, see Leibovici, *Nuestras Bodas*, 6.
27. For additional estimations regarding the total number of Moroccan Jews, see Burgard, "Les Sépharades dans les Études," 44; Cohen, "The Role of Music," 203.
28. Miles, "Between Ashkenaz and Québécois," 35.
29. Roumani, "'Le Juif Espagnol,'" 233; see also Cohen, "The Role of Music," 209.
30. Cohen, "Anahory Librowicz"; see Anahory Librowicz, "*Florilegio de Romances*."
31. Levy, "En Haketía con Simpatía-Programa RCJ_Poema Con los Apellidos Familias de Tánger," Paris (PAC, call no. 202-LG.TG21).
32. "Le Congrès Mondial de MABAT," 37.
33. Ibid., 38.
34. Ibid.
35. A brochure of the Conference, "MABAT-Primer Congreso Mundial, 22–25 Augosto 1983," PPC.
36. "Fédération Séphardie Canadienne," 37.
37. Serels, *A History*, 178.
38. Her notes are stored at the CJH archives in New York.
39. As they attest in an interview (31.1.2020), they felt like tourists fascinated by the country's culture, which they decided to capture on camara.
40. Interview with Gladys Pimienta, interviewed by the author, Israel, 2010.

41. Serels, *A History*, 181.
42. Mauricio Hatchwell, "En Torno a Sefarad 92, an interview for RCJ," Paris (PAC, call no. 202-LG.TG21).

EPILOGUE

1. Hanson, "Deciphering Venezuela's Emigration Wave," 356–59.
2. Candia, "Venezuela: Another Jewish Exodus," 22–25.
3. A total of 683 Venezuelans moved to Israel between 2013 and 2019 (see Reches, "From Ben-Gurion to Venezuelan Converts," 94–96).
4. While *Latinx* is a category often used interchangeably with *Hispanic* in popular and bureaucratic US discourses, it effectively excludes Spanish-speaking populations with origins outside of Latin America, mainly from Spain and former Spanish colonies in Africa.
5. Bokser Liwerant, "Latin American Jews in the United States," 133; Green, "Transnational Identity and Miami Sephardim," 135. Constituting a group of a few hundred in Israel as of 2020, Venezuelan Jews, of both Sephardi or Ashkenazi origins, became affiliated with the broader OLEI association, designed for Spanish-speaking Jewish immigrants from Spain and Latin and Central America in the country. An association called Beit Venezuela works to facilitate integration of Venezuelans into Israeli society.
6. Dahan, *From the Maghreb to the West*, 163–86.
7. An interview with Amram Amsalem, co-interviewed by the author, 2019, Miami.
8. Miami was incorporated as a branch already in 1982 due to a demand of leaders of the Cuban community in the region (see Bejarano, "Transnational Sephardi Zionism," 351–72).
9. Nae, "Verónica Maya," 5.
10. Aidi, "Let Us Be Moors," 43–52.
11. Author's conversation with Néstor L. Garrido, October 22, 2020.
12. Read more in the "editor's note" in a letter to the readers published in 2011, on the occasion of *Raíces*'s twenty-fifth anniversary (Jacobo Israel Garzón, president of the Federation of Jewish Communities of Spain [FCJE]; director of Roots between 1994 and 2005, accessed July 2020, http://www.revista-raices.com/sumarios/raices86/poema.htm).
13. *Tetuán* (Colección Zocos, Editorial Confluencias, 2017); *Los Judíos; Déjalo, Ya Volveremos* (Seix Barral, 2006); *Los Judíos de Tetuán* (2004); *Crónica de Una Familia Tetuaní* (2003). Another central figure was Ester Bendahan, a member of the community. As historian Adolfo Campoy Cubillo suggested, "Bendahan's novels can be read as a gradual attempt to come to terms with her own experience as a member of the Sephardic community" (Campoy Cubillo, *Memories*, 93). She published several novels on the interwoven ancient Sephardic past with modern-day Jewish experience in Spain and North Africa. Among her publications is *Soñar con Hispania* (with Ester Benari; Ediciones Tantín, 2002).
14. Many of these Israeli writers have engaged in contacts with Spanish institutions and published. Angy Cohen completed her important contribution to the study of this community in a shared program by the Hebrew University in Jerusalem and Complutense University of Madrid (see Cohen, "Recordar, Resistir.")
15. Weisz, *Jews and Muslims*, 77.
16. The Casa-Sefard-Israel also helped bestowing finance and support on the part of the Spanish embassy in Venezuela on the CESC (the author's conversation with Néstor L. Garrido, October 22, 2020).

17. The numeral gap reflects a number of unaffiliated Jews who are not registered in communal organizations.
18. Weisz, *Jews and Muslims*, 79.
19. Dominguez Diaz, "Once Upon a Time." The Spanish law was restricted to a period of three years (2015–18) and later extended for one year (see "Ley 12/2015, de 24 de Junio," *Boletín Oficial del Estado* 151, Sec. 1: 52557, accessed May 17, 2020, https://www.boe.es/eli/es/l/2015/06/24/12/dof/spa/pdf).
20. They were followed by Colombia with 2,673 applications and Argentina with 1,686. A total of 1,381 applications came from across the US and 149 from Canada. Only 868 applications were made in Turkey and only 860 from Israel (see Gesser Schammah, "Virtually Sephardic?" 200, 214).
21. "Viven Momento Histórico."
22. The author's conversation with Néstor L. Garrido, October 26, 2020.
23. Kerem, "Portugal's Citizenship," 5.
24. "The First Israeli is Entitled to a Spanish Passport."
25. Kerem, "Portugal's Citizenship," 5.
26. In 2010, Amazônia Judaica Historical Archive was founded by the center (www.amazoniajudaica.com.br).
27. *Amazônia Judaica* 20, 5, 12, 29.
28. Author's conversation with Elias Salgado, February 2022.
29. For a more in-depth exploration of these developments and complexities, refer to Elbaz, "Looking at the 'Other,'" 406–407. For further exploration of the dispute regarding the Hispanic and North African origins of northern Moroccan Jews, refer to Campoy Cubillo, *Memories*, 90–93.
30. See, for example, one of the several articles published on this initiative: https://zamane.ma/tanger-rencontre-internationale-dediee-a-lhistoire-des-juifs-du-nord-du-maroc-zamane/

CONCLUSIONS

1. Khachig Tölölyan, "Elites and Institutions in the Armenian Transnational," *Diaspora: A Journal of Transnational Studies* 9, no.1 (2000): 107–36; Judith Bokser Liwerant, "Globalization, Diasporas, and Transnationalism: Jews in the Americas," *Contemporary Jewry* (2022): 1–43.
2. Tölölyan, "Diaspora Studies"; Brubaker, "The 'Diaspora' Diaspora," 6; Miles and Sheffer, "Francophonie and Zionism."

ACKNOWLEDGMENTS

1. Vered, "The Little-Known Cuisine of Spain's Moroccan Jews."
2. Axel, "The Context of Diaspora," 29.

BIBLIOGRAPHY

ARCHIVES AND SELECTED PRIMARY SOURCES

Archives

American Jewish Committee Oral History Collection, New York Public Library [**OHC**]
Anu, Museum of the Jewish People, Tel Aviv
Ben-Abu's Private Collection
Benoliel's Private Collection
Center for Jewish History, YIVO, New York [**CJH**]
The Central Archive for the History of the Jewish People, Jerusalem [**CAHJP**]
The Central Zionist Archives, Jerusalem [**CZA**]
Centre de la Culture Judéo-Marocaine, Brussels [**CCJM**]
Centro de Easudios Sefaradies de Caracas archives [**CESC**]
Communauté Sépharade Unifiée du Québec archives [**CSUQ**]
Division of Oral History at the Avraham Harman Institute of Contemporary Jewry, the Hebrew University of Jerusalem [**ICJ**]
Historical Jewish Press, the National Library of Israel; Tel Aviv University [**JPress**]
Israel State Archive, Jerusalem [**ISA**]
Jimmy Pimienta's Audio Collection [**PAC**]
The Joint Distribution Committee Archives, Jerusalem [**JDCA**]
Ladino Periodical Collection and Manuscripts Department, Ben-Zvi Institute, Jerusalem [**BZLPC**]
Manuscripts Department, National Library of Israel, Jerusalem [**MDNL**]
Moreno's Private Collection [**MPC**]

Music Collection and Sound Archives, National Library of Israel, Jerusalem [**SA-JUNL**]
National Library of Israel [**NLI**]
Pimientas' Private Collection [**PPC**]
Serial and Government Publications Division, Library of Congress, Washington, DC [**PDLC**]

Newspapers and Periodicals Consulted

A Columna (Brazil, Archive: JPress)
Adelante (Morocco, Archive: JPress)
BaMa'aracha (Israel, Archive: MDNL)
Boletín de la Asociación a de Venezuela (Archive: CAHJP)
Boletín de la Sociedad Hajnasat Orhim (Morocco, Archive: MDNL)
Boletín Oficial de la Comunidad a de Tánger [*Boletín Oficial*] (Morocco, Archive: MDNL)
Carta de France MABATT (France, Archive: PPC)
El Mundo (Venezuela, Archive: MDNL)
España (Morocco, Archive: PDLC)
HaOlam (UK, Archive: JPress)
Israel (Argentina, Archive: MDNL)
Kol Israel (Morocco, Archive: BZLPC)
La Voix des Communautés (Morocco, Archive: JPress)
La Voix Sépharade (Canada, Archive: CSUQ)
MABAT Revista (Israel, Archive: PPC)
Maguén-Escudo [*Maguén*] (Venezuela, Archive: CESC)
Noar (Morocco, Archive: JPress)
Nuevo Mundo Israelita (Venezuela, MDNL)
Or-Luz (Morocco, Venezuela, Spain, Archive: BZLPC)
Raíces (Spain, MDNL)
Renacimiento de Israel (Morocco, Archive: BZLPC)
Revista de Filología Hispánica (Spain, Archive: PDLC)
Sephardic Highlight (USA, Archive: CJH)

Interviews

Alegría Bendelac, 1992, USA, OHC, OHL, call# **P (Oral Histories, Box 122, No. 4)
Carlos (pseudonym), 2009, Israel, interviewer: Aviad Moreno
Carlos Ben-Dahan, 1990, Venezuela, interviewer: Monica Botbol, ICJ (213)26
Carlos Gueron, 1991, Venezuela, interviewer: Clara Serfati, ICJ (213)51
Clarice (pseudonym), 2009, Israel, interviewer: Aviad Moreno
———, 2010, Israel, interviewer: Aviad Moreno

Daniel (pseudonym), 2010, Israel, interviewer: Aviad Moreno
Daniel Bendahan, 1990, Venezuela, interviewer: Monica Botbol, ICJ (213)21
David (pseudonym), 2009, Israel, interviewer: Aviad Moreno
———, 2010, Israel, interviewer: Aviad Moreno
Fortuna Bendayan de Furhman, 1989, Venezuela, interviewer: Debora Yurman, ICJ (213)25
Gladys Pimienta, 2010, Israel, interviewer: Aviad Moreno
Gonzalo Benaim Pinto, 1989, Venezuela, interviewer: Segal Ariel, ICJ (213)7
Hélène (pseudonym), 2009, Israel, interviewer: Aviad Moreno
Isaac Ben-Dayan, [1990?], Venezuela, interviewer: Rachel Gemer ICJ (213)29
Isaac Chocrón, 1989, Venezuela, interviewer: Leonardo Senkman, ICJ (213)11
Isaac Sananes, [1990?], Venezuela, interviewer: Rachel Gemer, ICJ (213)44
Lea Almosny Mercedes, 1990, Venezuela, interviewer: Clara Serfati, ICJ (213)30
Mary Taurel, 1989, Venezuela, interviewer: Debora Yurman, ICJ (213)39
Moisés Garzón Serfaty, 1990, Venezuela, interviewer: Leonardo Senkman, ICJ (213)12
Nina (pseudonym), 2009, Israel, interviewer: Aviad Moreno
Nisim Matut, 1990, Venezuela, interviewer: Leonardo Senkman, ICJ (213)41
Nusia Waher, 1990, Venezuela, interviewer: Leonardo Senkman, ICJ (213)38
Perla (pseudonym), 2009, Israel, interviewer: Aviad Moreno
Perla Sultan, 1989, Venezuela, interviewer: Merche Bendayan, ICJ (213)45
Ruth (pseudonym), 2009, Israel, interviewer: Aviad Moreno
———, 2010, Israel, interviewer: Aviad Moreno
Salomón (pseudonym), 2009, Israel, interviewer: Aviad Moreno
Sara (pseudonym), 2010, Israel, interviewer: Aviad Moreno
Sidney Pimienta, 2010, Israel, interviewer: Aviad Moreno
Simi (pseudonym), 2009, Israel, interviewer: Aviad Moreno
———, 2010, Israel, interviewer: Aviad Moreno
Simone Melo-Foinquinos, 2009, Israel, interviewer: Aviad Moreno
Yaakov Bentolila, 2010, Israel, interviewer: Aviad Moreno

Radio Broadcasting

Alberto Pimienta, "La Zarzuela y Los Judíos en el Teatro Cervantes de Tánger," Tangier
Alberto Pimienta, "Su Acción de Recoger Cantes Judeoespañoles de Marruecos," Tangier 1993
"Beit Hatfutsot, MABAT Israel, Fiesta de Hanukká -Live," Tel Aviv
Embajador de Israel en España-Shelomó BenAmí, "Patrimonio Judeoespañol, Marroquí de Habla Española," Madrid
Mauricio Hatchwell, "En Torno a Sefarad 92, an interview for RCJ," Paris 1992
Momy Benayón, Presidente de Mabat Israel, "Interview sobre Mabat Israel," Paris

Solly Lévy, "En Haketía con Simpatía-Programa RCJ_Poema Con los Apellidos Familias de Tánger," Paris

Sr. Ahmed Goudian, "Un Musulman Se Acuerda de los Antiguos Judíos Tangerinos," Tangier

REFERENCES

Abensur, Philip. "Les Eleves de la École de l'Alliance Israelite Universelle de Tanger entre 1864 et 1879." *Etsi* 12, no. 47 (March 2009).

Abitbol, Michel, and Alan Astro. "The Integration of North African Jews in France." *Yale French Studies* 85 (1994): 248–61.

Abu-Haidar, Farida. "La Coexistance Linguistique chez les Marocains en Grande Bretagne." In *Migrations Internationales entre le Maghreb et l'Europe*, edited by M. Berriane and H. Popp, 39–42. München; Rabat: Technische Universität München, Université Mohammed V.

Aderet, Ofer. "The First Israeli Is Entitled to a Spanish Passport after Proving a Connection to Spanish Exiles." *Haaretz*, January 23, 2016. https://www.haaretz.co.il/news/education/1.2827852 [Hebrew].

"Adherentes de Tánger." *Boletín de la Sociedad Hajnasat Orhim* 2 (1913): 16.

"Adherentes de Tánger." *Boletín de la Sociedad Hajnasat Orhim* 3 (1921): 10–23.

"Adherentes del Extranjero." *Boletín de la Sociedad Hajnasat Orhim* 2 (1921): 19–30.

Adila, Mustapha. "Datos Para la Historia de la Inmigración Española en Tánger." *Yuyaykusun* 5 (2012): 133–48.

Aharoni, Simha. *The Aliyah of the Jews of Morocco, 1961–1964*. Paris, France: The Jewish Agency, Immigration Department, 1965 [Hebrew].

———. *The Aliyah of the Jews of Morocco, 1961–1972*. Jerusalem: The Jewish Agency, Immigration & Absorption Department, 1973 [Hebrew].

Ahrens, Jill, and Russell King. *Onward Migration and Multi-Sited Transnationalism: Complex Trajectories, Practices and Ties*. Cham, Switzerland: Springer Nature, 2023.

Aidi, Hisham. "Let Us Be Moors: Islam, Race and 'Connected Histories.'" *Middle East Report*, no. 229 (2003): 42–53.

———. "Tangier's Jazzmen—and Their Phantom Producer." *Africa Is a Country*. October 30, 2017. https://africasacountry.com/2017/10/tangiers-jazzmen-and-their-phantom-producer.

Aizenberg, Edna. "Sephardim and Neo-Sephardim in Latin American Literature." In *Sepharadism: Spanish Jewish History and the Modern Literary Imagination*, edited by Yael Halevi Wise, 129–42. Stanford, CA: Stanford University Press, 2012.

Aizenberg, Isidoro. "Judíos en la América Precolombiana." *Maguén-Escudo* 29, October 1972.

———. "Venezuela y los Judíos Curazoleños." *Maguén–Escudo* 95, April–June 1995.
Alarcón, Pedro Antonio. *Diario de un Testigo de la Guerra de África*. Madrid, Spain: Gaspar Y Roig, 1859.
Albazzaz, Muhammad Alamin. "Tangier during the International Administration Period." *Revue Dar al-Niaba* 18 (Spring 1988): 24–14 [Arabic].
Albet Mas, Abel. "Three Gods, Two Shores, One Space: Religious Justifications for Tolerance and Confrontation between Spain and Colonial Morocco during the Franco Era." *Geopolitics* 11, no. 4 (December 2006): 580–600.
Alexander, Clair. "Beyond 'The "Diaspora" Diaspora.'" *Ethnic and Racial Studies* 40, no. 9 (1546): 1544–55.
Alexander, Tamar, and Yaakov Bentolila. *La Palabra en su Hora es Oro—El Refrán Judeo-español en el Norte de Marruecos*. Jerusalem, Israel: Ben-Zvi Institute, 2008.
Allain, Jean-Claude. "Les Europeens Au Maroc a la Vielle du Protectorat: Quelques Chiffres Et Quelques Eflexions." *Revue Dar al-Niaba* 12 (1986): 1–4.
Alsultany, Evelyn, and Ella Shohat, eds. *Between the Middle East and the Americas: The Cultural Politics of Diaspora*. Ann Arbor, MI: University of Michigan Press, 2013.
Alterman Blay, Eva. "Judeus na Amazônia." In *Identidades Judaicas no Brasil Contemporâneo*, edited by Bila Sorj, 25–56. Rio de Janeiro, Brazil: Imago, 1997.
Alvar, Manuel. "A Propósito del Diccionario de Jaquetía; Una Espléndida Cosecha." *Maguén-Escudo* 94, April–June 1995.
Álvarez, Ana María López. *La Comunidad Judía de Tetuán, 1881–1940: Onomástica y Sociología en el Libro de Registros de Circuncisiones del Rabino Yishaq Bar Vidal Haserfaty*. Madrid; Toledo: Ministerio de Educación y Cultura, Dirección General de Bellas Artes y Bienes Culturales, Subdirección General de Museos Estatales; Museo Sefard, 2003.
Ames, Lynne. "Spain's King Honors Sephardic Rabbi for Study of Traditions." *New York Times*, December 29, 1996. Accessed July 2020. https://www.nytimes.com/1996/12/29/nyregion/spain-s-king-honors-sephardic-rabbi-for-study-of-traditions.html.
Anahory Librowicz, Oro. *Florilegio de Romances Sefardíes de la Diáspora: una Colección Malagueña*. Madrid, Spain: Cátedra-Seminario Menéndez Pidal, 1980.
Anjali, Bhatt M., Amir Goldberg, and Sameer B. Srivastava. "A Language-Based Method for Assessing Symbolic Boundary Maintenance between Social Groups." *Sociological Methods and Research* (2021).
Armistead, G. Joseph, H. Silverman Samuel, Oro Anahory Librowicz, and Israel J. Katz. *Romances Judeo-Españoles de Tánger (Recogidos por Zarita Nahón)*. Madrid, Spain: Cátedra-Seminario Menéndez Pidal, 1977.
Armistead, Samuel G. "Judeo-Spanish Traditional Literature: Half a Century of Fieldwork and Scholarship." *European Judaism* 44 (2011): 98–106.

Arques, Enrique. "Indianos de Tetuán." *El Munto Israelita*, December 10, 1949.
———. "Indianos de Tetuán." *El Munto Israelita*, December 10–31, 1949.
———. "Indianos de Tetuán." *El Munto Israelita*, December 17, 1949.
———. "Indianos de Tetuán." *El Munto Israelita*, December 24, 1949.
———. "Indianos de Tetuán." *El Munto Israelita*, December 31, 1949.
Arsan, Andrew, John Karam, and Akram Khater. "On Forgotten Shores: Migration in Middle East Studies and the Middle East in Migration Studies." *Mashriq & Mahjar* 1, no. 1 (2013): 1–8.
A. S. "Como Era Nuestra Comunidad—¿Cual Eran Sus Preocupaciones? Y Nosotros Hoy, Aquí, ¿Que Hemos Podido Reactualizar?" *MABAT Revista* 1, 1989–90.
Avishai, Mordechai. "The Jews Are Back in Madrid." *Hedim* 11 (December 1975): 8–9 [Hebrew].
———. "The King of Spain Met with Delegates from the SF." *Hedim* 14 (April 1976): 18 [Hebrew].
———."Sephardi Roots and Public Activity." *Hedim* 42 (December 1979): 8 [Hebrew].
Avital, Amada. "A Boy from the Judería of Tetouan Has Become a Successful Industrialist." *MABAT Revista* 1, 1989–90 [Hebrew].
———. "Porque MABAT." *MABAT Revista* 1, 1989–90.
———. "Sionismo en Transición." *MABAT Revista* 1, 1989–90.
Axel, Brian Keith. "The Context of Diaspora." *Cultural Anthropology* 19, no. 1 (February 2004): 26–60.
Azaryahu, Maoz, Kenneth Foote, Reuben Rose-Redwood, and Derek Alderman. "Historical Space as Narrative Medium." *Geojournal* 73, no. 3 (January 2008): 179–94.
Babis, Deby. "The Paradox of Integration and Isolation within Immigrant Organisations: The Case of a Latin American Association in Israel." *Journal of Ethnic and Migration Studies* 42, no. 13 (2016): 2226–43.
Bahar, Baser, and Amira Halperin. "Diasporas from the Middle East: Displacement, Transnational Identities and Homeland Politics." *British Journal of Middle Eastern Studies* 46, no. 2 (March 2019): 215–21.
Balán, Jorge. "The Role of Migration Policies and Social Networks in the Development of a Migration System in the Southern Cone." In *International Migration Systems: A Global Approach*, edited by Mary M. Kritz, Lin Lean Lim, and Hania Zlotnik, 115–31. Oxford, UK: Clarendon, 1992.
"BaMa'aracha's Editor Is Due to Visit the Sephardic Communities in the Diaspora." *BaMa'aracha* 6, May 1962 [Hebrew].
Bartal, Israel. *Galut in the Land—Settlement in Eretz-Israel Prior to Zionism: Studies and Essays*. Jerusalem, Israel: Zionist Library, 1994 [Hebrew].
Bashkin, Orit. *Impossible Exodus*. Stanford, CA: Stanford University Press, 2020.

Bassan El Khuffash Alvarez, Edduar. "Venezuela, La Partición Del Mandato Británico De Palestina y el Nacimiento Del Estado De Israel." *Contra Relatos Desde El Sur* 12, no. 14 (2016): 29–37.

Bejarano, Margalit. "The Position of the Sephardi Community among the Jewish Settlement in Argentina." *Pe'amim: Studies in Oriental Jewry* 76 (1998): 30–51 [Hebrew].

———. "The Sephardic Communities of Latin America: A Puzzle of Sub-Ethnic Fragments." In *Contemporary Sephardic Identity in the Americas: An Interdisciplinary Approach*, edited by Margalit Bejarano and Edna Aizenberg, 19–52. Syracuse, NY: Syracuse University Press, 2012.

———. "Transnational Sephardi Zionism in a Historical Perspective: Salomón Garazi and the Cuban Chapter of FESELA in Miami." *Judaica Latinoamericana; Estudios Histórico-Sociales* 8 (2017): 351–72.

Belilty, Samuel. "Nety Bargraser: la Fuerza de Mover Montañas." *Revista Haguesher*, 1986.

Benabu, Abraham. "Notas de Viaje." *MABAT Revista* 1, 1989–90.

Ben-Ami, Shlomo. "ASF Hosts World Sephardi Meeting." *Sephardic Highlight* 3, no. 2 (October 1989): cover page.

———. *Fascism from Above: Dictatorship of Primo de Rivera in Spain, 1923–1930*. Oxford, UK: Oxford University Press, 1983.

———. *The Origins of the Second Republic in Spain*. Oxford, UK: Oxford University Press, 1978.

Benarroch, Carlos. "La Real Academia Española y los Judíos." *Maguén-Escudo* 12, May 1971.

Benarroch, Elías S. "Qué es y qué ac eel K.K.L." *Maguén-Escudo* 3, August 1970.

Benarroch Pinto, Isaac. *Indianos Tetuaníes, Edición e Introducción de Jacobo Israel Garzón*. Madrid, Spain: Hebraica; Casa Sefarad-Israel, 2008.

Benazeraf, Raphaël. "Episodes in the History of Jewish Press in Morocco." *BaMa'aracha*, July 22, 1975 [Hebrew].

———. *Refranero: Recueil de Refranes (proverbes) Judéo-espagnols du Maroc (Hakitía)*. Paris: Imprimerie Continentale, 1978.

Benbassa, Esther, and Aron Rodrigue. *Sephardi Jewry: A History of the Judeo-Spanish Community, 14th–20th Centuries*. Berkeley: University of California Press, 2000.

Benchimol, L. "La Langue Espagnole au Maroc." *Revue des Écoles de Alliance Israélite* 2 (1901): 126–33.

Benchimol, Samuel. *Eretz Amazonia: Os Judeus na Amazônia*. Manaus, Brazil: Valer, 1998.

Bendayan, David. *Une Jeunesse à Tanger*. Saint-Denis, France: Éditions Latitudes, 2000.

Bendelac, Alegría. *Diccionario del Judeoespañol de los Sefardíes del Norte de Marruecos*. Caracas, Venezuela: Centro de Estudios Sefardíes de Caracas, 1995.

———. *Los Nuestros: Sejiná, Letuarios, Jaquetía y Fraja: Un Retrato de los Sefaradíes del Norte de Marruecos a Través de Sus Recuerdos y de Su Lengua (1860–1984)*. New York: P. Lang, 1987.

———. *Mosaics: A Jewish Girl Grows in Tangiers*. Jerusalem, Israel: Center for Programming, Department of Development and Services, WZO, 1986.

———. *Voces Jaquetiescas*. Caracas, Venezuela: Centro de Estudios Sefardíes de Caracas, 1990.

Beneish, David Isaac. "Los Macabeos, Equipo Judío de Futbol de Larache 1920–1930." *eSefarad*, accessed May, 11, 2020. https://esefarad.com/los-macabeos-equipo-judio-de-futbol-de-larache-1920-1930/.

Bengio, J., and J. L. Miège. "La Communauté Juive de Tanger dans les Années 1860, 'Les Actas.'" *Revue Maroc-Europe: histoire, économies, sociétés* 6 (1994): 151–65.

Bengio, Joseph. "Juifs Marocains en Argentine." In *Mosaïques de Notre Mémoire: Les Judéo-Espagnols du Maroc*, edited by Sarah Leibovici, 233–49. Paris, France: U.I.S.F., Centre Don Isaac Abravanel, 1982.

Benhamú Jiménez, David. *La Jaquetía de la Comunidad Judía de Melilla en el Siglo XXI*. Instituto de las Culturas de la Ciudad Autónoma de Melilla, 2018.

Bénichou, Paul. *Creación Poética en El Romancero Tradicional*. Madrid, Spain: Gredos, 1968.

———. "Notas Sobre el Judeo-Español de Marruecos en 1950." *Nueva Revista De Filología Hispánica* 14, no. 3–4 (1960): 307–12.

———. "Observaciones sobre el Judeo-Español de Marruecos." *Revista de Filología Hispánica* 7 (1945): 209–58.

———. *Romanceros Judéo-Españoles de Marruecos*. Buenos Aires, Argentina: Instituto de Filología de la Universidad de Buenos Aires, 1946.

———. *Romanceros Judéo-Españoles de Marruecos*. Madrid, Spain: Castilia, 1968.

———. *Romanceros Judeo-Español de Marruecos, 2a ed*. Madrid, Spain: Editorial Castalia, 1968.

Benmaman, Joseph D. "El Símbolo del Sefaradísmo." *Or-Luz*, February 1, 1956.

———. "Un Hombre Conocido y Venerado en Todos los Hogares Judíos." *Or-Luz*, February 15, 1956.

Benmayor, Rina, and Dalia Kandiyoti. "Ancestry, Genealogy, and Restorative Citizenship. Oral Histories of Sephardi Descendants Reclaiming Spanish and Portuguese Nationality." *Genealogies of Sepharad* 18 (December 2020): 219–51.

Bennoune, Mahfoud. "Maghribi Workers in France." *Merip Reports* 34 (January 1975): 1–12.

Benoliel, José. "Dialecto Judeo-Hispano-Marroquí o Hakitia." *Boletín de la Real Academia Española* 13 (1926): 209–33.

———. "Dialecto Judeo-Hispano-Marroquí o Hakitia." *Boletín de la Real Academia Española* 14 (1927): 137–68, 196–234, 357–73, 566–80.

———. "Dialecto Judeo-Hispano-Marroquí o Hakitia." *Boletín de la Real Academia Española* 15 (1928): 47–61, 188–223.

———. *Dialecto Judeo-Hispano-Marroquí O Hakitía*. Madrid, Spain: Raphaël Benazeraf, 1977.

Benoliel, Leon. "Présence Judéo-Marocaine au Venezuela." In *Mosaïques de Notre Mémoire: les Judéo-espagnols du Maroc*, edited by Sarah Leibovici, 219–31. Paris, France: U.I.S.F., Centre Don Isaac Abravanel, 1982.

Ben-Rafael, Eliezer, and Stephen Sharot. *Ethnicity, Religion and Class in Israeli Society*. Cambridge, UK: Cambridge University Press, 1991.

Bensabat, Salomon. "Conozcamos Nuestro Pasado." *Or-Luz*, February 29, 1956.

Bensoussan, Georges. *Jews in Arab Countries: The Great Uprooting*. Bloomington: Indiana University Press, 2019.

Bentolila, Yaakov. "The Archive of Rabbi Yehuda Jalfon from Tetouan." In *Studies in the Culture of North African Jewry Vol. 2*, edited by Moshe Bar-Asher and Steven D. Fraade, 1–14. New Haven, CT; Jerusalem, Israel: 2011 [Hebrew].

Bentolila, Yossi. "The Immigration of the Jews from Tetuan and Tangier to Israel, Spain, Canada and Venezuela in the Twentieth Century." PhD diss., Bar-Ilan University, 2007 [Hebrew].

Bentolila Jalfón, Estrella. *Haketía: A Memoir of Judeo-Spanish Language and Culture in Morocco*. Translated by Ron Duncan Hart and Venessa Paloma. Santa Fe, NM: Gaon, 2011.

Benumeya, Rodolfo Gil (under the pseudonym Benomar). "El Futuro Problema de Marruecos." *Revista Hispano Africana* 25–26 (January–February 1927): 2.

Ben-Ya'akov, Michal. "Cazès-Benathar, Hélène." In *Encyclopedia of Jews in the Islamic World*, edited by Norman A. Stillman. Brill Online, 2013. Accessed February 12, 2020. https://referenceworks.brillonline.com/entries/encyclopedia-of-jews-in-the-islamic-world/cazes-benathar-helene-SIM_000660?s.num=0&s.f.s2_parent=s.f.book.encyclopedia-of-jews-in-the-islamic-world&s.q=Caz%C3%A8s-Benathar%2C+H%C3%A9l%C3%A8ne%2C.

Berdugo, Alberto S. "La Juventud Judía de Tánger y los Deportes." *Adelante*, February 15, 1931.

Bernecker, Walter L., and Jacqueline Cook. "The Change in Mentalities during the Late Franco Regime." In *Spain Transformed: The Franco Dictatorship*, edited by N. Townson, 67–84. London, UK: Palgrave Macmillan, 2007.

Bin-Nun, Yigal. "The Contribution of World Jewish Organizations to the Establishment of Rights for Jews in Morocco (1956–1961)." *Journal of Jewish Modern Studies* 9 (2010): 251–74.

———. "La Négociation de L'évacuation en Masse des Juifs du Maroc." In *La Fin du Judaïsme en Terres D'islam*, edited by Shmuel Trigano, 303–58. Paris, France: Denoël Médiations 2009.

———. "Moroccan Press Debate about the Rights of Jews, 1965–1955." *Kesher* 40 (2010): 86–101 [Hebrew].

———. "The Movement for Integration of Jews in Moroccan Society after Independence (1956–1967)." *Pe'amim Studies in Oriental Jewry* 125–27 (2011): 235–84 [Hebrew].

Blanc, Jaim. "El Desarrollo del Idioma Hebreo." *Or-Luz*, February 29, 1956.

Blank, Lily. "The Integration of Ashkenazi and Sephardi Jews in Venezuela through the Decision-Making Process in the Educational System." *Jewish Political Studies Review* 5 (1993): 209–45.

Bodenhamer, David. "Narrating Space and Place." In *Deep Maps and Narratives*, edited by David Bodenhamer, 7–27. Bloomington: Indiana University Press, 2015.

Bokser Liwerant, Judit. "Globalization, Diasporas, and Transnationalism: Jews in the Americas." *Contemporary Jewry* 41 (2021): 711–53.

———. "Latin American Jews in the United States: Community and Belonging in Times of Transnationalism." *Contemporary Jewry* 33, no. 1–2 (2013): 121–43.

Borestein, Tomas. "Noche de Pesca en el Kineret." *Or-Luz*, February 29, 1956.

Botbol, Alberto. "Conferencia Mundial de las Comunidades Judías pro Judíos de la Unión Soviética." *Maguén-Escudo* 2, July 1970.

Botbol Hatchuel, Abraham. "El Judeo-Español, el Ladino y la Haketia." *Maguén-Escudo* 44, July–September, 1982.

———. "La Comunidad Judía de Tetuàn y el Sionismo." *Maguén-Escudo* 21, February 1972.

———. "Los Sefardíes y Su Aporte al Desarrollo Económico y Cultural de Venezuela." *Maguén-Escudo* 85, October–December 1992.

Boum, Aomar. "From 'Little Jerusalem' to the Promised Land: Zionism, Moroccan Nationalism, and Rural Jewish Emigration." *The Journal of North African Studies* 15, no. 1 (2010): 51–69.

Brender, J. "El Famoso actor de cine, Danny Kaye en Tiberiades y Tel Aviv." *Or-Luz*, May 31, 1956.

Brodsky, Adriana M. *Sephardi, Jewish, Argentine: Community and National Identity, 1880–1960*. Bloomington: Indiana University Press, 2016.

Brubaker, Roger. "The 'Diaspora' Diaspora." *Ethnic and Racial Studies* 28, no. 1 (2005): 1–19.

Burgard, Antoine. "Les Sépharades Dans Les Études Démographiques." In *Les Sépharades Du Québec: Parcours d'Exils Nord-Africains*, edited by Yolande Cohen, 33–55. Montréal, Canada: Del Busso Éditeurs, 2017.

Bürki, Yvette. "Haketia in Morocco: Or the Story of the Decline of an Idiom." *International Journal of the Sociology of Language* 239 (2016): 121–55.

Calderwood, Eric. *Colonial Al-Andalus: Spain and the Making of Modern Morocco Culture*. Cambridge, MA: Belknap Press of Harvard University Press, 2018.

———. "Moroccan Jews and the Spanish Colonial Imaginary, 1903–1951." *Journal of North African Studies* 24 (2019): 1–25.
Campos, Michelle. *Ottoman Brothers: Muslims, Christians, and Jews in Early Twentieth-Century Palestine.* Stanford, CA: Stanford University Press, 2010.
Campos, Michelle, Orit Bashkin, and Lior Sternfeld. "MENA Jewry after 'the Middle Eastern Turn': Modernity and Its Shadows." *Jewish Social Studies* 28, no. 2 (2023): 3–40.
Campoy Cubillo, Adolfo. *Memories of the Maghreb.* New York: Palgrave Macmillan, 2012.
Campoy Cubillo, Adolfo, and Sampedro Vizcaya. "Entering the Global Hispanophone: An Introduction." *Journal of Spanish Cultural Studies* 20, no. 1–2 (2019): 1–16.
Candia, Carla. "Venezuela: Another Jewish Exodus." *World Policy Journal* 28, no. 4 (2011): 22–25.
Carciente, Jacob. *La Comunidad Judía de Venezuela: Síntesis Cronológica, 1610–1990.* Caracas, Venezuela: Asociación Israelita de Venezuela; Centro de Estudios Sefardíes de Caracas, 1991.
———. *Presencia Sefardí en la Historia de Venezuela.* Caracas, Venezuela: Asociación Israelita de Venezuela; Centro de Estudios Sefardíes de Caracas, 1997.
Carrion, Santos. "Imágenes de Sefarad." *Or-Luz*, May 15, 1956.
Cazes Bénatar, Hélène. "Spanish Morocco." *American Jewish Yearbook* 54 (1953): 394–95.
———. "Tangier." *American Jewish Yearbook* 56 (1955): 453–56.
"Cerca de Cien Niños Asisten a los Cursos de la AIV." *Maguén-Escudo* 28, September 1972.
Chatty, Dawn. *Displacement and Dispossession in the Middle East.* Cambridge, UK: Cambridge University Press, 2010.
Chazan, Meir. "Aliya from 'Affluent Countries' and David Ben-Gurion's Descent from the Political Scene." *Israel Affairs* 27, no. 3 (2021): 402–26.
Chen Dekel, Jonathan. "Rethinking Boundaries in the Jewish Diasporas from FSU." In *The New Jewish Diaspora: Russian-Speaking Immigrants in the United States, Israel, and Germany*, edited by Zvi Gitelman, 77–88. New Brunswick, NJ: Rutgers, 2016.
Chetrit, Joseph. "Judeo-Arabic and Judeo-Spanish in Morocco and Their Sociolinguistic Interaction." In *Readings in the Sociology of Jewish Languages*, edited by J. Fishman, 261–79. Leiden, the Netherlands: Brill, 1985.
Chocrón Serfaty, Isaac. "Una Carta en Jaquetía para un Personaje-autor." *Maguén-Escudo* 162, January–March 2012.
Cimenti, Elisa. "Sarita Benzquen: Cuento." *MABAT Revista* 1, 1989–90.
Clifford, James. "Diasporas." *Cultural Anthropology* 9, no. 3 (1994): 302–38.

Cohen, Ángeles (Angy) M. "Recordar, Resistir, Apostar: Conversaciones con Judíos Hispano-Marroquíes en Israel y Argentina." PhD diss., Hebrew University of Jerusalem and Autónoma de Madrid, 2017.

Cohen, Angy. "On Belonging and Other Dreams. The Ambiguous Positions of the Jews in 'Spanish Morocco.'" *Contemporary Jewry* 40, no. 4 (2020): 547–78.

Cohen, David. "Spanish-Speaking Zionist Leaders in Casablanca." *Shorashim Bamizrah* 5 (2002): 262–67 [Hebrew].

Cohen, Judith R. "Anahory-Librowicz, Oro." In *Encyclopedia of Jews in the Islamic World*, edited by Norman A. Stillman. Brill Online, 2013. https://referenceworks.brillonline.com/entries/encyclopedia-of-jews-in-the-islamic-world/anahory-librowicz-oro.

———. "The Role of Music in the Quebec Sephardic Community." In *Contemporary Sephardic Identity in the Americas: An Interdisciplinary Approach*, edited by Margalit Bejarano and Edna Aizenberg, 202–22. New York: Syracuse University Press, 2012.

Cohen, Rubin. *Global Diasporas*. New York: Routledge, 2008.

Cohen, Yolande, and Stephanie Tara Schwartz. "Scholarship on Moroccan Jews in Canada: Multidisciplinary, Multilingual, and Diasporic." *Journal of Canadian Studies* 50, no. 3 (2016): 592–612.

Comité Judío Americano, ed. *Comunidades Judías de Latinoamerica, 1973–1975*. Buenos Aires, Argentina: Oficina Sudamericana Del Comité Judío Americano, 1977.

"Conferencias de Rabi Baruj Garzón." *Maguén-Escudo* 25, June 1972.

"Congreso de Tangerinos en Terremolinos." *Costa Del Sol*, July 17, 1987.

Coriat, León. "Mi Comunidad: Breve Reseña Histórica y Sentimental de la Comunidad Judía de Tetouan." 1954, 1. (Found at the Raphaël Benazeraf Collection, Yad Ben Zvi, Jeruslaem, file: 35.) Accessed July 2020. https://northafricanjews-ww2.org.il/ar/doc/1039.

Crespo, Gérard. *Les Espagnols au Maroc, 1859–1975 de la Guerre d'Afrique à l'indépendance du Sahara Espagnol*. Saint-Denis, France: Editions Edilivre, 2016.

Dahan, Izthak. *From the Maghreb to the West: Moroccan Jews between Three Continents*. Tel Aviv, Israel: Resling, 2022 [Hebrew].

Danon, Abraham. "Recueil de Romances Judeo-Espagnoles Chantées en Turquie." Revue des études juives 32 (1896): 102–23.

Danon, Dina. *The Jews of Ottoman Izmir: A Modern History*. Stanford, CA: Stanford University Press, 2020.

De Haas, Hein. "Morocco's Migration Experience: A Transitional Perspcetive." *International Migration* 45, no. 4 (2007): 39–70.

De Haas, Hien, Stephen Catles, and Mark J. Miller. *The Age of Migration: International Population Movements in the Modern World*. New York; London: Guilford, 2020.

"Delegados de Hajnasat Orhim." *Boletín de la Sociedad Hajnasat Orhim* 2 (1913): 11.

Della Pergola, Sergio. "Jewish Out-Marriage: Mexico and Venezuela." In *Jewish Intermarriage around the World*, edited by Shulamit Reinharz and Sergio DellaPergola, 153–70. New Brunswick: Transaction Publishers, 2009.

———. "'Sephardic and Oriental' Jews in Israel and Western Countries: Migration, Social Change, and Identification." In *Sephardic Jewry and Mizrahi Jews: Volume XXII*, edited by Peter Y. Medding, 3–43. New York: Oxford University Press, 2008.

"Del Romancero Judeoespañol." *Maguén-Escudo* 15, August 1971.

"Del Romancero Judeoespañol." *Maguén-Escudo* 20, January 1972.

"Documentos Que Hacen Y Son Historia Acuerdo De La Creación Del Centro De Estudios Sefardíes En Caracas." *Maguén-Escudo* 37, October–December, 1980.

Dominguez Diaz, Marta. "Once Upon a Time Our Home Was in Spain: Comparing Diaspora Discourses among Morisco Descendants and Sephardim Today." In *Jewish-Muslim Relations in Past and Present: A Kaleidoscopic View*, edited by Meri Josef, 206–29. Leiden, the Netherlands: Brill, 2017.

"Donativos Varios." *Boletín de la Sociedad Hajnasat Orhim* 3 (1921): 31.

Dubnov, Arie M. "Review Essay: Zionism on the Diasporic Front." *Journal of Israeli History* 30 (September 2011): 211–24.

Duvshani, Moshe. "The Jewish School in Caracas." *Hachinuch: Educational Psychology Review* 1 (1954): 202–7 [Hebrew].

Duyvendak, Jan. *The Politics of Home: Belonging and Nostalgia in Europe and the United State*. London, UK: Palgrave Macmillan, 2011.

"Editorial-Deja Salir a Mi Pueblo." *Maguén-Escudo* 2, July 1970.

"Editor's Note." *Hedim* 1 (January 1974): 2 [Hebrew].

Efron, John M. *German Jewry and the Allure of the Sephardic*. Princeton, NJ: Princeton University Press, 2016.

"El Apostolado de Nuestro Ilustre Colaborador, el Senador Español Dr. Ángel Pulido." *Israel*, May 13, 1921.

Elbaz, I. "El Asilo Laredo-Sabah (Adelante 1931)." *MABAT Revista* 1, 1989–90.

Elbaz, Vanessa Paloma. "Jewish Music in Northern Morocco and the Building of Sonic Identity Boundaries." *Journal of North African Studies* 27 (2022): 1027–59.

———. "Looking at the 'Other' through the Ear: Contemporary Traces of Protectorate Politics through Music." In *Mélanges Festschrift for Professor Mohammed Kenbib*, edited by Khalid Ben Sghir, 401–27. Rabat: Faculté de lettres et sciences sociales Mohammed V (2021).

"El Bosque de MABAT." *MABAT Revista* 1, 1989–90.

"El Discubrimiento de America y los Judíos." *Adelante*, August 15, 1931.

"El Dr. Pulido en el Libro de Oro-Copiamos de la Revista 'Israel' de Buenos Aires." *Renacimiento de Israel*, March 3, 1927.

"Elecciones de la Asociacion Hispano-Hebrea." *Kol Israel*, April 17, 1914.

"El Grupo Herzl de la AIV y sus Actividades." *Maguén-Escudo* 1, June 1970.

El Guabli, Brahim. "Morocco Reimagined: When Moroccan Jews Could Theorize the Moroccan State." *Journal of Religious Minorities under Muslim Rule* 1, no. 1 (2023): 41–66.

"El Keren Kayemet Le-Israel." *MABAT Revista* 1, 1989–90.

"El Mundo Sefaradí-el Dr Pulido y los Sefardíes." *Noar*, May 12, 1952.

"El Viaje a España de la Juventud Tangerina." *Adelante*, January 1, 1931.

Ennaji, Moha. *Muslim Moroccan Migrants in Europe: Transnational Migration in its Multiplicity*. London, UK: Palgrave Macmillan, 2014.

"En Tetuán." *Adelante*, November 1, 1929.

Epstein, Diana Lia. "Instituciones y Liderazgo Comunitario de los Judíos de Origen Marroquí en Buenos Aires." In *Árabes Y Judíos en Iberoamérica: Similitudes, Diferencias y Tensiones*, edited by Raanan Rein, 135–58. Sevilla, Spain: Fundación Tres Culturas del Mediterráneo, 2008.

———. "Los Judeo-Marroquíes en Buenos Aires: Pautas Matrimoniales 1875–1910." *EIAL* 6 (1995): 113–33.

"Estado Financiero." *Boletín de la Sociedad Hajnasat Orhim* 2 (1913): 12–13.

Even-Sapir, M. "Venezuela—a Land of Oil and Prosperity." *Haboker*, May 28, 1955 [Hebrew].

Evri, Yuval. *The Return to Al-Andalus: Disputes of Sephardic Culture and Identity between Arabic and Hebrew*. Jerusalem, Israel: Magnes, 2020 [Hebrew].

Falbel, Nachman. "Jewish Agricultural Settlement in Brazil." *Jewish History* 21 (2007): 325–40.

"Fédération Séphardie Canadienne." *La Voix Sépharade*, August–September 1984.

Federbush, Simon. *World Jewry Today*. Jerusalem, Israel: Massadah, 1959.

"Fondo Especial." *Boletín de la Sociedad Hajnasat Orhim* 3 (1921): 9–32.

Friedman, Michal Rose. "Orientalism between Empires: Abraham Shalom Yahuda at the Intersection of Sepharad, Zionism and Imperialism." *Jewish Quarterly Review* 109 (2019): 435–51.

———. "Reconstructing 'Jewish Spain': The Politics and Institutionalization of Jewish History in Spain, 1845–1940." *Hamsa Journal of Judaic and Islamic Studies* 1 (2014): 55–67.

"Futuro Incierto Para el Judaísmo Marroquí." *Maguén-Escudo* 31, December 1972.

Garzón Serfaty, Moisés. "El Romancero Sefaradí." *Maguén-Escudo* 64, July–September, 1987.

———. "FESELA a los 40 Años de su Fundación: Ideario, Logros y Retos." *Maguén-Escudo* 165, October–December 2012. Accessed May 27, 2018. https://

revistamaguenescudo.wordpress.com/fesela-a-los-40-anos-de-su-fundacion-ideario-logros-y-retos.

———. "Premio Gordo Numero." *Or-Luz*, February 1956.

"Gerardo Diego Triunfo en el Circulo Israelíta de Tetuán." *Or-Luz*, February 15, 1956.

Gerber, Jane S. "Introduction." In *Sephardi Studies in University*, edited by Jane S. Gerber, 11–12. Rutherford, NJ: Fairleigh Dickinson University Press, 1995.

———. *The Jews of Spain: A History of the Sephardic Experience*. New York: Free Press, 1992.

Gherman, Michel. "The Beginnings of Brazilian Zionism: Historical Formation and Political Developments." In *Jews and Jewish Identities in Latin America: Historical, Cultural, and Literary Perspectives*, edited by Margalit Bejarano, Yaron Harel, Marta F. Topel, and Margalit Yosifon, 190–207. Boston, MA: Academic Studies, 2017.

Gil, Eduardo. "El Romancero." *Maguén-Escudo* 64, July–September 1987.

Gil, Eyal. *The Disenchantment of the Orient*. Stanford, CA: Stanford University Press, 2006.

Gilson Miller, Susan. "'Apportioning' Sacred Space in a Moroccan City: The Case of Tangier, 1860–1912." *City & Society* 13 (2001): 57–83.

———. *A History of Modern Morocco*. Cambridge, UK: Cambridge University Press, 2013.

———. "Kippur on the Amazon: Jewish Emigration from Northern Morocco in the Late Nineteenth Century." In *Sephardic and Middle Eastern Jewries: History and Culture in the Modern Era*, edited by Harvey E. Goldberg. Bloomington, IN: Indiana University Press, 1996.

———. *Years of Glory: Nelly Benatar and the Pursuit of Justice in Wartime North Africa*. Stanford, CA: Stanford University Press, 2021.

Goldberg, Jacqueline, and Wiktoria Hubschman. "Las Instituciones Fundadoras de la Kehilá Ashkenazí." *Nuevo Mundo Israelita*, September 2003.

———. "Los Pilares Fundacionales de la Kehilá (Parte II)." *(Noticias de una Diáspora 6), Nuevo Mundo Israelita*, September 2003.

Goldstein Sabah, Sasha. *Baghdadi Jewish Networks in the Age of Nationalism*. Leiden, the Netherlands: Brill, 2021.

Gómez Escalonilla, Delgado L. "Educación Para el Desarrollo. OCDE, Asistencia Exterior y Reforma de la Enseñanza en la España del Tardofranquismo." *Foro de Educación* 18, no. 2 (2020): 127–48.

———. "International Organizations and Educational Change in Spain during the 1960s." *Encounters on Education* 21 (2020): 70–91.

Gonzalez, Allyson. "Abraham S. Yahuda (1877–1951) and the Politics of Modern Jewish Scholarship." *Jewish Quarterly Review* 109 (2019): 406–33.

González González, Irene. "Escuelas, Niños y Maestros: La Educación en el Protectorado Español en Marruecos." *Awraq* 5–6 (2012): 117–33.

———. *Spanish Education in Morocco, 1912–1956: Cultural Interactions in a Colonial Context*. Brighton, UK: Sussex Academic Press, 2015.

"Gran Bazar La Caraqueña." *Renacimiento de Israel*, October 25, 1931.

Green, Henry A. "Transnational Identity and Miami Sephardim." In *Contemporary Sephardic Identity in the Americas: An Interdisciplinary Approach*, edited by Margalit Bejarano and Edna Aizenberg, 124–40. Syracuse, NY: Syracuse University Press, 2012.

Guberek, Simón. *Crónica Testimonial Sobre el Judaísmo Venezolano*. Bogotá, Colombia: Fundación Cultural Simón y Lola Guberek, 1980.

Guedj, David. *The Hebrew Culture in Morocco, 1912–1956*. Jerusalem, Israel: Zalman Shazar Center, 2022.

Guershon, Isaac. "The Foundation of Hispano-Jewish Associations in Morocco: Contrasting Portraits of Tangier and Tetouan." In *Sephardi and Middle Eastern Jewries: History and Culture in the Modern Era*, edited by H. Goldberg, 181–89. Bloomington: Indiana University Press, 1996.

"Hace 26 años: Instalado el Comité Venezolano Pro-Palestina." *Maguén-Escudo* 23, April 1972.

Haim, Abraham. *Particularity and Integration: The Sephardi Leadership in Jerusalem under British Rule, 1917–1948*. Jerusalem, Israel: Carmel, 2000 [Hebrew].

Halevi Wise, Yael. "Through the Prism of Sepharad." In *Sepharadism: Spanish Jewish History and the Modern Literary Imagination*, edited by Weise-Halevi, 1–34. Stanford, CA: Stanford University Press, 2012.

Haller, Dieter. "Place and Ethnicity in Two Merchant Diasporas: A Comparison of Sindhis and Jews in Gibraltar." *Global Networks: A Journal of Transnational Affairs* 3 (2003): 75–96.

Halliday, Fred. "The Millet of Manchester: Arab Merchants and Cotton Trade." *British Journal of Middle Eastern Studies* 19 (1992): 159–76.

Halstead, Charles. "A 'Somewhat Machiavellian' Face: Colonel Juan Beigbeder as High Commissioner in Spanish Morocco, 1937–1939." *Historian* 37 (November 1974): 46–66.

Hamilton, Michelle. "Hispanism and Sephardic Studies." *Journal of Medieval Iberian Studies* 1 (2009): 179–94.

Hanson, Rebecca. "Deciphering Venezuela's Emigration Wave: As Venezuela's Crisis Deepens, Many Are Leaving. What Are the Politics behind Conflicting Numbers of Migrants?" *NACLA Report on the Americas: Women Rising in the Americas* 50, no. 4 (2018): 356–59.

Hassán, I. "Más Hebraísmos en la Poesía Sefardí de Marruecos: Realidad y Ficción Léxicas." *Sefarad* 37 (1977): 373–428.

Hassan Cohen, Abraham. "Los Judeo Españoles De Marruecos, Ante 'El Reencuentro' de 1992." *La Carte de France Mabatt* 3, December 1990–January 1991, 1–3.

Hazkani, Shay. *Dear Palestine: A Social History of the 1948 War*. Stanford, CA: Stanford University Press, 2021.

Heckman, Alma R. *The Sultan's Communists: Moroccan Jews and the Politics of Belonging*. Stanford, CA: Stanford University Press, 2020.

Heffes, Gisela. "Botbol Hatchuel, Abraham." In *Encyclopedia of Jews in the Islamic World*, edited by Norman A. Stillman. Brill Online, 2013. Accessed March 3, 2013. http://www.paulyonline.brill.nl/entries/encyclopedia-of-jews-in-the-islamic-world/botbol-hatchuel-abraham-SIM_0004530.

Hernández Sandoica, Elena. *Pensamiento Burgués y Problemas Coloniales en la España de la Restauración (1875–1887)*. Madrid, Spain: Universidad Complutense, 1982.

Herzog, Ben. "Symbolism and Policy: Reading the Ben-Gurion-Blaustein 'Exchange' in Relation to Citizenship Laws in the United States." *Israel Studies* 25, no. 3 (2020): 49–64.

"Hilula de Rebbi Meir Baal HaNes en el Club Israelita de Venezuela." *Maguén-Escudo* 1, June 1970.

"Hilula de Rebbi Shimon Bar Yohai en la Sinagoga Tiferet Israel." *Maguén-Escudo* 1, June 1970.

Hissong, Kristin. *Nationalism and Jewish Identity in Morocco: A History of a Minority Community*. London, UK: I. B. Tauris, 2022.

Ich Yehudi. "Tolerancia No Es Ni Crea Derecho: Sobre El Edicto de Expulsión de 1492." *Adelante*, July 1, 1929.

Ilan, Nahem. "The Voice of the Mizrah: The Hebrew Periodicals of Sepharadi-Mizrahi Jews." *Pe'amim: Studies in Oriental Jewry* 93 (2003): 113–48 [Hebrew].

"Inauguration of First (Jewish) School in Spain." *Hedim* 1 (January 1974): 6 [Hebrew].

"Indice de Revistas Ibéricas Sefaradíes." *Adelante*, January 31, 1930.

"In Latin America." *Hedim* 1 (January 1974): 15 [Hebrew].

Israel Garzón, Jacobo. "Carta de un Caminante: Raíces y la Sociedad Civil Judía." *Raíces, Revista Judia de Cultura*. Accessed January 13, 2021. http://www.revista-raices.com/sumarios/raices86/poema.htm.

———. "Destinos de Emigración de Los Judíos de Norte de Marruecos entre 1700 y 1956." *Maguén-Escudo* 136, July–September 2005.

———. *Los Judíos de Tetuán*. Madrid, Spain: Biblioteca Metropoli, 2005.

———. *Los Judíos Hispano-Marroquíes: 1492–1973*. Madrid, Spain: Hebraica Ediciones, 2008.

Issawi, Charles. "The Historical Background of Lebanese Emigration, 1800–1914." In *The Lebanese in the World: A Century of Emigration*, edited by Albert Hourani and Nadim Shehadi, 13–32. London, UK: Centre for Lebanese Studies in association with I. B. Tauris, 1992.

"Jornaes." *A Columna*, May 4, 1917.

Jouin, Jan. "Le Costume de la Femme Israélite, au Maroc." *Journal de la Société des Africanistes* 6, no. 2 (1936): 167–86.

"Juanito Valderrama." In *The Encyclopedia of Popular Music*, edited by Colin Larkin. New York: Oxford University Press, 2016. https://www.oxfordreference.com/display/10.1093/acref/9780195313734.001.0001/acref-9780195313734-e-74951.

"Jucios y Opinions Sobre Nuesto Número Extraordinario." *Adelante*, April 13, 1930.

Kahn, Ava F. "They Came, They Saw, They Organized: The Association of American and Canadians in Israel." *American Jewish Archives* 43 (1991): 41–54.

Karkason, Tamir. "The Iberian Diasporas in the Eighteenth and Nineteenth Centuries." In *Jewish Literatures in Spanish and Portuguese: A Comprehensive Handbook*, edited by Ruth Fine and Susanne Zepp, 319–51. Berlin, Germany: De Gruyter, 2022.

Kasbarian, Sossie. "The Myth and Reality of 'Return'-Diaspora in the 'Homeland.'" *Diaspora: A Journal of Transnational Studies* 18, no. 3 (2015): 358–81.

Katz, Ethan B. *The Burdens of Brotherhood: Jews and Muslims from North Africa to France*. Cambridge, MA: Harvard University Press, 2015.

Kerem, Yitzchak. "Portugal's Citizenship for Sephardic Jewry: A Golden Fountainhead." *Contemporary Jewry* (October 2021): 1–24.

Klecker de Elizalde, Alejandro. "Aspectos Demográficos y Poblacionales de Ceuta y Melilla." *Cuadernos de Estrategia* 91 (1997): 51–66.

Kleinbort, Alberti. "Romances Tradicionales En Latinoamérica: Algunos Ejemplos Sumes V Criollos." *Maguén-Escudo* 57 (October–December 1985): 18–25.

Kobrin, Rebecca. *Jewish Bialystok and Its Diaspora*. Bloomington: Indiana University Press, 2010.

Kodesh, Shlomo. "A Great Lesson from a Small Mission." *Hachinuch: Educational Psychology Review* 41 (June 1969): 459–66 [Hebrew].

Kosansky, Oren, and Aomar Boum. "The 'Jewish Question' in Postcolonial Moroccan Cinema." *International Journal of Middle East Studies* 44, no. 3 (2012): 421–42.

Kozma, Liat, Cyrus Schayegh, and Avner Wishnitzer, eds. *A Global Middle East: Mobility, Materiality and Culture in the Modern Age, 1880–1940*. London, UK: I. B. Tauris, 2015.

Kristol, Irving. "Einstein: Pasión de la Razón Pura." *Or-Luz*, June 15, 1956.

Kutz, William. "State and Territorial Restructuring in the Globalizing City-Region of Tangier, Morocco." MA diss., University of Miami, 2010.
"La Asociación Cultural Sefarad -España." *Maguén-Escudo* 63, April–June 1987.
"La Asociacion Israelita de Venezuela Registra a su Socio No. 1000." *Maguén-Escudo* 12, May 1971.
"La I Semana Sefaradí de Caracas." *Maguén-Escudo* 44, July–September 1982.
"La Jaquetía Que Hablábamos." *Maguén-Escudo* 94, February 1995.
La Porte, Pablo. "Colonial Dreams and Nightmares: British and French Perceptions of Republican Policies in Spanish Morocco (1931–1936)." *International History Review* 41, no. 4 (2019): 821–44.
"La Primera Etapa: 'Adelante' Festeja su Primer Aniversario: En Fraternal Banquete se Reúnen los Redactores, Colaboradores, y Miembros de su Comité." *Adelante*, February 15, 1930.
"La Proclamación de la Independencia del Perú (28 de Julio de 1821)." *Adelante*, August 18, 1930.
"Larache en Fiesta, la Marcha de los Exploradores de Tánger." *Adelante*, September 9, 1930.
Laredo, Abraham I. *Bereberes y Hebreos en Marruecos*. Madrid: Instituto de Estudios Africanos, 1954.
———. "Lápidas Sepulcrales Antropomorfas de los Cementerios Israelitas de Alcazarquivir y Tánger." *Sefarad* 9, no. 2 (1949): 421–55.
———. *Les Noms des Juifs du Maroc*. Madrid, Spain: CSIC, 1978.
"La Situación de los Judíos en los *Países Árabes*." *Maguén-Escudo* 24, May 1972.
Laskier, Michael M. *The Alliance Israelite Universelle and the Jewish Communities of Morocco, 1862–1962*. Albany: State University of New York Press, 1983.
———. *North African Jewry in the Twentieth Century: The Jews of Morocco, Tunisia and Algeria*. New York: New York University Press, 1994.
———. "S. D. Lévy and Moïse Nahón: Two Sephardic Intellectuals in Modern Moroccan History." *Michael: On the History of the Jews in the Diaspora* 9 (1985): 51–86.
Las Migraciones Laborales en Venezuela: Diagnóstico Demográfico. Washington, DC: Organizacion de los Estados Americanos, Secretaria General, 1985.
"La Visita de Jo Amar." *Maguén-Escudo* 12, May 1971.
"Le Congrès Mondial de MABAT Tel Aviv 22–25 août 1983." *La Voix Sépharade*, November–December 1983.
"Le Dr Bension élu Membre de l'Académie Espagnole." *Adelante*, July 29, 1932.
"L'edition de Notre Journal." *Adelante*, August 1, 1929.
Lehmann, Matthias B. *Emissaries from the Holy Land: The Sephardic Diaspora and the Practice of Pan-Judaisim in the Eighteenth Century*. Stanford, CA: Stanford University Press, 2014.

———. "Rethinking Sephardi Identity: Jews and Other Jews in Ottoman Palestine." *Jewish Social Studies* 15, no. 1 (2008): 81–109.
Leibovici, Sara. "De Tetuán a Bujara: El Itinerario de Rebbi Yosef Mamán." *Maguén-Escudo* 61 (October–December 1986): 55–56.
———. "La Emigración a América de los Sefardíes de Marruecos." In *Diáspora Sefardí*, edited by Maria Antonia Bel Bravo et al., 241–49. Madrid, Spain: Editorial MAPFRE, 1992.
———. "Refranes Judeo-Españoles." *Noar*, November 4, 1951.
Lejter, Nelly C. "Jewish Discourses in Argentina and Venezuela, 1940s-1990s: A Comparative-Historical Analysis." PhD diss., Brown University, 2000.
Leon, Nissim, and Uri Cohen. "From the Mizrahi Middle Class Rehabilitation to the Israeli Center Renewed: Rethinking Center and Periphery." In *The Long History of the Mizrahim: New Directions in the Study of Jews from Muslim Countries*, edited by Aviad Moreno, 67–87. Ben-Gurion Institute for the Study of Israel and Zionism, Sde Boker Campus, 2021 [Hebrew].
Lesser, Jeff H. "From Pedlars to Proprietors: Lebanese, Syrian and Jewish Immigrants in Brazil." In *The Lebanese in the World: A Century of Emigration*, edited by Albert Hourani and Nadim Shehadi, 393–409. London, UK: Centre for Lebanese Studies in association with I. B. Tauris, 1992.
Levin, Yehuda. "From Tunisia to Argentina: The Origins of the Agricultural School in Djedeida and the Settlement of a Group of Its Graduates in Mauricio." *Pe'amim: Studies in Oriental Jewry* 101–2 (2015): 39–62 [Hebrew].
———. "Labor and Land at the Start of Jewish Settlement in Argentina." *Jewish History* 21 (2007): 341–59.
Levy, André. "Happy Mimouna: On a Mechanism for Marginalizing Moroccan Israelis." *Israel Studies* 23, no. 2 (2018): 1–24.
———. "Homecoming to the Diaspora: Nation and State in Visits of Israelis to Morocco." In *Homecomings: Unsettling Paths of Return*, edited by Anders H. Stefansson and Fran Markowitz, 92–108. Lexington, KY: Lexington Books, 2004.
———. *Return to Casablanca: Jews, Muslims and an Israeli Anthropologist*. Chicago, IL: University of Chicago Press, 2015.
Levy, Jacob. "La Juventud Judía y los Deportes." *Adelante*, March 1, 1931.
Levy, Joseph J. "Informe del Secretario Contador." *Boletín de la Sociedad Hajnasat Orhim* 3 (1921): 2–3.
Levy Benshimol, Abraham, and Jacqueline Goldberg. *Diccionario de Cultura Judía en Venezuela. Una Mirada Inconclusa*. Caracas, Venezuela: Asociación Israelita de Venezuela: Centro de Estudios Sefardíes de Caracas, 2014.
Liberman, Maria. "Moroccan Jews in the Brazilian Amazon." In *Recherches sur la Culture des Juifs d'Afrique du Nord*, edited by Issachar Ben-Ami, 105–12. Jerusalem, Israel: Communaute Israelite Nord-Africaine, 1991.

Lisbona Martín, José Antonio. "La Especificidad de las Migraciones Judías de Marruecos a España (1956–1970)." In *Atlas de la Inmigración Magrebí en España*, edited by Ana I. Planet Contreras and Ángeles Ramírez Fernández, 74–75. Madrid, Spain: Taller de Estudios Internacionales Mediterráneos; Universidad Autónoma de Madrid, 1996.

———. *Retorno a Sefarad: la Política de España hacia Sus Judíos en el Siglo XX*. Barcelona, Spain: Riopiedras, 1993.

Livneh, Eliezer. "Does Zionism Have a Future?" *Tradition: A Journal of Orthodox Jewish Thought* 6, no. 2 (1964): 30–41.

López García, Bernabé. "Españoles de Marruecos: Demografía de una Historia Compartida." In *Españoles en Marruecos, 1900–2007: Historia y Memoria Popular de una Convivencia*, edited by Oumama Aouad y Fatiha Benlabbah, 17–48. Rabat, Morocco: Editions & Impressions Bouregreg, 2008.

———. "Españoles en el Marruecos Actual." In *Atlas de la Inmigración Magrebí en España*, edited by Ana I. Planet Contreras and Ángeles Ramírez Fernández, 38–39. Madrid, Spain: Taller de Estudios Internacionales Mediterráneos; Universidad Autónoma de Madrid, 1996.

"Los Cheutas y Su Actual Situación; Mallorca y sus Judíos Viejos." *Or-Luz*, May 15, 1956.

"Los Judíos de Lengua Española y la Supresión, del Edicto de Expulsión de 1492." *Adelante*, April 15, 1931.

Lourido Díaz, Ramon. "Los Judíos en Marruecos Durante el Sultanato Sidi Muhammad B. Abd Allah (1757–1790)." *Revue Dar al-Niaba* 12 (1986): 23–37.

"MABAT Realice Su Florilegio de Romances." *MABAT Revista* 1, 1989–90.

Malo de Molina, Julio, and Fernando Domínguez. *Tetuán: El Ensanche: Guía de Arquitectura, 1913–1956*. Andalucía, Spain: Consejería de Obras Públicas y Transportes, 1996.

Marglin, Jessica. "Modernizing Moroccan Jews: The AIU Alumni Association in Tangier, 1893–1913." *Jewish Quarterly Review* 101, no. 4 (2011): 574–603.

Mateo Dieste, Josep Lluís. *La "Hermandad" Hispano-Marroquí: Política y Religión Bajo el Protectorado Español en Marruecos (1912-1956)*. Barcelona: Edicions Bellaterra, 2003.

Mays, Devi. *Forging Ties, Forging Passports: Migration and the Modern Sephardi Diaspora*. Stanford, CA: Stanford University Press, 2020.

Meddeb, Abdelwahab, and Benjamin Stora. *A History of Jewish-Muslim Relations: From the Origins to the Present Day*. Princeton, NJ: Princeton University Press, 2013.

Medina, Salomon. "Añoranzas de un Sabbat." *Or-Luz*, May 31, 1956.

———. "Bahia de Elath." *Or-Luz*, March 1956.

———. *Latidos de Andalucía*. Tetuán, Morocco: Cremades, 1954.

Meir Glitzenstein, Esther. *The "Magic Carpet" Exodus of Yemenite Jewry: An Israeli Formation Myth*. Brighton, UK: Sussex Academic Press, 2014.

Meyuhas Ginio, Alisa. *Between Sepharad and Jerusalem*. Leiden, the Netherlands: Brill, 2014.

Miccoli, Dario, ed. *Contemporary Sephardic and Mizrahi Literature: A Diaspora*. Philadelphia, PA: Taylor & Francis, 2017.

Miège, Jean-Louis. "L'activité Maritime a Tanger Première Moitie du XIX Siecle." In *Tangier 1800–1956: Contribution à L'histoire Récente du Maroc*, 55–76. Rabat, Morocco; Tetouan, Morocco: Université Mohammed V; Rabat et l'École Supérieure Roi Fahd de Traduction de Tanger; Université Abdelmalek Es-Saadi, 1991.

———. *Le Maroc et l'Europe: 1830–1894*. Paris, France: Universitaires de France, 1961–64.

Miles, William F. S. "Between Ashkenaz and Québécois: Fifty Years of Francophone Sephardim in Montréal." *Diaspora: A Journal of Transnational Studies* 16, no. 1–2 (2007): 29–66.

Miles, William, and Gabriel Sheffer. "Francophonie and Zionism: A Comparative Study in Transnationalism and Trans-statism." *Diaspora: A Journal of Transnational Studies* 7, no. 2 (1998): 119–48.

Mirelman, Victor A. "Sephardic Immigration to Argentina Prior to the Nazi Period." In *The Jewish Presence in Latin America*, edited by Gilbert W. Merkx and Judith Laikin Elkin. Boston, MA: Allen and Unwin, 1987.

Mogar. "Alegrías de Cádiz." *Or-Luz*, May 31, 1956.

———. "Tetuán Conserva con la Mayor Pureza sus Costumbres y Tradiciones, Declara el Dr. Laluf de la Argentina." *Or-Luz*, May 31, 1956.

Monaco, C. S. *Moses Levy of Florida: Jewish Utopian and Antebellum Reformer*. Baton Rouge: Louisiana State University Press, 2005.

Monk, Abraham, and Jose Isaacson. *Comunidades Judías de Latinoamérica*. Buenos Aires, Argentina: Oficina Latinoamericana del Comité Judío Americano—Instituto de Relaciones Humanas, 1966.

"The Monthly News: A Jewish Museum Opens in Spain." *BaMa'aracha* 124, July 1971 [Hebrew].

"Morenica." *Maguén-Escudo* 27, August 1972.

Moreno, Aviad. "Beyond the Nation-State: A Network Analysis of Jewish Emigration from Northern Morocco to Israel." *International Journal of Middle East Studies* 52 (February 2020): 1–21.

———. "De-Westernizing Morocco: Pre-Migration Colonial History and the Ethnic-Oriented Self-Representation of Tangier's Natives in Israel." *Quest: Issues in Contemporary Jewish History* 4 (2012): 67–85. https://www.quest-cdecjournal.it/de-westernizing-morocco-pre-migration-colonial-history-and-the-ethnic-oriented-self-representation-of-tangiers-natives-in-israel/

———. *Europe from Morocco: The Minutes of the Leadership of Tangier's Jewish Community (the Junta), 1860–1864*. Jerusalem, Israel: Ben-Zvi Institute, 2015 [Hebrew].

———. "Expanding the Dimensions of Moroccan (Jewish) Migration: Postcolonial Perspectives from Venezuela." *The Journal of North African Studies*, 2022, 1–28.

———. "The Ingathering of the Jewish (Moroccan) Diaspora: Zionism and Global Hometown Awareness among Spanish-Moroccan Jews in Israel." *European Judaism* 52, no. 2 (2019): 143–55. https://doi.org/10.3167/ej.2019.520211.

———. "Remapping 'Tradition': Community Formation and Spatiocultural Imagination among Jews in Colonial Northern Morocco." *Jewish Culture and History* 22, no. 4 (2021): 378–400. https://doi.org/10.1080/1462169X.2021.1993542.

Moreno, Aviad, and Noah Gerber. "Studying Jews from Muslims Countries in Israel: Developments and Divergences." In *The Long History of the Mizrahim: New Directions in the Study of Jews from Muslim Countries*, edited by Aviad Moreno, 7–39. Ben-Gurion Institute for the Study of Israel and Zionism, Sde Boker Campus, 2021.

Moya, José C. "The Jewish Experience in Argentina in a Diasporic Perspective." In *The New Jewish Argentina*, edited by Adriana Brodsky and Raanan Rein, 7–29. Leiden, the Netherlands: Brill, 2013.

Nae, Natán. "Verónica Maya, Primera Mujer en Presidir esta Organización; Fesela Reconoció Trayectoria de Moisés Garzón Serfaty." *Maguén-Escudo* 180, July 2017–January 2018.

Nahón Serfaty, Isaac. "Las Identidades de Isaac Chocrón: a Propósito de Rómpase en Caso de Incendio." *Maguén-Escudo*, January–March 2012.

Narvoni, Andrey. "The Jewish Communities in Spain Join the WSF." *Hedim* 13 (February 1976): 5–6 [Hebrew].

Nassí, Mario F. *La Comunidad Ashkeanzi de Caracas: Breve Historia Institucional.* Caracas, Venezuela: Unión Israelita de Caracas, 1981.

"The National Movement in Spain and Morocco." *Doar Hayom*, October 29, 1921 [Hebrew].

Noga Alberti-Kleinbort, Eleonora. "Romances Tradicionales En Latinoamérica: Algunos Ejemplos Sumes V Criollos." *Maguén-Escudo* 57, October–December 1985.

"Notas de Tetuán." *Renacimiento de Israel*, October 25, 1931.

Noy, Amos. *Experts or Witnesses: Jewish Intellegentsia from Jerusalem and the Levant in the Beginning of the Twentieth Century.* Tel Aviv, Israel: Resling, 2017 [Hebrew].

"Nuestras Doctrinas: El Respeto Sabático." *Adelante*, June 1, 1931.

"Nuestro Compatriotas en Buenos Aires: Rasgos Filantrópicos." *Renacimiento de Israel*, March 13, 1925.

"Nuevos Socios." *Boletín de la Asociación a de Venezuela*, April 1967.

Ojeda Mata, Maite. "Jewish Tetouan: Place, Community, and Ethnic Boundaries from the Minutes Book of The Community Board, 1929–46." *Jewish Culture and History* 22, no. 4 (2022): 358–77.

———. *Modern Spain and the Sephardim: Legitimizing Identities.* Maryland: Lexington Books, 2018.

———. "The Sephardim of North Morocco, Zionism and Illegal Emigration to Israel through the Spanish Cities of Ceuta and Melilla." *Contemporary Jewry* 40, no. 4 (2021): 519–45.

Onieva, Antonio J. *Guía Turística de Marruecos: Plazas de Soberanía, Protectorado Español, Tánger.* Madrid, Spain: Artes Gráficas Arges, 1947.

Onne, Elia. *Jewish Communities in Spanish Morocco: An Exhibition Catalog.* Tel Aviv, Israel: Beit Hatfutsot, 1983.

"Or Hailadim." *El Mundo Israelíta*, December 24, 1949.

"Origen y Significado de Algunos Apellidos Sefardíes." *Maguén-Escudo* 13, June 1971.

Ortega, Manuel L. *Los Hebreos en Marruecos: Estudio Histórico, Político y Social.* Madrid, Spain: Editorial hispano africana, 1919.

Ouaknine-Yekutieli, Orit, and Yigal S. Nizri. "My Heart Is in the Maghrib: Aspects of Cultural Revival of the Moroccan Diaspora in Israel." *Hespéris Tamuda* 51, no. 3 (2016): 165–94.

Padrón, Elena. "Whiteness in Latina Immigrants: A Venezuelan Perspective." *Women & Therapy* 38, no. 3–4 (2015): 194–206.

Palacín, A. Larrea. *Cuentos Populares del Norte de Marruecos.* Tetuán, Morocco: Editora Marroquí-Instituto General Franco de Estudios e Investigación Hispano-Arabe, 1952.

———. *Romances de Tetuán: Recogidos y Transcritos.* Madrid, Spain: Instituto de Estudios Africanos, 1952.

Peretz, Pauline. *Let My People Go: The Transnational Politics of Soviet Jewish Emigration during the Cold War.* London; New York: Routledge, 2017.

Phillips Cohen, Julia. *Becoming Ottomans: Sephardi Jews and Imperial Citizenship in the Modern Era.* New York: Oxford University Press, 2014.

Phillips Cohen, Julia, and Sarah Abrevaya Stein. *Sephardi Lives: A Documentary History, 1700–1950.* Stanford, CA: Stanford University Press, 2014.

Pimienta, Gladys. "Espagnol et Haketía à Travers Les Chansons Judéo-Espagnoles du Nord du Maroc." *Yod (Hommage à Haïm-Vidal Sephiha)* 1992: 33–34.

———. "Kantoniko de Haketia." *Aki Yerushalayim* 75 (July 2004): 63–66.

———. "Kantoniko de Haketia—La Kopla 'Nuestro Señor Elohenu.'" *Aki Yerushalayim* (April 2010). http://www.aki-erushalayim.co.il/ay/087/087_16_haketia.htm.

———. "Los Cantes de Matesha (Resumen)." *MABAT Revista* 1, 1989–90: 65–66.

———. *Un Aljófar y una Perla. Facetas del Tesoro Cultural de los Judeoespañoles de Marruecos: Documentos Recogidos y Comentados por Gladys Pimienta.* Jerusalem, Israel; Paris, France: Colección JEM; Editor Erez, 2019.

Pinto Abecasis, Nina. "From Grandmother to Grandson: Judeo-Spanish Anecdotes in Israel Today: Emigration, Cultural Accomodation and Language Preservation." *European Journal of Jewish Studies* 9 (2015): 100–118.

———. *The Peacock, the Ironed Man and the Half-Woman: Nicknames, Humor and Folklore in the Day-to-Day Speech of Tetouan's Haketia-Speaking Jews*. Jerusalem, Israel: Ben Zvi Institute, 2015 [Hebrew].

———. "The Piropo as a Bridge between Cultures in Tetouan (Northern Morocco)." *Jerusalem Studies in Jewish Folklore* 30 (2016): 75–100 [Hebrew].

———. "Transformations in the Noche de Paños Ceremony: From Street Ritual to the Visual Genealogy Tree." *Pe'amim: Studies in Oriental Jewry* 150–52 (2017): 139–62 [Hebrew].

Pouso Balleto, Ramón. "El Príncipe Muley Hassan y los Ministros del Gobierno Marroquí en la Fiesta del C.R.I." *Or-Luz*, April 18, 1956.

———. "S. M. Mohamed V en Tetuán." *Or-Luz*, April 18, 1956.

Pulido, Ángel. *Españoles Sin Patria y La Raza Sefardí*. Madrid, Spain: Tipografico de E. Teodor, 1905.

———. *Los Israelitas Españoles y el Idioma Castellano*. Madrid, Spain: Sucesores de Rivadeneyra, 1904.

Quintana, Aldina. "El Mellah de Tétouan (1860) en Aita Tétouan (1905) de Benito Pérez Galdós: Cambios de Actitud Frente a los Estereotipos Antisemitas en la España de la Restauración." *El-Presente* 2 (2008): 103–6.

"Raíces Nos Invita a Cruzar un Puente Entre Dos Mundos." *Raíces, Revista Judía de Cultura*. Accessed January 13, 2021. http://www.revista-raices.com/intro/intro.php.

"Realizose con Éxito el Primer Seminario Para Dirigentes Sefaradíes." *Maguén-Escudo* 20, January 1972.

Reches, Danni. "From Ben-Gurion to Venezuelan Converts: The Law of Return and the State of Israel's Jewish Identity." *Autores Convidados* 49, no. 1 (2021): 82–96.

Refael Shmuel. *Ladino Here and Now: Ladino Speakers in Israel in Light of Their Past and Culture*. Tel-Aviv, Israel: Tel-Aviv University Press, 2020 [Hebrew].

Rein, Raanan."Diplomacy, Propaganda, and Humanitarian Gestures: Francoist Spain and Egyptian Jews, 1956–1968." *Iberoamericana* 6, no. 23 (2006): 21–33.

Rein, Raanan, and Molly Lewis. "Complementary Identities: Sephardim, Zionists and Argentines in the Interwar Period." In *Contemporary Sephardic Identity in the Americas: An Interdisciplinary Approach*, edited by Margalit Bejarano and Edna Aizenberg, 99–116. Syracuse, NY: Syracuse University Press, 2012.

Ricard, Robert. "Cartas de Ricardo Ruiz Orsatti a Galdós Acercade Marruecos (1901–1910)." *Anales Galdosianos* 3 (1968): 99–115.

———. "L'émigration des Juifs Marocains en Amérique du Sud." *Journal de la Société des Américanistes* 20, no. 1 (1928): 427–29.

———. "L'émigration des Juifs Marocains en Amérique du Sud." *Journal de la Société des Américanistes* 24, no. 1 (1932): 201–2.

———. "L'émigration des Juifs Marocains en Amérique du Sud." *Journal de la Société des Américanistes* 28, no. 1 (1936): 259.

Rivodriya, Daniel. "Spain and the Argentine Jews in Morocco, 1980–1914." *Shorashim Bamizrah* 4 (1998): 113–20 [Hebrew].

"Roberto Ricard." *Diccionario Filosófico—Manual De Materialismo Filosófico, Una Introducción Analítica*. Accessed June 2020. http://filosofia.org/ave/001/a385.htm.

Roby, Bryan K. *The Mizrahi Era of Rebellion: Israeli's Forgotten Civil Rights Struggle 1948–1966*. New York: Syracuse University Press, 2015.

Rodrigue, Aron. *Jews and Muslims: Images of Sephardi and Eastern Jewries in Modern Times*. Seattle: University of Washington Press, 2003.

Rohr, Isabelle. *The Spanish Right and the Jews, 1898–1945: Antisemitism and Opportunism, Eastborne*. Brighton, UK: Sussex Academic Press, 2007.

Rojas Marcos, Albert Rocío. "Literatura Española en Tánger. Desde el Siglo XIX Hasta Nuestros Días." PhD diss., Universidad de Sevilla, 2017.

"Romancero Judeoespañol de Marruecos." *Maguén-Escudo* 5, October 1970.

Ronen, Mati. "The Founding Convention of the ASF." *BaMa'aracha* 146 (April 1973): 6 [Hebrew]

Rosen Lapidot, Efrat, and Harvey E. Goldberg. "The Triple Loci of Jewish-Maghribi Ethnicity: Voluntary Associations in Israel and in France." *Journal of North African Studies* 18, no. 1 (2013): 112–30.

Rossetto, Piera. "Mémoires de Diaspora, Diaspora de Mémoires: Juifs de Libye Entre Israël et l'Italie, de 1948 à Nos Jours." PhD diss., Ca' Foscari University of Venice, 2015.

Roumani, Judith. "'Le Juif Espagnol': The Idea of Sepharad among Colonial and Postcolonial Francophone Jewish Writers." In *Sephardism: Spanish Jewish History and the Modern Literary Imagination*, edited by Yael Halevi-Wise, 213–34. Stanford, CA: Stanford University Press, 2012.

Salama, Ibraim. "El Yishuv Judio en Brasil, la Participación de los Sefaradíes." *Maguén-Escudo* 32, January 1973.

"Samuel Serfaty: Jugador de Baloncesto en la Actualidad Entrenador del Atlético de Tetuán." *Or-Luz*, May 15, 1956.

Sananes Almoslinos, Moisés, and Carlos García-Eugenio. *El Discurso de El Mundo Israelita*. Caracas, Venezuela: Centro de Estudios Sefardíes de Caracas, 2003.

Sánchez, José Luís. "The Sephardi Berberisca Dress, Tradition and Symbology." *Datatèxtil* 37 (2017): 37–54.

Saposnik, Arieh Bruce. "Europe and Its Orients in Zionist Culture before World War One." *Historical Journal* 49 (2006): 1105–23.

Sayahi, Lotfi. "Aqui Todo el Mundo Hablaba Español: History of the Spanish Language in Tangier." *Journal of North African Studies* 9 (2004): 36–48.

Schammah Gesser, Silvina. "Virtually Sephardic? The Marketing and Reception of the New Iberian Laws of Nationality in Israel." *Lusotopie* 18, no. 2 (2020): 192–217.

Schammah Gesser, Silvina, and Teresa Pinheiro. "Guest Editors' Introduction to the Special Issue, Jewish (In) Visibility in Iberia: A View from the Margins." *Contemporary Jewry* 40, no. 4 (2021): 1–15.

Schammah Gesser, Silvina, and T. Pinheiro. "Revisiting Isomorphism: The Routes of Sefarad in Spain and Portugal." In *Iberian Studies: Reflections across Borders and Disciplines*, edited by Núria Codina Solà and Teresa Pinheir, 295–320. Berlin, Germany: Peter Lang, 2019.

Schapkow, Carsten. *Role Model and Counter Model: The Golden Age of Iberian Jewry and German Jewish Culture during the Era of Emancipation*. Lanham; Boulder, CO; New York; London: Lexington Books, 2016.

Schmelz, U. O. S., S. Della Pergola, and U. Avner. *Ethnic Differences among Israeli Jews: A New Look*. Jerusalem, Israel: Institute of Contemporary Jewry, the Hebrew University of Jerusalem, and the American Jewish Committee, 1991.

Schorsch, Ismar. "The Myth of Sephardi Supremacy." *Leo Baeck Institute Yearbook* 34 (1989): 47–66.

Schroeter, Daniel J. "From Sephardi to Oriental: The 'Decline' Theory of Jewish Civilization in the Middle East and North Africa." In *The Jewish Contribution to Civilization: Reassessing an Idea*, edited by Jeremy Cohen and Richard I. Cohen, 125–48. Oxford, UK: Littman Library of Jewish Civilization, 2008.

———. "Philo-Sephardism, Anti-Semitism, and Arab Nationalism: Muslims and Jews in the Spanish Protectorate of Morocco during the Third Reich." In *Nazism, the Holocaust, and the Middle East*, edited by Francis R. Nicosia and Bogac A. Ergene, 179–215. New York: Berghahm, 2018.

———. "Renacimiento de Israel (Tangier)." In *Encyclopedia of Jews in the Islamic World*, edited by Norman A. Stillman. Brill Online, 2013. Accessed February 6, 2020. https://referenceworks.brillonline.com/entries/encyclopedia-of-jews-in-the-islamic-world/renacimiento-de-israel-tangier-SIM_0018320.

———. "The Shifting Boundaries of Moroccan Jewish Identities; on the Different Role of French Colonialism in Constructing Modern Jewish Identities." *Jewish Social Studies* 15, no. 1 (January 2008): 145–64.

———. "Trade as a Mediator in Muslim-Jewish Relations: Southwestern Morocco in the Nineteenth Century." In *Jews among Arabs: Contacts and Boundaries*, edited by Mark R. Cohen and Abraham L. Udovitch, 113–40. Princeton, NJ: Darwin Press, 1989.

Schulze, Kirsten E. *The Jews of Lebanon: Between Coexistence and Conflict.* Brighton, UK: Sussex Academic Press, 2009.

Segal, Ariel. *Jews of the Amazon, Self-Exile in Earthly Paradise.* Philadelphia, PA: Jewish Publication Society, 1999.

"Semana de Judaísmo Latinoamericano en Israel." *Maguén-Escudo* 11, April 1971.

Sephiha, H. V. "Extinction du Judéo-Espagnol Vernaculaire du Maroc ou Hakitía." *Yod* 2, no. 1 (1976): 83–88.

———. "Le Judéo-Espagnol du Maroc ou Haketiya." *Combat pour la Diaspora* 6 (1981): 77–80.

Serels, Mitchell M. *A History of the Jews of Tangier in the Nineteenth and Twentieth Centuries.* New York: Sepher-Hermon, 1991.

———. *Jews of Cape Verde: A Brief History.* Brooklyn, NY: Sepher-Hermon, 1997.

———. "Nesry, Carlos De." In *Encyclopedia of Jews in the Islamic World*, edited by Norman A. Stillman. Brill Online, 2013. Accessed April 11, 2013. http://referenceworks.brillonline.com/entries/encyclopedia-of-jews-in-the-islamic-world/nesry-carlos-de-SIM_0016700.

Seroussi, Edwin. "Archivists of Memory: Written Folksong Collections of Twentieth-Century Sephardi Women in Magrini, Tullia." In *Music and Gender: Perspectives from the Mediterranean*, edited by Tullia Magrini, 195–214. Chicago, IL: University of Chicago Press, 2003.

———. *Sonic Ruins of Modernity.* London and New York: Routledge, 2022.

Setton, Guy. *Spanish-Israeli Relations, 1956–1992: Ghosts of the Past and Contemporary Challenges in the Middle East.* Sussex, UK: Sussex Academic Press, 2016.

Shabat, Reuven. "Learning Is Never Boring." *Etrog-Education Journal* (December 2008) [Hebrew]. http://www.itu.org.il/?CategoryID=1461&ArticleID=12590.

Shalom Chetrit, Sami. *Intra-Jewish Conflict in Israel: White Jews, Black Jews.* London and New York: Routledge, 2010.

Shaul, Moshe. "Lingüística—La Haketia." *MABAT Revista* 1, 1989–90.

Shcroeter, Daniel. "Moroccan Jewish Studies in Israel." *Hesperis Tamuda* 51, no. 2 (2016): 85–89.

Shenhav, Yehuda. "World Organization of Jews from Arab Countries (WOJAC) in the Context of the Palestinian National Struggle." *British Journal of Middle Eastern Studies* 29, no. 1 (2002): 27–56.

Shiloah, Amnon. *Jewish Musical Traditions.* Detroit, MI: Wayne State University Press, 1995.

Shohat, Ella. *On the Arab-Jew, Palestine, and Other Displacements: Selected Writings of Ella Shohat.* London, UK: Pluto Press, 2017.

———. "Sephardim in Israel: Zionism from the Standpoint of Its Jewish Victims." *Social Text* 19–20 (1988): 1–35.

———. *Taboo Memories, Diasporic Voices*. Durham, NC: Duke University Press, 2006.
Shukrun, Roy, and Aviad Moreno. "Rethinking Moroccan Transnationalism: Sephardism, Decolonization, and Activism between Israel and Montreal." *American Jewish History* 107, no. 2–3 (2023).
Sieskel, Dov M. "'El Jala': An Arabic-Language Zionist Periodical in Argentina." *Kesher* 10 (1991): 80–85 [Hebrew].
Silver, Christopher. *Jews, Muslims and Music across Twentieth-Century North Africa*. Stanford, CA: Stanford University Press, 2022.
Sitton, David. *Sephardi Communities Today*. Jerusalem, Israel: Council of Sephardi and Oriental Communities, 1985.
"Social: De la Llegada de S.M Mohamed V a Tetuán." *Or-Luz*, April 18, 1956.
Sofer, Yehezk'el. "Intensifying Activities by the WSF Worldwide and in Israel." *BaMa'aracha* 19, 1979.
"Spain." *B'nai B'rith Messenger*, September 4, 1914.
"Spanish Award for Radio Broadcasting." *Ma'ariv*, December 23, 1985 [Hebrew].
Sperling, Jessica. "Conceptualising 'Inter-Destination Transnationalism': The Presence and Implication of Coethnic Ties between Destination Societies." *Journal of Ethnic and Migration Studies* 40, no. 7 (2014): 1097–1115.
Spilerman, Seymour, and Jack Habib. "Development Towns in Israel: The Role of Community in Creating Ethnic Disparities in Labor Force Characteristics." *American Journal of Sociology* 81 (January 1976): 781–812.
Sternfeld, Lior B. *Between Iran and Zion: Jewish Histories of Twentieth-Century Iran*. Stanford, CA: Stanford University Press, 2020.
Stillman, Norman A. "The Academic Study of Islamicate Jewry." In *Jewish-Muslim Relations in Past and Present*, edited by Josef Meri, 13–47. Leiden, the Netherlands: Brill, 2017.
———. *The Jews of Arab Lands in Modern Times*. Philadelphia, PA: Jewish Publication Society, 1991.
Tapiero, J. "Folklore." *Noar*, November 4, 1951.
"Telegrama Rabat-New York." *Or-Luz*, February 15, 1956.
Teller, Adam. *Rescue the Surviving Souls: The Great Jewish Refugee Crisis of the Seventeenth Century*. Princeton, NJ: Princeton University Press, 2020.
Toledano, Isaac R. "Recuerdos de Tánger." *Maguén-Escudo* 4, September 1970.
———. "Recuerdos de Tánger." *Maguén-Escudo* 7, December 1970.
———. "Recuerdos de Tánger." *Maguén-Escudo* 10, March 1971.
Tölölyan, Khachig. "Elites and Institutions in the Armenian Transnational." *Diaspora: A Journal of Transnational Studies* 9, no. 1 (2000): 107–36.
"Tomo 1." *Israel* 4, July 1917.

Trevisan, Semi Emanuela, Dario Miccoli, and Tudor Parfitt, eds. *Memory and Ethnicity: Ethnic Museums in Israel and the Diaspora*. Newcastle upon Tyne, UK: Cambridge Scholars, 2013.

Triandafyllidou, A., and M. Veikou. "The Hierarchy of Greekness: Ethnic and National Identity Considerations in Greek Immigration Policy." *Ethnicities* 2, no. 2 (2002): 189–208.

Troper, Harold. "The Canadian Jewish Polity and the Limits of Political Action: The Campaigns on Behalf of Soviet and Syrian Jews." In *Ethnicity, Politics, and Public Policy: Case Studies in Canadian Diversity*, edited by Harold Troper and Morton Weinfel, 224–52. Toronto, Canada: University of Toronto Press, 2016.

Tsuda, Takeyuki. "Conclusion: Diasporic Homecomings and Ambivalent Encounters with the Ethnic Homeland." In *Diasporic Homecoming: Ethnic Return Migration in Comparative Perspective*, edited by Takeyuki Tsuda, 325–50. Stanford, CA: Stanford University Press, 2009.

Tsur, Yaron. "The Israeli Historiography and the Ethnic Problem." In *Making Israel*, edited by Benny Morris, 231–77. Ann Arbor, MI.: University of Michigan Press, 2007.

———. *A Torn Community: The Jews of Morocco and Nationalism 1943–1954*. Tel Aviv, Israel: Am Oved, 2001 [Hebrew].

Tsur, Yaron, and Hagar Hillel. *The Jews of Casablanca: Studies in the Modernization of the Political Elite in a Colonial Community*. Ramat-Aviv, Israel: Open University, 1995 [Hebrew].

"Una Feliz Inciativa." *Adelante*, November 1, 1931.

"Una Plaza y Una Avenida para Maimónides." *Maguén-Escudo* 75, April–June 1990.

"Un Libro de Samuel J. Benchetrit, La Leyenda de Epecúen." *Adelante*, December 15, 1929.

"Vacaciones." *Carta de France-Mabatt* 1. Private collection of Jimmy Pimienta (July 1990): 3.

Vagni, Juan José. "El Colonialismo Español En Marruecos Y Las Migraciones Árabes Y Sefardíes en el Cono Sur: Primeros Contactos a Principios del Siglo XX." *Nuevo Mundo Mundos Nuevos*. https://doi.org/10.4000/nuevomundo.85403.

Vallicrosa, Millas J. M. "Lápidas Sepulcrales Antropomorfas en los Cementerios Israelitas de Xauen y Tetuán." *Sefarad* 6 (1946): 63–72.

Veidlinger, Jeffrey, ed. *Going to the People: Jews and the Ethnographic Impulse*. Bloomington: Indiana University Press, 2016.

Vered, Ronit. "The Little-Known Cuisine of Spain's Moroccan Jews." *Haaretz*, May 15, 2015 [Hebrew]. https://www.haaretz.com/.premium-the-little-known-cuisine-of-spain-s-moroccan-jews-1.5362133.

Vilar, Juan Bautista. "Fernando VII, La Inquisición y los Judíos de Gibraltar." *Maguén-Escudo* 34, March 1973.

———. "Galdós y los judíos de Aitta Tetauen." *Maguén-Escudo* 36, May 1973.

———. "La Emigración Judeo-Marroquí a la América Latina en la Fase Pre-Estadística (1850–1880)." *Sefardica* 11 (1996): 39–44.

———. "Primeros Emigrantes Judeo-Marroquíes en América." *Maguén-Escudo* 18, November 1971.

"Viven Momento Histórico Dice Su Representante en Latinoamérica." *Lavanguardia*, October 8, 2015. https://www.lavanguardia.com/20151008/54437119039/sefardies-viven-momento-historico-dice-su-representante-en-latinoamerica.html.

Wahnon, Medina. "Maimónides Profeta de la Medicina Contemporánea." *Or-Luz*, May 15, 1956.

Weich-Shahak, Shoshana. *Cantares Y Romances Tradicionales Sefardíes de Marruecos*. Madrid: Tecnosaga, 1991. CD.

———. *En Buen Siman! Panorama del Repertorio Musical Sefaradí*. Haifa, Israel: Pardes, 2006.

———. "Investigación de la Tradición Musical Sefaradí de Marruecos." *MABAT Revista* 1, 1989–90: 61–62.

———. "Passage-Rites in the Judeo-Spanish Repertory of Morocco." *Pe'amim: Studies in Oriental Jewry* 30 (1987): 105–24 [Hebrew].

———. "Riqueza Temática del Romancero Sefardí de Alcazarquivir." In *Romances de Alcácerquibir*, edited by Kelly Benoudis Basílio, 89–112. Lisbon, Portugal: Colibri-Centro de Estudos Comparatistas, 2007.

Weich-Shahak, Shoshana, and Paloma Díaz Más. *Romancero Sefardí de Marruecos: Antología de Tradición Oral*. Madrid, Spain: Editorial Alpuerto, 1997.

Weisz, Martina L. *Jews and Muslims in Contemporary Spain: Redefining National Boundaries*. Wein: De Gruyter Oldembourg, 2019.

Wessendorf, Suzanne. "Pioneer Migrants and Their Social Relations in Super-Diverse London." *Ethnic and Racial Studies* 42, no. 1 (2019): 17–34.

Wieland, Yaakov. "On a Remote Jewish Collective: The Wealthy Grocers of Venezuela." *Hamishmar*, April 9, 1952 [Hebrew].

Yehuda, Zvi. "Zionist Activity in Morocco on the Eve of the Protectorate." In *The Jews of North Africa in the Nineteenth and Twentieth Centuries*, edited by Michel Abitboul. Jerusalem, Israel: Ben Zvi Institute, 1980 [Hebrew].

"Yona Benshimol (z"l)." *MABAT Revista* 1, 1989–90.

Zenner, Walter P. *A Global Community. The Jews from Aleppo, Syria*. Detroit: Wayne State University Press, 2000.

———. "Streams of Immigration: Sephardic Immigration to Britain and the United States." In *From Iberia to Diaspora: Studies in Sephardic History and Culture*, edited by K. Yedida and Norman A. Stillman, 139–50. Leiden, the Netherlands: Brill, 1999.

Zytnicki, Colette. *Les Juifs du Maghreb: Naissance D'une Historiographie Coloniale*. Paris, France: PUPS, 2011.

NAME INDEX

Abensur, Philip, 146–47
Abraham, Amram, 193n59
Aguilar, Manuel, 113
Aizenberg, Edna, 123
Alaoui, Moulay Ali, 79
Alberti-Kleinbort, Eleonora Noga, 193n72
Albo, Carlos, 84–85
Alexander, Tamar, 5, 136
Altit, Aldo, 147
Alvar, Manuel, 48, 119
Alvarez Buylla, Vicente, 183n34
Amar, Jo, 100
Anahory Librowicz, Ora, 149–50, 193n72, 197n26
Arias Montano, Benito, 45
Armistead, Samuel G., 48, 149, 193n72
Arraiz, Antonio, 7
Asayag, Pinhas, 7, 36, 37
Attías, Moshé, 193n72
Axel, Brian Keith, 14, 34, 49, 174
Azancot, Moshé, 151
Azencot, Abraham, 152
Azziza, Mimoun, 10, 22

Baal Hanes, Meir, 100
Bar Yochai, Shimon, 100
Barnuevo, Luis Yánez, 115

Beigbeder, Juan, 5
Bekkai, Emnarek, 87
Benabu, Abraham, 139
Benacerraf, Yaacov Raphaël, 69, 77
Benaím, Elías, 121
Benaím Pinto, Gonzalo, 98, 105, 193n59
Benaím Pinto, John, 98
Ben-Ami, Shlomo, 113–14, 116, 145, 194n21
Benardete, Maír José, 40
Benarroch, Benjamin, 25
Benarroch, Carlos, 121
Benarroch Benshabat, Salomon, 46
Benarroch Pinto, Isaac, 66, 197n26
Benatar, Rafael, 125
Benayoun, Solomon Momy, 116
Benazeraf, Raphaël, 46
Benchaya, Ramón, 63
Benchetrit, Samuel J., 63
Benchimol, Yona, 126, 133, 197n26
Bendahán Israel, Moisés J., 121
Bendayan Benayoun, Isaac, 42
Bendelac, Alegría, 22, 28, 67, 119, 152
Ben-Gaulid, Yitzhak, 52
Bengio, Joseph, 129, 133
Bengio, León, 119

Bengio, Mordojay, 36, 131
Benguigui, Yehuda, 161
Ben-Gurion, David, 94
Benhamú Guanich, Saadía, 121
Benharroch, Mois, 158
Benhayon, Salomon, 130
Bénichou, Paul, 6, 117, 125, 146
Benjelloun, Abd-el-Kader, 79
Ben Labrat, Dunash, 88
Benmamán, Jacob, 45
Benmaman, Yosef D., 47
Benoliel, José, 7, 39, 42, 75, 119, 125, 193n72, 197n26
Ben-Porat, Mordechai, 105
Bensabat, Solomon, 88–89
Ben Saruk, Menahem, 88
Benshimol, Amram Abraham Levy, 193n59
Ben-Simhon, Shaul, 130
Bension, Ariel, 74
Bentata, Jacobo, 66, 84
Bentolila, Yaakov, 15, 16, 134, 136
Bentolila Jalfón, Estrella de, 16
Benzaquen, Léon, 86, 88
Benzaquen, Sarita, 133
Benzecri Benmergui, Alfonso, 97
Berdugo, Alberto, 26, 42
Beregovski, Moyshe, 40
Berliavski, Y., 73
Bialik, Hayim Nahman, 89
Bin-Nun, Yigal, 89
Binnuna, M'hammad, 44
Blanco, Andrés Eloy, 97
Boaknin Benaim, Luna, 40
Boas, Franz, 7, 34, 40
Bolívar, Simón, 103
Botbol (Hachuel), Abraham, 117–18, 120–121, 193n59
Brauner, Ignacio, 74
Brodsky, Adriana, 58, 76
Brubaker, Rogers, 13
Bürki, Yvette, 24

Cagan, Solomon, 77
Calamaro, Paul, 83–84
Calderwood, Eric, 44, 88
Caracol, Manolo, 25
Cárcer [de Tejada], Manuel Aguirre, 42

Carciente, Jacob, 56, 122, 193n58
Castilho, Alvaro, 72
Castro, Estrellita, 25
Cazés, Alberto, 183n34
Cazes Bénatar, Hélène, 66, 84–85
Chagall, Mark, 89
Chávez, Hugo, 154, 157
Chocrón, Isaac, 118, 123–24
Chocrón, Samuel A., 62
Chocrón Cohén, José, 159
Cohen, Hassan, 1–3, 17, 153
Cohen, Judith, 149
Cohen, Rubin, 13–14
Cohen, Samuel, 179n29
Cohén Pariente, Amram, 122
Cohén Serfaty, Aharón, 119
Cohén Toledano, Jaime, 193n59
Cohén Toledano, Pinhas, 193n59
Cohén Zrihen, Saadia, 159
Columbus, Christopher, 1, 175n2
Coriat, León, 46
Curiel, Morris E., 156

Dahan, Paul, 161
Delacroix, Eugène, 35
Diego, Gerardo, 24
Dumas, Alexandre, 35

Einstein, Albert, 9
Elbaz, Isaac, 42
Elbaz, Venessa Paloma, 181n66
España, Alberto, 25
Essayag, Savador, 63
Evri, Yuval, 38

Fernaud, Ana, 125
Flores, Lola, 25
Franco, Francisco, 6–7, 11, 19, 21, 26, 44–45, 66, 70–71, 80, 82, 87, 109, 111–13, 115, 120, 138, 158, 165, 167
Friedman, Michal Rose, 38

Gabizón, Menáhem, 107
García, Issac, 63
Gardel, Carlos, 25
Garrido, Néstor, 158
Garzón, Benito (Baruj), 121, 160

NAME INDEX

Garzón de Benarroch, Lucy, 119
Garzón Serfaty, Moisés, 24, 26, 48, 92, 99, 102–3, 107, 119, 121–22, 124–25, 156
Gatmon, Alex, 9
Gil, Eduardo, 125
Gilson Miller, Susan, 60, 151–52
Gombau, Gerardo, 25
Gonzalez, Allyson, 38
Gonzalez, Marcelo, 114
Gordon, Esther, 13
Graterón, Salvador Garmendia, 123
Grebler, David, 115
Guabli, Brahim El, 87

Hadati, Saadia, 140
Halevy, Yehuda, 118
Halioua, Philippe, 107
Hassán, Iacov, 113, 125
Hassan, Mulay, 87–88, 90, 91
Hassan, Simón, 107
Hassán, Yosef, 179n29
Hassan Cohen, Abraham, 1–3, 17, 153
Hassán family, 45
Hatchel, Mauricio, 107, 115, 121
Heckman, Alma Rachel, 86
Herzl, Theodor, 75

Ibn-Gabirol, Solomon, 118
Imperio Argentina. See Nile del Río, Magdalena
Iragorry, Mario Briceño, 97
Israel Garzón, Jacobo, 113, 127, 158–59

Jalfón (Halfon), Yehuda (León), 73–74
Jouin, Jan, 36

Karim, Abd al, 5
Karsenty, Eliyahu (Eli), 52
Katz, Israel J., 48
Kaye, Danny, 9
Keinan Ofri, Esti, 15
King Hassan II, 79, 105, 137
King Juan Carlos I, 113
Kohan, Horacio, 113
Kohan, Liliana, 113

Landau, Rom, 23
Laredo, Abraham Isaac, 45–46, 86, 179n29
Laredo, Claudio. See Cohen, Samuel
Lascar, Alberto, 42, 48
Lasry, Joe, 69
Leibovici, Sara, 146–47
Levi, Momy, 153
Levy, André, 176n2
Lévy, Clémence, 150
Levy, Daniel, 69, 145
Levy, Jacob, 72
Levy, Leon, 107
Levy, Meir, 57
Levy, Samuel A., 72, 76
Lévy, S. D., 70–71, 77–78, 83, 92
Lévy, Solly, 149–50, 158
Lewis, Hal, 115
Liberman, Arnold, 113
Lima, Blanca de, 159
López Álvarez, Ana María, 113
Lorca, Federico García, 24
Lugaro, Agustín, 179n29

Machín, Antonio, 25
Macías, Uriel, 113
Maimonides (Moses Ben-Maimon), 5, 47, 118, 122
Mangual, Jose, 25
Mann, Herbie, 25
Manrique, Lara de, 193n72
Mariana, Jesuíta Juan de, 118
Masó, Fausto, 123
Mazin, Max, 110
Medina, Salomon, 48, 89
Menéndez Pidal, Ramón, 39, 193n72
Mercader, Trina, 24
Mérenfeld, Rubén, 99, 102
Moreno, Marcos, 125
Moryoussef Fereres, Sara de, 119
Musa, Ibrahim, 156
Muyal, Jacques, 25

Nahón, Isaac Benjamín, 119
Nahón, Samuel M., 62
Nahón, Zarita, 7, 34–35, 39–40, 125, 149
Nahón Avital, Amada, 126
Nahón de Toledano, Suzanne (Simy), 40

NAME INDEX

Nahón Sabáh, Jack (Jacobo), 42
Nasser, Gamal Abd al-, 109
Nataf, Elie, 77
Navon, Yitzhak, 114–16
Negrete, Jorge, 25
Nerín, Gustau, 6
Nesry, Carlos de, 46, 87, 89
Nile del Río, Magdalena (Imperio Argentina), 25
Nucete Sardi, José, 97

Ojeda Mata, Maite, 32
Onieva, Antonio J., 18, 31
Onís, Federico de, 40
Oriol, Antonio, 112
Ortega, Manuel L., 23, 35, 38–39, 44, 64–65, 73, 193n72, 197n26
Otero Silva, Miguel, 97

Palacín, Larrea, 193n72
Palacio, Lucila, 97
Peñalver, Diana, 125
Pères, Shimon, 137
Peréz, David Jose, 72
Pérez Jiménez, Marcos Evangelista, 96
Perl, Asher, 41, 43
Pierre, M. André, 75
Pimienta, Alberto, 49
Pimienta, Gladys, 39, 133, 135, 137, 152
Pimienta, Jimmy, 147, 152–53, 178n56
Pimienta, Sidney, 152
Pinto, Abraham, 65–66
Pinto Abecasis, Nina, 28, 158
Pinto Cohen, Gustavo, 97
Pisa, Isaac, 54, 60–61
Pulido, Ángel, 4, 36, 39, 44, 64–65, 70, 73, 76, 88, 106

Queen Sofía of Spain, 112
Querub, Isaac, 115

Rabbi Vidal, 61, 75
Rabbi Yamín, 28
Ricard, Robert, 64–65, 125, 146
Ricardo, Marcos, 113
Rivera, Miguel Primo de, 5
Romanelli, Samuel Aaron, 35

Romero, Elena, 193
Ronen, Mati, 190n38
Rotenberg, Abrasha, 113
Ruiz, Martínez J., 193n72

Sabah, Alfonso, 69, 83–84, 126, 133, 143, 189n87, 194n2
Sabah, Jack, 84
Sabah, Leopoldo, 84
Sabak, Mohamed, 24
Salama (Yavin), Jacob, 145
Salgado, David, 160
Salgado, Elias, 160, 173
Sananes, Moisés, 97
Sandoval, Alfredo, 125
Schroeter, Daniel J., 132
Sedero Cohen, Leon, 62
Semach, Y. D., 64–65
Serels, Mitchell, 122, 151
Serfaty, Abraham, 86
Serfaty, Leon, 59
Serfaty, Samuel, 26, 107, 191n1
Serrano, José, 125
Sevilla, Carmen, 25
Shaul, Moshe, 131, 136
Shohat, Ella, 177n34
Shriqui, León, 107
Silva, Fernando, 125
Silver, Chris, 47
Silverman, Joseph H., 48, 193n72
Skuditski, Zalmen, 40
Spanien, Raphael, 82–85
Stefano, Victoria de, 123
Stern, Alia, 151
Stern, John, 151
Sultán Amar, Kelly, 149
Sultan Mohammed V, 47, 79, 87–88, 91
Szenes, Hana, 89

Tapiero, Joseph, 69
Taurel, Léon, 63, 84
Tchernichovsky Gutmanovich, Shaul, 89
Thurscz, Jonathan, 77–78
Timsit, Maurice, 69
Toledano, Issac R., 106, 179n29
Toledano, Meyer, 186n1
Toledano, Rahma, 70, 92

NAME INDEX

Toledano, Samuel, 107, 112, 115
Toledano Hatchuel, Mauricio, 107, 121
Torres Benumeya, Rodolfo Gil, 65
Tudela, Benjamín de, 118

Valadares, Paulo, 161
Valderrama, Juanito, 25
Valdez, Carlos "Patato," 25
Varela, José, 26
Vázquez, Ángel, 119
Veidlinger, Jeffrey, 40
Velázquez Riviera, Ignacio, 140
Ventura, David, 107
Vidal Israel, Jaime, 75
Vidal Sphiha, Haim, 146

Wahnon, David, 62
Wahnon, Medina, 47
Wahnon, Shlomo, 140
Weich Shahak, Shoshana, 15, 133–34, 137, *138*, 152
Weinblatt, Jimmy, 15
Weisz, Martina L., 159
Weizmann, Chaim, 75

Yahuda, Avraham Shalom, 38, 74
Yosef, Ovadia, 113
Yousef, Mohammed ben, 47

Zapatero, José Luis Rodríguez, 158

SUBJECT INDEX

Aadas y Adafinas (radio show), 114, 116, 145, 147
Adelante (newspaper), 16, 26–27, 41–44, 63, 65, 75, 84, 143
África: Revista de Tropas Coloniales, see La Revista de Tropas Coloniales
Aki Yerushalayim (journal), 136
Algeria, 32, 52–53, 78; Oran, 52–53, 57
Alhambra Decree (1492), 1–2, 4, 7, 16, 40, 44, 46, 48, 112, 114–115, 118, 124, 130
Aliyah, 81, 94, 130, 144
Alliance Israélite Universelle's (AIU), 20, 42, 51, 70, 77, 93, 144
Alliance of Tunisian Immigrants in Beersheba and the South, 129
Amazônia Judaica (newsletter), 160–161
American Sephardi (journal), 111, 117
Amistad (magazine), 121
Amitiés Marocaines, Les (association), 86
Arab-Jewish conflict, 44, 77, 109
Argentina, 2, 7, 11, 25, 53–54, 56, 58–64, 66, 71–77, 84, 100, 112, 141, 150, 156, 165; Asociación Comunidad Israelita Latina de Buenos Aires, 59; Buenos Aires, 41, 54, 58–59, 62–63, 65, 72, 76, 113, 122, 185n44; Córdoba, 46, 63, 118, 139; Margarita, 72; Mauricio, 77; Rosario, 72; Vila Mercedes, 72
Arias Montano Institute for Arabic and Hebraic Studies, *see* Maimonides Institute'

Association for Professional Training, 80
Asociación Hispano-Hebrea (Hispanic-Hebrew Association), 36–38
Association of Americans and Canadians in Israel, 144
Australia, 83
L'Avenir Illustrée (periodical), 77–78

Bachad (Alliance of Religious Pioneers), 80
Balfour Declaration, 74–75
BaMa'aracha (periodical), 101
Belgium, 10, 137, 174
Bene Kedem, 75
Berber Dahir (Berber Edict), 44, 77
Berberisca, 31–32, 35–36
Black Panthers (movement), 100–101, 130, 145
Bnei Akiva (youth organization), 80, 98
B'nei B'rith América, 98
Boletín Oficial (newspaper), 41
Bolivia, 103
Bonei Yerushalaim (club), 73
Boundary work, 10, 130
Brazil, 2, 7, 11, 51, 53–54, 61–62, 64, 67, 72, 76, 83, 118, 141, 151, 156, 160, 165, 184n2, 184n12, 185n36; Centro de Estudos Judaicos da Amazônia (CEJA), 160; *Columna A* (newspaper), 72; Harmonía y Fraternidad de Brasil, 62; Itacoatiará, 62; Manicoré, 62; Parintins, 62
Brit Yotsei Maroko (association), 130

Bukhara, 51
Bulgaria, 32

Canada, 3, 13, 16, 83, 95, 122–123, 141, 148–151, 155–156, 168, 199n20; Association of Americans and Canadians in Israel, 144; Canadian Sephardi Federation, 107, 151; Montreal, 148–151, 158; Ontario, 122, 151; Ontario Sephardi Association, 151; Petah Tikvah Anshe Castilla Synagogue, 152; Quebec, 123, 148–149; Toronto, 150–151; Vancouver, 150
Canary Islands, 51, 56
Casa Sefarad (association), 74, 158, 198n16
Centro Hispano-Israelita, 59
Charles Netter Zionist youth movement, see Éclaireurs Israelites
Chile, 72, 83, 156
Colombia, 83, 103, 155–156, 199n20
Colonialism, 2, 4, 5, 10–11, 24, 27, 28, 31, 33, 34, 53, 75, 79, 83, 85, 93, 107, 109, 120, 134, 135, 148, 149, 163–165, 169; anticolonial, 87; French, 13, 38, 44, 53, 74, 94, 117, 146, 148, 167, 168; postcolonial, 3, 8, 9, 10–11, 13, 47, 48, 85, 86, 87, 106, 107, 108, 110, 113, 116, 117, 120, 125, 134, 142, 146, 148, 149, 157, 166, 167; precolonial, 38, 39, 41, 164; Spanish, 3, 4, 5, 6, 7, 10–11, 18, 20–21, 22, 23, 24, 33, 35, 36, 38, 39, 41, 42, 43, 44, 46, 48, 50, 65, 66, 70, 74, 86, 87, 89, 94, 107, 111, 116, 125, 139, 146, 157, 164, 165, 166, 167
Comisión de Organización Internacional, 142
Congregación Israelita Latina (see also Asociación Comunidad Israelita Latina de Buenos Aires), 59
Consolidation phase, 13–14
Convivencia, 4–5, 44, 87–88
Crisol Judío (newspaper), 41

Dépêche Marocaine (periodical), 43
Desván de los Recuerdos: Cuadros de una Judería Marroquí, El (book), 120
Diario de Africa, El (newspaper), 102
Diario de Tánger, El (newspaper), 41
Diario Marroquí de Larache (periodical), 43
Diaspora, 3, 8, 12, 13–14, 16, 34, 35, 49, 71, 94, 108, 127, 141, 143, 144, 153, 161, 162, 163, 164, 167, 169; Jewish, 8, 9, 12, 14, 65, 80; MENA, 9, 10, 164; Hispanic Moroccan Jews, 2, 3, 10, 25, 34, 47, 64, 65, 82, 85, 92, 95, 105, 116, 125, 132, 139, 140, 142, 158, 161, 166, 168, 169; postcolonial, 3, 107; Sephardi, 4, 5, 9, 10, 36, 52, 65, 101, 103, 107, 108, 113, 114, 116, 117, 118, 121, 151, 159, 164, 166, 167, 169
Dominican Republic, 156
Dror (youth organization), 80
Druze, 51

L'Echo de Tánger (periodical), 43
Éclaireurs Israelites (youth organization), 80
Eco Israelita, El (newspaper), 41, 143
Eco Mauritano de Tánger Heraldo de Marruecos, El (periodical), 43, 179n29
Ecuador, 103, 155
Egypt, 52, 109; Cairo, 53
Emigdirect, see HICEM
Emigration (see also Aliyah, Immigration), 22, 35, 48, 51–52, 68, 82, 92, 109, 112, 119; from Marocco, 52–53, 56–57, 60–61, 79, 81–83, 85, 96, 103, 120, 128; from Venezuela, 154, 157, 170; to Israel, 12, 78, 81, 84–85, 91–92, 95–96, 168; to Latin America, 51, 54, 57, 59–60, 83–84, 128; to Venezuela, 56, 84, 103
England, see Great Britain
Eretz Israel, see Palestine
España (newspaper), 24, 70
España de Tánger (newspaper), 66, 81, 179n29
Esperanza (newspaper), 52
Estatuto de Tánger, El (periodical), 43
European Economic Community, 114

Federación Hispano-Marroquí Sionista, 74
France, 1, 3–4, 10, 13, 16–17, 21, 22, 37, 48, 53, 80, 83, 123, 125, 140, 146, 148, 149, 150–151, 155, 168; France-MABATT, 1, 147, 151, 152, 153; North African migration, to 9, 96, 141, 146, 147, 177n34; Paris, 1, 38, 57, 64, 95, 112, 114, 135, 147, 150, 153

General Franco Institute for Hispano-Arab Studies, 45, 66
Germany, 10, 123; Nazi Germany, 71, 84
Gibraltar, 41, 52, 56, 57, 74, 108, 110, 127, 139
Gordonia (youth organization), 80

Great Britain, 10, 51
Great Depression (1930s), 61, 62
Greece, 32
Guinea, 13, 142

Habonim (youth organization), 80
Hadassah-WIZO, 95, 98
Haketia (Judeo-Spanish dialect, *see also* Linguistics), 2, 6–7, 13, 15, 22, 23, 30, 33, 34, 69, 75, 120, 123, 125, 127, 130, 132, 146, 149, 158, 162, 165, 168, 196n54; preservation, 11, 16, 38, 39, 119, 127, 131, 133, 135–136, 142, 150, 161; revival, 38, 134; teaching, 160
Hamisgeret (organization), 79, 89
Hashomer Hatzair (youth organization), 80, 98
Havaad Hazioni (club), 73
Hebreos en Marruecos, Los (book), 35, 39, 64
Hedim: Kehilot Sefaradiyot Ba'Olam (journal), 101
Heraldo de Marruecos, El (periodical), 23
Hesed ve-Emet, 58
Hesed Shel Emet Sefaradit (burial society), 58
Hevra Kedusha Ashkenazi, 58
HIAS (United Hebrew Immigration Aid Society), 79, 82–84, 94
HICEM, 83
Hispanization of Jewish names, 27
Hispanophone world, 7, 13, 20, 25, 52, 56, 64, 68, 71, 142, 164–166
Hispanotropicalism, *see* Colonialism
Holocaust, 44, 80, 85, 93, 104, 109, 130
Homeland, 8, 13, 14, 16, 42, 62, 76, 85, 108, 140, 152, 161, 163–164, 169; Jewish, 3, 8, 76; Spain and Morocco as entwined homelands, 7, 10, 137, 168; Venezuela and Morocco as entwined homelands, 103, 106
Horria, El (newspaper), 41
Hovevei Zion (Zionist group), 71, 73

Iberia, 7, 14, 34, 40, 46, 50, 64–65, 88–89, 106, 115, 116, 118, 122, 124, 125, 149, 157, 159; pre-1492 Iberia, 1–2, 4, 36, 38, 117, 118, 121, 153, 165, 169; Iberian Peninsula, 2, 13, 108, 118, 120, 124, 142, 147, 156
Immigration (*see also* emigration, Aliyah), 14, 35, 61, 101, 108, 144, 165; from MENA, 1, 12, 13, 15, 51, 79, 96, 100, 106, 113, 134, 135, 140, 141, 160, 169; internal migration within Morocco, 29, 52–53, 70, 76, 80; immigration to Europe, 10, 52, 127, 146, 147, 149; to Israel/Palestine, 9, 15, 22, 69, 74, 77, 78–79, 80–81, 82, 83, 84, 85, 89, 92, 93–94, 100, 106, 114, 126, 127–129, 130, 131, 132, 135, 142, 143, 145, 147, 152, 155, 159, 160, 166, 168, 169; to North Africa, 19, 27, 53, 73, 77, 139–140; to South and North America, 3, 53, 55–56, 58–59, 61, 64, 65, 66, 67, 71, 72, 75, 82, 84–85, 95–96, 97, 98, 100, 102, 106, 120, 148, 149; to Spain, 3, 48, 64, 109, 110–111, 112, 113, 149, 159
Indiano, al Kadi y la Luna, El (trilogy), 66
International Monetary Fund, 111, 154
International Organization for Migration (IOM), 154
Iran, 104, 157
Iraq, 78, 129
Islam, 26, 43, 44, 124, 171, 172, 175n2; Islamic countries, 19, 20, 21, 23, 29, 35, 51, 53, 86, 93, 100, 101, 102, 104–106, 126, 128, 132, 139–140; Islamic studies, 21; Islamic world, 52, 53, 85, 109, 114, 116, 123, 132, 157; Jewish-Muslim relations, 21, 22, 26, 38, 47, 86, 87, 88, 109, 161; Muslims in France, 96, 146; Muslims in Spain, 4, 12, 23, 44, 109, 110, 159, 167
Israel, 1, 2, 3, 7, 8, 9, 10, 12, 13, 14, 15, 16, 17, 20, 21, 22, 24, 28, 48, 67, 69, 70, 71, 72, 76, 77, 78, 79, 80, 81, 82, 83, 84, 85, 86, 87, 89, 91, 92, 93, 94, 95, 96, 97, 98, 100, 101, 102, 103, 104, 105, 106, 107, 108, 109, 113, 114, 115, 116, 123, 124, 126, 127, 128, 129, 130, 131, 132, 133, 134, 135, 136, 137, 138, 139, 140, 141, 142, 143, 144, 145, 146, 147, 148, 149, 150, 151, 152, 153, 155, 156, 158, 159, 160, 161, 162, 163, 164, 166, 167, 168, 169; Ashdod, 128, 129, 133; Ashkelon, 129, 134; Atlit, 128; Azur, 128; Bat Yam, 128, 133; Beersheba, 129; Dimona, 129; Eilat, 89, 129; Haifa, 100; Holon, 133; Jerusalem, 75, 87, 101, 115, 118, 122, 128, 131, 132, 134, 140, 150, 151, 158, 160; Kfar Shmariyahu, 128; Kiryat-Malachi, 129; Law of Return, 155, 159; MAPAI, 130; Mizpe Ramon, 128; Netanya, 128, 129, 144; Netivot, 128; Or-Yehuda, 128; Petah Tikva, 128; Sderot, 128, 129; Tel Aviv, 1, 114, 122, 133, 134, 141, 147, 150, 152

Israel (newspaper), 72, 75, 76
Italy, 82

Jewish Agency, 81, 86, 105, 127, 194n3
Jewish-Arab riots (1929), 44, 77
Jewish Music Research Centre of the Hebrew University, 133
Jewish Colonization Association (JCA), 60, 77, 83, 185n36
Jewish National Fund (JNF), 70, 74, 76, 77, 98, 103, 144
Jews, 4, 6, 7, 8, 9, 10, 12, 14, 34, 35, 36, 38, 44, 47, 48, 51, 60, 64, 66, 69, 82, 84, 85, 93, 94, 101, *104*, 105, 108, 112, 113, 115, 118, 124, 125, 132, 144, 146, 153, 154, 156, 158, 161, 163, 165, 167, 168; Arab, 105, 136; European, 56, 58, 59, 72, 75, 77, 79, 80, 89, 94, 96, 100, *104*, 110, 118, 123, 130, 145; Hispanic Moroccan, 2, 3, 7, 10, 11, 12, 13, 15, 16, 17, 18, 19–21, 22, 24, 25, 27, 34, 51, 52, 67, 71, 73, 76, 95, 102, 103, 108, 116, 119, 125, 126, 127, 135, 139, 144, 149, 155, 156, 157, 158, 159, 160, 163, 164, 165, 168, 170; MENA *see* Middle Eastern, North African; Middle Eastern, 2, 3, 8, 9, 58, 59, 75, 93, 94, 95, 101, *104*, 109, 123, 129, 142, 145, 148, 149, 164; Moroccan, 1–2, 3, 6, 11, 12, 15, 18, 21, 22, 23, 25, 26, 27, 28, 29, 31, 34, 36, 37, 38, 39, 41, 42, 43, 44, 47, 48, 51, 52, 54, 57, 58, 59, 60, 61, 62, 63, 64, 65, 66, 67, 69, 70, 71, 72, 73, 74, 76, 77, 78, 79, 81, 82, 83, 85, 86, 87, 88, 89, 91, 92, 93, 93, 94, 96, 97, 98, 99, 100, 101, 102, 103, 105, 106, 108, 109, 110, 116, 117, 118, 119, 120, 121, 123, 124, 125, 126, 127, 128, 129, 130, 131, 135, 136, 139, 140, 141, 143, 144, 145, 147, 149, 150, 151, 153, 155, 156, 160, 161, 164, 165, 166; North African, 3, 8, 9, 65, 82, 83, 93, 96, 101, 123, 129, 131, 132, 133, 142, 145, 146, 148, 149, 160, 161, 164, 169; North American, 56, 94, 124, 140, 146, 154; Sephardi, 1, 4, 5, 12, 15, 16, 18, 20, 36, 40, 45, 46, 67, 69, 73, 74, 100, 103, 109, 115, 117, 118, 119, 121, 122, 123, 124, 130, 146, 158, 159, 163; Soviet, 93, 94, 95, 100, 126; Venezuelan, 56, 95, 97, 98, 99, 102, 103, 105, 106, 123, 124, 125, 154, 155, 156, 157, 158, 159, 162
Juif de Tanger et le Maroc, Le (book), 87

Junta (local Jewish community council), 36, 46, 76, 86, 87, 137

Keren Hayesod, *see* United Israel Appeal (UIA)
Kol Hanoar: Órgano de la Unión Universal de Juventudes Judías (newspaper), 41
Kol Israel (newspaper), 41, 182n17
Kol Yisrael (radio station), 114, 134, 136, 147, 152

Ladino, 4, 6, 36, 59, 75, 114, 119, 152, 160; preservation, 131; studies, 15, 132, 135, 136, 146
Latin America, (*see also* Argentina, Bolivia, Brazil, Chile, Colombia, Dominic Republic, Ecuador, Mexico, Panama, Paraguay, Peru, Urugay, Venezuela), 2, 6, 11, 12, 13, 25, 52, 56–57, 58, 62, 63, 65, 74, 76, 82, 91, 101, 103, 107, 113, 122, 123, 124, 125, 129, 130, 142, 148, 149, 153, 154, 155–156, 157, 159, 167, 169; emigration to, 51, 53, 54, 57, 59–61, 62, 63, 64, 65, 67, 68, 83, 84, 103, 124, 146, 165, 166, 167; immigration from, 66, 94, 112–113, 130, 165, 166; Zionism, 71, 72, 143, 156
Lebanon, 51, 54, 65, 184n2
Leningrad trials (1970), 94
Liberté, La (newspaper), 41, 143
Libya, 78
Linguistics, (*see also* Haketia), 4, 6, 7, 10, 20, 23, 23, 38, 41, 69, 87, 117, 136, 148, 150, 153; Hispanic, 13, 18, 30, 45, 58, 127, 129, 130, 131, 153, 175n7
Lycée Français (network of French state schools outside the country), 22, 81, 135

Ma'ale Adumim Institute for the Documentation of Judeo-Spanish Language and its Culture, 133
MABAT, 1, 2, 116, 126–140, 141–145, 146–147, 150–151, 152, 169, 194n10
MABAT Revista (booklet), 16, 131, 133, 135, 139, 143, 144, 145
Maccabi (youth movement), 98
Madagascar, 79
Magbit (Zionist fundraising organization), 81
Magen David (association), 73, 77

SUBJECT INDEX

Magrebí, El (periodical), 179n29
Maguén-Escudo (periodical), 16, 102–103, *104*, 105, 116–117, 119, 121, 122, 124, 158
Maguid Micharim (book), 52
Maimonides Institute, 45–46, 88, 122
MATAN – Netanya Tunisian Club, 129
Mebasser Tob, Le (newspaper), 41
Melilla, 3, 48, 62, 107, 110, 124, 127, 139–140, 149, 168
Mellah (Jewish Quarter), 181n64
MENA region, 2, 3, 8–9, 10, 12, 35, 76, 83, 100, 101, 116, 123, 129, 136, 142, 148–149, 151, 157, 164, 166
Mexico, 64, 156, 158, 159
Misgav Yerushalayim (Centre for Research and Study of Sephardi and Oriental Jewish Heritage), 132
Morocco Alcazarquivir, 20, 26, 37, 63, 147; Arcila, 20; Casablanca, 62, 69, 70, 73, 74, 76–77, 78, 79, 80, 81, 83, 84–85, 86, 91, 92, 128, 137, 166; Casino Israelita in Tangier, 24, 25, 81, 137, *138*; Casino Israelita in Tetouan, 46, 88, 89; Centre de Recherche et Archives sur le Judaïsme du Nord du Maroc, 161; Chefchaouen, 110; Cinema Alhambra, 25; Fez, 4, 43, 52, 130, 131; Football clubs, 25–26; French protectorate, 5, 19, 26, 47, 85; Gran Teatro Cervantes (theater), 24, 31, 32; Hahnasat Orhim, society, 62; Huceima, 110; Istiqlal Party, 47, 85, 88; Larache, 20, 26, 37, 48, 61, 73, 110; Marrakech, 81; Moroccan National Front in Tangier, 47; Nador, 110, 140; Parti Communiste Marocain (PCM), 86; Parti Démocratique de l'Independence (PDI), 47, 87; Petitjean, 78; Rabat, 62, 85, 137; Radio Tangier, 1; Spanish protectorate, 5, 19, 20, 21–22, 29, 36, 38, 41, 45, 47, 57, 66, 70, 80, 85, 106, 110, 127; Synagogues, 31, 58, 63, 76, 100; Tangier, 1, 7, 11, 15, 19–29, 30, 31, 32, 34–36, 38–43, 45–49, 49, 52–54, 56–57, 59–63, 65–68, 69–70, 72–73, 75–77, 79–81, 83–87, 105–107, 112, 114–116, 119, 122, 124, 126, 131, 133, 135, 137, *138*, 139, 141, 144–145, 147, 149, 151–152, 161, 164, 168, 175n12, 179n7; Tetouan, 3, 11, 15, 18–21, 23, 26–29, 37, 44–46, 48, 52–53, 56–57, 59–63, 66–67, 72–73, 75, 81, 88–89, 90, 91, 97, 99, 105, 107, 110, 113, 120, 134–135, 137, 139, 145, 147, 149, 158, 160, 164; Zionist Federation of Tangier, 22, 81
Mossad (Israel intelligence agency), 79
Mundo, El (periodical), 66, 97
Mundo Israelita, El (weekly), 99, 102

National Authority for Ladino, 136
National Council of Jewish Women, 95
Nativ (Israeli Liaison Bureau), 95
NATO, 114
Netherlands, 10
Noar (newspaper), 69–70, 78, 186n1
Nostalgic narratives, 4–5, 7, 13, 16, 20, 37, 44, 48, 59, 63, 70, 102, 105–106, 108, 117, 120, 122, 137, 140, 144, 146, 151, 163, 165, 167
Nuestras Bodas en Tetuán (anthology), 147
Nuevo Mundo Israelita (newspaper), 99, 102

Oeuvre de Nourriture et d'Habillement (charitable), 144
Oeuvre de Secours aux Enfants (Jewish humanitarian organization), 86
Operation Yakhin, 79, 81, 93, 109, 126
Or Hayeladim (educational institute), 66
Or-Luz (periodical), 16, 24, 26, 28–29, 29, 41, 47–48, 66, 87–89, *90*, *91*, 99, 102–103, 110
Organization for European Economic Cooperation, 111
Organización Latinoamericana en Israel (OLEI), 130
Ottoman Empire, 5, 36, 51, 59, 109, 164

Palestine, 38, 41, 44, 51, 72, 74, 77, 78, 81, 97
Panama, 103, 154, 155, 156
Paraguay, 72
Pe'amim (journal), 132
Peru, 2, 11, 51, 54, 60, 62, 63, 67–68, 101, 103, 155–156, 165
Philippines, 13, 142
Philo-Sephardi discourse, 4, 6, 36–38, 39, 44–46, 47, 64–65, 70, 73, 74–76, 89, 107, 164, 166
Popular de Larache, El (periodical), 43
Portugal, 16, 39, 52, 53, 54, 74, 82, 108, 113, 122
Porvenir de Tánger, El (periodical), 43

Présence, see Voix Sépharade, La
Prezente, El (journal), 136

Radio de la Communauté Juive (RCJ), 114
Raíces: Revista Judía de Cultura (periodical), 112
Reencuentro (Jewish rencounter with Spain), 4
Renacimiento de Israel, El (newspaper), 41, 63, 75, 76
Reveil du Maroc, Le (newspaper), 41
Revista de la Raza, La (bulletin), 73
Revista de Tropas Coloniales, La (newspaper), 65
Rómpase en Caso de Incendio (book), 118, 123
Russia, *see* Soviet Union

Sefarad (newspaper), 45
Sefarad Society for Preserving and Cultivating the Judeo-Spanish Heritage, 136
Sepharad, *see* Spain
Sephardi Community Council (SCC), 75, 101, 115, 132
Shaarei Zion (club), 73
Shivat Zion (club), 73
Sociedad Israelita de Socorros Mutuos Varsovia, 58
Sociedad Israelita según Ritual Sefardíta, 58
Sociedad Sefardí de Beneficencia, 67
Sociedad según Ritual Sefardita, *see* Congregación Israelita Latina
South America, *see* Latin America
Soviet Union, 9, 40, 73, 77, 93, 94–95, 100, 104, 109, 126, 163
Spain, 9, 38, 73, 88, 117, 118, 120, 122, 123, 124, 156; Algeciras, 41, 108; Barcelona, 54, 56, 107, 115, 121, 140, 150; Beth Yaacov synagogue, 112; Cadiz, 48, 108; Casa Sefarad-Israel, 158; Comisión Nacional Judía Sefarad '92, 115; Expulsion of Jews *see* Alhambra Decree (1492); Federación de Comunidades Judías de España, 158; Federation of Jewish Communities, 115, 160; Madrid, 26, 32, 38, 70, 74, 107, 110, 112–113, 115, 139, 140, 147, 149, 150, 158, 161; Málaga, 107, 108, 110, 138, 139, 149; Press Association of the High Commissioner of Spain in Morocco, 75; Radio Sevilla, 180; Royal Spanish Academy, 36, 74, 119; Samuel Halevi synagogue, 112; Second Spanish Republic (1931–39), 5, 19; Sefarad '92 Conference, 1, 153; Seville, 48, 107, 108, 110, 115, 117, 139; Spanish Restoration (1874–1931), 5; Tarifa, 108; Valencia, 26, 107, 110
Spanish Israelites and the Spanish Language, The (book), 36
Stateless Spaniards (book), 64, 73, 76
Sudan, 51, 52
Switzerland, 16, 120, 141, 150, 152
Syria, 51, 58, 58–59, 75, 95, 104, 113; Bene Emet, 58

Tétouanais, Le, see Maguid Micharim
Tetuán, en el Resurgimiento Judío Contemporáneo (1850–1870) (book), 120
Transregional networks, 8, 9, 10, 11, 14, 16, 17, 36, 57, 58, 60, 71, 72, 74, 79, 85, 93, 112, 113, 121, 127, 130, 136, 159, 161, 162, 163, 165, 166, 169
Treaty of Fez (1912), 4
Tunisia, 77, 78, 129, 146
Turkey, 32, 75, 158

UN Resolution, 181, 97
UNESCO, 111
L'Union Marocaine (newspaper), 77
Unión de Jóvenes Hebreos (youth movement), 98
United Israel Appeal (UIA), 86, 98
United States, 3, 7, 9, 13, 17, 22, 51, 67, 72, 94, 95, 101, 108, 111, 113, 115, 117, 119, 124, 125, 141, 148, 151, 154, 155, 156, 168, 170; American Jewish Committee (AJC), 87, 124; American Joint Distribution Committee (JDC), 46–47, 80, 85, 94; American Sephardi Federation (ASF), 101, 107, 115; Los Angeles, 151; MABAT-USA (Aficoman), 151; Miami, 155, 156, 198n8; New York, 40, 83, 87, 101, 105, 107, 115, 119, 122, 124, 149, 151; Seattle, 158; Washington DC, 158
Uruguay, 72

SUBJECT INDEX   245

Veloce en Tanger, Alger et Tunis, Le (book), 35
Venezuela, 2, 3, 7, 11, 12, 16, 17, 53, 56, 57, 59, 61, 62, 63, 66, 67, 82, 83, 84, 85, 92, 93, 95–100, 102–103, 105–108, 112, 116–123, 135, 140–141, 143, 149–150, 154–157, 159–160, 165, 167–168, 170; Asociación Israelita de Venezuela (AIV), 67, 95, 118; Caracas, 16, 56, 57, 59, 61, 62, 66, 67, 97, 98, 100, 102, 105, 119, 120, 121, 122, 124, 140, 147, 149, 156, 157, 158; Centro de Estudios Sefradíes de Caracas (CESC), 118–119, 122, 123, 156; Comité Venezolano de Asociación Sefarad-España, 121; Comité Venezolano pro-Palestina Judía, 97; Confederación de Asociaciónes Israelitas de Venezuela, La (CAIV), 99, 102; Department for Zionist and Social Activity among Sephardi and Mizrahi Communities, 101; La Federación Sefaradí Latinoamericana (FeSeLA), 101–102, 107, 122, 156, 159; El Grupo Herzl, 99; La Guaira, 56, 67; Maracaibo, 67; Puerto Cabello, 67; Sociedad Israelita de Venezuela, 67; Los Teques, 56, 67; Unión Israelita de Caracas (UIC), 95, 99, 102; Zionist Federation of Venezuela (FSV), 98, 100, 102
Vida Perra de Juanita Narboni, La (book), 119
Voces Jaquetiescas (book), 119
Voix Sépharade, La, 149

Wars, 61, 80, 85, 93, 109; Balkan Wars (1912–13), 109; Cold War (1947–91), 95; Rif War (1920–26), 5; Spanish-American War (1898), 4; Spanish Civil War (1936–39), 6, 19, 25, 45, 70; Spanish-Moroccan War (1859–60), 3, 13, 18, 53, 56–57, 108, 139; World War I (1914–18), 53, 61, 62, 63, 109; World War II (1939–45), 10, 19, 33, 47, 78, 79, 80, 83, 85, 86, 96, 109, 113, 146, 151
al-Wifaq (association), 86–89
Women's International Zionist Organization (WIZO), 95, 98
World Bank, 111
World Jewish Congress (WJC), 79, 84–85, 95, 114
World Organization of Jews from Arab Countries (WOJAC), 104–105
World Sephardi Congress, 160
World Sephardi Federation (WSF), 75, 101, 107, 122, 132, 148
World Zionist Organization (WZO), 75, 100, 101, 143

Yearnings of a Jew, The (book), 89
Yemen, 78, 129
Yiddish, 6, 72, 75, 77, 96, 124, 148
YOMAS (organization), 129

Zionism (*see also* Hovevei Zion, Shaarei Zion, Shivat Zion, World Zionist Organization), 8, 9, 12, 43, 70, 71, 73–74, 75–79, 80, 83–84, 86, 89, 91–92, 94–95, 97–102, 106, 109, 127, 142–143, 144, 156, 164, 166–167, 169; activists, 71, 74, 78, 83, 91, 92, 94, 98, 126, 143, 146; anti-Zionism, 86–87; European, 71, 73, 74, 75, 80, 82; local federations, 22, 74, 77, 81, 83, 95, 98, 100, 102, 132; newspapers, 69, 70, 72, 76, 87, 89; rise of, 11–12, 68, 166; Sephardi, 75, 76, 99, 100, 112, 145, 156; youth movements, 69, 80, 98, 143

AVIAD MORENO is a faculty member at Ben-Gurion University of the Negev. He is the author of *Europe from Morocco* (2015) and the coeditor of *The Long History of the Mizrahim* (2021).

For Indiana University Press

Tony Brewer, Artist and Book Designer
Brian Carroll, Rights Manager
Gary Dunham, Acquisitions Editor and Director
Anna Francis, Assistant Acquisitions Editor
Brenna Hosman, Production Coordinator
Katie Huggins, Production Manager
David Miller, Lead Project Manager/Editor
Dan Pyle, Online Publishing Manager
Stephen Williams, Marketing and Publicity Manager
Jennifer Witzke, Senior Artist and Book Designer

www.ingramcontent.com/pod-product-compliance
Lightning Source LLC
Chambersburg PA
CBHW030120240426
43673CB00041B/1345